Lecture Notes in Computer Science   15420

Founding Editors

Gerhard Goos
Juris Hartmanis

Editorial Board Members

Elisa Bertino, *Purdue University, West Lafayette, IN, USA*
Wen Gao, *Peking University, Beijing, China*
Bernhard Steffen ⓘ, *TU Dortmund University, Dortmund, Germany*
Moti Yung ⓘ, *Columbia University, New York, NY, USA*

The series Lecture Notes in Computer Science (LNCS), including its subseries Lecture Notes in Artificial Intelligence (LNAI) and Lecture Notes in Bioinformatics (LNBI), has established itself as a medium for the publication of new developments in computer science and information technology research, teaching, and education.

LNCS enjoys close cooperation with the computer science R & D community, the series counts many renowned academics among its volume editors and paper authors, and collaborates with prestigious societies. Its mission is to serve this international community by providing an invaluable service, mainly focused on the publication of conference and workshop proceedings and postproceedings. LNCS commenced publication in 1973.

Heide Lukosch · Maria Freese · Sebastiaan Meijer
Editors

Simulation and Gaming across Borders

55th International Simulation and Gaming
Association Conference, ISAGA 2024
Christchurch, New Zealand, July 8–12, 2024
Revised Selected Papers

Editors
Heide Lukosch ⓘ
University of Canterbury
Christchurch, New Zealand

Maria Freese ⓘ
Otto-von-Guericke-University Magdeburg
Magdeburg, Germany

Sebastiaan Meijer ⓘ
KTH Royal Institute of Technology
Stockholm, Stockholms Län, Sweden

ISSN 0302-9743   ISSN 1611-3349 (electronic)
Lecture Notes in Computer Science
ISBN 978-3-031-86554-1   ISBN 978-3-031-86555-8 (eBook)
https://doi.org/10.1007/978-3-031-86555-8

© The Editor(s) (if applicable) and The Author(s), under exclusive license to Springer Nature Switzerland AG 2025
Chapter "Simulating Complex Adaptive Software System Technical Debt" is licensed under the terms of the Creative Commons Attribution 4.0 International License (http://creativecommons.org/licenses/by/4.0/). For further details see license information in the chapter.

This work is subject to copyright. All rights are solely and exclusively licensed by the Publisher, whether the whole or part of the material is concerned, specifically the rights of translation, reprinting, reuse of illustrations, recitation, broadcasting, reproduction on microfilms or in any other physical way, and transmission or information storage and retrieval, electronic adaptation, computer software, or by similar or dissimilar methodology now known or hereafter developed.
The use of general descriptive names, registered names, trademarks, service marks, etc. in this publication does not imply, even in the absence of a specific statement, that such names are exempt from the relevant protective laws and regulations and therefore free for general use.
The publisher, the authors and the editors are safe to assume that the advice and information in this book are believed to be true and accurate at the date of publication. Neither the publisher nor the authors or the editors give a warranty, expressed or implied, with respect to the material contained herein or for any errors or omissions that may have been made. The publisher remains neutral with regard to jurisdictional claims in published maps and institutional affiliations.

This Springer imprint is published by the registered company Springer Nature Switzerland AG
The registered company address is: Gewerbestrasse 11, 6330 Cham, Switzerland

If disposing of this product, please recycle the paper.

Preface

The International Simulation and Gaming Association (ISAGA) Conference 2024, held in Christchurch, New Zealand, from July 8 to 12, 2024, brought together a vibrant and diverse community of scholars, practitioners, and enthusiasts from around the world.

Under the theme *Simulation and Gaming across Borders*, the 2024 conference underscored the global and interdisciplinary reach of simulation and gaming as tools for education, research, and social change. The proceedings presented here capture the breadth of this convergence, highlighting innovative applications, emerging ethical considerations, intercultural dynamics, and new frontiers in facilitation techniques. The collection of papers represents a selection of all conference contributions. Out of 23 full papers submitted, 19 have been accepted for the proceedings. All papers have been reviewed in a double-blind reviewing process by 2 members of the program committee each. The editors of the proceedings have provided additional feedback after the conference, which led to the final versions included here.

As the world continues to face complex global challenges, simulation and gaming offer powerful methodologies for bridging geographical, cultural, and disciplinary boundaries. The papers collected in this volume reflect the growing recognition of these tools not only as mechanisms for learning but also as critical platforms for fostering dialogue, collaboration, and understanding across borders. The conference in Christchurch showed that all types of technologies, from card games laying the foundation for an engaging conference community to the use of virtual reality allowing a glance into the past, are used to support play in the simulation and gaming field. This year's conference saw a notable increase in the exploration of *intercultural play*, where participants examined the role of cultural context in shaping game design and player experience.

Topics ranged from game adaptations to facilitate cross-cultural understanding to the challenges and opportunities presented by multiplayer environments that transcend national or cultural boundaries. Central to the discussions were questions of *ethics* in simulation and gaming, particularly the responsibility of game designers and facilitators to ensure equitable, inclusive, and respectful experiences. Contributors emphasized the need for critical reflection on the impact of gaming applications in diverse social contexts, urging a thoughtful approach to the development and use of games in both educational and professional settings.

The theme of *facilitation* emerged as another prominent area of focus, with contributions highlighting new methodologies for guiding participants through complex game-based learning experiences. From simulations of policy decision-making to serious games for corporate training, the role of the facilitator is crucial in shaping the outcome of a gaming session. Presenters shared insights into how facilitators can create inclusive, safe, and productive environments that maximize learning and engagement, while also adapting to the varying needs of a diverse audience.

These proceedings also feature a wide array of *game examples* that demonstrate the versatility and potential of simulations across different sectors, from healthcare to urban planning, environmental sustainability, and beyond. These examples not only showcase the innovative applications of simulation and gaming but also provide practical insights into how games can be designed and implemented to address real-world challenges. A recurring theme in the discussions around game examples was the importance of creating experiences that are not only engaging but deeply meaningful, aligning playfulness with tangible learning outcomes and societal impact.

As the field of simulation and gaming continues to evolve, this collection of papers offers a snapshot of current trends and future directions. It serves as both a reflection on the state of the art and a call to action for researchers, designers, and educators to deepen their engagement with the interdisciplinary and cross-cultural dimensions of gaming. The contributions presented here remind us that the potential of simulation and gaming lies not only in their ability to entertain but in their capacity to foster cross-border collaboration, empathy, and problem-solving in an increasingly interconnected world.

We are grateful to all those who contributed to the success of the ISAGA 2024 Conference, and we hope this volume will serve as both a valuable resource for ongoing research and a source of inspiration for future explorations of simulation and gaming across borders.

December 2024

Heide Lukosch
Maria Freese
Sebastiaan Meijer

Organization

General Chair

Heide Lukosch — University of Canterbury, New Zealand

Co-chair

Maria Freese — Otto von Guericke University Magdeburg, Germany

Local Chairs

Karen Anderson — University of Canterbury, New Zealand
Timothy McKenzie — University of Canterbury, New Zealand

Web Chair

Shunsuke Fukuden — University of Canterbury, New Zealand

Finances

Chris Buyarski — University of Canterbury, New Zealand

Student Volunteers

Yasas Wickramasinghe
Mac Greenslade
Dilshani Kumarapeli
Upulanka Premasiri
Hēmi McNeill

Keynote Speakers

Maria Freese	Otto von Guericke University Magdeburg, Germany
Heide Lukosch	University of Canterbury, New Zealand
Tom Logan	University of Canterbury, New Zealand
Melanie Langlotz	Geo AR Games, New Zealand
Carl Leducq (Chair)	NZGDC, New Zealand
Hori Te Ariki Mataki	Ariki Creative, New Zealand

Program Committee

Tobias Alf
Bryann Avendano-Uribe
Olivier Barretau
Nicolas Becu
David Crookall
Sylvain Dernat
Claire Dormann
Anne Dray
Vinod Dumblekar
Martin Gerner
Shesh Narayan Gupta
Ryoju Hamada
Casper Harteveld
Tuomas Harviainen
Toshiko Kikkawa
Willy Kriz
Elyssebeth Leigh

Chien Lu
James McNeill
Sebastiaan Meijer
Misha Mirza
Erika Speelman
Steven Sutherland
Yusuke Toyoda
Friedrich Trautwein
Giovanni Troiano
Kieron Wall
Marcin Wardaszko
Ivo Wenzler
Yasas Wickramasinghe
Marieke de Wijse
Helmut Wittenzellner
Birgit Zuern

Contents

Crossing Borders by Revisiting Ethical Issues of Simulation and Gaming 1
    Willy Christian Kriz, Mieko Nakamura, and Toshiko Kikkawa

Where to Begin? Integrating Simulation and Indigenous Knowledges
to Create New Approaches 19
    *Cat Kutay, Pavan Kumar Menugonda, Christian Gio Biag Lizada,
and Elyssebeth Leigh*

Understanding Behavioral Differences Between Machine Agents
and Human Participants Based on How They Play the Energy Transition
Game 31
    *Kengo Suzuki, Yuta Nakadegawa, Kento Miura, Takeshi Shibuya,
and Susumu Ohnuma*

Accounting for Psychological Safety in Serious Game and Simulation
Design 46
    Dale Linegar and Gillian Vesty

Enhancing Fair Play in Online Gaming: The Development
and Implementation of the No More Cheats Anti-cheat System 69
    Jakubowski Michał, Małgorzata Ćwil, and Szatkowska Weronika

Navigating Uncertainty: The Emergence of Effort and Emotion in Tabletop
Games 81
    Shruti Agrawal and Girish Dalvi

Co-designing an Applied Game About Volcanic Hazards for a Bi-cultural
Environment: 5 Minute Volcano 96
    *Kieron Wall, Heide Lukosch, Simon Hoermann, Kathryn MacCallum,
and Ben Kennedy*

Conflicted Courses: A Matrix Game for Course Design 110
    Richard Durham and Ruth Lemon

A Framework for Co-design of Edu Escape-Room Aimed at Exploring
Cultural Identity 128
    *Weronika Szatkowska, Małgorzata Ćwil,
and Blanka Błaszczak-Rozenbaum*

Theory Informing Practice – Theorizing Good Facilitation Practice 144
  Elyssebeth Leigh and Laurie L. Levesque

The Impact of Participants Motivation and Playfulness for the Facilitation
of Simulation Games 155
  Friedrich Trautwein and Tobias Alf

Pratiti …Becoming Aware: Promoting Simulations and Games on a Global
Platform 168
  Jigyasu Dubey, Elyssebeth Leigh, Vinod Dumblekar, Anand Rajavat,
  and Upinder Dhar

Analyzing Relationship to Nature Within a Game Frame: Proposal
and Application of a Conceptual Framework and its Evaluation Method 182
  Éléonore Sas and Nicolas Becu

Extraordinarily Large-Scale Gaming for the Youth 200
  Ryoju Hamada and Tomomi Kaneko

How Does Evaluating the Effects of a Participatory Simulation Raise
Questions About the Design Intentions of Participatory Processes that May
Involve Simulation/Gaming? 215
  Amélie Monfort

Digital Veggie Mart Game for Nutritional Education and Sustainable Food
Supply Chain 228
  Mizuho Sato and Hajime Mizuyama

How Entrepreneurs Learn About Artificial Intelligence by Using
an Analogue Card Game 239
  Maria Freese, Birgit Zürn, and Helmut Wittenzellner

The Impact of Simulation Games on the Success of Simulation Game
Courses 249
  Friedrich Trautwein and Tobias Alf

Feedback and Biofeedback Procedure and Results, Based on the Gearshfit
Engine 262
  Błażej Podgórski, Marcin Wardaszko, and Piotr Wątrucki

Simulating Complex Adaptive Software System Technical Debt 270
  David Gould, Tim French, and Melinda Hodkiewicz

Author Index 285

Crossing Borders by Revisiting Ethical Issues of Simulation and Gaming

Willy Christian Kriz[1](✉), Mieko Nakamura[2], and Toshiko Kikkawa[3]

[1] FHV University Vorarlberg, Hochschulstrasse 1, 6850 Dornbirn, Austria
`willy.kriz@fhv.at`
[2] Ryutsu Keizai University, Hirahata, Ryugasaki 301-8555, Ibaraki, Japan
`mnakamura@rku.ac.jp`
[3] Keio University, 2-15-45, Mita, Minato-Ku 108-8345, Tokyo, Japan
`tompei22@keio.jp`

Abstract. This paper explores the ethical issues of Simulation and Gaming. Although there has been an extensive discussion on this topic, it has recently gained increasing relevance within a time of defying borders. Therefore, a reexamination of these topics from this new point of view becomes necessary. Firstly, the importance of this research is further elaborated on. When we refer to a border, we may imagine a country's border. However, we have created many kinds of 'borders' around us, for instance the dividing lines we have drawn and continue to draw between different cultures or gender identities. The need for defying and crossing these self-imposed borders has become clearly evident in a world full of diversity. The issue of crossing and overcoming these boundaries can then be interpreted as to how sustainably and appropriately we deal with this diversity. Managing diversity, equity and inclusion thus becomes increasingly ethical issue also for the discipline of Gaming Simulation. In the paper, the presented ethical viewpoints are explored from three perspectives, namely the ones of game design, game facilitation and debriefing, and game content. Lastly, we conclude with some proposals for the Simulation and Gaming community based on our discussion.

Keywords: Borders · Diversity · Ethics · Simulation and Gaming · Game Design · Game Facilitation · Game Content

1 Ethical Issues for Crossing Borders

In this paper, we will explore some of the ethical issues of Simulation and Gaming (S&G). While many authors – including ourselves – have already discussed such ethical issues, [1–3], we need to reconsider these matters, taking into account the fact that we live in times in which we are becoming more aware of the harmfulness of the dividing lines we have drawn and continue to draw e.g. between different cultures or gender identities and several other aspects of diversity. The need for defying and crossing these self-imposed borders has become clearly evident and has raised new discussion points also for the community of S&G.

When we refer to the term border in this paper, we should realize the multiple meanings it has. First of all, we use the term to refer to the border between countries. However, in the current world where diversity matters, we realize other borders, or boundaries, that divide our world, whether we ourselves actively notice them or not.

For example – to pick one element of diversity – a harmful border between genders may have gained more and more awareness and criticism through equal rights movements and changes in many societies in the past 100 years. Nevertheless, even within processes in society and organizations that are related to this dimension of diversity and equality these borders have often not been addressed properly, as the metaphorical expression of 'the glass ceiling' implies. The term 'glass ceiling' describes the phenomenon of seemingly invisible barriers that prevent women from reaching the highest management positions. These invisible borders still lead to unfair and unethical consequences (e.g. still unequal payment for men and women for the same work in the majority of societies worldwide). Regarding S&G we must admit that systematic research is lacking. It seems that ISAGA and other S&G communities have just recently become aware of the need to discuss such issues of gender equality and how they are interconnected with gaming, e.g. in a reflection on female game players, facilitators, designers and female game characters and how gender is represented in games [4]. If we take a look into reported gender effects in game evaluation studies [5], we often find unconscious and unintended but very strong stereotypes in the behaviour of male and female players that lead to unintended outcomes of learning during and after the gameplay (see more detailed example below). Overall, a gender perspective is still underrepresented in gaming research and gaming practice.

The aspect of gender was taken here as only one exemplary case as basis for the argumentation, that all dimensions of diversity (see below) are not yet sufficiently taken into consideration in a systematic and scientifically sound manner by the research and practice regarding S&G. At the same time, these aspects regarding the differences between people's identity, culture, or background and S&G also have ethical implications. The issue of crossing and overcoming diversity-related borders and boundaries can then be interpreted as to how sustainably and appropriately we deal with these differences in the processes of S&G. Managing diversity is thus increasingly becoming an ethical issue also for our discipline.

The literature on diversity and its management often refers to so-called diversity dimensions. The 'Four Layers of Diversity' model according to Gardenswartz and Rowe [6] is a widely used way of dealing with diversity in organizations. When we discuss the topic in this paper, this approach seems to be well suited. In this model the individual personality of involved stakeholders (e.g. game designers, facilitators, players, sponsors and clients, etc.) is one of the four layers. Together with the second layer of internal dimensions – these are gender, age, race, ethnicity, sexual orientation and physical (dis)abilities – elements of diversity are defined that are relatively difficult or impossible to change for the individual person and they should be particularly protected against discrimination. The above example regarding gender is therefore only one of several inner dimensions of diversity. In general, the S&G communities have to deal with the ethical implications that result from the management of all different aspects of diversity, equity and inclusion in the processes of S&G. The third layer describes external dimensions which can be changed. However, they must be respected and taken into account for a fair and ethical treatment of people involved in S&G activities: religion, marital and parental status, income and socio-economic status, educational background and skills, work experience, appearance, personal habits, and geographic location. The last and fourth layer of organizational dimensions consists of attributes that normally change several times in the course of our professional and working life: functional level, job, seniority, working location, management status, work-related units or departments or groups, etc. Other research shows the additional relevance of the diversity regarding cultural backgrounds [7]. All these dimensions generate dangers for discrimination and unethical treatment often based on unconscious mental borders or stereotypes we draw.

For example, designing (and the designed content and game artifact), playing, and debriefing can intentionally (manipulation, indoctrination) or unintentionally promote certain stereotypes, lead to harmful and discriminating effects (e.g. exploitation of 'tokens', normalization of unethical behaviour, negative shifting of moral standards, negative effects on emotions, metal models and self-confidence of involved people, etc.).

We need to reconsider and cross borders related to all of the different diversity dimensions, and interconnected ethical issues must be discussed for the process of S&G. Within this process, several critical factors for designers, facilitators, and evaluators of simulation games determine if an ethical and sustainable learning environment for participants and users can be created. Therefore, in the paper, the presented ethical viewpoints are explored from three perspectives, namely the ones of game design, game facilitation and debriefing, and game content.

2 Ethical Issues of Game Design

In general, there can be many different forms of intended and unintended unethical use of S&G. One aspect of this is manipulation and various possible motivations for being manipulative in gaming. For example, players and facilitators as main actors of a gameplay might attempt to realize a personal gain, to attain feelings of power and superiority in relationships with other participants, to be in control, or to boost own self-esteem and – in competitive simulation games – to win the game [8].

In this section we will explore some issues connected to game design. There are several interconnections between S&G and ethics from the perspective of design science [9]. From the design science point of view games are used to foster learning on individual, collective, and organizational levels and to support decision making, policy development and transformation processes of large socio-technical systems. Simulation games may be designed as a media of communication to support certain behaviour and/or to create certain awareness and mindsets. This can lead to fruitful learning and change of dysfunctional systems towards a better future of individuals, groups, organizations, and societies. However, all media can be used for manipulation, too (see also Sect. 4). This includes building or reinforcing specific stereotypes and attitudes due to the values or interests of the game designers or their sponsors. The aims could reach from political and ideological indoctrination to criminal economic and financial interests through the application of games. It is obvious that game designers have to prevent the game from being fake and designed for manipulation.

The founding father of ISAGA, Richard Duke, has already reflected on some aspects of ethics in his influential 1974 book [10]. One main focus of concern lies on legal issues like copyrights and intellectual property rights regarding designers and their game products. Furthermore, Duke [10] points out that "Since games entail demands on individuals in terms of time, cost, and psychological resources, it is incumbent upon the profession to develop an ethical code governing appropriate use of games." (p. 102). Such a commonly agreed on ethical code or standard is still missing. According to Duke, a simulation game designer has an obligation to the game participants and facilitators to present them with a game of clear content. "The game designer has a further obligation to produce a non-manipulative, neutral design. By neutrality of design, what is meant is that there must be safeguards against the game designer constructing a situation which is self-serving, whether self be the designer or the client" (p. 103). For example, if a game is intended to be in use to convey information or to be a tool for a training of skills, but is then used (within a hidden agenda) as a psychological testing device or as tool for personnel selection, basic ethical principles have been violated. Duke also argues that the designer has a special obligation to provide the game facilitators with information which will allow them to use the game with optimal quality and results. This includes a thorough game concept report, a facilitator manual and materials and information to run the game in a fully operational way.

Duke [10] discusses that for the game design, the validity of the simulated system conveyed must be established. Klabbers [9] stated that the issue-driven science of design approach emphasizes the usability of simulation games. In this perspective their development and use in practical contexts is of high importance. Here, it is necessary to focus on local knowledge and unique, individual circumstances to derive customized solutions to practical problems. A potential ethical problem can occur if sponsors of the game follow some own interests and try to intentionally or unintentionally influence the designed game artifact to represent their own mental models or interests.

Many game design frameworks recommend to already include a variety of stakeholders in the whole game design process (e.g. the well-known 21-step policy game design method of Duke and Geurts [11]). Important stakeholders are the sponsors or clients, all people that are representatives and experts for the content, simulated system and case situation in reality and also representatives of the target group (future players and users of the game). They should be partially taken into the design team as members. Other stakeholders are included through regular meetings and presentations of the game development progress. If a concept report has been prepared based on the reviews of stakeholders the game has been designed to accurately reflect the conceptual map of the referenced reality from the point of view of the relevant experts. The game design is an iterative process that involves cycles of development and testing the model and gameplay. This agile approach ensures some guarantee of validity. Here it is necessary to partially integrate the stakeholders in the prototype testing phases, too. However, the designer has to be aware of and to handle and balance different interests and sometimes has to deal with unethical misuse of power and micropolitics of stakeholders that are taking part in the development of the simulation game model. Often they aim to enforce a specific interest and one-sided interpretation on the reality.

As an example of integrating stakeholders, we shortly point out a game design project of Kriz and Eberle [12]. The German children's television channel (KiKA) ran programs with the theme 'Living together, now and in the future'. The editorial office of KiKA proposed a 30-min special broadcast to address the following questions: How can people of different origins, skin colors and religions harmoniously live together in Germany, given that their value systems may differ?; and How do we want to live together in the future?. For this special broadcast, KiKA asked for the design of a simulation game. The gameplay and debriefing of which would be recorded and shown on the television show. One of the implemented design principles was to include the relevant stakeholders in the design process. A diverse group of children was selected as representatives of the target audience (with different cultural backgrounds, religions, genders and identities), because the game itself focused on dealing with the potential conflicts that might arise in a culturally diverse society. They acted as co-designers. Some of the children had immigrated to Germany, others did not have German as their native language. From an ethical perspective it is important that children are given opportunities to explore alternative futures that go beyond the conditions set by adults, to deal with the increasing complexity of society, as well as with the issues of co-existence and conflict resolution from the perspective of diversity.

As one of the game elements the players assumed the role of a self-determined character. To create an in-game avatar, the so-called "player passport" was used. Here the players have considerable freedom; they can use their "true self" as a template, or design a completely different, fictional persona by choosing a name and gender, leisure preferences, religion (or atheism), nationality, and languages to be spoken in their homes. The inclusion of several diversity variables was important for the realism of the game, but could also be stressful. Therefore the designers decided to not explicitly simulate race or skin color. Although these attributes play an important role in the real world, they were not directly simulated due to their sensitive nature, as some of the kids reported that these aspects caused some distress. This shows how important it is to integrate the perspectives of the target group and to seriously take their emotions and experiences into account. Another important principle was to not manipulate the possible future game outcomes. In other words, the authors tried to avoid biasing the simulation towards a particular model of society.

To prevent unethical influences, designers have to ensure real multi-perspectives and dialogue in the design process and within the design team. A diversity of perspectives will not only increase fidelity and relevance to reality, it will increase the usability and potential of the game for fulfilling its primary goals. At the same time, in order to cross borders, the selection of design team members, test players and experts has to take the diversity dimensions into consideration that were discussed above. Ideas to combine stakeholder management and diversity management [13] should be used for the process of game design. This can help to design a simulation model (representation of the simulated system) and a didactic model (how to apply the game in the situation of play through facilitation and debriefing) that take ethical aspects of the simulated reality into account. Designers, test-players and selected stakeholders that represent a maximum mix and variety of diversity dimensions and bring them into the process will increase the awareness for sensible aspects of the game and enhance the game's potential to cross borders in an appropriate way.

Duke [10] also became well known for his concept of 'multilogue' (or focused solution-oriented and holistic multi-dialogue). He argued that existing communication modes do not address complex problems adequately. Duke proposed S&G as a future language for better understanding and changing of complex malfunctioning systems because it is a form of gestalt-communication, a multilogue, which is more than adequate for dealing with systems and communicating complex interrelationships of reality. Multilogue is the primary interaction pattern in S&G [14]. In his framework, communication through a gaming model entails not only multilogue among the players, but also multilogue between players, facilitators and designers. In order to foster this kind of communication within the design process we need to apply 'meta-debriefing' and formative evaluation throughout the whole design process [15, 16]. In such a continuous meta-debriefing, game designers, facilitators, participants (players) and other stakeholders reflect on shared feedback, on the game outcomes and discuss the game process. It helps to understand how and why the game works in specific contexts and how the game quality can be improved for specific target groups. Such an approach guarantees the best opportunities to check whether there are sensible and potentially discriminating elements in the game. Elements that may make users feel uncomfortable can be identified and ideas for solving potential threats can be generated.

As an exemplary case for the usefulness of meta-debriefing and formative evaluation in the design process, we make use of the research of Kriz and Auchter [17] who performed a series of evaluation studies in which nearly 8200 students participated in more than 300 startup business games in a game-based entrepreneurship program that was conducted together with approximately 150 universities under the auspices of the German Federal Ministry of Economics and Technology. As an example, we briefly discuss here some of the effects related to gender that were found in the evaluation studies. In contrast to the program's intentions of increasing entrepreneurial motivation, the analysis revealed reduced motivation among female participants. Compared to their male peers, women had a better knowledge of business administration and created better business plans; however, the predisposition to start a business was found significantly less among women than among men, both before and after the simulation. Compared to men, women demonstrated less inclination to take risks; their willingness to take on a leadership role in the simulation games was also less pronounced. Specific gender stereotypes contributed to these outcomes. The formative evaluation and meta-debriefing led to special seminars that were conducted for women only. Furthermore, the male facilitators were replaced with female facilitators (as better role-models). Additionally, a board-based simulation game (same learning goals and simulated variables, but as a board game instead of the previously used digital computer-assisted game) was applied. The debriefing was also modified in response to conducted interviews. The interview results showed that women were more content-oriented (learning from the game), whereas men were more competition-oriented (winning the game). Women desired a more detailed discussion of the game results. The extended debriefing process was likely responsible for the significantly improved outcomes, compared with the traditional mixed-gender seminars. These findings demonstrate how an iterative adaptation of simulation games in the design, as well as the facilitation of gameplay and debriefing settings, can diminish negative effects and help to reach the desired learning outcomes. The introduction of board-based simulations and extended debriefing sessions for the women-only seminars resulted in significant reductions in gender differences and improved learning; it also led to higher motivation and desire to launch start-up businesses. Several design aspects of the special test games were later included in the regular mixed-gender program. These changes had no negative impact on the participating male students, it was possible to implement significant optimisations with benefits for both male and female students.

Another pioneer of simulation game design - next to Dick Duke - was Cathy Greenblat; both of them also worked together closely in several projects. An important concept that Greenblatt contributed to the discussion is called 'multiple reality' [18]. She discussed game design and game use as a social construction of reality and disputed the existence of a common reality underlying game design and use. The different involved actors negotiate reality in design, use, and debriefing. Different individual mental models provide the base for multiple realities, and multiple realities tend to arise from the conflicting goals of different stakeholders. To increase diversity in the design process may bring the risk of more conflicts, but it also has the potential to increase awareness about borders and the chance to overcome unconscious limitations caused by implicit assumptions, bias and stereotypes. Therefore, game designers need to have professional skills to moderate and to handle group dynamics for using the diversity in the design team to create games that have a better opportunity of overcoming unethical and restrictive conditions in games and to foster a beneficial participatory design and use of games.

The proceedings of the second ISAGA conference 1971 in Utrecht have already discussed several aspects that are still relevant in the modern game design. The summary of a discussion at the conference by Becker [19] describes, that design related decisions have to be made that imply the need to cross and overcome borders. Some decisions lead to core issues when it comes to defining the purpose and objectives and target groups of the designed artifact. In the aspect of validity and usefulness, our predecessors struggled with the option to make games more complex and to increase realism, or to make games more simple and playable for the goal of learning (taking into account the difference between a purpose of educational game models versus policy game models). For game design ethics it is the consensus, that the design should minimize all unnecessary complexity, uncertainty and ambiguity in the scenario and the gaming materials, that is not needed for reaching the intended results. At the same time, a valuable simulation game should offer the players an appropriate level of uncertainty that activates the participants to develop strategies for acting and deciding, but that is not overburdening through too much complexity. This partly depends on the prior knowledge and level of skills the target group of participants will bring into the game. Another furthermore important design decision is the focus on the issue, whether the simulation game should contribute to the status quo (like in many so-called rigid-rule games) or should aim for social change (as in so-called free form games). This leads to an ethical principle, that the game should be preferably designed in a way that game elements like rules and steps of play are less rigid and normative and more open to ensure that there is enough freedom for facilitators and participants to contribute and to tailor their own learning process. This will also provide more chances for crossing borders and for dealing with diversity more flexibly, and for handling unforeseen game and group dynamics that lead to discrimination, inappropriate reinforcement of all kinds of boundaries and harmful experiences. In open and free form games some key elements can be rapidly adapted in order to react to the emotional needs, mental capabilities and skills of the involved players in interconnection with certain diversity dimensions of the game users. If rigid rule games are applied, at least a debriefing process has to be designed, that allows to realize the constraints of the game model.

3 Ethical Issues Regarding Facilitation

Facilitation is getting more important and more challenging than ever before. In this age of diversity, facilitators are in the position of running S&G with participants who have multiple backgrounds in various aspects such as professional knowledge and skills, culture, gender identity, religion, and values. The differences among participants create very different perspectives and can provide precious opportunities of learning if properly addressed. On the other hand, if the correct presentation of such differences fails, the game could result in miserable discomfort and unresolved miscommunication in both participants and facilitators.

First, we would like to emphasize to facilitators the importance of preparation. Collecting information related to participants would help facilitators to select a suitable game and be sufficiently prepared for the running and debriefing of the game. For example, age, gender, native language, academic backgrounds, etc., of participants would be useful to prepare for the session of S&G. In addition to these characteristics, facilitators should try to consider participants' experiences in S&G. People who have experienced many S&G sessions tend to exhibit more readiness, for example, and are less hesitant to jump into the situation provided by the game and more open to take action. They would be faster to understand the procedure of a role-sharing system or a scoring system than those who have little experience of S&G sessions. When the level of experience of S&G among participants are varied, facilitators can ask people who have much experience to support other members and encourage people who are not accustomed to S&G to ask for help from others. Facilitators are responsible for noticing the differences among participants and building an atmosphere that is respecting of each other and that appreciates the differences as they bring new viewpoints into the session.

Facilitators are responsible for explaining how the session will proceed and what will happen during the session beforehand so that participants can grasp an idea of the session even if it is vague. The participants would feel safe to know that they are not the only ones to be left alone in an unknown world. In some games, facilitators are not allowed to give much information beforehand. In that case, although the facilitators cannot explain the details, they are still responsible for creating a space where participants feel free to act as they like. Kriz [20] mentioned establishing a contract with participants, either verbal or written, "assigning in what ways participants will interact with each other to optimally support learning" (p. 668). The idea of such a "full value contract" is to build a safe environment, free from bullying, physical violence, etc., and to organize a collaborative learning environment of constructive feedback among participants. Sometimes we can even draw in participants' attention by saying that physical violence is strictly prohibited, to give a warning that participants will be frustrated during the session and be expected to endure the frustration.

Facilitators need to pay attention to the methods to convey information to participants. Rules can be explained literally, verbally, visually, etc. Several medias such as audio, paper, screen, etc. would help participants to understand the meaning of information. Some people easily understand the meaning of information by seeing rather than listening or the other way around. Pictures and illustrations help most people to grasp the meaning of words. Some people may prefer to read the definition of things in words. If facilitators prepare several tools to convey information, it contributes to raising the level of participants' understanding. Some participants would be overwhelmed with tons of information at the beginning. The facilitator can in this case help them to prioritize the crucial information by asking them a question to make them focus on the most essential element needed to make a good plan [21]. In addition, it is very important to tell participants that playing is the best way to understand how things work. Facilitators need to decide when to stop briefing and go to the next stage, that is, game execution. Jones [1] advised "keep the briefing brief" (p. 34). Thiagarajan [22] insisted to keep instructions within 4 min, named the "4-min rule". This is because spending too much time on briefing will interfere with the flow of the game run. Even if this rule may be applicable only for shorter games with less complexity, also comprehensive simulation games with a duration of several days should use not too much time in the briefing and may provide written information beforehand for preparation. Thus, one possible option is to provide basic information at the beginning and add more information later. Anyway, participants will deepen their understanding of how to play the game during the session. Table 1 shows the four phases which facilitators deal with for S&G session and what facilitators do in these phases. There are many other things to do, such as room arrangement, team organization, etc. If you are interested in the detailed list of facilitation, please refer to Nakamura [23].

Table 1. The four phases of facilitation, the time, and what facilitators do in a S&G session

Phases	Time	What facilitators do
1. Preparation	Before Game run	Gathering information and preparing games (selecting, adjusting, or designing games, and preparing materials)
2. Briefing	Before Game run	Clarifying the purpose of the session, explaining the rules, and organizing teams
3. Execution	During Game run	Observing the flow of the game and handling troubles if needed
4. Debriefing	After Game run	Escaping from the game world, looking back at what happened, sharing opinions, deepening thoughts, and building up the connections to the real world

As for the briefing, facilitators should keep in mind that the expression 'game' has a wide range of meanings. The participants may not share a common view of the S&G session. Facilitators are responsible for fostering a more common and better understanding of S&G among participants at the beginning of the session. In Table 1, briefing requires facilitators to clarify the purpose of the session: the reason why S&G is used, a brief account of the game that is to be played, etc. After that, the rules will be explained, and teams will be organized. To reduce the anxiety among participants, facilitators can offer a trial run before the real run [24]. Participants can therefore test their ideas, get feedback, and understand the mechanics of the game at least partially.

How to organize teams depends on the situation. Suppose, for instance, there are five female participants and ten male participants. When we ask them to form a group of three, we can ask them to combine one female and two male participants in a group. This indicates that facilitators expect each team to be gender-diverse. For another example, suppose there are two non-native speakers among 20 participants. When we ask them to form a group of five, we can ask the two non-native speakers to be in the same team. This indicates that facilitators expect the two participants to help each other and understand the situation better. Based on the information obtained during the preparation, facilitators should plan ahead for team organization. Facilitators should remember that their way of handling the differences among participants will set the atmosphere for the session.

In game execution, a facilitators' main role is to observe the flow of the game vigilantly. Superficially regarded, they do nothing but standing. Quietly and carefully, they listen and watch what is happening and are prepared to support participants and/or handle troubles if needed. They try not to draw attention to themselves so that participants can concentrate on their works. They stay close by just in case participants need their help. If they notice that a certain participant has a difficulty to catch up with other members, they may need to decide whether to lend a helping hand to the participant or to ask surrounding members to help the participant. Facilitators are responsible for avoiding unintended harm that may arise and develop rapidly. For example, cultural differences may cause unintentional misunderstandings. Silence implies agreement in some cultures and it does not in other cultures. In today's global society, facilitators are required to pay much more attention to cultural differences. In case of an emergency—such as a certain participant becoming mad at someone's behaviour and seeming to lose control—the facilitator should step in and get the situation under control. However, if conflicts are within the scope of prior assumptions regarding how the game is expected to play out, the facilitator should not take any visible action. The main role of the facilitator during the game run is to monitor miscellaneous events for debriefing.

If the purpose of the S&G session is learning, then debriefing is essential. Crookall [25] said, "[the] game design should start with the place where the participants are going to learn, that is, with the debriefing. At the very least, the debriefing should be a design consideration right from the start." (p. 908). Crookall [26] also mentioned that running S&G without debriefing participants fully is unethical.

For debriefing, facilitators can start by explaining what to do during debriefing. When some participants have never experienced debriefing, a brief instruction would be helpful. The debriefing proceeds from the moment of stepping out of the game world, to looking back at what happened during the game, sharing opinions among participants, deepening thoughts, and it ends with building up the connection to the real world.

If a facilitator's manual shows a list of questions for debriefing, these provide a good start. Facilitators can begin by picking some questions from the list and creating a new list of questions referring to the given list. There is a so-called common flow of debriefing as starting from concrete experiences during the game, generalizing them, and applying them to real-world behaviours. Keeping in mind the common flow, facilitators can prepare a list of questions before the S&G session and arrange it during the session.

During debriefing, facilitators should be sensible about who is speaking. Being a minority usually makes people quiet. Facilitators need to provide an opportunity for everyone to make a statement. Being part of a majority can be problematic in the sense that people might often miss the real issue. Facilitators need to mention the importance of different perspectives, especially those of the minority, to get to the real issue. The phase of debriefing has to be planned ahead and pre-designed as a kind of 'choreography' to ensure a variety of perspectives being discussed and contributed by participants. For the diversity of perspectives and inclusion of all participants it may be necessary to use a mixture of debriefing methods in the different steps of the reflection [20], e.g. a combination of written and oral debriefing formats with a variation of group sizes (from individual, pairs, small groups to plenary) during the debriefing steps.

Stewart's advice [27] is valuable to remember: debriefers should guide the pace and the depth of the debriefing to minimize discomfort whenever possible, because debriefing sometimes may be an uncomfortable activity for participants. Some participants may misunderstand debriefing as looking for the person who is responsible for a 'bad' result. This perception is totally wrong. The world created by S&G is a condensed world where something is designed to happen so that participants can experience it during the session and learn new perspectives through debriefing. Debriefing exists to collect data and share how this looks from different viewpoints. To reflect on the influence of diversity and ethical aspects during play, facilitators can address related issues in the debriefing. This will increase sensibility and awareness about communication and behaviour in the gameplay and lead to an understanding of how boundaries and stereotypes were reinforced or overcome. These insights for dealing with diversity in a humane and adequate way can be transferred to situations in the real world. Through "what if"-questions participants can explore alternative rules, behaviours and decisions. New rules, for example, would bring different effects and outcomes to subgroups and minorities with a different mix of diversity. The conclusion obtained from debriefing is meant to be different each time. Kriz, Kikkawa, & Sugiura [8] call participants the co-designers of S&G. We would furthermore call both participants and facilitators co-learners. Facilitators need to have leaner attitudes. S&G is never the same. Without a learner's mind, facilitators will miss what they could learn from S&G. In summary, facilitators need to be as prepared as possible off-site and as flexible as possible on-site.

4 Ethical Issues of the Contents of the Games

Here we discuss the ethical issues from the perspective of game content, both intentional and unintentional. Yet, it is impossible to fully cover all problematic cases, therefore we focus on some of the evident ethical issues that have arisen in recent years, exploring them in more detail. They are fourfold: Ethical issues regarding culture, stereotypes, intentional manipulation, and lastly regarding unintentional manipulation.

4.1 Issues Relating to Culture

We start this section with an anecdote that one of our colleagues experienced when he conducted a workshop in a rural agricultural village in Vietnam. The workshop consisted of several games for local people to improve their understanding of risk-related environmental issues. Some of the people seemed to be affected by their religion. He used GARBAGE by Thiagarajan [28] in the workshop. However, all Muslims refused to play it, since the rule contains cheating. Muslims living in developed countries understand perfectly well the environmental issues in developed countries and the rules in games. The creed of Islam does not allow cheating.

The above anecdote tells us that we should be more aware of cultural issues since even popular games contain risks of being interpreted as unethical depending on the culture. In other words, we must be careful when using games for people with different cultures. We need as much of a preparatory investigation into issues of culture as possible when we plan the game workshop. If local cultural elements are reflected in the materials that are used and in how games are played, games may be of better use and fulfill more educational goals. Localization would be indispensable when games are introduced in actual, e.g., rural, settings. That is, the essence of games – that they can be brought in as is – is global but materials and tools to be used need to be localized, e.g., to fit the local culture.

Games relating to cultural awareness themselves may cause ethical issues nowadays. For example, BAFÁBAFÁ [29] is a classic and one of the most frequently used games for increasing awareness of cultural differences, such as the ones we raised by exemplifying the aforementioned anecdote. However, when the game was developed 1974, we lived in a more homogeneous society and had less of a chance to encounter other cultures. Therefore, while the game experience has offered an invaluable opportunity to notice the cultural difference. Nowadays we are more aware of the differences in culture, including religion, and a game that contains such exclusions as BAFÁBAFÁ may raise ethical issues for players. In other words, it is too close to the reality. Experiencing exclusion may not be educative anymore, but rather considered unethical.

BARNGA [30] is a game that has also been used for improving cultural awareness and could overcome this ethical issue. In most cases, players may experience embarrassment when entering a new group that has a different set of rules in the game. However, the game has the possibility that newcomers to a group can change the rules, i.e., the culture of the group by silently persuading other players. This is indeed a matter of 'silent' persuasion, since the game rule forbids verbal communication among players, though it frequently occurs in practice.

4.2 Considerations Related to Increasing Prejudice or Stereotypes

Awareness of ethical issues has been increasing in the world of entertainment games. In the entertainment games field, there is greater awareness of ethical issues as they relate to game development and how the game is perceived by its customers. For example, board game companies 'Board & Dice' [31] and 'Hans im Glück' [32] announced that they would stop selling the games of a particular designer and collaborating with their work unless the designer acknowledged wrongdoing and corrected instances of discriminatory wording. In addition, 'Hans im Glück' [33] later apologized for the use of a black dice in their popular game, 'Marco Polo', as there was the possibility that the dice could be interpreted as black slaves and the trafficking of slaves.

These kinds of ethical issues are especially difficult when the theme of a game deals with history. Ethical issues related to board games have been pointed out in numerous studies [34], as well as inclusion and diversity issues [35]. The game industry has been paying more attention to this matter, as the ever-increasing gaming population assumes a more global character. Related changes have already been occurring in practice. For example, when you carefully look at game packages, you notice that more attention has been paid to addressing ethnicity and that there is a greater diversity in the game characters and the colour of their skin, to be more inclusive, rather than stereotypical.

4.3 Intentional Manipulation of Games

We must be careful to guard ourselves against manipulation that is hidden from us in our time. For instance, during WWII, many games were developed for propaganda purposes, i.e., for justifying wars and increasing aggression toward other countries, religions, and ethnicities. For example, Kikkawa [36] previously discussed a German game that had been designed to teach children to avoid shopping at Jewish shops (Fig. 1). The objective of the game was for children to learn that Jewish people earn a lot of money and that they should therefore be discriminated against and even deported out of town. Here, the game was used for Nazi propaganda and as a manipulative educational tool.

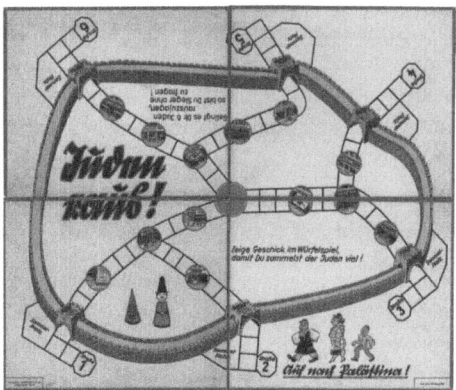

Fig. 1. 'Juden Raus' game

The LANDLORD'S GAME, which later became MONOPOLY®, would be another good example. The original game was developed to teach that an economy that rewards the creation of wealth is better than one in which monopolists work under few constraints [37, 38]. This differs completely from the objective of today's MONOPOLY®.

Recently, the surface value of the games has attracted marketing experts' attention. Many companies have used games to increase their sales whether the games are digital or analog. Games are used for propaganda purposes even in contemporary times. For example, before the 3.11 Fukushima disaster in 2011, the Japan Atomic Energy Agency used games to promote and foster public acceptance of nuclear energy. One of them was developed in 2008 using the Japanese traditional 'Sugoroku' games, whose rules are similar to that of 'snake and ladders' (Fig. 2). The name of the game is 'Kuru-kuru Uran game', whose direct translation is 'Cycle of the Uranium'.

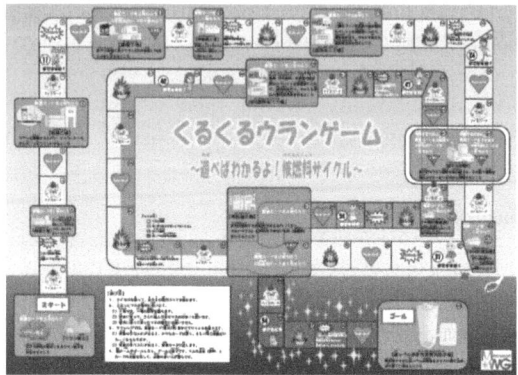

Fig. 2. "Uranium Energy Recycling" game

The purpose of the game is to gain public acceptance of the nuclear fuel cycle, which the government has strongly enforced and has still stuck to. The targeted players could be young school students, considering its content and phonetic subscripts added to the Chinese characters to increase readability. We would argue that analog games, in particular, are frequently used for propaganda purposes since they are easier to be included in school education programs than digital games. We must be careful in using these games whose themes deal with controversial issues, especially when introducing them within the educational system.

4.4 Unintentional Manipulation of Games

Since winning is an objective of many games, one can implicitly or unintentionally manipulate participants by setting a specific winning condition. For example, if you want to have disciplined children/students, you can design a game in which a player who shows obedience to the teacher wins.

More subtly, you can design a game for "moral" education. The implication of the term 'moral' would be 'good'; thus, teachers would be likely to welcome such a game, at face value, as an educational tool. However, before using the game for instructional purposes, we must scrutinize the "morals being taught by the game and keep in mind that the learning point may completely change with the rules or winning conditions.

Even in the case of games dealing with SDGs (sustainable development goals of the United Nations) where people agree that expanding public understanding and practice of these goals is necessary, we have to scrutinize the contents to determine whether the game contents fit the spirits of the original SDGs. It is plausible that some people misinterpret the SDGs and deliver the wrong messages to the players.

An extensive example of the unintentional manipulative and unethical use of S&G in the field of business management simulation games is described in Kriz, Kikkawa & Sugiura [8]. As games are powerful and effective tools if properly used, S&G experts should be careful with the contents without being deceived by their surface value.

5 Conclusion and Proposals

Although we have a rich tradition of excellent games, only a few of which we have discussed here as examples, we cannot rely on this heritage to protect game users from the ill intent and manipulation of some people within the gaming industry. A code of ethics is necessary for the gaming community to ensure the enjoyment, usefulness for learning and a gain for personal development, well-being, and trust of game participants in using the designed game product. This code has been proposed previously by ISAGA founding father Richard Duke (see Sect. 2) in his book from 1974 [10]. Maybe now in 2024, 60 years later, ISAGA could start a new initiative to develop a code of ethics for game design, game facilitation and game evaluation.

More importantly, games should be redesigned or newly designed to minimize any ethical concerns. Nowadays, ethical issues have to be interconnected with issues of diversity to avoid any kind of discrimination and related negative effects of games for all participating stakeholders and actors involved in S&G. From its origins, the 'DNA' of ISAGA consists of a great variety of research topics and methodological approaches; a wide spectrum of simulation game forms (e.g. face-to-face to online web-based gaming, role-playing games, board-based games, frame games, computer-assisted games, policy exercises, behaviour games, computer simulations, and digital games); an international network of scientists with various disciplinary backgrounds, gaming professionals, and practitioners (designers, facilitators, trainers, consultants, etc.); an association in which all members share an interest to benefit from each other's knowledge; a community that strives for meta-disciplinary perspectives to solve complex problems and to change dysfunctional systems. This already existing diversity is a strength and supports the ability to cross various borders [9]. Therefore, ISAGA seems to be ideally suited to take on the difficult task of combining diversity management and ethical considerations and applying these principles to communities that develop and use simulation games. Our paper is aimed to revisit some ethical aspects related to S&G and intended to provoke a new discussion.

Regarding S&G we must admit that systematic research is lacking on the processes that lead to the creation of borders and strategies to overcome boundaries. Especially dangerous seems to be the unconscious and invisible borders we draw based on stereotypes about other human beings and social groups that nevertheless lead to unintended unethical consequences and manipulation in the design, content, facilitation and play of simulation games. Like the first attempt of Lukosch, Schmitz, & Bostan [4] for issues regarding gender and culture we propose to adopt a comprehensive framework from diversity management, e.g. the 'Four Layers of Diversity' model with its several dimensions and elements from Gardenswartz and Rowe [6]. Those elements should be systematically transferred and applied to reflect on implications for designers, facilitators and players with certain diversity characteristics and to reflect on how these diversity dimensions are represented in the game content and steps of play, facilitation and debriefing.

Considering that Duke's book title, 'Gaming is the Future's Language' [10] is the basis of our ISAGA community, we still have hope that S&G will contribute to solving the recent issues of crossing borders related to diversity with the updated ethical principles. Especially elements like meta-debriefing and a formative evaluation in the design and facilitation can help to create a multilogue communication not only during gameplay and debriefing, but as an interconnected learning community of designers, facilitators and players in a loop of continuous iterative reflection and improvement of games and their application. This kind of multilogue aims to minimize intended or unintended manipulation and to be more aware of some culture-related boundaries and constraints. In this way it is possible to uncover and bridge across obstructing psychological and social stereotypical dynamics.

As further implications for ISAGA, we propose to establish an ethics committee for dealing with copyright, intellectual property rights, and all unethical aspects including forms of manipulation and discrimination in the processes of S&G (including design, facilitation and evaluation phases). ISAGA could establish a (certified) train-the-trainer program that also deals with ethics of design, facilitation and debriefing. If this is not feasible, ISAGA could at least develop and publish an official code of ethics that is based upon recent knowledge from diversity management and that gives orientation about standards for ethics in game design, facilitation and debriefing. Finally, ISAGA could support the building of a repository of best-case and worst-case examples of games and their application that show and educate future generations in S&G about issues of ethics and dealing with diversity.

We are aware that regarding to the understanding and use of the term ethics in this article, we position ourselves with a focus on postmodern, applied and practical ethics [39] to explore relevant considerations of moral principles for game design, facilitation and debriefing. We are not taking a normative ethical perspective. For ISAGA as an organization, a suitable ethical positioning would have to be discussed further.

Acknowledgments. This study was funded by the Fusion of Science and Technology (Japan). We thank Katharina Ananda Kriz for editorial and language proof support.

Disclosure of Interests. The authors have no competing interests to declare that are relevant to the content of this article.

References

1. Jones, K.: Games and Simulations Made Easy: Practical Tips to Improve Learning Through Gaming. Kogan Page, London (1997)
2. Peters, V., van de Westelaken, M., Bruining, J.: Simulation games as a safe environment. Stud. Simul. Gaming **22**, 59–64 (2012)
3. Kikkawa, T., Kriz, W.C., Sugiura, J. (eds.): Gaming as a Cultural Commons: Risks, Challenges, and Opportunities. Springer, Singapore (2022)

4. Lukosch, H.K., Schmitz, C., Bostan, O.: Women (and a little bit of culture) in simulation gaming. In: Kikkawa, T., Kriz, W.C., Sugiura, J. (eds.) Gaming as a Cultural Commons: Risks, Challenges, and Opportunities, pp. 57–72. Springer, Singapore (2022)
5. Auchter, E., Kriz, W.C.: Gender aspects by using start-up simulations for entrepreneurship education. Results of theory-based evaluation studies. J. Asia Entrep. Sustain. **9**(1), 39–56 (2013)
6. Gardenswartz, L., Rowe, A.: Managing Diversity: A Complete Desk Reference and Planning Guide, 3rd revised edn. Society for Human Resource Management, Alexandria (2010)
7. Harvey, C.P., Allard, M.J.: Understanding and Managing Diversity: Readings, Cases, and Exercises. Pearson, Upper Saddle River (2015)
8. Kriz, W.C., Kikkawa, T., Sugiura, J.: Manipulation through gamification and gaming. In: Kikkawa, T., Kriz, W.C., Sugiura, J. (eds.) Gaming as a Cultural Commons: Risks, Challenges, and Opportunities, pp. 185–199. Springer, Singapore (2022)
9. Klabbers, J.: The Magic Circle: Principles of Gaming & Simulation, 3rd edn. Sense Publishers, Rotterdam (2009)
10. Duke, R.D.: Gaming: The Future's Language. Sage, New York (1974)
11. Duke, R.D., Geurts, J.L.A.: Policy Games for Strategic Management. Dutch University Press, Amsterdam (2004)
12. Kriz, W.C., Eberle, T.: Case example: KIKATOPIA game - a simulation game on diversity and living together with children as co-designers. In: Kikkawa, T., Kriz, W.C., Sugiura, J. (eds.) Gaming as a Cultural Commons: Risks, Challenges, and Opportunities, pp. 93–106. Springer, Singapore (2022)
13. Jolanta, M.A.J.: Diversity management's stakeholders and stakeholders management. In: Proceedings of the 9th International Management Conference "Management and Innovation for Competitive Advantage", pp. 780–793. Bucharest (2015)
14. Duke, R.D., Kriz, W.C. (eds.): Back to the Future of Gaming. W. Bertelsmann Verlag, Bielefeld (2014)
15. Kriz, W.C.: Creating effective learning environments and learning organizations through gaming simulation design. Simul. Gaming **34**(4), 495–511 (2003)
16. De Wijse-van Heeswijk, M., Kriz, W.C.: A design science perspective on formative evaluation in simulation games. In: Angelini, M.L., Muñiz, R. (eds.) Simulation Applications in Education: Towards a Collaborative Approach to Teaching and Learning, pp. 215–251. Springer, Cham (2023)
17. Kriz, W.C., Auchter, E.: 10 years of evaluation research into gaming simulation for German entrepreneurship and a new study on its long-term effects. Simul. Gaming **47**(2), 179–205 (2016)
18. Greenblat, C.S.: Designing Games and Simulations. Sage, Beverly Hills (1988)
19. Becker, H.A.: Summary of discussion. In: Becker, H.A., Goudappel, H.M. (eds.) Developments in Simulation and Gaming, pp. 155–160. Utrecht University, Utrecht (1972)
20. Kriz, W.C.: A systemic-constructivist approach to the facilitation and debriefing of simulations and games. Simul. Gaming **41**(5), 663–680 (2010)
21. Nakamura, M.: The effects of structured instruction on team performance. In: Dhar, U., Dubey, J., Dumblekar, V., Meijer, S., Lukosch, H. (eds.) Gaming, Simulation and Innovations: Challenges and Opportunities, pp. 15–27. Springer, Cham (2021)
22. Thiagarajan, S.: Secrets of effective and engaging games and simulations [Keynote address]. In: ISAGA 52th Conference, Indore (2021)
23. Nakamura, M.: Code of conduct for facilitators and the ethics of debriefing. In: Kikkawa, T., Kriz, W.C., Sugiura, J. (eds.) Gaming as a Cultural Commons: Risks, Challenges, and Opportunities, pp. 127–147. Springer, Singapore (2022)

24. De Wijse-van Heeswijk, M., Leigh, E.: Ethics and simulation games in a cultural context: why should we bother? In: Kikkawa, T., Kriz, W.C., Sugiura, J. (eds.) Gaming as a Cultural Commons: Risks, Challenges, and Opportunities, pp. 149–167. Springer, Singapore (2022)
25. Crookall, D.: Serious games, debriefing, and simulation/gaming as a discipline. Simul. Gaming **41**(6), 898–920 (2010)
26. Crookall, D.: Engaging (in) gameplay and (in) debriefing. Simul. Gaming **45**(4–5), 416–427 (2014)
27. Stewart, L.P.: Ethical issues in postexperimental and postexperiential debriefing. Simul. Gaming **23**(2), 196–211 (1992)
28. Thiagarajan, S.: Garbage: a card game that simulates the trade-off between competition and concern. Simul. Gaming **22**, 112–11 (1991)
29. Shirts, R.G.: BafáBafá: a cross culture simulation. Simulation Training Systems, Del Mar (1977)
30. Thiagarajan, S., Thiagarajan, R.: Barnga: A Simulation Game on Cultural Clashes. Intercultural Press, Boston (2006)
31. Board & Dice: Official statement regarding Daniele Tascini (2021). https://boardanddice.com/news/statement-on-daniele-tascini/. Accessed 31 Jan 2024
32. Hans im Glück: Statement zu Rassistischen Äusserugen (2021). https://www.hans-im-glueck.de/news/statement-zu-rassistischen-aeusserungen.html. Accessed 24 Sept 2021
33. Hans im Glück: Marco Polo - The black dice (2021). Accessed 24 Sept 2021
34. Draper, K.: Should board gamers pay the roles of racists, slavers and Nazis?: After the cancellation of Scramble for Africa, where do board gamers go from here?, 1 August 2019. https://www.nytimes.com/2019/08/01/style/board-games-cancel-culture.html. Accessed 31 Jan 2024
35. Hargrave, E.: Inclusion, diversity, and representation in board gamers and beyond (2020). https://stonemaiergames.com/inclusion-diversity-and-representation-in-board-games-and-beyond-guest-post-by-elizabeth-hargrave/. Accessed 31 Jan 2024
36. Kikkawa, T.: Subtle manipulation in games. In: Kikkawa, T., Kriz, W.C., Sugiura, J. (eds.) Gaming as a Cultural Commons: Risks, Challenges, and Opportunities, pp. 171–183. Springer, Singapore (2022)
37. Pilon, M.: The monopolists: obsession, fury, and the scandal behind the world's favorite board game. Bloomsbury (2015)
38. Kriz, W.C.: Historical Roots and New Fruits of Gaming and Simulation. Simul. Gaming **48**(5), 583–587 (2017)
39. Ryberg, J.: Applied Ethics. Oxford Bibliographies Online Research Guide. Oxford University Press (2010)

Where to Begin? Integrating Simulation and Indigenous Knowledges to Create New Approaches

Cat Kutay[1], Pavan Kumar Menugonda[1], Christian Gio Biag Lizada[1], and Elyssebeth Leigh[2]

[1] Charles Darwin University, Darwin, NT, Australia
cat.kutay@cdu.edu.au
[2] University of Technology, Sydney, NSW, Australia

Abstract. Developing programs using participatory action research can be assisted by considering the delivery as working within Cynefin domains of alternating shared and specialist knowledge. This provides a way of planning and preparing resources for that is a fluid process requiring sensitivity to the aspirations and engagement of other cultures. This paper looks at using this approach for training in game making in remote Aboriginal communities.

We consider the resources available for each domain of approach to support the training in ethe respective specialist knowledge. Given the use of AI in creating resources for game making and the open sharing of material which removes many barriers to entry into the area of game making, it is timely to be researching how to engage those with creative ideas in controlling their own game development.

The analysis provides a way to monitor the progress of training and to assist in moving from one complex or complicated domain to another with ease, and with awareness of what is suitable and supported at any time.

Keywords: First Nations Storytelling · Ambiguity in games · Games for playful learning

1 Introduction

The uptake of media communication by First Nations in Australia has been substantial. Radios, cassette tapes and CD's, were followed by cloud sharing, a process which reflects the long history of adaption of communication technology by a culture that values communication (Kral and Ellis, 2021). This work describes the planning for a participatory action research (PAR) project in remote communities in the NT of Australia. The project is based on efforts to share new information and communication technology for community use through games.

PAR is a process of collective and self-reflective inquiry, in which game makers and community members will try to understand and improve upon their practices and context of training. This process then leads to action which should empower the people and community to have increased control over their learning and eventually their lives (Baum et al. 2006). Given the history of dispossession in Australia it is important that efforts are made to provide support for such power shifts especially focused on knowledge sharing through different media.

Through use of up-to-date communication technology First Nations are continuing their practices of knowledge sharing across a wide expanse of peoples and lands. The audience for such media has been invariably First Nations, and little engagement occurs outside this community. This may be because the format created in First Nations media is still very much embedded in the culture and is quite foreign to the new settlers in Australia.

We look at game development as this provides an environment well understood by all, where First Nations can create a new world to represent their Dreaming Stories which are set in a timeless space representing the common patterns of the environment in which they live. The game can also present some aspects of the spiritual world that cannot be seen without a deep knowledge of the country, such as the transformation between people and their totems, or between spirit beings and the landscape. Previously John Bradley worked with various communities[1] to develop animations using a game engine, which illustrated this adaption of the technology.

The purpose of this project is to establish what games might be developed using community narratives, what tools assist in creating gaming components and what scripts can enable the gaming components to be integrated in a systematic way to assist the development. The aim is not to provide for game development solely in community at this stage, but a staged process. This paper looks at how to ensure a robust participatory approach to both the development of the tools to be used and workshop formats arising from the juxtaposition of the two knowledge systems. We are developing the games into a series of workshops to share skills in gaming media in remote communities.

The project starts with students and community members creating a storyline. These are usually based on local Dreaming stories, stories of care for country. The authors will have their own totem, the perspective from which they will tell this story. They may make 3D models of the totems, using software tools. They may record animations extracted from videos. They may draw background locations or extract this from google maps. All these components will build up the game and the previous work has been developing the tools that the developers will need to make these artefacts into games.

This gaming format of sharing knowledge through games will be more amenable to cross-cultural learning and bring the knowledge from First Nations communities into mainstream experience (Watson and Milward 2019). Also, the ambiguity in gaming and the playfulness of the media are both synonymous with First Nations learning methods (Kutay 2014), while the media is again appropriate for an oral tradition. The aim is thus to encourage the sharing of knowledge in a format that will increase truth telling and mainstream engagement with First Nations culture, values, beliefs, morals and ethics while using a process that reflects the original cultures' knowledge sharing skills.

2 Background

In 2011, the Australian national curriculum called for greater inclusion of Indigenous cultures, histories, values and knowledges. However recent attempts to provide improved services to First Nations due to these different and changing circumstances, have failed. To embed this cultural education in our curriculum and into society, requires that relevant material be collected in a format that will engage people (Bradley 2020). The media of

---

[1] https://www.monash.edu/arts/monash-indigenous-studies/wunungu-awara.

game is seen as a suitable means of reaching a broader audience than just schooling (Emery and Habel 2017).

This complex historical background requires that our game makers in the project receive cultural induction training before they go out to community to work with participants and also receive ongoing mentoring. The game makers will collect models, designs, and animations around a local story. The lead trainer/developer is First Nations, but the project team will be working on country that is not in the country or location of their knowledge. Hence, they will also be an outsider learning. The workshops will be done with people in community who are interested in using technology, for instance to teach language, and who are willing to share material around a relevant story.

When in community we have invited school students, staff and others to share stories. These are the likely participants for the project. Their stories will be rendered into games in visual 3D extracts of country from world data using the Unity Game engine. This will ensure the visuals match the true country as much as possible which has been a request from community in relation to animations (Bradley et al. 2010). Clay models of local characters (eg animals), backdrops from local artwork and animations extracted from videos using AI will provide the gameplay environment.

The project is using a participatory action research approach so that the skills and techniques of gaming can be shared without non-Indigenous technologies engulfing the local approaches to storytelling through overuse of mainstream methods. The present stage of this research is focusing on how to develop a game framework based on Unity, various plugins and other features, which provide a more accessible approach to community generating their own stories using their own creations. This will allow people from different communities to share games and gaming skills as well as opening participants to avenues for employment in design and programming. This is important as both the knowledge and the learning need to be collaborative (Sang et al. 2023).

There is however a proviso with this paper. This is written about the planning for the development and training process, it does not deal with our background in developing training for and with community or the process of developing a relationship with different communities where the project will start. This process depends on location and personnel so is not relevant to this paper.

2.1 Narratives as Themes

We expect the games will be based around the local Dreaming stories which are the traditional knowledge sharing process for First Nations in Australia. These stories are told to community members from a young age, and expand in detail as the child grows, until they provide a vehicle to share the knowledge required to care for that country. These provide an entirely different method of knowledge construction in the listener to the western cultural linear storyline methods. As noted in Duke (1974) the understanding of present technology and processes require a more complex communication tool:

"Consider our great urban centres as they exist today-multisystems within multisystems, alternative upon alternative presenting an incomprehensible, many-futured state which is being rearticulated daily-a great multifaceted sphere of complexity that cannot be managed, but must be. Management of such an environment requires a holistic perspective that cannot be obtained through traditional sequential communication forms". (pp. 4–5 Duke 1974).

We propose that the storytelling of First Nations provides just such a tool that allows those who learn with it to retain a much more complex and holistic picture of the domain they are studying (Kelly 2016). The use of non-linear storylines, focused on reinforcement learning within a consistent narrative framework, allows those learning through the story to experience a system where they gain a holistic understanding of the environment and its care. We plan to show the same narrative development through the gameplay.

The overall design is like Never Lone (Bryant 2014) where the knowledge of the community contributors will be accessed through related challenges in the game. The knowledge, the progression and the challenges are all part of the storyboard design with community.

2.2 Planning

In developing a process to negotiate game development with community we have various challenges. The one that we consider in this paper is how to prepare and manage workshops where *both way* learning occurs between those who are skilled in game making and those who know the stories, games and processes that can be shared with those outside the community.

Both way learning is a way in which knowledge can be shared between the two cultures, without imposing one knowledge system over another. This is a PAR approach which is critical to the work. We are dealing with two very different knowledge systems where we want each group to participate and engage in the knowledge of the others, so we wish to analyse these domains of knowledge. The project is considered as a melding of gaming and design skills, as well as the local knowledge that we wish to represent in the games.

There is also synergy between these two domains that suggest they will be a productive mix. Firstly, the ambiguity of games (Klabbers 2009) matches the technique of storytelling in Aboriginal communities which provides a way of sharing knowledge to those who may or may not have the prior knowledge to follow a story. The use of ambiguity allows in depth material to be shared in a story that is remembered, even if its significance is not understood at the time of telling. First Nations talk about how they remember the stories, and only later in life realise the significance of the stories.

Secondly the First Nations' stories are playful based, as they are in their beginning a communication to the young of basic principles, told within a story that grows with the listener over time. The use of totem animals, which are the responsibility of the person with that totem, also not only represents the animal or material being described (caring for country and wildlife) but also provides a gameful rendition of the moral and physical aspects of the story.

Finally the audio-visual nature of the game allows us to provide translations into the local language for those using or learning this language. The funding of languages in schools was reduced soon after the program started (Dickson 2012). This was after evaluation suggested this approach did not improve learning in English after a year 3 review. This is generally not long enough to evaluate an educational change. In the Decade of Indigenous Languages, we are hoping this will be reversed and implemented across the country.

Another feature is the orical aspects of storytelling that enable the listener to remember the themes of the story, and provide a way to persuade the listener of the importance of the moral and practical aspects being conveyed. Similarly in games various rhetorical methods are used to convey meaning to the player (Klabbers 2009). These rhetorical strategies have been transferred to mobile apps use (Kral and Ellis 2021) and may also be set into games.

2.3 Description of Knowledge Domains

We now look at how to blend the two knowledge domains. The main focus is on how to determine what approach to take at any stage of the training, when to focus on community knowledge or when to focus on gaming knowledge and how to assess when each approach will be most useful.

We consider the knowledge of each group (game makers and community) at times as either in depth, secret knowledge or as shared knowledge. These different levels of knowledge form different domains or aspects of the workshops we are proposing (domains shown in Fig. 1). We envisage we will have to pass through all these knowledge domains at some time in the work, but we are not sure where to start.

In our work our shared knowledge is in the "Obvious" domain where we understand each other's knowledge, if not approach. Each person's specialty is their own complicated domain but they form a mutually complex domains for the other participants. Also, in the Cynefin model the starting point is the central "Disorder" region where we decide where we need to work next. Hence, we want to consider what is creating this disorder so how we select where to move.

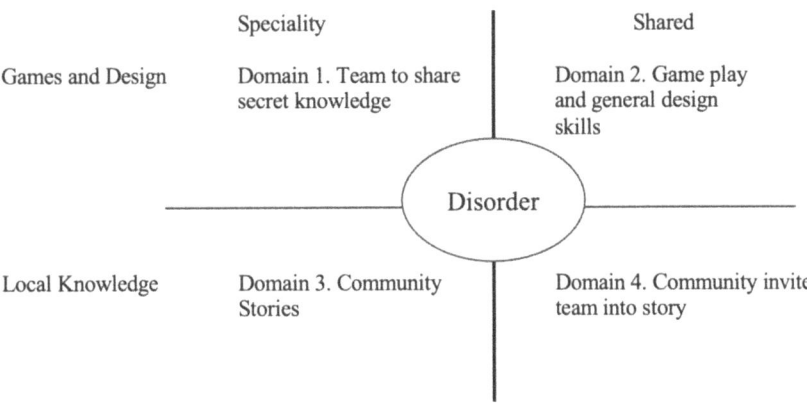

Fig. 1. Adapted from Cynefin domains of problem solving.

When providing skills from western technology to those in community, we are opening areas that have often been "secret" to First Nations. This is the specialised knowledge of the technology and is knowledge that is sought by people in community, but not presented in terms they know. That is, this specialist knowledge (eg of gaming) is often not shared, as mainstream game makers do not trust the First Nations students to understand. The entire lesson is dumbed down due to lack of prior shared knowledge.

However much of the knowledge of game playing, what makes good game play, how to design figures and background, are well developed in community and can be easily transferred into a game engine using existing tools. Hence this project is a timely approach to what is now a feasible way to share skills around the use of this technology.

On the other hand, community has many stories of country that they may wish to share. Those which they decide may be too important to share remain "secret" from those they do not trust to use the knowledge with respect. There will therefore be some shared knowledge in the team already around the process of stories and how they develop over time, but more needs to be understood to produce the games in an authentic form.

What we consider most important for clarifying the process is the central Disorder domain where we are not aware of how much is secret, the unknown unknowns, or how much the other participants trust us to share the knowledge required. At each stage in the project there will need to be a certain level of sharing to advance the project, and this must be done in a trustful environment. One step is to make this domain known to all as a place of temporary discomfort that needs to be considered with care, and then take the necessary steps to define what knowledge domain we are working in at any time, and to move between them to disperse power relations by working withing domains which are 'complicated' but not unknown to each of us.

3 Gaming Prototypes

We started the project with building a game like ones available to play in community. While the existing games bear little relation to First Nations knowledge systems, we chose themes relevant to the urban First Nations we were working with. These will provide something the participants can engage in as we wish to expand understanding of what is possible in gaming. The games we have built as exemplars are around community stories that are widely shared if not common knowledge.

The two games are designed to share First Nations' knowledges around specific areas, the Brewarrina Fish Traps[2] and the Budj Bim eel traps[3]. We can use these as games for the community participants to play to introduce the idea of designing their own game. The first game was developed working with members of the Brewarrina community to write the narrative, design the badges related to the eight-ways learning used in that area (Yunkaporta n.d.) and play test the game. The second game was based on material recorded online on Budj Bim and a previous animation made on the dreaming of that area[4].

Also, this project is tied to training around tools for language learning (King et al. 2023), hence the collection of resources and games for language sharing in context may be a good way to engage participants.

These games have provided a template in Unity which we can adapt to new narratives. We have seen that much of the actions and scripting that are needed to create these games are set up for a new story to be slotted in. However, we realise that there may be quite a different approach used by those in remote areas, as opposed to the urban work we have

---

[2] https://www.mpra.com.au/brewarrina-fish-traps.
[3] https://deadlystory.com/page/culture/history/gunditjmara_people_build_sophisticated_budj_bim_eel_trap_system
[4] Games Material https://test-game.dalang.com.au/.

been doing, hence we have developers involved in the workshops to supply new tools and templates as needed.

4 Process

Participatory action research is significant in this context. For many years study has been made of First Nations communities, without much feedback or engagement of local researchers, to consider what if any bearing the results have on reality, and what is the effect of such an outsider's impression of the community. Hence myths abound about how community people might engage with such a project, or how a project should be set up.

Furthermore, the skills to be shared are quite novel in community, while many will have played games, very few have had the chance to be creatives on the computer. The approach is to enable existing processes of storytelling, drawing and dance to provide the material for the game and to grow the narrative and game with the authors in a steady flow, to ensure that the authors have control over both the product and the process of creation. After each workshop in community we will create more tools and examples that will assist the authors in the process they develop.

Also the process of developing these workshops as participatory and incrementally developed, is very much up for debate. Hence, we provide a "process" that starts in each domain above and consider how it will progress. Here each domain is a region with experts and novices from either group, the community or game makers, and the project is to bring these two groups closer together in understanding and skills. This is both-way learning.

4.1 Starting in Domain 1

At university we are required to design the unit that we can take out to community, preparing a curriculum of some sort and designing the learning progression. Hence this is the domain or topic where we usually start as it ensures we have the material needed for the learning when we are 'remote'. However, if we start in this domain we have already (under-)estimated the skills brought by community to the project. Hence, we do not wish to design a process from the start, we are providing the tools for the community to be their own defenders of their knowledge system, to control how it is represented in gaming. Working in this domain includes the following resources which will enable the authors to create as much of the artefacts and gaming as possible within the community. Some aspects will need to be done back on campus.

Resources. The resources we plan for the project are crucial as these will need to be prepared prior to travel. They include:

Models. We are using clay to model avatars for the game and tools like Polycam or other 3D camera scanning programs which upload a series of photos taken around the model to the cloud, to be stitched together to form a 3D model. These are tools easily accessible to those in community who are creative and understand the stories.

Modelling tools such as Blender are complex to learn however they provide a way to rapidly manipulate 3D exports and clean them up, as well as rig them for animations. Also animations can be extracted for Unity from videos through AI resources such as DeepMotion[5] to provide relevant actions that relate closely to ceremonial forms.

In generating the environment of the game we want to emulate the real world as close as possible (Szapiro et al. 2020). The stories we are simulating are stories about country hence to respect the knowledge and the original transfer method of sharing knowledge 'on Country' is an important part of the project. Terra World is a Unity plugin which is the chosen development platform. It creates "close to reality environments using real-world data from Environmental Systems Research Institute,(ESRI), National Aeronautics and Space Administration (NASA) & OpenStreetMap along with built-in algorithms for procedural generation and placement of 3D assets in scene." (TerraWorld n.d.)

Scripting Tools. We are using a centralised dialogue control system, rather than a system where speech acts specify the next act to initiate. This approach provides robust branching scenarios for interactions. However, this reduces the ability to build the script from the characters, and requires the entire sequence be mapped out, with any repetition included in the dialogue tree. We use Visual Scripting to provide spoken/written interaction with characters and any information sharing with player.

Game Generation. The aspects of gaming that will need to be provided in the framework designed to support a plug and play approach to development, are provided here as the process that can be shared, and supported by the framework we are developing for these games.

1. Training in
    a. importing new terrain through Terra World
    b. cleaning and rigging a model in Blender.
    c. placing models in a scene in Unity
    d. generating animations from a video and attaching to a model
    e. edit videos to add more information from recordings.
    f. adding scripts for character interaction in Visual Scripting
    g. generating and exporting a game (to PC or STEAM)
2. Build skills in:
    a. Generating storyline in game
    b. Storyboarding the script
    c. Building relevant challenges

As noted, this domain is the standard domain where we normally start our training, and it provides us with an idea of what and who to take out to community. However, at times we may come to a stage of Disorder and need to give more control to the community members.

Output. This domain is where the physical manifestation of the game is produced for each story, and the game framework is designed and verified. It is the traditional learning environment of game making in university however may not be the final area we work in for this project. Considering the work that will be required to put the game online (or Steam) with correct permission, the final stage may lie more in Domain 3.

---

[5] https://www.deepmotion.com/.

4.2 Starting in Domain 2

If we start from where the participants are in their game play, we will provide a more robust connection to prior knowledge and relevance to their life. However, this may not extend beyond the realm of the present game consumption in communities. To engage in game creation requires new tools and new processes, and a great number of skills. This approach would be more around a "need to know" approach as the participants try and implement the ideas they create in their game design.

This is a domain where transformation learning, reflection and change of perspective will play a major part and hence likely to have the most impact on learning (Brandon et al. 2023). The idea of extending from a zone of proximal development is appealing. But also the fact that the genre of games will change significantly in the process suggests learning will be strong.

Resources. The background in language learning and teaching in the team will help provide an opening to discuss more learning focused games and allow community members to see the project as the knowledge sharing opportunity it is. The existing games that have been created both in English and for collecting and learning local languages will be shared in discussions with the participants from community. Similarly, the university team are from different language backgrounds so will have some experience of this process of game-based learning.

Another aspect is the need to consider suitable teaching styles in this domain. For example Warren and Young (2008) talk about the need to focus on experiential learning, oral format and the need to use the language of the domain to give participants an "opportunity to move out of their low socio economic circumstances and act as 'activists for real social change'".

Output. The output of this domain will be a design of the specific games and challenges, those that the community consider represent the knowledge or language they wish to either share or merely to emphasize to those around them. This will also help modify the gaming framework as we will need to support the processes and gaming aspects that the community members want to instantiate in the game.

4.3 Starting in Domain 3

Here we start with another aspect of the knowledge to be shared. This will be time spent telling and hearing stories. The stories will be the children's version of the Dreaming stories, the safe version with no secrets, as the game makers are too "young" in the culture to advance further into the knowledge. However, this means the true value of the story will not be shared. It will only be understood by the game makers to the extent to which the complexity of the game system needs to be understood, if a fuller version of a story can be shared. This is the domain in which relationships are formed, which is crucial to any knowledge sharing (Webb and Gordon 2023).

While spending the time to hear and learn the simple stories will help game makers gain the trust of the community, it will take a long time for this to have any impact on the game makers understanding. Working within this domain is more important for

First Nations in determining what story they can share in Domain 4, based on the game makers comprehension when told the children's version of the Dreaming stories.

Resources. This will be controlled by the community participants and is where the visiting game makers will be listening and learning from outside their domain of expertise. The importance of this domain is to be aware of the need to encourage these discussions and not to interrupt when community members offer such knowledge. The preparatory training will also include some examples of these stories and how they work as knowledge sharing to assist the game makers to appreciate the complexity of what they are taking part in.

As discussed above the stories are told at different levels and the university team will be coming in as 'children' into the knowledge system of the community. Importantly this is also the level that many of the game players will be located if the game is shared outside the community. Hence this will help them design the game as an oral knowledge sharing framework.

Output. There may not be much time for both way learning in this domain, as the vast knowledge being conveyed will require long listening and the necessary ambiguity in this mode of teaching will mean the use of questioning or comments will not be appropriate. Hence the learning will be both a specific story that the university group will learn part of, and some time for the two groups to understand each other better and form a relationship on which to develop the workshops.

4.4 Starting in Domain 4

As a first step we can ask what story the community would like to share. As it will be shared broadly it has to be knowledge they can trust giving to strangers through the gameplay. We can work with community people to establish the story and how much they wish to share and how they want to tell this story in the new medium. This will have the advantage of ensuring the community is happy with what the participants are working on, and hence it will be more likely available to share publicly when completed.

Again, this is a main design factor in the project, where unless trust is maintained and the community aware they are always dealing with a broad audience, the initial stories will not be sharable and hence it will be hard to promote the project and the game framework even within First Nations communities. However, this is the point, to make a shareable tool.

This has already started in the communities where we plan to start training, as initial training in IT has drawn out people's stories they wish to display in visual and text format. There is a natural inclination to share this knowledge where possible, as it is most crucial to survival of the country and people, in these places.

Resources. The game will be chosen by community participants, but we expect there will be further discussion in the community about the correctness of sharing this story and how to set up the challenges. It will be important for the university members to remember when we speak to those developing the game, that we are in fact talking to a whole community through their representatives. Community governance is a participatory democratic process, another feature that would be good to share in the way the games are experienced when shared with non-First Nations.

Output. This will require more thorough understanding of the specific story by the game makers. The actual narrative of the game will be collected in this domain, sometimes through videos to be inserted, or in the storyboard dialogue. As mentioned above, this may be the final domain where we ensure that the meaning of the story is retained truthfully for the players.

5 Discussion

Our work in each domain is clearly marked out with our stakeholders being those with the knowledge who are training and those without who are listening and doing. The tools and resources that we can use in each domain will assist in the flow between domains in the workshops. Also, these will increase awareness of what domain we are working in at any time and the output we should be aiming for in a session.

While we have called the team who is off country the game makers, the aspiration is that as the project develops, all will be game makers. Also, to some extent those from off-country will become part of the community knowledge, so that they too can respect the culture and care for the country where the stories lie.

We consider the project will only provide a forum for cultural sharing if the game makers from both the university and community are able to understand and engage with the knowledge of the other party. Only then can we hope to provide a true translation of First Nations stories into mainstream play.

The main outcome will be the template system that is being developed in Unity that will have to tools and components needed to support game creation from artefacts. This will develop as we understand what community want to represent in games. One aspect will be how the player will learn, the progress through the game and the understanding to be achieved which will be the focus of the game play.

Examples of the significance of these stories would be if we can develop games to emulate or exemplify the participatory approach to knowledge sharing in the community, as well as the knowledge sharing structure, in a way that the player will be enlightened about these different approaches. This will reduce the perception of deficit towards First Nations in Australia and assist in true cross-cultural learning around caring for country, a very old land and sea that is rapidly being destroyed.

6 Conclusion

When laying out clearly the path that we take when starting in each domain we have a way to identify where we have initially chosen each day to start to PAR process, maybe intuitively. This approach will also assist us to identify when we are focusing too much on any one domain, or avoiding any domain, for instance not allowing the community to discuss stories in their own time (Domain 3) so they can consider how to present these to the broader world, and also develop what is most suitable to the game format that is being shown to them.

Importantly it provides some flexibility to our planning so that we are ensuring the community have some control of their specialist knowledge and how they share it and what to keep secret. Using these workshops to develop a gaming framework will also help develop a community of game story tellers and provide entry into an industry that allows much opportunity for economic and social development of the community. Furthermore, there is the benefit that this will be a collaboration with other communities as the workshops will be run across different countries in the NT region.

References

Baum, F., MacDougall, C., Smith, D.: Participatory action research. J. Epidemiol. Community Health **60**, 854–857 (2006)

Bradley, J.: Writing from the edge: writing what was never meant to be written. In: Kearney, A., Bradley, J. (eds.) Reflexive Ethnographic Practice, pp. 39–64. Palgrave, MacMillan (2020)

Bradley J, Families, Y.: Singing Saltwater Country: Journey to the Songlines of Carpentaria. Allen and Unwin (2010)

Bryant, H.: Never alone: using games as an invitation for courageous learning. KTOO Public Media (2014). Accessed 10 Jan 2023. https://www.ktoo.org/features/never-alone/

Duke, D.: Gaming: The Futures Language. Halsted Press, Ultimo (1974)

Dickson, G.: Ngurrju! Manymak! Pupuni! NT drops 'First Four Hours' policy. Accessed 30 Jan 2024. https://www.crikey.com.au/2012/07/12/ngurrju-manymak-pupuni-nt-drops-first-four-hours-policy/

Emery, S., Habel, C.: Video games and Indigenous education: Let's bridge the 'epistemology gap. Ergo **4**(1) (2017)

Hill, B., Nilson, C., Uink, B., Fetherston, C.: Transformation at the cultural interface: exploring the experiences of Aboriginal and Torres Strait Islander university students. Aust. J. Indigenous Educ. **52**, 2 (2023)

Kelly, Lynne (2016) The Memory Code. Allen and Unwin

King, L., Kutay, C., Smith, D., Tuladhar, L., Manandhar, S.: Collecting resources for teaching aboriginal languages. In: Presentation at Puliima, Darwin (2023)

Klabbers: The Magic Circle: Principles of Gaming and Simulation (2009)

Kral, I., Ellis, E.M.: In the Time of Their Lives: Wangka kutjupa-kutjuparringu: How talk has changed in the Western Desert. Newsouth Books (2021)

Kutay, C.: One Person's Culture is Another One's Entertainment, 1–8 (2014). https://doi.org/10.1145/2677758.2677793

Sanga, K., Reynolds, M., Malefoasi, A., Paulsen, I.: Curating a connected community in virtual space: solomon islands research mentoring tok stori. Aust. J. Indigenous Educ. **52**, 1 (2023)

Szapiro, D., Kutay, C., Garcia, J., Raffe, W., Green R.: Learning on country a game-based experience of an australian aboriginal language. In: Proceedings of the International Conference of Innovation in Media and Visual Design (IMDES 2020). Atlantis Press (2020)

TerraWorld. (n.d.). https://unityunreal.com/unity-assets/tools/1859-terraworld-2021-automated-level-designer.html

Warren, E., Young, J.: Oral language, representations and mathematical understanding: indigenous Australian students. Aust. J. Indigenous Educ. **37**(1), 130–137 (2008). https://doi.org/10.1017/S1326011100016173

Watson, P., Milward, D.: Old stories, new tech: Indigenous storytelling in videogames (2019). Accessed 12 Jan 2024. https://www.acmi.net.au/stories-and-ideas/old-stories-new-tech-indigenous-storytelling-videogames/

Webb, G., Gordon, B.: Embedding speech pathology in an Aboriginal community-controlled playgroup: perceptions from the community. Aust. J. Indigenous Educ. **52**, 2 (2023)

Yunkaporta, T.: (n.d.). https://www.8ways.online/

Understanding Behavioral Differences Between Machine Agents and Human Participants Based on How They Play the Energy Transition Game

Kengo Suzuki[1(✉)], Yuta Nakadegawa[1], Kento Miura[1], Takeshi Shibuya[1], and Susumu Ohnuma[2]

[1] University of Tsukuba, 1-1-1 Tenno-Dai, Tsukuba, Ibaraki, Japan
kengo@risk.tsukuba.ac.jp, {s2220534,s2320554}@u.tsukuba.ac.jp,
shibuya@iit.tsukuba.ac.jp
[2] Hokkaido University, Sapporo, Hokkaido, Japan
ohnuma@let.hokudai.ac.jp

Abstract. This study investigates the behavioral differences between machine agents and human participants when they play the same game. We aim to experimentally clarify the advantages and disadvantages of agent-based simulation (ABS) and gaming simulation (GS) and to identify the suitability of each method for various types of research topics. A multi-player game, which models the energy technology selection and price competition of energy companies in a liberalized market, was implemented via ABS and GS under two conditions: with and without carbon tax conditions. The machine agents identified better strategies of energy technology selection in the without-tax condition, whereas the human participants identified better strategies in the with-tax condition. In terms of price competition, the behaviors of machine agents were adaptive and rational, whereas those of human participants were not. These results suggest that the ABS is suitable for determining relatively simple strategies and investigating the adaptive behavior under strategic situations; conversely, the GS is suitable for investigating the real behaviors of humans in relatively complex situations and for inferring the socio-political failures caused by their psychological aspects.

Keywords: Energy Transition · Agent-based Simulation · Gaming Simulation · Behavioral Science · Machine Learning

1 Introduction

The energy transition from fossil fuels to backstop resources, such as renewables and nuclear power [1], is expected to play a significant role in achieving the Sustainability Development Goals [2] while the global carbon emissions has reached the highest level in history in 2022 [3]. This situation indicates that energy transition is not progressing as expected despite the vast amounts of investments in green technologies.

The role of social dynamics and human behavior on energy transition has attracted considerable attention because energy transition involves various types of stakeholders [4], is motivated by different types of narratives [5], and requires public acceptance of policies and systematic change [6]. These discussions indicate that energy technology selection by users and societies is an important research theme to complement the conventional energy-related studies that primarily focuses on technological development.

Based on these backgrounds, the process of energy transition has been regarded as multi-agent systems comprising egoistic decision makers. In several cases, these multi-agent systems satisfy the definition of a game: a system in which players engage in an artificial conflict, defined by rules, that results in a quantifiable outcome [7]. The studies on multi-agent systems, or games, are called agent-based simulations (ABS) when players are machine agents. The ABS have been applied to investigate various types of energy transition issues, such as solar panel installation in households [8], interactions between investors and policymakers surrounding power plant investment [9], and heating technology selection by local consumers [10]. Conversely, when players are human participants, such experimental approaches are called gaming simulations (GS). GS have also been applied to model energy issues such as negotiations between various types of stakeholders in urban districts [11], the effects of incentives for implementation of renewable energies [12], and carbon pricing on power source selections [13].

ABS and GS exhibit distinct advantages and disadvantages. An ABS can be run multiple times with varying market and agent characteristics [14]; a larger number of conditions can be tested with relatively lesser costs and efforts [15]. Conversely, a GS can consider soft factors such as the irrational behavior and complex psychological features of humans [16], which cannot be easily implemented in machine agents. However, these discussions are mainly based on the comparison between studies using different games; in-depth insights on the differences in ABS and GS are expected to be induced by directly comparing their results by using the same games. One study with such direct comparison have proposed the combined use of ABS for short-time scale and GS for long-time scale [17]. Another study has pointed out that ABS enables to test innovative situations largely different from current status while GS better helps in the concerted planning of the implementation of innovations [18].

This study investigates how the behaviors of machine agents and human participants vary when they play the Energy Transition Game. By directly comparing the results of ABS and GS, we aimed to obtain deep insight on the suitability of the two methods for various types of multi-agent systems. Such a direct comparison can contribute to cross the border between information and behavioral sciences and provide interdisciplinary solutions to promote energy technology selections for a sustainable world. Note that this study omitted a considerable part of the results, such as the test of convergence in the ABS and questionnaire surveys in the GS, because the main concern of this study was to clarify the methodological difference between the ABS and GS. The discussions and policy implications from each type of simulation will be published in future papers.

2 Method

2.1 Energy Transition Game

Concept of the Game

The multi-player "Energy Transition Game" is designed to model the temporal and social conflicts that prevent energy transition in the real world. The temporal conflict is a choice between current and future interests, and the social conflict is a choice between private and public interests [19]. In the context of energy transition, fossil fuel is economically reasonable for individual consumers in a short term. However, the price of fossil fuels is expected to rise in the future because of resource shortage [20], and the CO_2 emissions from fossil fuels are a threat to public welfare in the future [21]. Therefore, the temporal and social conflicts in terms of energy transition is represented as a technology selection problem between fossil fuels and backstop energies. These conflicts are well known as the obstacles to climate change policies [22].

The players of the Energy Transition Game act as energy companies in a competitive market whose purpose is to maximize their own profit during the game. The energy companies produce a final energy from either fossil fuels or backstop energy, and sell the final energy to consumers. There assumed to be only one type of fossil fuel, backstop energy, and final energy. The game proceeds by repeating time steps called "rounds." In each round, players observe the current market status, produce final energy from either energy sources, and sell the final energy to consumers. In this study, the number of players (N) was set to four, and the length of a game (T) was set to 30 rounds.

In the first round of the game, the energy transition was assumed to not have begun; the price of fossil fuels was cheaper than that of backstop energy. However, the price of fossil fuels increased each round because of resource depletion. Conversely, the price of backstop energy was reduced as the players consumed a larger amount of backstop energy; this rule represents the cost savings incurred by technological developments.

The total final energy demand in the market was assumed to be constant during the gameplay. Further, the final energy demand was evenly distributed to all energy companies at the beginning of games. The energy companies had a duty to satisfy all final energy demands they had received; they were required to procure a sufficient amount of fossil fuels or backstop energy to satisfy the demand of their customers. Further, the final energy demand moved between energy companies as a result of price competition. Players could lose a part of their demand when they set a relatively higher retail price or gain a certain amount of demand when they set a relatively lower retail price.

Climate change was assumed to occur as fossil fuels were consumed; however, the environmental damages occurring from climate change did not did not directly decrease their profits. This assumption represents the externality of environmental damage, which is often observed in the real world. The environmental damage was assumed to be internalized to the market by only the carbon tax rule that charges an additional cost on the purchase of fossil fuels. The carbon tax rate was assumed to increase in steps as the game proceeds because the carbon tax in the real world is also introduced in stages to soften the social resistance and mitigate socioeconomic uncertainties [23].

The Energy Transition Game was played under two scenarios, both in the ABS and GS studies. The first was the "control scenario," in which the carbon tax rule was not incorporated, and the second was the "tax scenario," which included the carbon tax rule. The optimal solution in the control scenario was to continue the strategy of using 100% fossil fuels until the end of the game, whereas that in the tax scenario was a gradual shift in the energy source from fossil fuels to backstop energy. Thus, the optimal strategy for each player corresponded to the socially desirable solution in the tax scenario. Note that this study defines the word "scenario" as a unique environment where a specific strategy becomes an optimal solution for players. Further, this study uses the term 'optimal' to indicate the solutions or strategies that maximizes the profit of players under the certain scenario. Similarly, the term 'rational' is used to indicate the behaviors of players that contribute to achieve the optimal solution.

Formal Model

The model of our study is elaborately explained below. The units of energy, profit, and prices are set as [E], [G], and [G/E], respectively.

The purpose of players is to maximize their cumulative profit, $V_{i,t}$, until the end of games; i and t are suffixes to identify players and rounds, respectively. In each round, the profit by selling the final energy, $D_{i,t-1} \, ps_{i,t}$, is added to $V_{i,t}$, and the procurement cost of fossil fuels and backstop energy, $eb_{i,t} \, Pb_{t-1}$ and $(D_{i,t-1} - eb_{i,t}) \, Pf_{t-1}$, are subtracted from $V_{i,t}$ as follows:

$$V_{i,t} = V_{i,t-1} + D_{i,t-1} ps_{i,t} - eb_{i,t} Pb_{t-1} - (D_{i,t-1} - eb_{i,t}) Pf_{t-1}, \quad (1)$$

where $D_{i,t}$ is a final energy demand of a player, and Pb_t and Pf_t are the procurement prices of the backstop energy and fossil fuels, respectively. $Ps_{i,t}$ denotes the retail price of the final energy, which is set by player i. $eb_{i,t}$ and $(D_{i,t-1} - eb_{i,t})$ are the amounts of backstop energy and fossil fuels, respectively, that are consumed by player i to produce the final energy.

The final energy demand is reallocated among players in every round; the change in the demand of players is in proportion to the difference between the retail prices of each player and their market average:

$$D_{i,t} = D_{i,t-1} + \alpha(\mu_t - ps_{i,t}), \quad (2)$$

$$\mu_t = \Sigma_i(D_{i,t-1} ps_{i,t}) / \Sigma_i D_{i,t-1}, \quad (3)$$

where μ_t is average retail price in round t and α is a parameter determining the intensity of competition. The maximum value, minimum value, and maximum change rate per round of retail price, which are denoted as Ps_{max}, Ps_{min}, and m, respectively, are exogenously given as

$$Ps_{min} \leq ps_{i,t} \leq Ps_{max}, \quad (4)$$

$$ps_{i,t-1} - m \leq ps_{i,t} \leq ps_{i,t-1} + m, \quad (5)$$

where $Ps_{min} = 8$ [G/E], $Ps_{max} = 14$ [G/E], and $m = 1$ [G/E].

The price of backstop energy and fossil fuels are common to all players. The price of backstop energy, Pb_t, exponentially decreases with the knowledge stock K_t, which is a function of the cumulative consumption of the backstop energy.

$$Pb_t = Pb_0(1 + \beta K_t)^{-\delta}, \tag{6}$$

$$K_t = K_{t-1}\left(\Sigma_i eb_{i,t}/N\gamma\right)^{\varepsilon}, \tag{7}$$

where Pb_0 is the initial price of the backstop energy and β, γ, δ, and ε are parameters to determine the rate of learning. These formulas represent a one-factor learning function representing the learning-by-doing effect [24]. The price of fossil fuels, Pf_t, exponentially increases as a function of t.

$$Pf_t = Pf_0 \exp(\sigma t) + TAX_t, \tag{8}$$

where Pf_0 is the initial price of fossil fuels, TAX_t is the carbon tax on fossil fuel consumptions, and σ is a parameter to determine the rate of increase in the price.

The environmental damage C_t is represented as a quadratic function of the cumulative consumption of fossil fuels Ef_t.

$$C_t = \zeta Ef_t^2 + \eta Ef_t \tag{9}$$

$$Ef_t = Ef_{t-1} + \Sigma_i(D_{i,t-1} - eb_{i,t})/N, \tag{10}$$

where ζ and η are parameters to determine the rate of environmental destruction.

In each round, players decide the backstop energy consumption, $eb_{i,t}$, and retail prices of final energy $ps_{i,t}$. The amount of fossil fuel consumption ($D_{i,t-1} - eb_{i,t}$) is automatically calculated because players must satisfy the assigned demand using either backstop energy or fossil fuels. The players cannot observe the decisions of other players in advance because they simultaneously input the values to the game application. Figure 1 shows the basic structure of the Energy Transition Game.

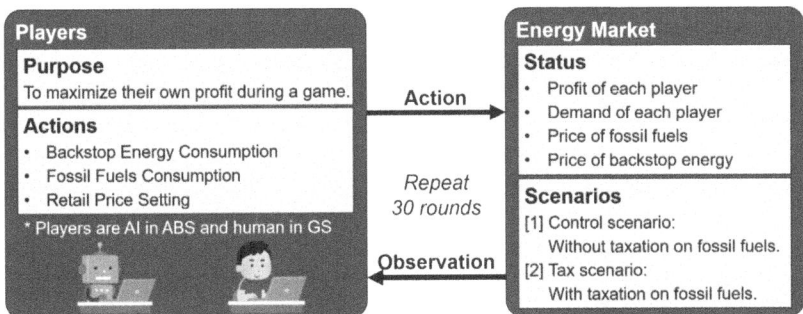

Fig. 1. The basic structure of the Energy Transition Game.

Scenario Design

In the formal model, a unique set of parameters is regarded as one scenario; the uniqueness of a parameter set ensures the uniqueness of game dynamics. Therefore, the differences between scenarios can be resolved to differences between parameter sets. In this study, the difference between the control and tax scenarios was defined as the difference in the parameter TAX_t, which represents the carbon tax rate in round t. TAX_t was zero for all t in the control scenario, whereas it was greater than or equal to zero in the tax scenario. Parameters other than TAX_t were given the same values in both scenarios.

In this study, an optimal solution for a scenario was defined as the time-series behavior of players, $eb_{i,t}$ and $ps_{i,t}$ for all i and t, that maximizes the average profit of all players at the end of the game. To estimate the optimal solutions, this study developed two types of nonlinear mathematical programing models with different objective functions, as formulated in Eqs. (11) and (12), and common constraints, which are presented in Eqs. (1) to (10).

$$\max \Sigma_t \Sigma_i V_{i,t}/N, \tag{11}$$

$$\max \Sigma_t \Sigma_i V_{i,t}/N - C_T. \tag{12}$$

The procedures to determine parameters are explained subsequently. First, a parameter set corresponding to the control scenario is heuristically adjusted so that the objective function (11) is maximized when $eb_{i,t} = 0$ for all i and t. Thus, the profits of players are maximized by the 100%-fossil-fuels strategy. In this step, the carbon tax rate, TAX_t and environmental damage parameters, ζ and η, are fixed to zero. Further, N, T, Ps_{min}, Ps_{max}, and m are fixed as explained in the Formal Model subsection. Other parameters are adjusted through trial and error. Second, the parameters ζ and η, which determine the magnitude of environmental damage C_T, are adjusted so that the objective function (12) is maximized when $eb_{i,t}$ is gradually increased and becomes equal to the final energy demand at the end of game. Thus, the profits of players are maximized when they complete energy transition by the end of game. The problem here is that players are not involved in the social and temporal conflicts if the 100%-backstop strategy is easily recognized as the best strategy. Therefore, the optimal solution was adjusted so that players did not choose the 100%-backstop strategy at the first half of the game; they had to discern the timing of transition to maximize their profit. Third, the parameter TAX_t is adjusted so that the objective function (11) is maximized when $eb_{i,t}$ exhibits a trend similar to that in the second step. That is, the carbon tax rate is determined so that the profits of players are maximized when they behave as if they have considered the environmental damage. The parameter set obtained in the third step corresponds to the tax scenario where environmental damage is internalized by the carbon tax.

2.2 Simulation Methods

Agent-Based Simulation (ABS)

In the ABS, the Energy Transition Game was played by machine agents that autonomously learn adaptive strategies through the Q-Learning algorithm [25]. At the beginning of learning process, machine agents randomly act because they are given only the rules of the game. However, by playing the same game numerous times, they gradually update their strategy: the relationships between the current status, their subsequent actions, and the rewards from these actions under current status. In this study, machine agents observed three variables (backstop energy price Pb_t, fossil fuels price Pf_t, and average retail price μ_t), decided two actions (backstop energy consumption $eb_{i,t}$ and retail price $ps_{i,t}$), and received rewards in proportion to obtained profits. This learning process is regarded to be converged when the agents stop updating their strategies. In this study, one set of ABS consists of two million gameplays; this number was confirmed to be enough to converge their learning processes. We performed 50 sets of ABS and reported the finally converged gameplay of each set as their adaptive strategy.

All the simulation environments were developed as a Python application. Before starting the ABS, the learning ability of the machine agents was tested via single-agent simulations where the number of agents N was set to 1. In principle, the results of single-agent simulations are equal to the optimal solutions because of a lack of interactions between agents. Fifty sets of simulations were performed per scenario; the results of the simulation were compared with the optimal solutions of each scenario. The test results indicate that the designed agents could identify the optimal strategies of the two scenarios; the agents did not use fossil fuels at all in the control scenario and gradually increased the usage of backstop energy in the tax scenario. The machine agents perfectly learned the optimal solution of the control scenario; however, a few deviations from the optimal solution were observed in the tax scenario.

Gaming Simulation (GS)

In the GS, the Energy Transition Game was played by human participants. Forty-eight students of the University of Tsukuba were voluntarily participated in the GS. They were evenly assigned to two scenarios, divided into four-person groups, and played the game only once. Consequently, six games were played for each scenario. The web application version of the Energy Transition Game was developed using oTree [26], which is a Python-based platform to develop web applications for behavioral science studies such as dynamic questionnaire surveys and turn-based games. The developed application was uploaded to a platform service of Heroku. The game could be played using any type of terminal with a web browser and an access to the internet. In this study, the participants played the game in an experimental room using tablet terminals prepared by the authors. They sat around a table and could talk to each other freely.

The procedure of GS was as follows. First, the abstract of our study and rules of the game were explained. Next, the basic rules of the game were explained via its demo version. Here, participants were only qualitatively informed about the structure of the game; however, the rate and timing of the carbon tax were quantitatively explained. After the explanations, participants played the game only once under either the control or tax scenario. After gameplays, they received prize money in the range of JP¥2,000–4,000, which is approximately €12.5–25, according to the final profit in the game. This prize is expected to give participants an incentive to pursue their own interests.

3 Results

3.1 Summary of ABS and GS Results

Figure 2 shows the results of the ABS and GS in the two scenarios; fifty sets of ABS and six GS gameplays were performed per scenario, respectively. The horizontal and vertical axes indicate the cumulative backstop energy consumption and profit per player until the end of the games, respectively; the averaged values of four players are shown here. The blue circular and triangular plots are the results of the ABS in the control and tax scenarios, respectively. The red circular and triangular plots are the results of the GS in the two scenarios, respectively. The black circular and triangular plots indicate the optimal solutions for these scenarios, respectively. Table 1 lists the means and standard deviations of the ABS and GS results in each scenario. The values in the optimal solutions are also listed. As defined in Sect. 2.2, the optimal strategy in the control scenario is to never consume backstop energy, whereas that in the tax scenario is to consume a certain amount of backstop energy. The profit for the optimal solution of the tax scenario is lower than that of the control scenario because of the carbon tax.

Before starting the simulations, the authors speculated that the results of ABS will be closer to the optimal solutions than these of GS owing to two reasons. First, the machine agents in the ABS played the same game several times, whereas the human participants in the GS played the game only once. Second, the machine agents were programed to simply maximize their profit, whereas the behavior of human participants could be affected by various types of psychological factors.

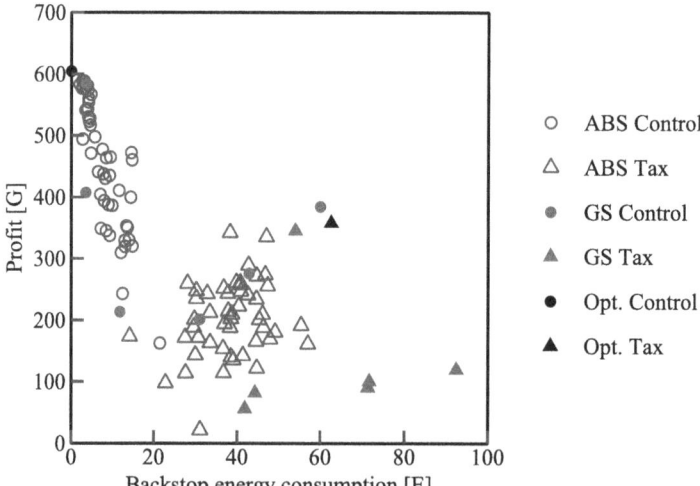

Fig. 2. All results of agent-based simulations (ABS) and gaming simulations (GS) in the control and tax scenarios. The horizontal and vertical axes indicate the cumulative backstop energy consumption and profit per player until the end of games, respectively. The averaged values of four agents or participants in each game are illustrated. The [E] and [G] are virtual units of energy and profits.

This inference was accurate in the control scenario, but incorrect in the tax scenario. In the control scenario, both the mean backstop energy consumption and profit in the ABS were closer to the optimal solution than those in the GS as the machine agents consumed a smaller amount of backstop energy and obtained a larger amount of profit. Conversely, in the tax scenario, the mean backstop energy consumption in the GS was equal to the optimal solution, whereas that in the ABS was significantly lesser than the optimal solution. When considering the profit, the mean value in the ABS was closer to the optimal solution than in the case of the GS. Interestingly, the human players consumed almost an optimal amount of backstop energy, although they failed to maximize their profit. These results also indicate that the results of the GS were more scattered than those of the ABS. As shown in Fig. 2, the results of the GS are spread cross a wider range of values than those of the ABS in spite of the fewer numbers of gameplays. Further, Table 1 shows that the standard deviations in the GS were higher than these in the ABS for both the backstop energy consumption and profit in both scenarios. These results indicate that, in contrast to the ABS, a wider area in the solution space of games was explored by a fewer numbers of gameplays compared in the GS.

Table 1. Means and standard deviations of the ABS and GS results: backstop energy consumption [E] and profit [G] in each scenario. The values of the optimal solutions are also listed.

	Control scenario				Tax scenario			
	Backstop energy consumption		Profit		Backstop energy consumption		Profit	
	Mean	S.D.	Mean	S.D.	Mean	S.D.	Mean	S.D.
ABS	7.6	4.5	458	105	38.6	8.2	202	60
GS	25.4	23.1	344	145	62.6	19.4	132	107
Opt	0.0		605		62.6		358	

3.2 Backstop Energy Consumption

Figure 3 shows the time-series changes in the backstop energy consumption per player in the control and tax scenarios in the ABS and GS in terms of the mean values of all gameplays. The optimal strategies for each scenario, which is the values of $eb_{i,t}$ in the optimal solutions, are also shown. The optimal solution was to depend on fossil fuels throughout the game in the control scenario, whereas energy transition had to be completed by the sixteenth round in the tax scenario. The energy transition is regarded to be completed when the backstop energy consumption reaches a value of five because the average energy demand per player is five in the games.

The results of the ABS and GS were approximately similar to the optimal solutions both in the control and tax scenarios. In the control scenario, the backstop energy consumption was maintained at a low level until the end of the games; the results of the ABS were relatively closer to the optimal strategy as compared to those of the GS. In the tax scenario, the backstop energy consumption was maintained at a low level in the first half of the games and rapidly increased in the latter half of the games; the results of the GS were relatively similar to the optimal solution than those of the ABS.

The machine agents in the ABS learned the quantitative relationship between the observed situation and rewards for available actions under the situation from the vast numbers of trials and observed errors. This learning algorithm is more effective when the best action in a current round is affected by only current situations in contrast to when the best action is affected by past situations and actions. Therefore, machine agents appear to experience difficulty in quantitatively predicting long-term profit of investing in backstop energy in such multi-agent systems.

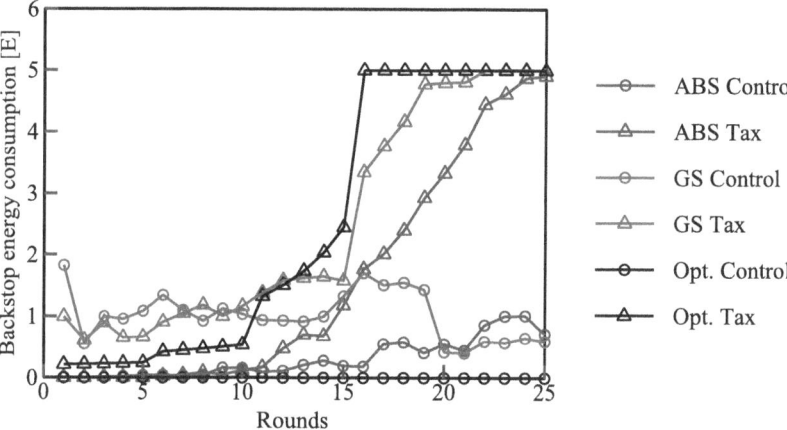

Fig. 3. Time-series changes in the backstop energy consumption per player in the control and tax scenarios obtained from the ABS and GS. The optimal solutions for each scenario are also shown. The [E] is virtual unit of energy.

Conversely, human participants in the GS did not experience a trial-and-error learning process; they played the game only once relying on the qualitative explanations provided to them before starting the experiments. In such a situation, the actions of human participants can be affected by several factors. First, human participants can perform actions based on such qualitative information without learning quantitative relationship between situations, actions, and rewards. Such a heuristic behavior of human players may be more suitable for determining the best strategy when the target system is too complex to be understood through trials and errors. Second, the human participants may be affected by the norms and values in the real world; for example, they understand that energy transition is necessary for a sustainable world. Although the motivation of participants was controlled by the prize, this psychological aspect of human participants must also be considered in the GS. Third, the actions of human participants might be affected by more local norms; some of them might have cared about how they were perceived by others. Humans often behave cooperatively because they do not want be regarded as uncooperative individuals. Considering these possible explanations, the behavior of human participants can be affected by a wider range of factors when compared to that of machine agents who behave rationally in a narrow sense.

3.3 Retail Prices

Figure 4 shows the time-series changes in the average retail price of the final energy in the control and tax scenarios in the ABS and GS in terms of the mean values of all sets of simulations. The colors and shapes of plots are identical to those in Fig. 3. The optimal strategy for each scenario are also shown. In both scenarios, the optimal strategy is to increase the retail price to the upper limit, 14 [G/E], at the maximum rate, 1 [G/E] per round, and maintain the price level until the end of the game.

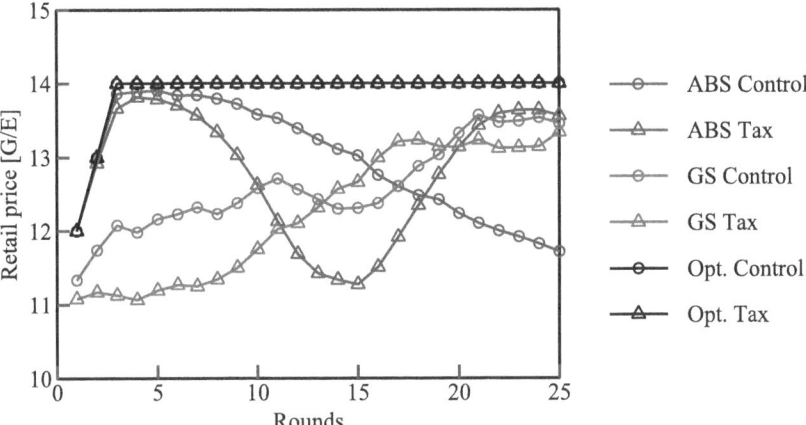

Fig. 4. Time-series changes in the average retail prices of final energy in the control and tax scenarios obtained from the ABS and GS. The optimal solutions for each scenario are also shown. The [G/E] is a virtual unit of energy price.

The results of the ABS were similar to the optimal solution at the early phase of the game in both scenarios; machine agents cooperatively raised their retail prices to 14 [G/E] at the maximum rate. However, once the average retail price reached the upper limit, they changed their strategies to reduce the prices, that is, they began price competitions. The retail price continuously decreased until the end of the game in the control scenario, whereas it tended to increase after the fifteenth round in the tax scenario. These results indicate that machine agents continued price competition until the end of the games in the control scenario, whereas they stopped competing in the second half of the games in the tax scenario. Conversely, the results of the GS were significantly different from the optimal solutions; human participants set lower retail prices, at around 11 [G/E], at the beginning of the games, and gradually increased the prices as the game proceeded. Few differences were noted between the trends in the two scenarios as the price level in the tax scenario was relatively lower in the first half of the games. These results indicate that human participants competed with each other regardless of the inclusion of carbon tax;

the additional cost due to the taxation was not shifted to the final consumers because of price competitions.

The results of the ABS suggest that machine agents learned the adaptive strategy based on the social conflicts surrounding retail prices. At the beginning of the games, they cooperatively increased the retail prices because all agents can increase their profit based on this strategy. However, after the retail price reached the upper limit, they were required to expand the market share by competing against each other to further increase their own profit. Therefore, they started lowering their retail prices to exploit the demand of other agents after the fifth round. The difference in the trend of lowering retail prices between scenarios can be explained by the difference in the energy supply cost. As the games proceeded, the agents in the tax scenario were required to pay more energy supply cost than these in the control scenario because of the increasing carbon tax rate. Therefore, they had to increase the retail price again to maintain their profit; thus, the price competition was suppressed by the taxations. As such, the behaviors of machine agents can be explained assuming that they learned the adaptive strategy under the multi-agent environment. Such an adaptive strategy is similar to the Nash equilibrium in the field of Game Theory, where the total profit of all agents is not maximized because of competitions between agents.

The price competitions in the early part of games in the GS suggest that their behaviors are affected by psychological factors such as norm, trust, and communications [27]. Because the social conflicts surrounding retail prices were qualitatively explained to the human participants before the start of the experiment, they were aware that they could maximize their total profit by cooperatively increasing the retail prices. However, they do not behave cooperatively as they do not trust others even when cooperative action is apparently the best choice for public profit [28]. Conversely, the actions of machine agents are not affected by such psychological factors because they mechanically learn the action that can maximize their own reward under given situations.

The results of the GS also suggest that human participants prioritized competing against each other rather than recovering the additional cost by the carbon tax. Theoretically, the retail price in the tax scenario is expected to be higher than that in the control scenario because the energy procurement cost is increased by taxation. However, human participants set similar levels of retail prices in both the scenarios. Such non-cooperative behaviors may have been caused by the side effects of carbon tax; moreover, incentives on cooperative actions, such as a carbon tax, are suggested to actually decrease desirable behaviors by undermining social norms and trust [29–31].

4 Discussion

4.1 Behavioral Differences Between Machine Agents and Human Participants

In the tax condition, the energy source selections of human participants were significantly more similar to the optimal strategy as compared to these of machine agents. This result suggests that the GS can identify better solutions through fewer numbers of simulations than the ABS as games become more complex. As long as the best strategy for players is relatively linear and short-sighted, as in the control scenario, machine agents can easily find such a strategy. However, when the best strategy is nonlinear and requires long-term considerations, as in the tax scenario, the heuristics of human participants appear to overwhelm the vast number of trials and errors by machine agents.

The pricing strategies of both machine agents and human participants were quite different from the optimal strategy. The strategies of machine agents can be easily explained; they focused on price competition to further increase their profit. However, the strategies of human participants appear to be more complex; they competed against each other even at the early stages of the games. This result suggests that the ABS and GS can simulate different types of socio-political barriers to the socially optimal solution. The ABS can represent the strategic situation where rational players cannot reach the socially optimal solutions. Conversely, the GS can represent more complicated situations where the perceptions and behaviors of humans play a critical role.

4.2 Suitability of ABS and GS for Various Types of Multi-agent Systems

When the purpose of simulating multi-agent system is to identify better strategies for the stakeholders of a target system, we must identify the complexities of the better strategies. When the players behave in a nonlinear and anticipatory manner, the GS appears to be a better simulation method; the heuristics of human participants are expected to help in untangling the complex situations. However, the parallel use of ABS appears to be helpful; the machine agents may identify simpler strategies with similar performances as compared to those identified by humans. Conversely, when the purpose of simulations is to determine the risk of failure or side effects of new policies, we must identify the cause of such failures and effects. The ABS appear to be the better approach provided the failures and side effects are assumed to be caused by a strategic situation, whereas the GS is the better approach when these undesirable results are assumed to be caused by the psychological aspects of humans. These implications remind us that the studies in multi-agent systems must carefully plan which aspects of the real world should be clarified before deciding the research method.

4.3 Limitations

The limitation of this study is that the results of the ABS appear to depend on the computational resources and learning algorithms. For example, if the authors can be free from the limitation of computational resources, the Deep-Q-Network algorithm [23] can be adopted instead of Q-Learning. Such an upgrade in the ABS will aid machine agents to learn more complex strategies and enable them to identify strategies similar to those determined by the human participants. However, even when the computational resources and learning algorithms are updated, the decision-making processes of machine agents is significantly different from these of human participants. Therefore, discussions related to the psychological aspects of humans are still supported despite the infinite computational resources available in the ABS.

5 Conclusions

This study aimed to clarify the suitability of the ABS and GS when investigating different research topics by directly comparing the behaviors of machine agents and human participants playing the same game. The ABS appear to be suitable for identifying relatively simple strategies and investigating the socio-political barriers under strategic situations. Conversely, the GS appears to be suitable for finding relatively complex strategies and inferring the failure and side effects of new policies caused by the psychological aspect of humans. These insights are expected to cross the border between information and behavioral sciences and contribute to interdisciplinary studies in the future. For example, the gameplays by human participants can be used as the training data for machine agents by adopting the supervised learning algorithm. Such an integration of the ABS and GS is expected to compensate the disadvantages of individual methods and enables more flexible modeling of multi-agent systems in the real world.

Acknowledgments. This study was funded by the Foundation for the Fusion of Science and Technology (FOST) (grant number 2020–01) and JSPS Kakenhi (grant number 22H03807/23K25061).

Disclosure of Interests. There are no conflicts of interest to declare.

References

1. van der Ploeg, F., Withagen, C.: Is there really a green paradox? J. Environ. Econ. Manag. **64**(3), 342–363 (2012)
2. Nerini, F.F., et al.: Mapping synergies and trade-offs between energy and the sustainable development goals. Nat. Energy **3**(1), 10–15 (2018)
3. Liu, Z., Deng, Z., Davis, S., Ciais, P.: Monitoring global carbon emissions in 2022. Nat. Rev. Earth Environ. **4**, 205–206 (2023)
4. Geels, F.W., Sovacool, B.K., Schwanen, T., Sorrell, S.: The socio-technical dynamics of low-carbon transitions. Joule **1**(3), 463–479 (2017)
5. Holden, E., Linnerud, K., Rygg, B.J.: A review of dominant sustainable energy narratives. Renew. Sustain. Energy Rev. **144**, 110955 (2021)
6. Steg, L., Perlaviciute, G., van der Werff, E.: Understanding the human dimensions of a sustainable energy transition. Front. Psychol. **6**, 805 (2015)
7. Salen, K., Zimmerman, E.: Rules of Play: Game Design Fundamentals, p. 84. MIT Press, Cambridge (2003)
8. Rai, V., Robinson, S.A.: Agent-based modeling of energy technology adoption: empirical integration of social, behavioral, economic, and environmental factors. Environ. Model. Softw. **70**, 163–177 (2015)
9. Li, P.H., Barazza, E., Strachan, N.: The influences of non-optimal investments on the scale-up of smart local energy systems in the UK electricity market. Energy Policy **170**, 113241 (2022)
10. Fouladvand, J., Ghorbani, A., Sari, Y., Hoppe, T., Kunneke, R., Herder, P.: Energy security in community energy systems: an agent-based modelling approach. J. Clean. Prod. **366**, 132765 (2022)
11. Bekebrede, G., Van Bueren, E., Wenzler, I.: Towards a joint local energy transition process in urban districts: the GO2Zero simulation game. Sustainability **10**(8), 2602 (2018)

12. Marrero-Trujillo, V., Arias-Gaviria, J., Arango-Aramburo, S., Larsen, E.R.: Gamification model for communicating and evaluating renewable energy planning. Utilities Policy **84**, 101624 (2023)
13. Suzuki, K., Ishiwata, R.: Impact of a carbon tax on energy transition in a deregulated market: a game-based experimental approach. Sustainability **14**(19), 12785 (2022)
14. Kowalska-Pyzalska, A., Maciejowska, K., Suszczyński, K., Sznajd-Weron, K., Weron, R.: Turning green: agent-based modeling of the adoption of dynamic electricity tariffs. Energy Policy **72**, 164–174 (2014)
15. Hansen, P., Liu, X., Morrison, G.M.: Agent-based modelling and socio-technical energy transitions: a systematic literature review. Energy Res. Soc. Sci. **49**, 41–52 (2019)
16. Anatolitis, V., Welisch, M.: Putting renewable energy auctions into action – an agent-based model of onshore wind power auctions in Germany. Energy Policy **110**, 394–402 (2017)
17. Barreteau, O., Abrami, G.: Variable time scales, agent-based models, and role-playing games: the PIEPLUE river basin management game. Simul. Gaming **38**(3), 364–381 (2007)
18. van den Hoogen, J., Meijer, S.: Gaming and simulation for railway innovation: a case study of the dutch railway system. Simul. Gaming **46**(5), 489–511 (2015)
19. Milfont, T.L., Wilson, J., Diniz, P.: Time perspective and environmental engagement: a meta-analysis. Int. J. Psychol. **47**(5), 325–334 (2012)
20. Brockway, P.E., Owen, A., Brand-Correa, L.I., Hardt, L.: Estimation of global final-stage energy-return-on-investment for fossil fuels with comparison to renewable energy sources. Nat. Energy **4**(7), 612–621 (2019)
21. The Intergovernmental Panel on Climate Change (IPCC) Assessment Report Six Synthesis Report. https://www.ipcc.ch/report/sixth-assessment-report-cycle/. Accessed 25 Jan 2024
22. Nordhaus, W.D.: The Climate Casino: Risk, Uncertainty, and Economics for a Warming World, pp. 316–326. Yale University Press, New Haven (2013)
23. Carattini, S., Carvalho, M., Fankhauser, S.: Overcoming public resistance to carbon taxes. Wiley Interdisc. Rev. Climate Change **9**(5), Article e531 (2018)
24. Rubin, E.S., Azevedo, I.M.L., Jaramillo, P., Yeh, S.: A review of learning rates for electricity supply technologies. Energy Policy **86**, 198–218 (2015)
25. Sutton, R., Barto, A.: Reinforcement Learning: An Introduction, 2nd edn. The MIT Press, Cambridge (2018)
26. Chen, D.L., Schonger, M., Wickens, C.: OTree-an open-source platform for laboratory, online, and field experiments. J. Behav. Exp. Financ. **9**, 88–97 (2016)
27. Dawes, R.: Social dilemmas. Annu. Rev. Psychol. **31**, 169–193 (1980)
28. Yamagishi, T.: The provision of a sanctioning system in the united states and Japan. Soc. Psychol. Q. **51**(3), 265–271 (1988)
29. Tenbrunsel, A.E., Messick, D.M.: Sanctioning systems, decision frames, and cooperation. Adm. Sci. Q. **44**(4), 684–707 (1999)
30. Mulder, L.B., van Dijk, E., De Cremer, D., Wilke, H.A.M.: Undermining trust and cooperation: the paradox of sanctioning systems in social dilemmas. J. Exp. Soc. Psychol. **42**(2), 147–162 (2006)
31. Kitakaji, Y., Ohnuma, S.: Demonstrating that monitoring and punishing increase non-cooperative behavior in a social dilemma game. Jpn. J. Psychol. **85**, 9–19 (2014)

Accounting for Psychological Safety in Serious Game and Simulation Design

Dale Linegar(✉) ⓘ and Gillian Vesty ⓘ

RMIT University, Melbourne, Australia
`S3820265@student.rmit.edu.au, gillian.vesty@rmit.edu.au`

Abstract. Serious games and simulations are increasingly used in fields such as education, healthcare, defence and business training. Serious games and simulations transcend entertainment games, by offering a platform to engage with complex issues in a safe, controlled environment. However there are also risks associated with serious games and simulations, such as those posed to the psychological safety of learners.

In relation to games or simulations, psychological safety refers to being able to engage without fear of negative personal consequences. How do you ensure that a serious game or simulation is safe, and fosters a sense of security and trust?

This paper explores the ways that psychological safety can be considered when designing a serious game. By synthesising insights gathered from interviews with multiple acclaimed serious game developers with the current literature regarding psychological safety in serious game and simulation design, specific frameworks, approaches and challenges are examined. By examining these issues, this paper aims to increase the understanding of how various aspects of simulation and game design can impact psychological safety.

Keywords: Serious games · Simulation · Psychological safety

1 Introduction

The concept of learning through experiential play has deep historical roots, traceable back to the philosophies of Plato. However it was not until 1969 that Clark Abt coined the term "serious games", stating in his seminal work that serious games "provide us with a rich field in which serious intellectual and social issues can be explored in a risk-free, positive manner" [1]. The word 'can' is crucially significant, as whilst serious games can be a powerful tool for learning, there is substantial evidence suggesting that serious games and simulations can also present risks and negative experiences if the proper considerations are not taken [2–4].

This is especially evident when looking at the current practices of many game developers. Approaches to ensuring players' psychological safety and well-being are often informal, ad hoc and lack the necessary consistency. This approach raises concerns about the effectiveness and safety of these games as teaching tools. The question for this paper then becomes: How are serious game and simulation developers considering players' psychological safety? This arguably involves not only creating engaging content, but also understanding the impact of game mechanics, narrative, and interactions on players' psychological and emotional states.

In 1965 Schein and Bennis defined psychological safety as "an atmosphere where one can take chances (which experimentalism implies) without fear and with sufficient protection (…) thus a climate is built which encourages provisional tries and which tolerates failure without retaliation, renunciation, or guilt" [5].

Improvements in this area are not just desirable, they are needed [6–8]. As the use of serious games expands into a variety of educational and professional training areas, the responsibility of developers to create safe, effective, and positive learning environments becomes increasingly important. It is important to consider the psychological impact these games and simulations have to ensure that serious games and simulations are living up to their potential by providing a better way of experiential learning.

2 Literature Review

2.1 Serious Games

Serious games have one key factor that makes them successful: they impart knowledge while keeping participants engaged [9].

Serious games are ideal for contemplating social, ethical, and political matters [10] due to their ability to communicate complex and difficult topics through an engaging, interactive and responsive medium. Unlike more traditional forms of media, such as books or movies where the reader plays more of a passive role, serious games allow the player to become an active moral agent [11].

Serious games are used in a wide range of fields including education, health, social change, business and defence [12–15], and there is a wide range of evidence that suggests they provide significant improvements in knowledge acquisition and retention due to the way they facilitate active participation and engagement in the learning process through relevant and meaningful activities [16].

Serious games are often used as a compulsory part of education, much like a textbook or other class materials are. It is therefore important that serious games are designed in a way that suits all players or learners equally [17] to ensure equality of opportunity. Developing a game that achieves this involves consideration of a wide range of factors.

The way that the elements that make up a game are considered and designed, including characters, storylines, strategies and rewards, form the values of the game and create the learner experience [18, 19]. So the experience of playing games is both derived from the design of the game, as well as the player's interaction with the game [17], as illustrated by Hunicke et al. [20] (Fig. 1).

In summary, serious games offer enhanced learning experiences due to their engaging, immersive and interactive nature, which promotes active participation. However there are a wide range of considerations necessary to ensure that serious games are providing equal learning opportunities for all players.

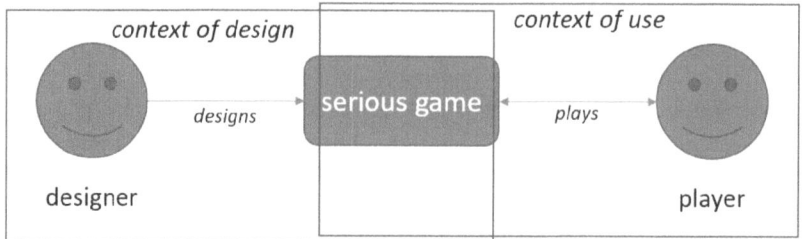

Fig. 1. Formal Approach to Game Design and Game Research [20]

2.2 Psychological Safety in Serious Games and Simulations

Psychological safety refers to how secure and comfortable people feel to act and make mistakes without fear of negative consequences. In the workplace, this means employees feel safe in interpersonal interactions, and are able to contribute new ideas, share knowledge, and take initiative, enhancing the way organisations both learn and then perform. This is becoming increasingly important as organisations pay growing attention to the way they learn and innovate. In the workplace a lot of this responsibility lies with leadership, as well as the strategy, vision and goals of the organisation, but is also influenced by outside forces such as culture [21].

In serious games and simulations psychological safety is known to have an impact on the ability of learners' confidence and problem solving skills [22]. Psychological safety, promoted by characteristics such as diversity, trust and virtue, encourages learners to experiment and correct themselves, as there is no fear of being punished for mistakes [23].

One of the major benefits of serious games and simulations is that they are able to provide safe, immersive learning environments that allow for the application of skills, knowledge and behaviours without the limitations and consequences of the real world. [24, 25]. Because they offer learners the opportunity to become actively engaged as moral agents [11], serious games provide a range of opportunities for creating experiences which reduce psychological distance, which can be used to bring learners closer to specific topics, such as climate change [26] or ethical dilemmas in the workplace [27]. They can evoke strong emotions, which are known to be effective for transformational learning [28, 29]. There is evidence that games and play can increase psychological safety and resilience when done correctly [30–32], and that psychological safety is important for not just the transfer of learning, but also social cohesion [33, 34]. However if a serious game or simulation, or the context they are being used in is not psychologically safe, then the opposite is true [4]. There is also recognition that in serious games and simulations psychological safety is known to have an impact on the ability of learners' confidence and problem solving skills [22]. While psychological safety, promoted by characteristics such as diversity, trust and virtue, encourages learners to experiment and correct themselves, as there is no fear of being punished for mistakes [23].

For example, in the management of psychological safety in serious games development, the Yerkes-Dodson law can be used to visualise the importance of maintaining appropriate levels of psychological safety for effective learning. In essence, if a task is too easy, then the learner won't be sufficiently aroused (stressed), and the transfer of information will be less than optimal. Likewise if the task is too difficult, the heightened arousal (stress and discomfort) interferes with memory retrieval [35] and increases the cognitive load of players [36]. Figure 2 shows the relationship between task performance and arousal levels. If the stress of a task is too low the learner will feel too secure and performance will suffer, and likewise if the arousal is too high then the learner will experience feelings such as unease, pressure, fear, nervousness, frustration, sorrow, indifference, remorse and paralysis, and the learner is no longer able to learn or perform at an optimal level [24].

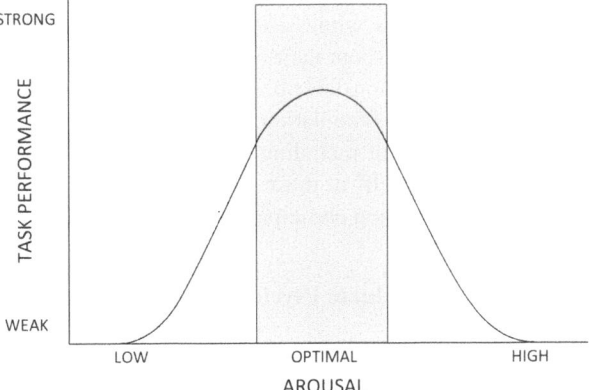

Fig. 2. Yerkes-Dodson law bell curve [Adapted from 36]

Carrera et al. [38] look at a range of vignettes of simulations, including health, business, transport, drama and construction, challenging the conception that simulations are held in a 'safe container'. They found that simulations could create tangible threats to psychological safety at interpersonal, individual and historical levels, including;

- Relational Risks: These are risks that arise in interactions or communications among individuals.
- Personal Risks: These involve self-regulatory challenges or issues specific to an individual.
- Legacy Risks: These are risks linked to past experiences or historical events in one's life. [38]

One such example is in first aid training, when an intensely vivid simulation triggers flashbacks of past traumatic events. The authors conclude with a recommendation that more research be done involving participants who have experienced trauma during simulations, and additional resilience training to prevent damage from occurring in the first place.

The 'Embedded Design' model [39] also used by Linegar et al. [27], provides an approach which bypasses players' psychological barriers to increase the games persuasive effectiveness, using methods such as intermixing, obfuscating and distancing. However there is evidence that these methods also come with their own risks.

Naweed et al. [40] provide an example of a simulation workshop for healthcare professionals where the aim was to explore the potential physical and psychological risks associated with simulation-based exercises, and provide an opportunity to practise ways to mitigate and manage these safety concerns as they emerge. The simulation 'obfuscated' part of the lesson by embedding a confederate who simulated a panic attack in response to a simulated physical injury, and continued to display symptoms after the simulation had 'officially' been stopped using safe words. The somewhat unintended consequences of this were that some participants felt stress and fear during the scenario, and then afterwards, a sense that they had been deceived [40].

This reaction is counter to what has been experienced with the Bogart accounting ethics game [27, 31], where players are deliberately deceived into unethical behaviour by the game mechanics. Reactions witnessed are generally more along the lines of bemusement and instant reflection about their own behaviours that led to that result.

Arguably for the former simulation described by Naweed et al., the negative reactions were the result of the realism of the simulation, its deviation from what are considered healthcare simulation norms by not including an accurate pre-briefing [41], and the way the simulation involved the 'self' of those participating, they were involved not as characters in a game, but as workshop participants [42].

2.3 User-Centred Design to Evaluate Psychological Safety in Serious Games and Simulations

User-centred design (closely related to human-centred design and design thinking depending on context[1]) is also recommended as a way to ensure games have a player centric focus which result in an efficacious impact on feelings of belonging and psychological safety [44, 45].

Research suggests that stakeholders are included as part of the design process, giving feedback that can form part of an iterative design process [17, 46], and that a so-called 'player centric design' process can create a positive playing experience by putting the needs of the player above those of the developer [47]. Dekker et al. [48] discuss some of the limitations of this approach, including how sometimes the learners or players don't necessarily know what's best for them, and it's better to ask experts (informants). The example they provide is that clinicians often possess knowledge about dealing with psychological issues that patients do not, or would not willingly take part in.

Peters et al. [24] provides an overview of measures for simulation game designers and facilitators when designing for psychological safety. These are outlined in Table 1.

Table 1 provides a useful framework for examining the attention serious games and simulation developers may or may not give to psychological safety during the design process and whether they take a user-centred design perspective in order to mitigate any potential dangers to learners. Although more than 10 years since this framework was developed, its effectiveness as a tool has not been widely explored or tested in

---

[1] User-centred design is focussed on a particular audience for a product or service. Human-centred design focuses on all humans as users of a product or service. Design thinking looks more at product design. All can be considered as part of the game design process, where the term 'player-centred design' is now in regular use [43].

Table 1. Summary of psychological hazards to be considered during the design phase of simulation games [24].

Element	Considerations
The intake	Check whether there are for the particular target group, elements that may make them feel uncomfortable. In case of a tailor made simulation game, this can be one of the issues addressed in the intake with the client
	Check whether major issues play "under the surface" (e.g. conflicts or major differences in viewpoints, the threat of downsizing or reorganisation)
The scenario	Stay close to the real life situation or use a metaphor; using a metaphor increases the distance to the real life situation; no participant has worked in the metaphoric situation before, so all are equal in regard to knowledge of the situation
	Reduce (unnecessary) ambiguity in the scenario and the gaming materials
	For some participants an atmosphere of competition in the simulation game may cause insecurity, for others an atmosphere of cooperation. Choose an atmosphere which fits the group
The roles	Is the game designed in such a way that each role is performed by one person, or does it allow for more participants per role? In the latter case participants may feel a shared responsibility
The gaming materials	Consider the required level of complexity of the materials (forms, indicators and symbols)
	The way procedures and role descriptions are presented and the way participants are introduced in their role; present all information at once or make the participants step by step acquainted with the materials they have to deal with
The steps of play	Elements that may help (or hinder) to increase complexity gradually, so that participants can get the hang of it step-by-step before the chaos starts (throw them in the deep, or let them get gradually into the water) - the complexity of the scenario and the assignments - the pace of the game
Assessing the performance	Build assessment and monitoring functions into the game (e.g. a Council), so that evaluation of actions, results and behaviour is done from a role inside the simulation game instead of by an external person
The flexibility of the game	Consider whether the 'boundaries of the system' have to be defined narrowly or that they allow the facilitator to stretch the limit of these boundaries

(*continued*)

Table 1. (*continued*)

Element	Considerations
	The extent to which game elements are designed (open) and the extent to which participants can contribute
General considerations	The fun factor in the simulation game, take care for moments of relaxation in the flow of activities
	The tone of the game: the ideal for any adequate (not too light, not heavy, but doable, you learn the most)

the literature. Using in-depth interviews with leading serious games developers, Peters et al. [24] is put to the test in this paper to determine its applicability and whether the framework needs to be extended.

Drawing on this background, the following research question is posed: How are serious game and simulation developers considering players' psychological safety?

3 Methodology

A theory of valuing, or sociology of worth, provides the theoretical lens for this study [49] and is useful in examining the distinct values, or world views of individual game developers. This theoretical lens explains the justification that actors make for their decisions, particularly when making game design decisions. There may be times when they may draw on distinct measurement tools or other experts to agree with their design choices and overall world view, which is ranked in order of worthiness. That is, what is most important from a game designer perspective? This could be game design decisions that prioritise the game's market worth (e.g. maximise return on investment of the game); it could be to elevate design choices that ensure longevity in business (e.g. focus more on costs and efficiency in game development). Further, it could be all about the unique, innovative contribution of the game, where creative risks may be taken. Decisions could be taken on the basis of building fame and recognition in the industry. Alternatively, game developers may consider the public good. One particular order of worth that aligns with this study prioritises the individual psychological issues. In this order of worth, game designers make choices, akin to acting as a familial father figure whose main role is to look out for others that they have immersive control over. How important this order of worth is to game developers is interesting for this study.

Ten serious game developers who had been recognised by their peers through nomination for industry awards (including the Game Developer Australia Awards, Serious Games Showcase & Challenge Australasia, Serious Games Showcase & Challenge, and Games for Change Awards) were interviewed for this study. They were asked open-ended questions (Appendix 1) guided by the sociology of worth literature [49]. The questions take each developer on a 90 min journey through their own creations, asking them to consider how their values, and the values of other stakeholders influenced the design of their game. Interview transcriptions were then coded to draw out the inductive themes which emerged whilst examining the transcripts.

4 Results: How Game Developers Considered Psychological Safety

Table 2 outlines the number of references to 'psychological safety' in the interviews conducted. 'Psychological safety' emerged as one of the key inductive themes which eight of the ten developers had considered, with 30 individual references contained in their interviews.

Table 2. References for emergent theme 'psychological safety' in interviews with key game developers.

No.	Topic	Technologies	References
1	First aid training	Virtual Reality	2
2	Disability Support & Early Childhood Education	Augmented Reality Mobile/Tablet app	2
3	Disability Support & Early Childhood Intervention	Mobile/Tablet app	5
4	Social Impact & Youth Work	PC Mobile/Tablet app	1
5	Play-based learning and team building	Real world	4
6	Learner driver training	Virtual Reality PC	12
7	Space	Virtual Reality	3
8	Physiotherapy	Exergaming Wearables/IoT Mobile app	1
9	Environmental Awareness & Social Change	PC Mobile/Tablet app	0
10	Agriculture	PC Mobile/Tablet app	0
Total references			30

The following is a summary overview of the psychological hazards that each of the 8 out of 10 game developers identified in the interviews.

4.1 First Aid Training

In one game, the audience were army medics. In this scenario incorrect treatment of a patient could cause the virtual patient to deteriorate or die. This was seen as an important part of the scenarios as the developer wished for the learners to be able to experiment and learn from their mistakes. As the target audience were army medics, a certain level of psychological resilience was assumed.

One such example is that the learners had the ability to administer ventilation to a child patient who had measles, which is not a common disease here in Australia, but can be found in many of the regions where the Australian Army is conducting humanitarian missions, such as the South Pacific. This was not the correct course of action, and for those who made the mistake this was an educative moment in the gameplay. The ability to make (often common and deliberately placed) mistakes with a patient who wasn't really suffering or dying was seen as one of the major benefits and reasons to use a serious game. However, although the game was playable in a somewhat immersive VR headset, the fidelity and realism of the simulation wasn't high which perhaps made the adverse results more palatable.

4.2 Disability Support and Early Childhood Education

On the other hand, a developer who made applications for young children and people living with mental impairment deliberately created games with no fail state. The games all allow players to progress according to their own abilities, with no external judgement. The game interface was simple and used lots of bright colours and icons, to allow for low literacy levels and simplify use.

After finishing the game the developer slowed it down by four times to allow for the audience to play it. However after user acceptance testing they had to slow it down even further to allow for all the potential players to enjoy the game without being overwhelmed. Likewise certain player actions were limited so as not to cause players too much stress. This reflects the consideration from Peters et al. [24] to keep games 'doable', and also the advice given by Sandovar et al. [17] to use user-centred design methods to ensure that "Ethical stewardship requires including stakeholders as co-creators of the game from the beginning" [17].

Another particular game dealt with the topic of emotions, and in this game feeling sad or other emotions that could typically be viewed as negative were never treated as such, as the object of the game was to encourage those playing it to share their emotions.

4.3 Disability Support and Early Childhood Intervention

A practitioner with psychological expertise who had developed games for young children reported similar challenges with the game they developed, which helped to diagnose and treat mental disorders. A major consideration for them was limiting any kind of anxiety or stress both for the sake of the learner, and also for the accuracy of the results. In their words "give me an adult or someone who's having issues with anxiety; their performance on an IQ test is going to be very different to what it is on a day they haven't got any anxiety."

The reports from these games were only seen by clinicians to prevent any distress caused by comparison to other players; "how great would you feel if your brother or sister who was younger than you performed better than you? It's difficult. It's a challenging space, at least in the context of these games."

Likewise consideration was given to ensuring that the game was played in a controlled environment, to avoid situations where they might be getting help (for example from a parent or sibling) during one play through, but then playing along the next time and not performing as well.

Another element raised by the practitioner was how consideration of issues, such as psychological safety, involves balancing the needs and wants of a wide range of stakeholders. In this case the patients weren't always the only group being considered, it was also the business owners, investors, clinical team and game developers who all had input.

4.4 Social Impact and Youth Work

One game developed to help young people find support services in their areas considered psychological safety in terms of how different cultures were represented in the digital world they created. The game involves communicating with a range of characters who represent the community through authentic stories, for example aboriginal, LGBTQ, or from a specific ethnicity. The developer acknowledged the importance of involving people from the community in making what were described as very difficult design decisions, whilst also acknowledging the limitations of this approach. As the developer stated,

"Co-design, I think, is the first thing people go to when thinking about diversity, okay, so just use co-design. Okay, okay, we'll get an Indian. Yeah, really, you're gonna get one Indian who's gonna speak for all Indians? Like, okay, so we need five Indians really? Five? We're gonna speak all night. Because like I said, there's limitations."

This developer observed that financial limitations play a large role in how many resources you can put into developing a serious game, and therefore how you can mitigate any risks.

"It is tricky, and it will stay tricky. And I think if you're, you know, if you're in the serious games, space, it's such an important part. But games are so expensive to make, you know, they're really difficult to make projects, and they're expensive. And so co-design is very expensive, as well, because it's lengthy. And it's not a straight line from A to B...it's a complicated curve that goes all kinds of directions and, and the risk is that it completely derails the very thing that makes your project strong and attractive. And so that's really difficult, and you know, people building that into the project is, I would say, by far the hardest thing."

4.5 Play-Based Learning and Team Building

A facilitator of real world games for corporate, team building sessions also considered psychological safety when designing his programs, particularly as many of these workshops were designed to bring up complex issues, and normalise and give people a safe space to talk about them. One such consideration he took was that he asked participants to share their favourite food during an icebreaker activity. This was deliberately chosen as a topic that people could easily share something quite personal, to whatever degree they chose; for example just 'pizza' or 'spaghetti like my mother used to make for me,' whilst minimising fear of negative interpersonal consequences. After sharing this with the group they were then more likely to continue to feel safe to share in the workshop.

Another consideration was that nobody feels pressured to participate in any activity they don't want to, with the forethought that he never really knew what sort of issues people had been through in their lives, and therefore couldn't reliably judge what is or isn't going to cause distress to any particular individual. One example raised was a workshop participant who had a very complex relationship with the concept of play due to her childhood, where she wasn't allowed to play. Through a sensitive approach which allowed that participant to contribute only when she wanted to, a positive outcome was achieved.

4.6 Learner Driver Training

In a driving simulation game, which was targeting young learner drivers aged 15–18 in a school setting, several measures were taken to protect the psychological safety of participants. This was deemed necessary due to the age of the participants, their lack of experience as drivers, and the setting the game was used in (secondary schools in Australia).

Drivers were unable to swerve off the road and crash in the game. As soon as they crossed the road lines, the game would stop and the learner would get a warning. The learner would then have to restart the driving task.

Likewise if the learners went 3 km over the speed limit, or if the learner was going to crash into another NPC (non-player character) vehicle the game would stop. All obstacles in the game's more advanced levels were designed as flat billboards with representative but not realistic images on them. The billboards sprung up from the ground on a hinge to make it clear they were signs and not real objects, and were not actually visible during the collision. Obstacles were introduced slowly throughout the game to avoid cognitively overloading the learner, allowing them to learn at their own pace without unnecessary distractions.

The game aesthetics were also carefully considered, with the driving taking place in a large skid pan, on a sunny, clear day. Audio prompts are deliberately bright and non-threatening. Nothing competitive, such as scores or points, was included in the game, as safety is not a competition.

The developers were very sensitive, partially due to their own experiences as learner drivers, that learning to drive can be a stressful experience. This along with considerations about who the audience was, where the program was to be delivered, and the real world risks attached to hazardous behaviour, meant they went to considerable lengths to mitigate any potential stressors. They worked closely with an SME who was passionate about road safety. The culture of the game was to remain calm and drive safety, and all of the design considerations reflected that culture.

4.7 Space

Another developer of space themed VR experiences had different considerations to consider, including fear of heights. Their experience placed people in a very realistic scenario where they are hanging from a space station, floating above earth. Although there are a wide range of background hazards associated with being in such a scenario, many of these were deliberately left out of the experience, for brevity and also focus, acknowledging that not all of the threats could be represented in a short experience that was essentially made for a public audience. The experience allowed players to learn how to navigate within the interior of the space station before they exited, and found themselves floating above the earth. Once floating above earth they were able to take 'selfies' of themselves hanging from the space station above earth.

They also found that the fear of heights wasn't as profound as in other VR experiences such as 'Richie's Plank Experience' as the fear of floating away in space was more of an inner existential feat than something that was more immediate and in your face, like walking on a plank above a busy city street and having spiders appear.

4.8 Physiotherapy

An 'exergame' created for physical rehabilitation was developed with a more general audience in mind. The lead developer acknowledged that this forced them to modify their original game so it would be accessible and acceptable to a wider audience. What was interesting and fun for the development team wasn't necessarily received the same way by their audience.

Their first iteration of one particular level included blood curdling screams every time an enemy capsule was 'shot' - which resulted in what they described as 'a simultaneously horrible and hilarious' sound which they described as follows;

"We hadn't had that much emotive reaction to much of the stuff that we've made in a long time. So we're like, damn, this is fun. This is really good."

They decided to make the enemy into realistic bear characters, but when testing decided that shooting realistic bears that scream was a little unsettling for a general audience. They experimented further, making the bears look more scary, before then going back to more cute looking 'cartoon zombie bears' that don't scream as a more palatable and less psychologically distressing enemy for their game.

4.9 Examples and Illustrative Quotes

In further analysing the interview data, Table 3, provides examples of each of the elements of Peters et al., [24] with illustrative quotes from the interviewees. In reviewing each of the coded references provided by the game developers, it is possible to determine if Peters et al. [24] is a useful guide for developers in providing a reflective tool for exploring experiences during the development of their serious games and simulations.

5 Discussion

The psychological hazards checklist by Peters et al. [24] has proven to be valuable in drawing out each of the developer's game design experiences. The analysis of the interview data also indicates that this tool could have been more valuable for the developers if being used as a checklist during the discovery and definition phases of game design. As identified in the findings, all the hazards in the checklist inductively emerged when coding the open-ended interview data, but this was often in retrospect, or done intuitively rather than systematically. There is certainly potential to use this table as a checklist, or to incorporate it into surveys for use during the discovery phase or iterative feedback loops.

Table 3. Summary of psychological hazards to be considered during the design phase of simulation games with columns added with examples from this study [Adapted from 24].

Element	Example	Illustrative quote
The intake	3. Considering that for some learners seeing that they aren't scoring as high as others could make them feel bad	"…how great would you feel if your brother or sister was a year younger than you and performed better than you? It's difficult."
	5. Being aware that workshop participants may have underlying issues	"I know that people have very complex relationships to certain experiences."
The scenario	4. Modelling simulations so the most important learning outcomes are based on reality	"…as long as those inputs are the same as the real world, we're reinforcing the message and, and relative values of how impactful some of those decisions can be."
	6. Making the driving environment stress free	"…we want to reduce anxiety so you can learn these lessons before you become too anxious because anxiety can affect the way you learn. So having someone in a big skid pan, with lots of room around, there's nothing to hit…."
	3. Ensuring the game is played in controlled conditions and only by the learner being assessed	" … so that you can have a three year old come up with perfect scores, but you find out it was a five year old who was doing it for them while they were sitting next to them, or the parent…."
The roles	5. Encouraging sharing amongst the group with simple activities to promote interpersonal skills	"Thinking about food creates a sense of safety. So I want to do that in the workshop. They've also shared something personal about themselves, even though it's their favourite meals, not deeply personal, something. And they've all made eye contact."

(*continued*)

Table 3. (*continued*)

Element	Example	Illustrative quote
The gaming materials	2. Consideration of UI elements to suit the target audience	"… 'adults with intellectual disabilities don't like playing kids games…They want something that they can engage with, as an adult and be treated like an adult, but have it be appropriate to them."
	6. Introducing concepts and obstacles one at a time	"It was always kind of, here's how to learn one more little thing, one more little thing, one more little thing. So eventually, they've learned 20, 30 things, but feeling like they're just learning one thing each time."
The steps of play	7. Allowing participants to learn what they can do within the space station before exiting into space	"But the structure of it is intended to be, you know, you teach people the pieces that they need to know in order to solve puzzles, those kinds of things, and then you give them as much as you can a sense of direction as to what they're supposed to be doing. You know, like, you lose contact with mission control, well, the very next thing you need to do is like, go and try and get control back."
Assessing the performance	6. All actions are given immediate feedback, with the learner driver only progressing once they have completed a task satisfactorily	"I should say the most, kind of fun part of the game, is there's sort of like a little obstacle course, but you have to not hit barriers, and you have to swerve left and right around the barriers…. But if you hit a barrier, you fail straight away."

(*continued*)

Table 3. (*continued*)

Element	Example	Illustrative quote
The flexibility of the game	6. Players must act safely and within the boundaries of the game, if they leave the road for example the game stops	"But they're constrained in speed by the barriers, like if you go too fast, you just hit a barrier and fail. So, yeah, and you can sort of go off the course, but again, you'll just fail if you get out of bounds."
	4. Consideration is given to how much players can stray from the core path, and how many resources are devoted to this	"…a lot of the time, it's just do we spend the time implementing features so that people can go against the intent of the project or do we focus more time on implementing or improving or polishing the core path they go down in order to make that core message more effective?"
General considerations	6. Allowing students to have some free play in the simulator at the end of the session	"…we have a dev mode that we can run where you can drive at any speed. It just turns off the road rules. And often kids, when they finished, they just wanted to play around, have a bit of fun with the driving."
	2. Game pace was adjusted according to feedback to make it doable by the target audience	"…I slowed those games down a lot. So in terms of how many actions a user can perform, I was like, four times slower than I would have done, and I still had to slow it down. Like it was probably like, 10 times slower than I would have done it."

User or player-centred design can and does work, with some limitations [17, 46, 47]. All developers interviewed employed varying degrees of testing with users. Some possibly left it a little too late, doing it as part of a user acceptance testing (UAT) process rather than embedding feedback in early on as part of a more iterative design process and had to make adjustments after the fact, but it didn't have a major impact in any of the cases discussed. Most of this also came down to budgets and simply not having the resources to produce multiple 'playable' versions of the game.

Financial resources appeared to be a major factor for serious games designers which demonstrated that other orders of worth are at play, and foregrounding psychological safety. The interviewees acknowledged the limitations and compromises involved. Careful consideration needs to be given to ensure resources are allocated in a way that allows for the maximum amount of psychological hazards to be identified and controlled in an appropriate manner. As the developer of the youth services game observed, games are expensive, complex, and difficult, and doing user-centred design is very expensive to do right. Then even when there are sufficient resources for involving users in an iterative design process, it still requires intervention by the developers to make the game content palatable, and avoid stereotypes. It's near impossible to create something that will be truly representative and considerate of all users, trade-offs are inevitable.

Complicating this further is the impact that multiple stakeholder groups have on the design of games and how 'user-centric' they end up being. For example the developer producing a game for physiotherapy had to balance the often competing needs of the physiotherapy business owners, practitioners, and the end users. Each of these may have different priorities in what they consider orders of worth in the final product. The game developer is then forced to make their own values judgement in terms of which stakeholder's desires, needs or views they prioritise.

Limited resources were also mentioned by many of the developers in regards to how much scope there was for evaluation of the games they had developed. There was an underlying admission that is every possibility that some of these games had psychological impacts which are unknown to the developers and undocumented.

Given the subjective nature of valuing by stakeholders, Barry et al. [50] emphasises the importance of transparency to ensure design choices support psychological wellbeing. Transparency can be made more powerful when prioritised in practice. It could potentially be useful to make use of the psychological hazards checklist throughout the design process in conjunction with stakeholders. This seems worthy of further research.

The interviews indicate how, "the playful is political" [51] and designing serious games and simulations that fully account for the psychological safety of everybody is challenging without understanding the politics at play and how the competing sets of values can be costly. It's up to the lead game developer to recognise these competing values by working closely with subject matter experts and the target audience, so that the transmission (design) and reception (use) of serious games and simulations are as synchronised as possible in prioritising psychological safety.

6 Conclusion

This paper highlights the need for careful consideration by game developers to ensure they are designing games in a way that is psychologically safe for players. In discussions of the broad range of case studies with game developers, it was apparent that game developers do consider psychological safety. However, it is often in an ad-hoc fashion, and not necessarily prioritised as theorised in the sociology of worth. This lack of prioritisation is evident in game developers who do not consider it at all, and for others the lack of rigour and the appropriate resources, such as the use of a formalised psychological safety tool as a game development checklist that can be debated with the design team through the inception of the game design and development stages. This would also serve to accommodate other orders of worth such as cost savings on unnecessary rework, negating any unwanted, negative publicity or fame as a result of unforeseen psychological harm.

Appendix 1 - Interview Script and Questions

Introduction – 2 min
Thanks for taking the time to participate in this interview.

My name is Dale Linegar and as you know I am doing a research project about ethical consideration in game design.

As stated in the Participant Information Sheet, your participation is completely voluntary, and you do not need to answer any questions you don't want to and can stop the interview at any time. You may also withdraw from this research project at any time before publication.

I would like to make you aware that any anecdotes you share in this interview may be traceable back to you if you provide details that will allow others to identify you. So please exercise discretion when responding.

All information you give here will be de-identified and I will be the only person who is aware of your involvement.

Do you have any questions for me before we start?

Can I confirm that you are okay to proceed with this interview being recorded?

Interview Questions (Based on Values at Play Framework) - 60–90 min
Okay so what we will do in this interview is start off narrow, then broaden as we go. The idea is to get you thinking about the game design process and all the games you have developed over the years, and to ask you what you have or haven't considered regarding values and ethics, and even what you didn't consider or become aware of until after deployment.

I will be interviewing between 20 and 30 developers who, like yourself, have been a finalist in either the Serious Games Showcase & Challenge, the Australian Games Developer Serious Game Awards, or Games for Change Awards. This is being used as a filter of sorts to make sure we are speaking with developers who have been recognised by their peers as worthy serious game developers.

DISCOVERY
How did the following affect the values of your game?

Key actors - the people involved in creating the game.

Functional description - the explicit statement describing the game.

Societal input - cultural contexts, standards, and other external factors bearing upon the game.

Technical constraints - software, hardware and other game elements that together constitute the game.

Financial constraints – the budget.

Any other constraints you can think of, for example time.

IMPLEMENTATION
I would like to take you through 15 different elements of game design and ask how you consider each of these elements when taking what you have learned during discovery and turning it into a game, in particular in regard to the values you want your game to express.

For each of these items I would like you to consider two things:

1. How did you pay attention to a particular game element?
2. How did you consider what you were trying to achieve and how your game conveys values to players (or others)?

1. **Narrative premise and goals**

    What is the story?
    What goals or motivations drive the playable or player character?
    Who or what is the playable character pursuing, and what happens along the way?
    How are the events ordered?
    What will the player have accomplished when the game is 'beaten' or 'won'?
    Are players paying attention to the narrative as they play?

2. **Characters**

    Can playable characters be customised or selected?
    If they can, how is this done and what options are provided?
    What are the characters' attributes and characteristics?
    What are the characteristics and roles of non playable characters (NPCs)?

3. **Actions in game**

    What can the player do (or cause playable characters to do) in a game?

4. **Player choice**

    What choices are available to the player?
    What choices aren't?
    From a values perspective, what does it mean to offer or withhold these choices?

5. **Rules for interaction with other players and NPCs**

    How do interactions with other players and NPCs reflect the values of the game?

6. **Rules for interaction with the environment**

    What types of interactions does the game afford between playable characters and the non sentient aspects of the game world?
    What resources are available?
    What types of interactions are incentivised through the game's rules and the capacity of the AI or ADM system?
    Is the player rewarded for exploring or appreciating, for depleting resources or replenishing them, or for destroying the game world or nurturing it?

7. **Point of view**

    How do players view the playable character?
    Do they survey the world from a first or third person perspective?
    Do players take on the view of a certain character or are they controlling the situation from a God's eye, top down view?
    Is it something in between or both?

8. **Hardware**

    How has the intended hardware shaped your game design?

9. **Interface**

    Interfaces can be thought of as the construct of the hardware and the software, the mode through which players interact with the game world.
    How did you consider your interface in regards to the values you wished to express through your game?

10. **Game engine and software**

    How did the software or games engine used affect how you designed your game?
    Do you think this changed the values of your game?

11. **Context of play**

    What is the 'culture' of your game? For example some games have mechanics which encourage kindness and collaboration, some have the opposite, where it's dog eat dog and you are going to be taunted if you aren't competing.

12. **Rewards**

    What are points awarded for?
    What are the game goals?
    If no points are given, how are players rewarded as they advance in a game?
    What is the end state of the game?
    How do you win?
    A game's reward structures can reveal what accomplishments are valued in the game.

13. **Strategies**

    What strategies can be usefully applied in the game?
    What approaches to the challenges in the game will help players progress or win?

14. **Game maps**

    Does your game feature a game map, and does it foster or prohibit certain values?

15. **Aesthetics**

    How do the aesthetics of your game infuse values into the game?

VERIFICATION

Do you go through a verification process for your games?
    What are the factors which allow for or constrain this?
    What is your process?
    Do you have evidence of the following?
    Has the game promoted the desired behaviours?
    Has the game enabled greater understanding and appreciation?
    Has the game elicited a particular affective or attitudinal response?

Final Questions

What do you think, broadly speaking, are ethical considerations that should be taken when designing a serious game?

Is it something you are conscious of, or more alerted to by something that seems obviously unethical?

How has your own ethics affected your approach to specific subjects or topics?

Have you ever had any unexpected feedback regarding the ethical implications of your serious game design decisions?

Have you seen other serious games and questioned the way that they considered the ethical implications of their game design?

Does the way that others will perceive your ethics affect the way you approach game design?

What are the challenges of being able to design serious games with appropriate ethical consideration?

How do you think we could measure the level of ethical consideration given to serious game design?

Is there anything else you would like to share regarding ethics and serious game design?

Conclusion – 1 min

Great, that was the last question and brings us to the end of the interview.

As I mentioned I will now transcribe this discussion and send it back to you for you to review. If you want to add, modify or remove anything that's fine, just let me know, the idea of this interview is to get your views.

This interview has given me a great amount to think about and is a really valuable contribution to the project.

Thank you for your time, it's really appreciated.

I will be in touch.

References

1. Abt, C.C.: Serious Games. University Press of America (1987). https://play.google.com/store/books/details?id=axUs9HA-hF8C
2. Bong, C.L., Fraser, K., Oriot, D.: Cognitive load and stress in simulation. In: Grant, V.J., Cheng, A. (eds.) Comprehensive Healthcare Simulation: Pediatrics, pp. 3–17. Springer, Cham (2016). https://doi.org/10.1007/978-3-319-24187-6_1
3. Tsai, C.-F., Yeh, S.-C., Huang, Y., Wu, Z., Cui, J., Zheng, L.: The effect of augmented reality and virtual reality on inducing anxiety for exposure therapy: a comparison using heart rate variability. J. Healthc. Eng. **2018**, 6357351 (2018). https://doi.org/10.1155/2018/6357351
4. Lateef, F.: Maximizing learning and creativity: understanding psychological safety in simulation-based learning. J. Emerg. Trauma Shock **13**(1), 5–14 (2020). https://doi.org/10.4103/JETS.JETS_96_19
5. Schein, E.H., Bennis, W.G.: Personal and Organizational Change Through Group Methods: The Laboratory Approach. Wiley, New York (1965)
6. Martens, M.A., Antley, A., Freeman, D., Slater, M., Harrison, P.J., Tunbridge, E.M.: It feels real: physiological responses to a stressful virtual reality environment and its impact on working memory. J. Psychopharmacol. **33**(10), 1264–1273 (2019). https://doi.org/10.1177/0269881119860156

7. Chang, T.P., Beshay, Y., Hollinger, T., Sherman, J.M.: Comparisons of stress physiology of providers in real-life resuscitations and virtual reality-simulated resuscitations. Simul. Healthc. J. Soc. Simul. Healthc. **14**(2), 104 (2019). https://doi.org/10.1097/SIH.0000000000000356
8. Silverman, B.: Toward realism in human performance simulation. In: Ness, J.W., Tepe, V., Ritzer, D.R. (eds.) The Science and Simulation of Human Performance, vol. 5, pp. 469–498. Emerald Group Publishing Limited (2004). https://doi.org/10.1016/S1479-3601(04)05009-X
9. Chen, S., Michael, D.: Proof of learning: assessment in serious games, October 2005. http://www.cedma-europe.org/newsletter%20articles/misc/Proof%20of%20Learning%20-%20Assessment%20in%20Serious%20games%20(Oct%202005).pdf
10. Darzentas, D.P., Urquhart, L.: Interdisciplinary reflections on games and human values. In: Proceedings of the 2015 Annual Symposium on Computer-Human Interaction in Play, pp. 805–810. Association for Computing Machinery, New York (2015). https://doi.org/10.1145/2793107.2810259
11. Boling, M.E.: Virtual Responsibility: Video Games and Ethical Considerations in Players. search.proquest.com (2016). https://search.proquest.com/openview/4b405a8360f99610ea2abc8ca8565a1b/1?pq-origsite=gscholar&cbl=18750
12. Gregory, S., et al.: Sustaining the future through virtual worlds. In: Brown, M., Stewart, T., Hartnett, M. (eds.) Presented at the Australasian Society for Computers in Learning in Tertiary Education Conference, pp. 361–368. ascilite - Australian Society for Computers in Learning in Tertiary Education, Australia (2012). https://eprints.qut.edu.au/53959/
13. O'Rourke, M.: Increasing engagement with vocational education and training: a case study of computer games-based safety training. 2013 postgraduate research papers: a compendium, pp. 113–133 (2013). https://library.bsl.org.au/jspui/bitstream/1/4639/1/GriffinT_2013-postgraduate-research-papers-compendium_NCVER-2014.pdf#page=115
14. Brooks, A., Vesty, G.: Kilgors: A Digital Performance Management Simulation, 17 August 2014. https://doi.org/10.2139/ssrn.2482085
15. Popescu, M.M., Romero, M., Usart, M.: Serious games for serious learning using SG for business, management and defence education. Int. J. Comput. Sci. Res. Appl. **3**(1), 5–15 (2013). https://www.academia.edu/download/52437524/Serious_Games_for_Serious_Learning_Using20170402-5997-1rmot7z.pdf
16. Wouters, P., van Nimwegen, C., van Oostendorp, H., van der Spek, E.D.: A meta-analysis of the cognitive and motivational effects of serious games. J. Educ. Psychol. **105**(2), 249–265 (2013). https://doi.org/10.1037/a0031311
17. Sandovar, A., Braad, E., Streicher, A., Söbke, H.: Ethical stewardship: designing serious games seriously. In: Dörner, R., Göbel, S., Kickmeier-Rust, M., Masuch, M., Zweig, K. (eds.) Entertainment Computing and Serious Games: International GI-Dagstuhl Seminar, Dagstuhl Castle, Germany, 5–10 July 2015, Revised Selected Papers, vol. 15283, pp. 42–62. Springer, Cham (2016). https://doi.org/10.1007/978-3-319-46152-6_3
18. Flanagan, M., Nissenbaum, H.: Values at Play in Digital Games. MIT Press (2014). https://play.google.com/store/books/details?id=iIYRBAAAQBAJ
19. Macklin, C., Sharp, J.: Games, Design and Play: A Detailed Approach to Iterative Game Design. Addison-Wesley Professional (2016). https://play.google.com/store/books/details?id=usQwDAAAQBAJ
20. Hunicke, R., Le Blanc, M., Zubek, R.: MDA: a formal approach to game design and game research. game-developers.org (2004). https://game-developers.org/wp-content/uploads/2022/09/MDA.pdf. Accessed 28 Dec 2023
21. Edmondson, A.C., Lei, Z.: Psychological safety: the history, renaissance, and future of an interpersonal construct. Annu. Rev. Organ. Psych. Organ. Behav. **1**(1), 23–43 (2014). https://doi.org/10.1146/annurev-orgpsych-031413-091305

22. Turner, S., Harder, N.: Psychological safe environment: a concept analysis. Clin. Simul. Nurs. **18**, 47–55 (2018). https://doi.org/10.1016/j.ecns.2018.02.004
23. Aranzamendez, G., James, D., Toms, R.: Finding antecedents of psychological safety: a step toward quality improvement. Nurs. Forum **50**(3), 171–178 (2015). https://doi.org/10.1111/nuf.12084
24. Peters, V., van de Westelaken, M., Bruining, J.: Simulation games as a safe environment: what can game designers and facilitators do to guard the psychological security of participants? シミュレーション&ゲーミング**22**(Special), 59–64 (2012). https://doi.org/10.32165/jasag.22.SPECIAL_59
25. Hummel, H.G.K., Nadolski, R.J., Eshuis, J., Slootmaker, A., Storm, J.: Serious game in introductory psychology for professional awareness: optimal learner control and authenticity. Br. J. Educ. Technol. J. Council Educ. Technol. **52**(1), 125–141 (2021). https://doi.org/10.1111/bjet.12960
26. van Beek, L., et al.: The effects of serious gaming on risk perceptions of climate tipping points. Clim. Change **170**(3), 31 (2022). https://doi.org/10.1007/s10584-022-03318-x
27. Linegar, D., Vesty, G., Tsahuridu, E.: Serious games, stealth interventions and accounting ethics. In: Games for Change Asia-Pacific Journal Volume 2, pp. 179–202. ETC Press (2023)
28. de Wijse-van Heeswijk, M., Leigh, E.: Ethics and simulation games in a cultural context: why should we bother? And what can we learn? In: Kikkawa, T., Kriz, W.C., Sugiura, J. (eds.) Gaming as a Cultural Commons: Risks, Challenges, and Opportunities, pp. 149–167. Springer, Singapore (2022). https://doi.org/10.1007/978-981-19-0348-9_9
29. Plass, J.L., Kalyuga, S.: Four ways of considering emotion in cognitive load theory. Educ. Psychol. Rev. **31**(2), 339–359 (2019). https://doi.org/10.1007/s10648-019-09473-5
30. Mukerjee, J., Metiu, A.: Play and psychological safety: an ethnography of innovative work. J. Prod. Innov. Manag. **39**(3), 394–418 (2022). https://doi.org/10.1111/jpim.12598
31. Le, A.N.: Developing Wellbeing Literacy for Remote Work Integrated Learning. researchrepository.rmit.edu.au (2023). https://researchrepository.rmit.edu.au/esploro/outputs/doctoral/Developing-Wellbeing-Literacy-for-Remote-Work/9922283212701341?institution=61RMIT_INST
32. Nelson, S., Padilla, C.: Level up: games for socially just leadership education. New Dir. Stud. Leadersh. **2022**(174), 121–128 (2022). https://doi.org/10.1002/yd.20505
33. Mayer, I., van Dierendonck, D., van Ruijven, T., Wenzler, I.: Stealth assessment of teams in a digital game environment. In: Games and Learning Alliance, pp. 224–235. Springer, Cham (2014). https://doi.org/10.1007/978-3-319-12157-4_18
34. Parker, H., du Plooy, E.: Team-based games: catalysts for developing psychological safety, learning and performance. J. Bus. Res. **125**, 45–51 (2021). https://doi.org/10.1016/j.jbusres.2020.12.010
35. Jeong, E.J., Biocca, F.A.: Are there optimal levels of arousal to memory? Effects of arousal, centrality, and familiarity on brand memory in video games. Comput. Hum. Behav. **28**(2), 285–291 (2012). https://doi.org/10.1016/j.chb.2011.09.011
36. Arity, V., Vesty, G., Moloney, B.: Digitized simulation and gamified pedagogy in a first year accounting core subject. In: Rana, T., Svanberg, J., Öhman, P., Lowe, A. (eds.) Handbook of Big Data and Analytics in Accounting and Auditing, pp. 361–393. Springer, Singapore (2023). https://doi.org/10.1007/978-981-19-4460-4_16
37. Yerkes, R.M., Dodson, J.D.: The relation of strength of stimulus to rapidity of habit-formation. J. Comp. Neurol. Psychol. **18**(5), 459–482 (1908). https://doi.org/10.1002/cne.920180503
38. Carrera, A.M., et al.: Constructing safe containers for effective learning: vignettes of breakdown in psychological safety during simulated scenarios. In: Intersections in Simulation and Gaming, pp. 15–29. Springer, Cham (2018). https://doi.org/10.1007/978-3-319-78795-4_2

39. Kaufman, G., Flanagan, M., Seidman, M.: Creating stealth game interventions for attitude and behavior change: an "Embedded Design" model. Trans. Digit. Games Res. Assoc. **2**(3), (2016). https://www.researchgate.net/profile/Geoff-Kaufman/publication/319995249_Creating_Stealth_Game_Interventions_for_Attitude_and_Behavior_Change_An_Embedded_Design_Model/links/5ac6b5224585151e80a37d0a/Creating-Stealth-Game-Interventions-for-Attitude-and-Behavior-Change-An-Embedded-Design-Model.pdf?_sg%5B0%5D=started_experiment_milestone&origin=journalDetail&_rtd=e30%3D
40. Naweed, A., Dennis, D., Krynski, B., Crea, T., Knott, C.: Delivering simulation activities safely: what if we hurt ourselves? Simul. Healthc. J. Soc. Simul. Healthc. **16**(1), 60–66 (2021). https://doi.org/10.1097/SIH.0000000000000460
41. Turner, D., Picton, G., Harrod, E., Bossy, M.: Using a breathing simulator to improve simulation-based education for noninvasive ventilation. Breathe (Sheff.) **17**(2), 200285 (2021). https://doi.org/10.1183/20734735.0285-2020
42. Lebois, L.A.M., et al.: A shift in perspective: decentering through mindful attention to imagined stressful events. Neuropsychologia **75**, 505–524 (2015). https://doi.org/10.1016/j.neuropsychologia.2015.05.030
43. Charles, D., et al.: Player-centred game design: player modelling and adaptive digital games. In: Proceedings of DiGRA 2005 Conference: Changing Views – Worlds in Play, pp. 285–298. Digital Games Research Association: DiGRA (2005). https://mural.maynoothuniversity.ie/12737/
44. Hardy, A., et al.: How inclusive, user-centered design research can improve psychological therapies for psychosis: development of SlowMo. JMIR Mental Health **5**(4), e11222 (2018). https://doi.org/10.2196/11222
45. Al Halabi, G., Tinç, K., Süngü, E.: The impact of human-centered design of game mechanics on feelings of belonging. In: Game + Design Education, pp. 167–177. Springer, Cham (2021). https://doi.org/10.1007/978-3-030-65060-5_14
46. Brauner, P., Ziefle, M.: Beyond playful learning – serious games for the human-centric digital transformation of production and a design process model. Technol. Soc. **71**(C), 102140 (2022). https://doi.org/10.1016/j.techsoc.2022.102140
47. Bayrak, A.T.: Compassionate game design: a holistic perspective for a player-centric game design paradigm for gameshealth. personales.upv.es (2020). http://personales.upv.es/thinkmind/dl/journals/intsys/intsys_v13_n12_2020/intsys_v13_n12_2020_1.pdf. Accessed 7 Jan 2024
48. Dekker, M.R., Williams, A.D.: The use of user-centered participatory design in serious games for anxiety and depression. Games Health J. **6**(6), 327–333 (2017). https://doi.org/10.1089/g4h.2017.0058
49. Boltanski, L., Thévenot, L.: On Justification. Princeton University Press (2006). https://doi.org/10.1515/9781400827145
50. Barry, M., Doherty, K., Marcano Belisario, J., Car, J., Morrison, C., Doherty, G.: mHealth for maternal mental health: everyday wisdom in ethical design. In: Proceedings of the 2017 CHI Conference on Human Factors in Computing Systems, pp. 2708–2756. Association for Computing Machinery, New York (2017). https://doi.org/10.1145/3025453.3025918
51. Chess, S.: Ready Player Two: Women Gamers and Designed Identity. University of Minnesota Press (2017). https://play.google.com/store/books/details?id=yil0DwAAQBAJ

Enhancing Fair Play in Online Gaming: The Development and Implementation of the No More Cheats Anti-cheat System

Jakubowski Michał(✉), Małgorzata Ćwil, and Szatkowska Weronika

Kozminski University, Warsaw, Poland
mcwil@kozminski.edu.pl

Abstract. The integrity of competitive online gaming and esports is increasingly compromised by the prevalence of cheating, a multifaceted problem that undermines fair play and diminishes the gaming experience for honest players. This paper provides a comprehensive overview of cheating in online gaming, tracing its evolution from the inception of video games to the current landscape dominated by sophisticated online multiplayer environments. Through an exploratory qualitative study involving semi-structured interviews with 30 gamers, predominantly male, from Poland, we delve into the motivations behind cheating, the various forms it takes, and the impact on the gaming community. Our findings highlight the most common and disruptive cheats, such as aimbots and wallhacks, and the psychological and material motivations driving players to exploit these unfair advantages. Furthermore, we assess the effectiveness of existing anti-cheat measures and propose the "No More Cheats" system, a conceptual framework for a more effective and less intrusive anti-cheat solution. The study emphasizes the need for ongoing innovation in anti-cheat technology, incorporating advanced detection algorithms and ethical considerations to maintain the integrity of competitive online gaming and esports. Through this discussion, we aim to contribute to the development of more sophisticated, fair, and transparent anti-cheat systems, ensuring a level playing field and preserving the spirit of competition that is fundamental to the gaming experience.

Keywords: anti-cheat · gaming · cheating

1 Introduction

Competitive gaming has been present on the video game market from its very beginning. Due to the limited number of mechanics and the generally low level of complexity, first games did not allow any player to gain an advantage by using unfair practices. Competitive gaming has a lot in common with sports competitions. Both areas use skills acquired over many hours of training to gain an advantage over an opponent. Video game tournaments have been played almost since the beginning, with the first one in 1972 using the game Pong [1]. Any cheating back then was also made more difficult by the way the games were run. Tournament players performed in the same room in front of their fans and using software and hardware, e.g. from the game producer or tournament sponsor.

Everything started to change in the 1990s, when games, in addition to graphical and technological improvements, gained one more key feature - the ability to play online [2]. The ability to play the match from the comfort of one's room made it difficult to control what exactly was running on the computer along with the game. The emerging software that modified the gameplay on the player's side made it possible to gain an additional advantage that was undetectable by the default settings of online gameplay. Despite this, online gaming was becoming one of the favorite ways to enjoy games. The motivation to be the best was suddenly no longer limited to the closest circle of friends, from now on you could test yourself with virtually anyone around the world. Ultimately, this led to the professionalization of online gaming, which we now know better as eSports.

The rapid development of the computer games and esports industry makes players more and more willing to appear, compete and participate in the largest leagues and tournaments [3, 4]. However, the path to the top is not easy. It requires dedication, training and sacrifices that affect their health, family and social life, education and professional career. In the current phase of esports development, professional organizations and clubs bringing together players, in cooperation with specialists in various fields, have managed to develop specific training programs for building a professional player's career [5], combining all the previously mentioned aspects and incorporating modern technological solutions.

Some cases of professional athletes cheating can be observed even during the official tournaments [6]. Cheating hacks and software are easily accessible to casual gamers, as many websites offer cheating software for a small or no fee. Even a small percentage of cheaters can ruin the gaming experience for a large percentage of players: if 6% of players are cheating, the chance of meeting at least one cheater is 42.7% in 5 vs. 5 matches [6]. That are the reasons why developing a new and innovative anti-cheating system is crucial.

2 Cheating in Gaming

2.1 Motivation for Cheating

Just like in traditional sports, esports is also exposed to attempts to shorten this path by using unfair practices of players who are influenced by the desire to be famous as quickly as possible, to gain attention and approval [7, 8]. The reasons why amateur and professional esports players cheat are very similar and in most cases are the result of human reflexes, upbringing and character.

The reasons why players cheat in video games can be divided into two categories: satisfaction of mental and material needs. In the sphere of tangible benefits that motivate cheating in esports, the basic factors are very good player statistics, position in rankings, and final results in tournaments and leagues. Achieving them often makes it easier for players to get a contract in a professional esports organization and potentially become famous. This, in turn, leads to the conclusion of new contracts with management agencies and sponsorship agreements. At the same time, we come to the financial issue, i.e. the desire to get rich quickly and achieve financial benefits.

2.2 Definition of Cheating

Though online cheating is getting more broadly used, it is hard to find one generally accepted definition on what a cheat is. Different companies and various researchers, use different criteria to determine which behavior is cheating. For example, some allow players to use macros to replay a series of keystrokes, or mouse moves and clicks, while others regard the use of macros as cheating [9].

According to Jeff Yan and Choi [10], "any behavior that a player uses to gain an advantage over his peer players or achieve a target in an online game is cheating if, according to the game rules or at the discretion of the game operator (i.e. the game service provider, who is not necessarily the developer of the game), the advantage or the target is one that he is not supposed to have achieved". This is the definition of a cheat that the researchers will use during this study.

2.3 Types of Cheating

Cheating in games can take various forms, and developers should employ different measures to prevent and detect cheating.

According to Yan and Randell [11], there are 15 main categories of cheats in video games.

1. Cheating by Exploiting Misplaced Trust – happens when a player tamper with game code, configuration data, or both, on the client side, when a cheater modifies the game client program, data, or both, and then replace the old copy with the revised but non-proper one for future use. This form of cheating happens due to placing too much trust is on the client side.
2. Cheating by Collusion – when players can collude with each other to gain unfair advantages over their honest opponents [12].
3. Cheating by Abusing the Game Procedure - may be carried out without any technical sophistication when a cheater simply abuses the operating procedure of a game. It can for example take a form of escaping - a cheater disconnects from the game when they are going to lose.
4. Cheating Related to Virtual Assets - virtual items acquired in online games can be traded for real money. A cheater might offer a virtual item, receive real money for the item but never deliver it as agreed.
5. Cheating by Exploiting Machine Intelligence - the advancement of computer chess research has produced many programs that can compete with human players at the master level. When playing chess online, a cheater can look for the best candidates for his next move by stealthily running a strong computer chess program.
6. Cheating by Modifying Client Infrastructure - a player can cheat by modifying the client infrastructure such as device drivers in their operating system, they can modify a graphics driver to make a wall transparent so that he can see through the wall, locating other players who are supposed to be hidden behind the wall (wallhacks).
7. Cheating by Denying Service to Peer Players - a cheater can, for example, delay the responses from his opponent by flooding his network connection.
8. Timing Cheating - a cheating player can delay his own move until he knows all the opponents' moves, and thus gain a huge advantage [13].

9. Cheating by Compromising Passwords - compromising a password gives a player a chance to have access to the victim's data and authorization.
10. Cheating by Exploiting Lack of Secrecy – players can cheat by eavesdropping on packets and inserting, deleting or modifying game events or commands transmitted over the network.
11. Cheating by Exploiting Lack of Authentication - if there is no proper mechanism for authenticating a game server to clients, a cheater can collect many ID password pairs of legitimate players by setting up a bogus game server.
12. Cheating by Exploiting a Bug or Loophole.
13. Cheating by Compromising Game Servers - a player can tamper with game server programs or change their configurations once he has obtained access to the game host systems.
14. Cheating Related to Internal Misuse - an employee of the game operator has the privileges of a system administrator and they can abuse this privilege, for example when generating super characters by modifying the game database on the server side.
15. Cheating by Social Engineering - cheaters attempt to trick a player into believing something attractive or annoying has happened to him and that as a result his ID and password are needed.

The available forms of cheating used by esports players are very closely related to the wealth of players, the stage of their career and the situation in which they have to decide to use cheats. Beginner players usually use publicly available free cheating software, which is easy to detect by the security measures of esports competition organizers. It is also easier for the administrators of these tournaments and leagues to analyze. More and more often, however, we can point to cases where professional players of the highest possible rank turned out to be cheaters. At this level, they make full use of paid cheats, which allow for better configuration and a much lower chance of detection. They are paid as part of monthly subscriptions worth from a dozen to several dozen dollars. Proving a violation of the rules to a player using such software is more difficult, takes more time and requires extensive analysis at the program level, as well as the assessment by experienced administrators of soft factors such as the player's movements and reactions from the recorded gameplay.

3 Methodology

This article presents the results of an exploratory qualitative study. The study aimed to recognize the phenomenon of cheating in online games, to learn about the experiences, observations and thoughts of players with a long history of playing these games, and to confront them with the idea for the "No More Cheats" system.

The study was conducted in the form of semi-structured individual interviews. The interview scenario was created around the following topics:

- demographics of respondents,
- interest in games,
- factors determining whether to play with other people,

- experiences with cheating in online games,
- experience with anti-cheat systems,
- discussion about the "No More Cheats" proposal.

30 people took part in the study, including 29 men and 1 woman. Respondents were recruited via social media in the form of private and public messages to the circle of people related to eSports. Everyone was informed about the purpose of the study, the anonymity of the processed information and the need to sign a confidentiality agreement.

The demographic structure of the respondents is approximately 30-year-old men from small and large towns in Poland. They represented various professional groups, with a predominance of IT workers. The majority of players have been playing video games since early youth (the record holder said he had been playing for 27 years). Many of them had experience playing professional or semi-professional tournaments.

The interviews were conducted entirely online using instant messengers such as Google Meet and Microsoft Teams. All the interviews lasted approximately 60 min. During the conversations, the researchers recorded initial observations, and then, by listening to the recordings, specific conclusions were transferred to the "Rainbow Sheet" tool. This made it easier to follow changes and new findings after subsequent interviews by the 3 researchers.

The following research questions were stated:

- What is the current state of the video game cheating phenomenon?
- What are the most common and most burdensome cheats according to gamers?
- What elements should a good anti-cheat system contain?

4 Findings

4.1 Most Popular Cheats

Respondents were asked to indicate all cheats they associated with, both those they had encountered and those they knew about from other sources. They were also asked which of them were the most bothersome. The collected results present an interesting picture of both the popularity of cheats and their perceived harmfulness.

In the majority of the interviews two main types of cheating where mentioned – aimbot and wallhack. At the same time, they are also perceived as the most burdensome (Fig. 1).

Aimbot involves software that automatically aims a player's weapon at opponents, ensuring near-perfect accuracy. It's commonly used in first-person and third-person shooter games.

Wallhack is a cheat consisting of obtaining the opportunity to observe the opponent's character through other game textures such as walls, obstacles, etc. Wallhacks allow players to gain an unfair advantage by being aware of the positions of opponents.

The third most often mentioned type of cheat is maphack - a scam involving obtaining a vision of more of the game map than should be actually visible to him or her. Enables, for example, omitting the so-called fog of war in RTS and RPG games.

The other types of cheats that were listed by the respondents are:

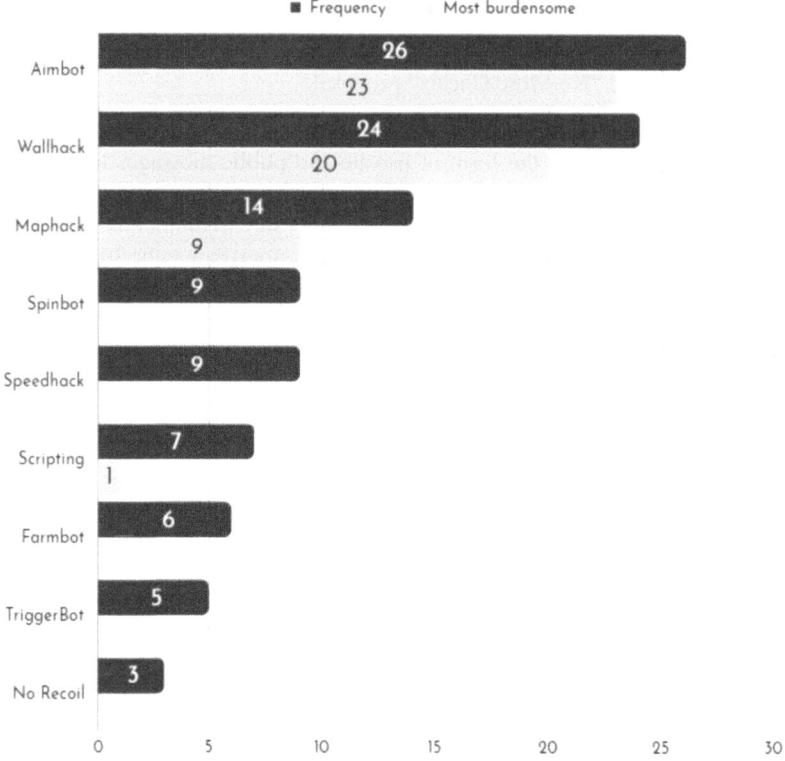

Fig. 1. Most frequent and most burdensome cheats.

- Spin bot - a cheat or hack that causes a player's in-game character to rapidly spin around within 360 degrees in an unpredictable manner, which can make it difficult for other players to aim at and hit the spinning player, giving them an unfair advantage. It is most often used in conjunction with the AIM bot.
- Speed hack - a game cheating technique where players modify the clock speed to move much faster than otherwise possible
- Scripting - the use of a program or game feature to automate certain actions or behaviors.
- Farmbot - a robot controlled through a computer or webapp that can be programmed to plant, water, and weed plants in a garden
- trigger bot - this cheat consists in simulating pressing the fire button when aiming at an opponent, guaranteeing immediate reaction and recoil control.
- no recoil - stops the movement of the crosshair, so recoil is not displayed on the screen.

And less often:

- Stream sniping - a situation when a player (stream sniper) follows a person broadcasting their gameplay on streaming websites and tries to find him in order to defeat him, harass him or disturb him in the game.

- Account Smurfing - frequently observed form of cheating among experienced players, in which they intentionally create new gaming accounts to challenge players with a much lower skill level.
- Account Boosting - involves taking advantage of the offer of an experienced player who, in exchange for a monetary payment, helps the commissioning person achieve very high places in the rankings by playing on that person's account.
- Fans' tips - a scam that involves fans providing voice prompts. During large live esports events with an audience, the noise is so high that players are able to predict the outcome of the game based on crowd reaction and sound.
- Communication by touch - non-verbal means of communication, e.g. by touching a fixed sign, most often used by coaches of esports teams, despite regulatory restrictions on communication with players during the match.
- Screen Sniping - a situation in which players participating in a stationary tournament look for the opportunity to view other image sources during a match to gain an advantage in predicting their opponent's movements.

Table 1. Comparison of Yan and Randell typology [8] and the results of our research.

Yan and Randell (2005) typology	Found in the research
Cheating by Exploiting Misplaced Trust	aim bot, spin bot, full removal hack, scripting
Cheating by Collusion	
Cheating by Abusing the Game Procedure	
Cheating Related to Virtual Assets	
Cheating by Exploiting Machine Intelligence	mobility hack,
Cheating by Modifying Client Infrastructure	wallhack, maphack, 3D box hack, extra sensory perception
Cheating by Denying Service to Peer Players	
Timing Cheating	trigger bot
Cheating by Compromising Passwords	
Cheating by Exploiting Lack of Secrecy	player warnings
Cheating by Exploiting Lack of Authentication	
Cheating by Exploiting a Bug or Loophole	
Cheating by Compromising Game Servers	
Cheating Related to Internal Misuse	
Cheating by Social Engineering	

It should be underlined that among the cheats mentioned in the research, only a few categories from Yan and Randell (2005) typology appeared. Table 1 summarizes the cheats found in the research and compares them with the afore-mentioned typology. During our research four main categories of cheating were mentioned: Cheating by Exploiting Misplaced Trust, Cheating by Exploiting Machine Intelligence, Cheating by Modifying Client Infrastructure and Timing Cheating. Aim bot, which was mentioned most often, belongs to the first category (exploiting misplaced trust) and the second most often mentioned – wallhack – is based on modifying client infrastructure.

The categories of Cheating by Collusion, by Abusing the Game Procedure, by Denying Service to Peer Players, by Compromising Passwords, by Exploiting Lack of Secrecy, by Exploiting Lack of Authentication, by Exploiting Lack of Authentication did not appear in our research. There can be various reasons for that happening. Maybe those categories are not that visible or prominent for the players. Or maybe they are just not perceived as cheats.

4.2 Most Burdensome Cheats

There are three types of cheats that are regarded by respondents as burdensome: aimbot, wallhack and maphack, and especially the combination of them. Using aimbot together with wallhack seems like the worst possible combination of cheats, when the player becomes almost or entirely unbeatable.

"Wallhack, Maphack - the opponent using them can see your every move and tactic. He can predict your thinking and quickly counter you, making it impossible for you to win. In the case of an aimbot in FPS games, for the cheater to win, he must first see your character, but this can be countered, for example, with a smoke grenade that covers you."

"Aimbot - is practically impossible to counter by another player. In the case of Wallhack and the ability to view another person's movements through walls, players who do not use cheats still have a chance to defeat such a cheater with their aiming skills."

"Aimbot, Wallhack - these two cheats, when combined with each other, provide virtually unlimited possibilities of controlling what is happening in the game and total domination over other players taking part in the game. You could call it the immortality mode of people who benefit from these two scams."

"Aimbot, Wallhack - the opponent has a much faster reaction time when aiming and is guaranteed to be able to effectively hit other players, which makes him practically impossible to eliminate. Wallhack, on the other hand, allows you to additionally predict the movements and positions of opponents on the map."

"Aimbot, Wallhack - due to their unique properties and the ability to gain a significant advantage over other players."

"Aimbot - bends all norms and limits of human capabilities in games. Wallhack can be easily confused with the so-called skill. Scanning the map, i.e. shooting blindly through various obstacles in the game, such as thin wooden walls. All cheats are equally irritating, only some are easier to catch and others are more difficult."

There were additional thoughts about the problems that the aforementioned scams cause. In the case of wallhacks and maphacks, the opponent can see every move and tactic based on them, he can predict the way of thinking and quickly counter, which makes it impossible to win. In the case of an aimbot - before the cheat can be used, the player must meet and see another player on the game screen. This allows for the possibility of countering with appropriate equipment (smoke grenade) or weapon (rapid-firing P90 rifle in Counter Strike). However, it is still very difficult and sometimes cheats are used simultaneously. An opponent with a wallhack and aimbot enabled is practically impossible to defeat.

4.3 Anti-cheat System

In the answers provided by the interviewees, there were three main problems with the way current anti-cheat systems work. The first of them, and the most important from the point of view of the essence of this phenomenon, is that despite increasingly better anti-cheat systems, it has not been possible to completely get rid of the use of cheats. Cheaters are still present, finding new loopholes in the game code, and it is a never-ending battle between game programmers and cheaters. A way to reduce this phenomenon may be to focus on the real causes and motivations for cheating, as well as better verification of user accounts and stricter bans for using cheats.

The second emerging problem concerns the "false positive" phenomenon, i.e. incorrect recognition of a player as a cheater. An error may occur both on the side of the automatic report verification system and on the side of the human who analyzes evidence of fraud. Sometimes players who did not use cheats get banned for playing exceptionally well or installing new drivers, e.g. for a mouse, which the algorithm will perceive as potential unknown software communicating with the game (because it did not have information about such a driver in the database yet). The reference point was to trace the history of the Runescape game and the problems with the anti-cheat system that occurred there. They resulted in a lot of false positive reports, which resulted from both the algorithm and human errors.

Finally, the third significant problem with existing anti-cheat systems is that they overload the computer's processing power, which leads to a slowdown in the system and the game. In the case of online games, response time is very important and any delay may cost you a loss. Players mentioned that they would prefer to play without anti-cheat support if it significantly affects the computer's performance.

The respondents were also asked to imagine a situation in which they had no budget, technological or time constraints and were to create a new anti-cheat system. According to their answers, such a system should be invisible to the end user and should not be noticeable while playing or using the application it supervises. It should be light, intuitive and should not burden the computer. They stated that there should be a possibility to disable the application if the game is not running. The system application should be able to be quickly accessed using an individual keyboard shortcut. The anti-cheating system should have as much information as possible from the software and devices connected to the computer. Some of the information can be analyzed by learning algorithms. Large portions of such visual data could be evaluated by image or video recognition scripts and thus help humans find fraudsters. The system should detect all new launches and check for potential threats. It should detect what keys are used and inform about strange ones that are not related to the game configuration. It should invalidate the results of matches during which fraud occurred.

The system should require more accurate user verification. It should be a better version of the antivirus. It should inform users about its effectiveness by showing statistics about how many disputes have been resolved, how many cheaters have been caught, etc. According to the respondents, the penalty for detected cheaters should be, preferably, a permanent ban on the IP address and other services and games of a given manufacturer, or even banning of the user's equipment for use in the game. The high penalty would effectively deter attempts at fraud.

In addition to using cheats, the anti-cheating system should also address other undesirable player behaviors such as using swear words, threats and other toxic elements of these interactions.

4.4 No More Cheats

The project aims to create a system that prevents cheating in competitive online computer games by combining technological and social methods for reporting fraud. This approach strengthens the identification of abuses, which has so far been the responsibility of entities creating and operating games, by making players aware that such behavior may have occurred and that they are capable of responding to it.

The operation of the No More Cheats-designed application is based on five stages:

Installation of the AntiCheat program on the player's computer: Activity related to the application begins when registering as a new user and defining specific preferences in their profile, such as the games supported by No More Cheats they wish to play. After meeting these criteria, the user will be asked to download and install the AC application on their device.

Operation of the launched application during and outside of gameplay: To use the AC software after installation, the user will be prompted to restart their computer. During this process, at a very early stage, an executable file that monitors the memory state at the system kernel level, i.e., before the operating system like Windows is loaded, will be launched. After each correct launch of the user environment, the application automatically activates, conducting active monitoring of the player's computer in search of potential unauthorized cheater software. If the application is closed during use, the user will be asked to restart their computer before attempting to launch the game again, as required by the AC application.

Active monitoring of the user's system environment, i.e., collecting data on installed software, hardware drivers, etc., and then detecting deviations from specified norms: The Anti-Cheat software will monitor the operating system environment to a much greater extent compared to popular antivirus programs. It will analyze all files and applications in the user's device memory, especially focusing on games and related data such as mouse drivers and other devices. Information about the player during a game will be continuously transmitted to the cloud computing, where it will be processed by monitoring systems. Based on this, preventive actions will be taken against players using unauthorized software in games, which will be processed into further stages of analysis, allowing for the construction of the final decision and drawing consequences against the user violating the game rules.

Built-in user rating system: In addition to the functions mentioned, the No More Cheats application will contain an implemented user rating system. Its main assumption is to build a sense of responsibility and awareness among users to motivate them to nurture and appreciate good attitudes in the virtual gaming environment and beyond. This functionality will also allow reporting negative ratings and stigmatizing reprehensible behaviors that significantly violate the regulations and norms set by the gaming community. The tool will enable to transparently evaluate users after a completed joint game, match, or event - based on predefined parameters in terms of skills, behavior, and other predispositions as a player and member of the gaming community.

Data analysis based on information sent in real-time: Data collected during the preceding steps will be transmitted and analyzed by appropriate algorithms in real-time with the support of the administration team. Based on this, evidence of fraud will be presented, with further consequences being appropriate actions taken against the specific user. The long-term goal of the project is to create an application and artificial intelligence algorithm that learns to detect fraud in online multiplayer games based on a detailed analysis of the user's profile built from the previously described levels.

The uniqueness of that solution lies in the combination of technological and social cheat prevention. Both of them were present in anti-cheat systems already, but never as one, consistent mechanism. Respondents were asked to share their opinions and feedback about that concept which led to the list of software design requirements as well as details of the rating system such as evaluation criteria or parameters. This part of the research had the biggest value for the development of anti-cheat prototype.

5 Limitations

One of the study's main limitations is the respondents' demographic structure. The vast majority are men from Poland. We managed to talk to only one woman and her statements had an interesting contribution to the overall understanding of the topic of undesirable behavior of players (issues of harassment, vulgarity towards women, etc.). While the first element is not of major importance - players' problems related to cheating are similar around the world, the issue of involving more women on the respondents' side should be addressed if this study is continued.

There were also some technical problems. Two recordings do not contain the respondent's voice, and one of the recordings recorded only 10 min of the entire conversation. The conclusions from these conversations were based on the researcher's notes (supplemented with conclusions after the interview), but these may be incomplete information that was provided during the conversation.

6 Conclusions

The research is informative for simulation game designers in several ways. Firstly, technological advancement enables the application of tailored methods to cheat in online games. When it comes to long-time, competitive simulation games, there may be attempts to modify the game or purchase modifications. Secondly, online cheating is available and there are multiple ways to pursue it.

Any attempts to cheat may damage the credibility of the educational tool. Cheating can create a frustrating and negative experience for players. It can lead to feelings of unfairness, frustration, and a lack of enjoyment, and also hinder the learning process. Thus, it is partially the responsibility of the designer and the facilitator to provide an environment to be resistant to cheating. Unfortunately, with technological development, it is barely possible to create a tool that will accurately limit cheating. That is why effective debriefing and building trust while applying simulation games is crucial.

References

1. Good, O.: Today is the 40th Anniversary of the World's First Known Video Gaming Tournament. Kotaku, 19 October 2012 (2012). https://kotaku.com/today-is-the-40th-anniversary-of-the-worlds-first-known-5953371
2. Raessens, J., Goldstein, J. (eds.): Handbook of Computer Game Studies. MIT Press (2011)
3. Precedence Research, Esports Market Size, Share, and Trends 2024 to 2033, June 2024. https://www.precedenceresearch.com/esports-market
4. Abramov, S., et al.: Analysis of video game players' emotions and team performance: an esports tournament case study. IEEE J. Biomed. Health Inform. **26**(8), 3597–3606 (2021)
5. Nagorsky, E., Wiemeyer, J.: The structure of performance and training in esports. PLoS ONE **15**(8), e0237584 (2020)
6. Jonnalagadda, A., Frosio, I., Schneider, S., McGuire, M., Kim, J.: Robust vision-based cheat detection in competitive gaming. Proc. ACM Comput. Graph. Interact. Tech. **4**(1), 1–18 (2021)
7. Lee, S.J., Jeong, E.J., Lee, D.Y., Kim, G.M.: Why do some users become enticed to cheating in competitive online games? An empirical study of cheating focused on competitive motivation, self-esteem, and aggression. Front. Psychol. **12**, 768825 (2021)
8. Passmore, C.J., Miller, M.K., Liu, J., Phillips, C.J., Mandryk, R.L.: A cheating mood: the emotional and psychological benefits of cheating in single-player games. In: Proceedings of the Annual Symposium on Computer-Human Interaction in Play, pp. 58–70, November 2020
9. Tang, S.: "Yes, I cheat, but not blatantly": the use of macros in racing games as transgressive play. In: Conference Proceedings of DiGRA 2023 Conference: Limits and Margins of Games Settings, June 2023
10. Jeff Yan, J., Choi, H.J.: Security issues in online games. Electron. Libr. **20**(2), 125–133 (2002)
11. Yan, J.J., Randell, B.: A systematic classification of cheating in online games. In: Proceedings of 4th ACM SIGCOMM Workshop on Network and System Support for Games, pp. 1–9, October 2005
12. Yan, J.: Security design in online games. In: Proceedings of 19th Annual Computer Security Applications Conference, pp. 286–295. IEEE, December 2003
13. Baughman, N.E., Levine, B.N.: Cheat-proof playout for centralized and distributed online games. In: Proceedings IEEE INFOCOM 2001. Conference on Computer Communications. Twentieth Annual Joint Conference of the IEEE Computer and Communications Society (Cat. No. 01CH37213), vol. 1, pp. 104–113. IEEE, April 2001

Navigating Uncertainty: The Emergence of Effort and Emotion in Tabletop Games

Shruti Agrawal(✉) and Girish Dalvi

IDC School of Design, Indian Institute of Technology Bombay, Mumbai, India
{shruti.idc,girish.dalvi}@iitb.ac.in

Abstract. Uncertainty is a core aspect of games; it shapes gameplay dynamics and influences players' experiences. Several dimensions of uncertainty have been studied, such as its relation to player engagement and motivation, sources, levels, and degrees. However, the relationship of uncertainty with effort and emotions that emerge as players navigate unpredictable game states remains underexplored. This study employs a qualitative methodology with eight players to examine the association between uncertainty and effort-emotion duo, analyzing two tabletop games, "Splendor" and "Azul." Based on collected data, we introduce adverb-verb phrases to capture players' emotions and mental exertions. Since uncertainty is a pervasive element in gameplay, it is challenging to attribute a particular emotion or the nature of mental effort solely to a specific kind of uncertainty. Hence, we group it into three distinct yet interconnected categories: continuous uncertainty, stage-specific uncertainty, and cumulative uncertainty. Our findings indicate that player emotions and efforts in tabletop games are neither static nor predictable based on game outcomes alone. Instead, they exhibit dynamic trajectories, fluctuating in response to the changing uncertainties. By highlighting the associations between uncertainty, effort, and emotion, this study offers a granular understanding of player experiences, underscoring the necessity of considering these elements in game design and analysis.

Keywords: Uncertainty · Effort · Emotions · Experiences · Emergent · Qualitative · Tabletop

1 Introduction and Motivation

Games come to life when players interact with them, giving rise to complex experiences. Rules and resources do not solely determine these experiences; they come together in players' minds as they engage with the game [1]. Various facets of player experiences range from broader states such as immersion, fun, and flow to subjective experiences encompassing players' feelings, emotional states, and motivations [2–5]. These experiences are often linked with aspects of games like difficulty, narrative, social interaction, mechanics, learning, and competition [6–10]. One such core aspect influencing gameplay is uncertainty [11–14]. While uncertainty is a recognized element in game design, its experiential implications, particularly in terms of the emotion and effort related responses it elicits, are less explored. Working through uncertainty is not only fundamental in games, but also the primary source of experiences generated while playing. Games necessitates players to exert effort in their open and ambiguous structure to have a play experience [15]. This study is an attempt to find nature of association between efforts that players put as they navigate uncertainty and emotions arising from the gameplay.

1.1 Previous Work on Uncertainty

Uncertainty has been considerably studied by game design scholars; it is recognized as one of the fundamental elements that significantly shapes player experience. Costikyan describes it as the essence of games, arguing that unpredictability is in "the path the game follows, in how players manage problems, in the surprises they hold" [11]. Aligning with this perspective, Schell posits that chance or uncertainty introduces surprises, making games pleasurable and fun [16]. Similarly, Juul explores the balance between skill and luck (a source of uncertainty), emphasizing that the interplay between these elements is crucial in designing fair and challenging games [17]. Multiple dimensions of uncertainty have been explored, including characterizing its nature not only in terms of sources and degree but also in terms of its association with other aspects like motivation, curiosity, engagement, and learning outcome [18–21, 24].

Greg Costikyan's taxonomy of sources of uncertainty is one of the central literatures on this topic [11]. He identifies sources such as 'performative uncertainty,' which challenges players' physical or skill-based capabilities, and 'solvers' uncertainty,' where players engage with the intellectual challenge crafted by game designers. 'Player Unpredictability' highlights the dynamic nature of social interaction in games, while 'Randomness' introduces elements of chance through dice and random arrangement of cards, shaping game dynamics. These categories highlight the diverse sources of uncertainty, from randomness and complexity inherent in games to the narrative surprises that keep players engaged. Similarly, Shalev et al. explore various dimensions of uncertainty in games, specifically focusing on tabletop games, highlighting elements like 'Betting and Bluffing' and 'Push Your Luck,' where risk-taking and strategic decision-making under uncertain conditions are essential [22]. They emphasize the importance of memory and hidden information, where players must navigate games with incomplete knowledge, enhancing the strategic depth. 'Hidden Roles' and 'Asymmetric Information' introduce intrigue and complexity to gameplay, while 'Communication Limits' and 'Probability Management' challenge players to make decisions with limited information and control. Debus explores the diversity in ontological and epistemological randomness, highlighting how uncertainty can arise from the game's inherent unpredictability and the limits of players' knowledge [23]. Salen et al. categorize game uncertainty into two levels: micro-level related to chance at isolated moments in games, such as dice roll, and macro-level uncertainty arising from the game's ultimate outcome [12].

Researchers have also studied uncertainty in games from a mathematical perspective to understand the logic behind each choice that is known and unknown to the players and how those choices affect the outcome [19, 25, 26]. Such approaches of analyzing games, though heavily prevalent, are also critiqued, especially by non-mathematics scholars, particularly due to their one-dimensional view of games which is often divorced from players' experiences.

1.2 Association of Uncertainty with Effort and Emotions

Caillois examines the difference between looking at play and real-life uncertain phenomenon through mathematical lens. Play, according to him, is irreducible to simple projections like 'A is better than B due to certain calculations' not only because accurate estimation is impossible in most games, but also because play is not reducible to the outcome of winning or making apt decisions. The pleasure of the game lies in the unknown outcome of the game i.e., the risk of losing. Through such arguments, Caillois questions the applicability of pure logic to understanding games, highlighting the importance of human elements like luck, caprice, and even the desire to lose. While he discusses the concept of uncertainty in a broader context of play and games as cultural and psychological phenomenon, Costikyan focuses more on the design aspects of games, specifically how uncertainty is an essential aspect of engaging games [11]. Expanding on the idea of uncertainty, he critiques Caillois' fixation on uncertainty of outcome as he expounds on various sources of uncertainty and detailed analysis of individual games. In his work, Costikyan theoretically identifies sources of uncertainties and applies it to a wide variety of games comprising digital, board, card, and even folk games. His insights, however, are confined to game design and how uncertainty can be engineered within games for improved experience.

Costikyan's taxonomy of uncertainty in terms of its sources works well in the context of identification and examination of uncertainty in various games. Nevertheless, application of this knowledge in game design requires a further study focused on player-centric understanding of sources of uncertainty. Emotions that arise concurrent to navigation of ambiguous paths in games should be examined from the players' perspective. This concept has been briefly touched upon by Salen et al. referred to as 'feelings of randomness.' This study addresses the gap by examining the nature of the relationship between uncertainty, its various sources, emotions, and effort, all of which coexist in a dynamic and entangled state. Understanding player emotions and effort under the lens of uncertainty in games suggest a complex, intertwined view of experiences that are influenced by the game's unfolding scenarios.

2 Methodology

2.1 Methodological Approach

This study adopts a qualitative, exploratory approach to delve into the complexities of player experiences in tabletop games, focusing on uncertainty, effort, and emotions. The qualitative method is chosen for its strength in capturing the depth and nuance of emotions and strategies. By analyzing descriptive detail and the subjective interpretations of participants, this approach facilitates an in-depth understanding of the dynamic interplay between game mechanics, player effort, and emotional responses. This methodology aligns with the work of scholars like Denzin and Lincoln, who in "The SAGE Handbook of Qualitative Research," advocate for qualitative research to explore complex phenomena in their natural settings, offering rich insights into participant behaviors and perceptions [29].

2.2 Selection of Games and Participants

We use tabletop games as primary focus in this for several reasons. Firstly, tabletop games have simple rules, making them accessible yet challenging platforms for studying decision-making under uncertainty. Moreover, dynamics afforded by tabletop games are more of an emergent nature rather than progressive giving rise to unpredictable game states with minimal rules, necessitating diverse and unique efforts across multiple scenarios [30]. Furthermore, the field of tabletop games, especially abstract strategy games, remains relatively underexplored in academic research compared to their digital counterparts. This gap presents a unique opportunity to contribute novel insights into game studies, particularly concerning how uncertainty influences player experience.

"Splendor" and "Azul" were specifically chosen for this study due to their abstract nature and strategic demands. These games have themes, yet they lack fictional narratives, thus primarily requiring navigation of challenge-based uncertainty. This characteristic makes them ideal subjects for dissecting uncertainty without the influence of narrative-driven emotional engagement. Other factors contributing to selection of these games are—availability and accessibility of games, length of gameplay, and the number of players. These are pragmatic considerations that significantly influenced the feasibility and scope of conducting this study within the constraints of time, resources, and participant engagement.

The participant group for this study comprises eight bachelor's students from an engineering institute, aged between 18 to 24 years. Proficiency in English was a crucial criterion, ensuring that participants could grasp the instructions and articulate their experience efficiently. Hobbyists who play tabletop games on a regular basis were chosen for this study due to their familiarity with typical game mechanics and strategies. This group's frequent engagement with tabletop games means they are more likely to notice subtle aspects of gameplay that less experienced players might overlook, making them ideal candidates.

2.3 Sessions

The study includes four gaming sessions, encompassing two sessions each for "Splendor" and "Azul." To accommodate varying group dynamics, one session for each game was conducted with four participants, while the other session had two participants. Throughout these sessions, data was collected from eight participants. Four of these participants engaged in both games, while the other four only played a single game. While the core of the study is built on eight distinct cases—each representing a unique participant's experience—the methodology yielded twelve separate entries. Each of these observations corresponds to an individual gameplay session, providing a granular view into the details of single gameplay experiences (Table 1).

Table 1. Details of Games and Gameplay Sessions

Games	Mechanics	Length	No	Session type 1	Session type 2
Splendor	Contracts, Open Drafting, Race, Set Collection	30–45	2–4	P1, P2, P3, P4	P5, P7
Azul	End-Game Bonuses, Open Drafting, Pattern Building, Tile Placement, Turn Order- Claim Action	30–45	2–4	P5, P6, P7, P8	P2, P3
Total Cases: 8	**Total Entries: 12**				

2.4 Data Collection

The study employed an experience sampling method with open-ended questions, allowing players to document their emotion and effort related experiences on a notepad throughout gameplay. Initially, participants were instructed to record their thoughts as they occurred naturally. This approach, however, led to varied data, with some participants providing extensive insights while others offered minimal input. To address this inconsistency, we modified our approach in the final sessions, setting specific intervals for reflection. For Azul, participants reflected at the conclusion of each round, while for Splendor, the roughly 30-min gameplay was segmented into four intervals for periodic reflection.

Participants were asked to articulate their experiences in the first person, detailing both their actions and the accompanying emotions, with prompts such as 'what are you doing and how does it make you feel as you're doing it?' This method aimed to delve into the players' experiences of effort and emotions without directly prompting thoughts on uncertainty. The rationale behind this approach was to mitigate bias and ensure that the data captured genuine experiences of players, free from the influence of the researchers' focus on uncertainty. The intention was to later draw connections between uncertainty and effort-emotion duo during the analysis phase. By not predefining the concept of uncertainty for participants, we allowed for a grounded emergence of themes and patterns.

3 Analysis and Findings

3.1 Emotion-Effort Describing Adverb-Verb Phrase

The analysis process began with transfer of hand-written analog data in digital format. This was followed by coding of the transcript. Coding of the data primarily included the first cycle of coding which encompassed two methods – elemental and affective [28]. A combination of process coding and emotion coding was performed within elemental and affective coding respectively [28]. Process coding involves breaking down the data into basic elements, focusing on the actions and processes described by players. Specific activities and strategies that players put effort into during gameplay were identified using this method. Emotion coding captures the feelings expressed in the data. The emotions were labeled based on either the way they were directly recalled/experienced by the participants or as they were inferred by the researcher about the participants. Based on the first level of coding, adverb-verb phrases were developed that describe the essence of effort and emotion in a single phrase. The use of adverb-verb phrase is a novel approach that aptly captures both the effort and emotional response in a concise format.

Process coding involves breakdown of data into basic elements, focusing on the action and process described. For the sentence "In the beginning I am not putting too much effort, since I know cards will be taken early before you can build to them, so I am just taking tokens," the process codes are – initial strategy development, anticipatory decision-making, and resource acquisition. Emotional codes, which involve identifying and categorizing the emotional states and attitudes expressed in the data are – relaxed or casual approach, anticipatory acceptance, and practical mindset. Bringing the two together, adverb-verb phrases were created. For this statement, for instance, the phrases were – casually exploring, tactically reserving, and cautiously observing. Various considerations were considered before assigning adverb-phrase to a chunk of data primarily being gameplay context, grammar, and other holistic considerations (Table 2).

Table 2. List of considerations for selection of adverb-verb phrase.

Type	Title	Explanation
Contextual Considerations	Game Phase Sensitivity	Tailoring phrases to the specific stages or shifts in the game
	Emotion Complexity	Capturing the multifaceted nature of emotions in gaming, acknowledging mixed or layered feelings
	Inter-player Dynamics	Reflecting how interactions with other players influence emotional and strategic responses
	Strategic Evolution	Highlighting how strategies evolve in response to game developments and their emotional impact
Grammar Considerations	Verb-Adverb Focus	Prioritizing the use of verb-adverb pairs for conciseness and direct emotional depiction

(*continued*)

Table 2. (*continued*)

Type	Title	Explanation
	Noun Inclusion/Exclusion	Deciding when to include nouns for clarity or exclude them for brevity
	Prepositional Phrasing	Assessing the need for prepositions to provide context or maintain simplicity without them
	Conciseness vs. Detail	Balancing between being succinct and providing enough detail for clarity and depth
	Grammatical Structure Adaptability	Flexibility in sentence construction to best convey the intended meaning and emotion
	Word Choice Precision	Selecting words that precisely convey the intended emotion or action, considering their nuances and connotations
	What is happening to him vs what is he doing	active engagement rather than passive engagement
Holistic Considerations	Narrative Flow	Ensuring that phrases collectively tell a coherent story of the gaming experience
	Reflective Depth	Capturing not just the surface emotions but also the underlying thought processes and reactions
	Consistency vs. Variety	Balancing consistency in style with enough variety to accurately reflect different emotional states
	Player Perspective Alignment	Aligning the phrases with the viewpoint and experience of the player, maintaining authenticity

Considering these factors, each phase of player statement was broken down into fragments describing effort-emotion duo using adverb-verb phrase. Twelve individual gameplay entries from eight sessions were analyzed to generate a comprehensive set of verb-adverb phrases. These phrases encapsulate the emotional and effortful experiences of the players as the game progresses. Following this, analysis was done to understand the relationship between various uncertainties and the combined dynamics of effort and emotion. Following segment illustrates data and analysis of one of the twelve entries (Table 3):

Table 3. Gameplay stages, emotion describing adverb-verb phrases, and explanation of the phrases ascribed to a player's description of the gameplay session of Splendor.

Stage	Emotion Describing Verb-Adverb Phrase	Explanation
1) Beginning: Initial Strategy	Casually exploring	Conveys an initial, relaxed approach to exploring options
	Tactically reserving	Indicates a strategic, careful start, avoiding overcommitment
	Cautiously observing	Reflects a watchful, measured approach in the early game
2) Few Turns: Focused Planning	Strategically intensifying	Shows an increase in mental effort and strategic focus
	Deliberately targeting	Captures specific aims, like reserving and acquiring particular cards
	Calculative planning	Indicates a more analytical approach in decision-making
3) Mid-Game: Steady Effort with Luck	Consistently exerting	Keeping a consistent level of effort in gameplay
	Opportunistically leveraging	Actively taking advantage of fortuitous card availability
	Adaptively playing	Adjusting play style to incorporate elements of luck and opportunity
4) Strategy Working	Confidently implementing	Actively executing a strategy with growing confidence
	Skilfully capitalizing	The player is adeptly making the most of their strategic position
	Focused narrowing	Actively concentrating on a singular, effective strategy
	Rewardingly executing	Reflects the satisfying experience of successfully implementing a winning strategy
5) Game End: Narrowed Options	Relievedly simplifying	Conveys a sense of relief as the game's complexity decreases and choices become more straightforward

(*continued*)

Table 3. (*continued*)

Stage	Emotion Describing Verb-Adverb Phrase	Explanation
	Resolvedly finalizing	Captures a sense of determination and clarity as the player makes decisive moves in the concluding phase
	Clearly prioritizing	Actively focusing on the most beneficial moves as options decrease

"In the beginning I am not putting too much effort, since I know cards will be taken early before you can build them, so I am just taking tokens. Now, after a few turns, there are a few cards I am aiming for, and reserving and taking tokens accordingly. So, my mental effort is increasing. About the same effort as previously mentioned, still quite a lot of effort but kind of reduced because of luck, since a lot of free cards are coming. I am feeling rewarded since my strategy is working (mostly unobstructed) and I got a noble card, the mental effort is going down since I am doubling down on one strategy. The effort is lower as the options I should take are reducing."

3.2 Complexity of the Influence of Uncertainty

To explore uncertainties encountered in tabletop games, we adopted the categorizations proposed by Shalev et al. and Costikyan G. [11, 22]. These frameworks offer structured taxonomy for dissecting player experiences in uncertainty, with Shalev's categorization providing particularly insightful perspectives on the sources of uncertainty in tabletop games. A vital analysis stage involved identifying each game's primary sources of uncertainty. It is essential to acknowledge that not all sources were relevant due to their lack or absence of influence in the two games. For instance, there are no hidden roles in either game. Although remembering the opponent's cards may help make better strategies, uncertainty due to memory did not seem to play a significant role in Splendor.

Close observation of the gameplay sessions made it apparent that while many uncertainty sources exist in these games – ranging from player unpredictability to hidden information – their influences on the experience of effort and emotion are interwoven and pervasive. This complexity suggests that it would be reductive to directly correlate specific effort-emotion responses describing phrases like 'confidently implementing' to individual uncertainty sources. The intertwined nature of these influences makes such direct associations overly simplistic and unrepresentative of the depth of the player's experiences. To address this complexity, we refined our approach to categorizing uncertainties into three broader categories: continuous uncertainty, stage-specific uncertainty, and cumulative uncertainty.

Continuous uncertainty refers to ongoing elements of unpredictability that persist throughout the game, such as the uncertainty of other players' strategies or random game events. Stage-specific uncertainty encompasses uncertainties that become particularly salient or relevant during specific game phases, significantly influencing decision-making and emotional responses during those stages. Cumulative uncertainty involves uncertainties that build up throughout the game. This categorization allows for a more comprehensive analysis of how uncertainties interact with player experiences, acknowledging the intricate and often inseparable nature of these game elements (Table 4).

Table 4. Sources and Nature of Uncertainty in Splendor

Source of Uncertainty	Continuous Uncertainty	Stage-Specific Uncertainty	Cumulative Uncertainty
Player Unpredictability	Players' strategies and choices vary, creating ongoing uncertainty in opponents' next moves	When a player makes a significant move, like a sudden change in gem collection strategy, influencing others' decisions	-
Randomness	The draw of development cards adds an element of randomness, as players cannot predict which cards will become available	-	-
Analytic Complexity	Players continuously assess the best strategic use of their resources (gems) throughout the game	Increased complexity when nearing the points threshold for winning, as strategic choices become critical	Decision-making becomes more intense as the game progresses, with potential strategies and counter-strategies changing in form (not necessarily increasing or decreasing)
Hidden Information	Not all development cards are visible; players must adapt to new information as cards are revealed	The revelation of new development cards can suddenly shift strategies at specific game moments	Players accumulate knowledge about potential card availability and opponents' strategies over time

(*continued*)

Table 4. (*continued*)

Source of Uncertainty	Continuous Uncertainty	Stage-Specific Uncertainty	Cumulative Uncertainty
Memory	Remembering opponents' past actions and remaining vigilant of their gem stocks and reserved cards	-	Memory plays a role in anticipating opponents' potential moves in later stages
Probability Management	Players assess the likelihood of obtaining certain cards based on available gems and visible cards	-	Players might adjust their strategies based on evolving probabilities as the game progresses
Variable Setup	Each game begins with a different set of development cards and noble tiles, requiring players to adapt their strategies	-	-

In light of the categorization into continuous, stage-specific, and cumulative uncertainties, each effort-emotion descriptor duo from Splendor and Azul was analyzed in relation to the different types of uncertainties experienced during gameplay.

Continuous Uncertainty. Certain game uncertainties are felt as a constant presence; they demand perpetual adaptation from players. We call it 'continuous uncertainty.' Acting as a pervasive force, they permeate the entire gameplay experience, influencing every decision and emotional reaction. These uncertainties shape player experience at a fundamental level as they constantly impact players' decisions. In terms of effort, continuous uncertainty typically requires broad and flexible strategies to accommodate a wide range of possibilities. Various emotions, such as anticipation, apprehension, and anxiety, were found to be associated with this category of uncertainty.

In Azul, the tiles available in the central display constantly change, not just after each round, but also within a single round, in each turn. Players continuously adapt to the randomness of the tile distribution, which significantly impacts their strategy. For instance, a player may plan to collect specific-colored tiles to complete a row. Still, depending on the availability of tiles on the central display, their plan may be hindered or facilitated. Similarly, in Splendor, continuous uncertainty primarily stems from the random distribution of cards and actions taken by opponents in acquiring those cards. The available cards continue to change throughout the game. The impact of continuous uncertainty is evident in Splendor when a development card that a player has been planning for a long time is acquired by an opponent, necessitating a shift in strategy. The difference in the manifestation of the impact of uncertainty lies in the fact that while uncertainty in Splendor comes from individual-level opportunities to build an engine of gem production, Azul's uncertainty is linked with shared central resources.

Another difference between the two games regarding continuous uncertainty is the immediate and tactical nature of tile selection in Azul and the long-term and strategic nature of card acquisition in Splendor. The analysis hints towards the emergence of a broader spectrum of emotions due to continuous uncertainty in Azul, like feeling 'fortuitous' and 'embarrassed' as it engages the players in dealing with more moment-to-moment uncertainty in Azul. On the other hand, being more about gradual unfolding of a planned strategy, emotions in Splendor are characterized by anticipation and strategic tension.

Stage-Specific Uncertainty. A set of critical junctures were identified as opposed to continuous uncertainties, which demand a higher level of player adaptability. Due to their temporal specificity, such circumstances have been termed 'stage-specific uncertainties.' These uncertainties explain the crucial events with novelty and uniqueness, primarily demanding immediate strategic adjustment. Stage-specific uncertainty may cause sudden spikes in excitement, frustration, or relief, distinct from continuous uncertainty in terms of the palpability of the experience. It is often short-lived with a heightened degree of emotion. Players respond to discrete and significant uncertainty, unlike continuous uncertainty in which ongoing adaptation to an ever-changing game environment exists.

In the undesirable situation in Azul, when many tiles of the same color are on the central display, any player who gets them incurs negative points. The game space becomes more intense, conversations increase, and at the same time, players strategize ways to minimize potential loss if they end up with those tiles. In Splendor, this form of uncertainty generally emerges with the appearance of certain cards or when a player is close to attaining a noble or a high-value development card, and they hope that their opponents do not pick them up. Since Azul has various rounds within a single gameplay, the end of each round, due to depleting tiles, often leads to high-stake, immediate benefit/loss situations compared to Splendor, in which there is a gradual reduction in the number of cards.

Emotional experience in continuous uncertainty is characterized by a general sense of apprehension, anticipation, vigilance, and strategic patience, exemplified by adverb-verb phrases like 'openly exploring' and 'methodically investing.' Stage-specific uncertainty is experienced in sharp spikes marked by heightened excitement and urgency. Adverb-verb phrases like 'surprisingly recalibrating,' 'intensifyingly focusing,' and 'humorously disrupting' illustrate this form of uncertainty.

Cumulative Uncertainty. As a game progresses, complexity and depth of strategies evolve in layers. The effect of previous moves adds up. Hence, it is called 'cumulative uncertainty' in this study. These accumulations, which happen over time, significantly affect decisions, and often lead to a profound strategic and emotional depth. The cumulative uncertainty often results in tension or satisfaction, depending on the player's situation. It is largely perceptible as a game reaches its conclusive phase. The build-up, however, may also happen in any other phase of the game.

As a game progresses, players' strategies get solidified, and positive or negative outcomes begin to surface. For instance, in Azul, as walls begin to fill and patterns emerge, the earlier uncertainty resulting in open exploration diminishes as gameplay shapes up to some form; players learn not only about the potential outcome of their strategy but can also predict opponents' game plans. Being non-hidden, players get an idea of which tiles their opponents need and plan their moves accordingly. Cumulative uncertainty is experienced differently in Splendor as the strategy is built invisibly in players' minds while Azul affords visualization of the game state.

One differentiating feature of emerging emotions and effort from cumulative uncertainty is the 'interconnectedness' of any stage with effort and emotions that emerged in previous game states. Unlike the general and immediate emotions of continuous and stage-specific uncertainty, cumulative uncertainty is more layered. Verb-adverb phrases accompanying the experience of this uncertainty reflect the association with previous decisions. Phrases like 'confidently implementing,' 'easily coasting,' 'edgily anticipating,' 'resolvedly finalizing,' and 'frustratingly derailed' hint at association with uncertainties that emerge from a chain of previous events. Game progression leads to the accumulation of strategic layers, leading to a complex interplay of effort and emotions, and players accordingly respond to unfolding game dynamics.

4 Discussion and Interpretation: Dynamic Uncertainty and Emergent Effort-Emotion

The intent of this study is to delve deeper into the feelings and exertions associated with navigation of uncertainty in games. We relied upon the frameworks by Shalev and Costikyan to define sources of uncertainty in two tabletop games - Splendor and Azul. Using experience sampling method, we collected data about players' experience of effort and emotions in those games. Analysis of the qualitative data in relation to uncertainty suggests that attempting to draw direct, cause-effect correlations between specific sources of uncertainty and distinct emotional or effortful responses oversimplifies the complexity of player experience. Moreover, a source of uncertainty like analytical complexity inherent in both Azul and Splendor cannot be singularly linked to feelings of frustration and strategic calculation. This is because the influence of any source of uncertainty is not isolated; rather, it is entangled with other uncertainties and their effects on player experience.

In light of this confluence of uncertainties in shaping gameplay and its experience, categorizing uncertainties into continuous, stage-specific, and cumulative enables an understanding of how uncertainty collectively influence player experience. Continuous uncertainty is the ongoing condition which demands constant exertions and emotions. Stage-specific uncertainty includes high stake game states which are typically accompanied by a spike in emotional and strategic intensity. Cumulative uncertainty emerges because of progression of game and layering of strategic and emotional depth.

The result of this study suggests that these categories of uncertainty are not discrete elements experienced in isolation with fixed temporal boundaries. They are dynamic interact in complex ways, influencing and being influenced by each other. By emergent, we mean that effort and emotions emerge not only from the designed mechanics but also from the ways in which players interact, strategize, and feel. In turn, dynamic uncertainty give rise to a spectrum of emotional responses and strategic efforts, which further shape game's unfolding landscape. For instance, a player's strategic decision (effort) in the face of uncertainty may lead to a sense of excitement (emotion), which then influences subsequent decisions and emotional responses, creating a cyclic pattern of influence that continuously reshapes the player's experience. Each turn or move brings new uncertainties, requiring players to continuously adapt their strategies and emotions. This ongoing adaptation results in dynamic emotional and effortful trajectories, as players navigate through a landscape that is in a constant flux.

This perspective of experience-oriented analysis of uncertainty helps in understanding the complexity of player experiences in tabletop games. Moreover, the uniqueness of each player's experience is inherently tied to their personal strategies, decision-making processes, and reactions to in-game events. Each player brings their own perspective, style, and emotional responses to the game, making their journey through it unique. This is exemplified in how one player might find "Mischievously Interfering" in "Azul" to be a delightful strategy, while another might see it as a risky move, leading to a different emotional and strategic pathway.

5 Conclusion

The findings suggest that player emotions and exertions fluctuate in response to various game stages and are not static or predictable based on game outcomes alone. For example, a player might experience a journey from optimism to frustration and then to excitement, all within a single game of Splendor or Azul, depending on the shifting game dynamics. Different types of uncertainties (continuous, cumulative, and stage-specific) influence player emotions and efforts in a distinct manner yet their effect is entangled.

Understanding the emotional and effort-related responses to uncertainties can inform more player-sensitive and engaging game design. For game analysts and researchers, this study provides an approach to examine games, emphasizing the qualitative aspects of player experiences.

References

1. Calleja, G.: Unboxed: Board game experience and design (2022)
2. Juul, J.: Half-Real: Video Games between Real Rules and Fictional Worlds. MIT Press (2011)
3. Why we play: affect and the fun of games: designing emotions for games, entertainment interfaces, and interactive products. In: Human-Computer Interaction, pp. 173–194. CRC Press (2009)
4. Deterding, S., Andersen, M.M., Kiverstein, J., Miller, M.: Mastering uncertainty: a predictive processing account of enjoying uncertain success in video game play. Front. Psychol. **13** (2022). https://doi.org/10.3389/fpsyg.2022.924953
5. Csikszentmihalyi, M.: Flow: The Psychology of Optimal Experience. Harper Collins (2009)
6. Perron, B., Wolf, M.J.P.: The Video Game Theory Reader 2. Routledge (2008)
7. Murray, J.H.: Hamlet on the Holodeck, updated edition: The Future of Narrative in Cyberspace. MIT Press (2017)
8. Sicart, M.: Play Computers. In: Games and Rules, pp. 47–64. Transcript Verlag (2018)
9. Gee, J.P.: What video games have to teach us about learning and literacy. Comput. Entertain. **1**, 20 (2003). https://doi.org/10.1145/950566.950595

10. El-Nasr, M.S., Drachen, A., Canossa, A.: Game Analytics: Maximizing the Value of Player Data. Springer (2013)
11. Costikyan, G.: Uncertainty in Games. MIT Press (2015)
12. Tekinbas, K.S., Zimmerman, E.: Rules of Play: Game Design Fundamentals. MIT Press (2003)
13. Costello, B., Edmonds, E.: A study in play, pleasure and interaction design. In: Proceedings of the 2007 Conference on Designing Pleasurable Products and Interfaces. ACM, New York (2007)
14. Rouse, R.: Game Design: Theory & Practice. Wordware Computer Books (2001)
15. Sharp, J., Thomas, D.: Fun, Taste, & Games: An Aesthetics of the Idle, Unproductive, and Otherwise Playful. MIT Press (2019)
16. Schell, J.: The Art of Game Design: A Book of Lenses, 3rd edn. CRC Press (2019)
17. Poker: Game of Skill or Game of Chance? – The Ludologist. https://www.jesperjuul.net/ludologist/2007/12/18/poker-game-of-skill-or-game-of-chance/. Accessed 13 Feb 2024
18. Kumari, S., Power, C., Cairns, P.: Investigating uncertainty in digital games and its impact on player immersion. In: Extended Abstracts Publication of the Annual Symposium on Computer-Human Interaction in Play. ACM, New York (2017)
19. Heinemann, F., Ockenfels, P.: Measuring strategic uncertainty in coordination games. SSRN Electron. J. (2004). https://doi.org/10.2139/ssrn.849404
20. Howard-Jones, P.A., Demetriou, S.: Uncertainty and engagement with learning games. Instr. Sci. **37**, 519–536 (2008). https://doi.org/10.1007/s11251-008-9073-6
21. Kumari, S., Deterding, S., Freeman, J.: The role of uncertainty in moment-to-moment player motivation. In: Proceedings of the Annual Symposium on Computer-Human Interaction in Play. ACM, New York (2019)
22. Engelstein, G., Shalev, I.: Building Blocks of Tabletop Game Design: An Encyclopedia of Mechanisms. CRC Press (2022)
23. Debus, M.S.: Unifying Game Ontology: A Faceted Classification of Game Elements. IT-Universitetet i København, 2019. 356 p (2019)
24. Alexandra, T., Safinah, A., Geoff, K., Jessica, H.: Integrating curiosity and uncertainty in game design. In: Dundee, Scotland: Digital Games Research Association and Society for the Advancement of the Science of Digital Games, August, no. 1, vol. 13 (2016)
25. de Alfaro, L., Godefroid, P., Jagadeesan, R.: Three-valued abstractions of games: uncertainty, but with precision. In: Proceedings of the 19th Annual IEEE Symposium on Logic in Computer Science, 2004. IEEE (2004)
26. Feltovich, N., Swierzbinski, J.: The role of strategic uncertainty in games: an experimental study of cheap talk and contracts in the Nash demand game. Eur. Econ. Rev. **55**, 554–574 (2011). https://doi.org/10.1016/j.euroecorev.2010.07.001
27. Caillois, R.: Man, Play, and Games. University of Illinois Press (2001)
28. Miles, M.B., Huberman, A.M., Saldana, J.: Qualitative Data Analysis: A Methods Sourcebook. SAGE Publications (2013)
29. Denzin, N.K., Lincoln, Y.S.: The SAGE Handbook of Qualitative Research. SAGE (2005)
30. Juul, J.: The open and the closed: game of emergence and games of progression. In: Computer Games and Digital Cultures Conference Proceedings, edited by Frans Mäyrä, pp. 323–329. Tampere: Tampere University Press (2002). http://www.jesperjuul.net/text/openandtheclosed.html

Co-designing an Applied Game About Volcanic Hazards for a Bi-cultural Environment: 5 Minute Volcano

Kieron Wall[1]( ), Heide Lukosch[1], Simon Hoermann[2], Kathryn MacCallum[3], and Ben Kennedy[4]

[1] HIT Lab NZ, University of Canterbury, Christchurch, New Zealand
kieron.wall@pg.canterbury.ac.nz
[2] School of Product Design, University of Canterbury, Christchurch, New Zealand
[3] School of Educational Studies and Leadership, University of Canterbury, Christchurch, New Zealand
[4] School of Earth and Environment, University of Canterbury, Christchurch, New Zealand

Abstract. This paper describes how applied games can be designed to communicate volcanic tsunami risk in the bi-cultural environment of Aotearoa (New Zealand). Background research shows that children are vulnerable to natural hazards, yet crucial in risk communication. Previous research shows that applied games can be developed to help children learn, yet the research gaps are extensive without evidence on designing effective risk communication interventions. We worked with a local school to co-design an applied game for school children about tsunami risk communication and evacuation strategies. The children engaged in workshops, through exploratory observational and qualitative interview methods. The prototype *5-Minute Volcano* was designed, incorporating Māori and Western cultural aspects. We performed an additional user study and observed a group of four children and a teacher playing the game, and the collected data was used to determine how applied games could be designed and used for learning and risk reduction.

Keywords: Hazards · Applied Games · Children · Learning · Co-Design

1 Introduction

Learning through the act of play is an intuitive process [22, 53]. Games designed for learning are used in schools globally and have been used to improve the understanding of particular topics, develop cognitive skills, promote interaction with peers, and for enjoyment purposes [13, 24, 32, 51, 56]. However, these games are often designed without including children as co-designers and tend not to address specific audiences. Co-designing with children is challenging, as distinct ways of making their knowledge, needs and preferences explicit need to be found. In this study, we aim to include children in the design process, as well as designing learning games that are fun, engaging, and relate to the unique bi-cultural learning environment of Aotearoa New Zealand. This will align them with the target audience and learning context. For this purpose, we report on our design process and considerations for a physical card game to communicate hazards related to volcanic activity in the Bay of Plenty region of New Zealand to primary school-aged children.

There are several reasons why it is important to communicate these hazards to children. Globally, educational practices of disaster risk reduction were officially recognized by the Hyogo Framework for Action 2005–2015 [58] and later by the Sendai Framework for Disaster Risk Reduction [59]. These frameworks have led to increasing numbers of disaster preparedness programs [10–12, 30, 45, 48, 57] to ensure that those affected by the risk of a volcanic eruption are well informed.

Communicating these hazards to school children in New Zealand is an important part of their learning. New Zealand is a geologically active country with a rich history of natural hazard events. A recent major event was the 2019 eruption of White Island, or Whakaari in Te Reo Māori, which is the nation's most active volcano since the 1960s [28]. The phreatic (steam) eruption occurred with little warning, causing the deaths of 22 people including locals and tourists [4, 8, 9]. Educational facilities are thus a crucial means to raise awareness of these hazards, and the risks posed by such events, and create risk reduction strategies in students and their communities [49]. Literature shows that the importance of disaster education at these educational facilities has increased due to the following [25, p. 59]: "…Children are one of the most vulnerable groups of a society during a disaster, children represent future resilience, schools serve as central locations within communities for meetings and group activities, and effects of education can be transferred to parents and the community".

These points are further reinforced by the accounts during events like the 2004 Boxing Day Tsunami. Due to her education on tsunamis, 10-year-old Tilly Smith, an English school girl, helped evacuate a Thailand beach when she saw the warning signs of the approaching tsunami. Even though she lived in England, where tsunami risk is very low, she had been taught about the hazard and thus saved over 100 lives [20, 31, 37, 50]. Of the survivors of the 2004 tsunami, 1 in every 3 were either women or under 15 years old [31]. Children are also the most impacted demographic for disasters globally [20, 37], which shows that increasing disaster awareness is significant to not only these children but their families and communities as well. As natural hazards are near impossible to predict, population preparedness is crucial for a community's, and thus a nation's, resilience [35]. Children are often overlooked within risk management, yet it is believed that their ideas are a vast source of information that when applied correctly, can assist in evacuation and mitigation strategies [6].

To communicate hazard risk to children, they need motivation to learn. Applied games have the potential to create safe spaces that provide interactive learning environments for children, all whilst teaching new skills needed for hazard and risk recognition [20]. This paper explores design elements within a physical card game co-designed with children from New Zealand to teach them about volcanic risks. Several local volcanic sources such as Whakaari/White Island, Tuhua/Mayor Island and undersea volcanoes related to the Kermadec arc are located within close proximity to the coastline. This makes them potential sources for volcanic events and tsunamis for the community where this study is based. This paper will examine literature about the design of games in this area and how games contribute to children's learning. In addition, we look at how New Zealand's bi-cultural influences could be used to develop learning games which are informative, inclusive, and enjoyable for children to play by using qualitative research approaches to construct observational and interview-style data collection methods.

2 Related Work

2.1 Applied Games

Especially in younger audiences, games have grown into an increasingly popular form of entertainment. This has led to learning, or applied, games becoming popular both at home and in the classroom. Applied games are games designed for learning and the teaching of skills, rather than entertainment value. They can be "…regarded as a particularly active, problem-solving, situated and social form of learning with rapid and differentiated feedback that also promotes the enjoyment of learning" [24, p. 151]. These games use logic and knowledge to confront real-world problems in a simulated experience [54]. They generally allow players to participate with others, learn to use communication, and learn decision-making skills without entertainment being a required factor [13], and are important as play is crucial to a child's physical, social, cognitive and creative growth [32, 51]. A literature review found that the majority of applied game papers focus on learning rather than entertainment [17], thus, many applied games are designed with little focus on 'fun' components and more on numbers and facts. This is important for teaching, yet the purpose of applied games is to get participants involved in the learning, and adding motivational and engaging components could raise their interest in the subject.

2.2 Previous Disaster Games

Disaster games have been used in learning before. Games such as "Stop Disasters!" [3], "Disaster Master" [1], and "Earth Girl" [2] all aim to teach children about the impacts and warning signs of natural hazards. Each attempts to motivate learners and engage them in an experiential learning experience, in which knowledge is formed through the learner's experience [29]. Many games, however, do not equip children to make adequate evacuation decisions [20]. Most hazard games also tend to focus on the impacts of these disasters as opposed to mitigation techniques, which is thought to be more effective than teaching response and recovery [33]. This gap in targeted information, hazard identification and evacuation should therefore be addressed [19].

Disaster-themed games that examine mitigation and evacuation strategies include Disaster Master Stop Disasters! and Stop Disasters Disaster Master (see Fig. 1). Disaster Master is an online interactive graphic novel where players experience the perspectives of six children across six regions of the U.S.A., whilst facing different hazards like tornadoes, blizzards, earthquakes, and more. The story integrates informative questions to test players' knowledge of disaster preparedness and response. For example, one child evacuates from a tsunami by running to higher ground, highlighting proper evacuation protocol. However, Disaster Master lacks gameplay strategy and mostly functions as

Fig. 1. Screenshots from the 'Disaster Master' game (top), showing strips of the ocean retreating and evacuation, and the 'Stop Disasters' game (bottom), showing the planning phase (left) and the tsunami impact (right) [20]

an illustrated novel. The single-nation focus and lack of any audio limits engagement, especially for non-U.S. audiences. Stop Disasters is a learning game published by the United Nations Office for Disaster Risk Reduction (UNDRR) for 9–16-year-old children. Players choose from 5 hazards (tsunamis, floods, earthquakes, wildfires, and hurricanes), 3 difficulties, and unlike Disaster Master, each hazard impacts different locations around the world. It teaches players to use limited resources to create a resilient community that is prepared for incoming disasters by building key structures like hospitals and schools, upgrading buildings, and preparing defences. After the disaster strikes, a score is given based on damage and death toll. The game overall is informative, with information accessed during the game, and the locations are real regions impacted by the hazards (for example, Indonesia is the location of the tsunami). The game allows players to use disaster risk reduction strategies (prevention/mitigation/preparedness and evacuation) to reduce the impact and increase awareness of these hazards, whilst giving players an incentive to keep playing to achieve a higher score [15, 16]. The game has had a positive impact on players and reportedly helped raise awareness of wildfire prevention techniques [36], yet research suggests players struggle to provide new knowledge during post-game questionnaires [15]. There are issues with some scenarios, such as the tsunami arriving with sound, yet the ocean doesn't retreat, no animals are fleeing from the coastal region, and more [20]. Games are not only digital. Card games such as "Sneaky Volcano" by the Earth Observatory of Singapore and "Volcanic Disaster" are examples of disaster-based volcano games which require some luck and planning respectively to play. Sneaky Volcano focuses more on the warning signs of an eruption, whilst Volcanic Disaster is about predicting eruptions whilst 'building up' volcanoes from across the world with appropriate hazards. For a New Zealand context, the main issue with games such as these is there are very few, if any hazard scenarios in a New Zealand setting. New Zealand is a geologically active region with multiple hazards and is thus a perfect location for such learning games. This is a gap to be addressed in this study as well as needing to align the game with the learning needs and preferences and its target group. Co-Design is one such way to achieve this.

2.3 Co-designing Games with Children

Co-design is a method in which *"diverse experts come together, such as researchers, designers or developers, and (potential) customers and users…to cooperate creatively."* [52], meaning players become participants in the design process. Regarding children, background work suggests that early in the design process, children are better suited as informants and idea generators rather than as co-designers due to children's lack of complex knowledge about specific topics and the design process, as this limits their ability to provide relevant suggestions [27, 47]. Khaled & Vasalou [27] highlight two case studies where they worked with children before and during the game design process. When working with children beforehand, they found the children had ideas that could be applied to a plethora of games as opposed to the one being made, and their ideas showed little understanding of the main topic (conflict resolution). This result was similar to experiences reported by Tan et al. [55] which stated that the children could provide valuable information for game ideas, but often fell beyond the game's intended objectives, including violent or competitive mechanics conflicting with the purpose of the game. The second user study in Khaled & Vasalou [27] worked with children after the designers had made a prototype game. This was more successful as the children generated ideas based on the game they just played, and thus had more of a focus than the previous user study. The researchers concluded that working with children during the middle of the design process allows them to set up the topic and guide the children's ideas to a higher degree than if the children co-designed from the beginning stages.

3 Game Design Process

For this research, we look at how applied games could be designed to communicate volcanic-tsunami risk to children. To do this, the game design process used for this study focuses on an exploratory co-design method, which uses observations and interviews to gain insight into unknown knowledge bases for the design process (see Fig. 2). We use exploratory research as it is designed to uncover poorly understood phenomena, as well as assist researchers in areas they may be unfamiliar with [23, 39, 43]. This type of research allows us to contribute new knowledge to games designed for New Zealand schools. To explore this area, we used both observational and interview methods [5, 7]. Observations allow participants to be viewed in a familiar and more natural setting, as well as allowing researchers to take notes and in most instances, interact with the children and hear their ideas. When evaluating children's behaviour, it is suggested that observational methods are most appropriate, though some techniques used for adults will not work with children. Expressions such as frowning and yawns are better indications of a lack of engagement than the child's response to questions [18]. A multitude of behaviours that could be used to measure a child's 'engagement' in the game include, but are not limited to smiles, laughter, signs of concentration, excitable bouncing and positive vocalisation. A lack of a child's engagement could be measured in frowns, signs of boredom (ear playing/fiddling etc.), shrugging and negative verbalisation [41].

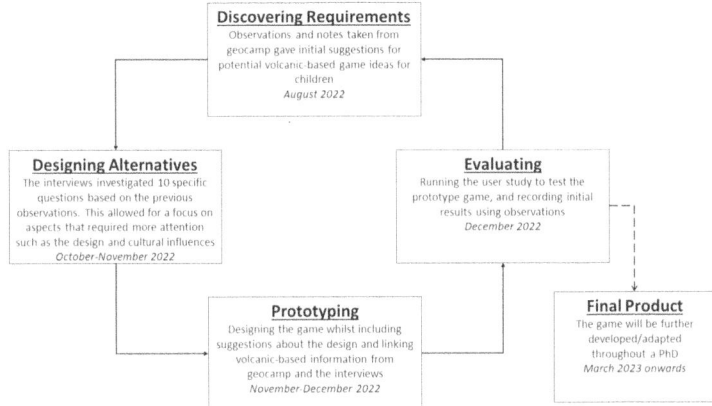

Fig. 2. A Simple Design Process model for this study, based on Preece [40]. This figure includes a description and dates of each step in the Simple Design Process.

This study worked with the primary school Te Kura O Te Paroa, located in Whakatane on the East Coast of New Zealand's North Island, during a week-long 'geocamp'. Geocamp was an opportunity to teach the children about geological processes and also build relationships between the school and the team. The children were observed to be digitally competent, but also very active and good at teamwork and collaborative activities. These observations allowed us to narrow our design ideas into questions asked in the interview process and incorporate them into the design process as a whole (see Fig. 2).

Semi-structured interviews were used to collect further information for the design process. The nature of these interviews allows for further exploration into new topics, more discussions, and allowing the interviewed participants to express themselves less formally [14, 26, 34, 38, 44, 46]. This study interviewed two experts and two teachers from the school. Analysis of these interviews showed that learning goals about geological hazards support core competencies (such as critical thinking and collaboration) laid out in the school curriculum. This meant the game would need to be simple to play and learn but have a strong focus on teamwork. The research team investigated existing games that could work as a blueprint for this. The game '5-Minute: Dungeon' by Wiggles 3D was used as a basis for this due to its quick-paced, easy to learn and collaborative nature and permission was obtained from the company to use this gameplay as a template for this research. Teachers and experts were questioned through emails and meetings throughout the design process to maintain a co-design approach, allowing important decisions to be supported by them.

4 Designing the Game

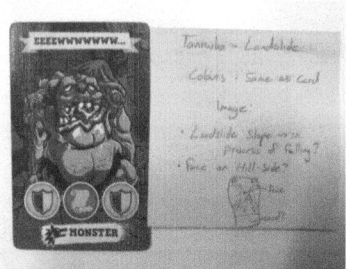

Fig. 3. This figure shows the original, brainstormed, and final card design for one of the taniwha cards used in 5-Minute: Volcano

'5-Minute: Dungeon' is a fast-paced cooperative game where players must use their cards and abilities to defeat a deck of creatures in under 5 minutes. Due to the collaborative nature of this game, we used this as a basis for our game design. The cards required change to fit not just a geological, but a New Zealand context too. Therefore, almost all cards were a simple change of the card name and art. Only a few required some more tweaking, but overall the game follows the same rules and mechanics as the original version. Due to the co-design focus, the children were the initial informants of the design, giving suggestions about the game style, goals, characters and gameplay. These ideas were further refined through interviews with the teachers. Methods from this stage of the process included observations, interviews, meetings and related work analysis that informed the design of the characters, cards, actions and animals created for the new version of the game. One such character in the game is the 'Māori Elder'. The Elder replaces the Valkyrie from the base game as its ability, allowing every other player to pick up two cards, means the Elder can assist all other players in the game. In addition, the Saddleback (or tīeke) was chosen as this character because a local teacher explained that Ngāti Awa (the local tribe around Whakatane, New Zealand) narratives say the bird led the first Māori settlers to the region of Whakatane, making it of cultural significance to the school we worked with. Other changes made through the design process included swapping 'fantasy' icons, such as swords and scrolls, for real-world ones, such as 'teaching' and 'research' respectively. Monsters from the base game were changed to taniwha (monsters or creatures in the Māori culture) which represented volcanic hazards such as tsunamis, lava and ash fall (see Fig. 3). The final bosses of the game are each replaced with a New Zealand vocal no, starting at Whakaari White Island, and ending with Taupō, New Zealand's largest volcano. This design resulted in the prototype for the game '5-Minute Volcano'.

5 Results

A user study was performed with a group of 4 children from Te Kura O Te Paroa. Each child was part of the geocamp event where we got our initial ideas from, and they played the prototype game six times. Before play, they were asked questions about what they could remember from 'geocamp' earlier that year. This phase showed that they could recall some terminology, but especially recalled activities they had been involved in. The children then learnt the game from one of the researchers, and after practicing for only a few minutes, were able to comprehend the game fully. To add a challenge for them, physical actions such as a fake evacuation were added after 'defeating' certain, more challenging, cards to reinforce the point of 'Long, Strong, Get Gone', a New Zealand-based warning about long or strong earthquakes causing tsunamis. During play, the children showed an increase in communication and cooperation once the timer was implemented. Initially, there seemed to be some confusion to how their character's abilities worked, but within two games, they even helped each other with using abilities and cards. One of the researchers observed the children and noted comments such as "*...nah I want to carry on*" when asked if they wanted a break, "*...was lucky I had this card!*" when a card allowed the team to win with nine seconds remaining, and "*...this is fun as!*" or "*...can we play again?*" after the games showed that the children enjoyed the excitement and quick-paced gameplay. The observed comments and reactions were all positive, but it should be noted that they could have responded in this manner because they wanted to give the researchers the 'correct' answer, or what they thought we wanted to hear [42]. However, from observations of engagement stated in Read 2002 [41] such as smiling and laughing, we can assume that the children genuinely enjoyed the game. The children even recognised a picture of the marae at 'geocamp' behind the Māori Elder character, which showed the importance of familiarity and co-designing with them, as the researchers wouldn't have done this otherwise. Two of the games were played post-questionnaire, with the children initially struggling to play the game again. However, within the first game, they found their rhythm and even tried different characters out. After play, children were asked five questions in a debrief about other characters, abilities, and highlights of the game. It was difficult to get the children to give meaningful answers, especially when not prompted by one of the teachers. One child said they enjoyed the tamariki (child) character because you can get "*...loads of cards in your hand*". Few answers were given regarding thoughts on the characters and abilities, yet when asked about additions, the children became more involved, bringing in their own ideas such as new characters, abilities, and volcanoes. One example of this is one child suggesting to "*split the scientist into a seismologist and volcanologist*", allowing for similar characters but with different abilities. The game didn't seem to help with the children's educational goals as few comments involved volcano science. However, it allowed for collaborative gameplay, and a key point brought up by the children was the importance of teamwork, with one child saying *"Don't rely on one person"* and *"Teamwork makes the dream work"*. They also suggested the addition of digital elements such as a timer app for cellular devices as this would make the game "*...way better*".

6 Discussion

For this study, we suggested a co-design process to help us design 5-Minute: Volcano with the children. Upon review of the co-design process, the researchers recognise that the process is more akin to a participatory approach, where end users are involved in and influence the design process decisions like co-design, but they do not assist in the creation of the game itself. This design approach will be looked at in greater detail during future studies. It should be noted as well that the initial goal of the game design was to create an evacuation learning game. However, due to the design direction influenced by the school and 5-Minute Dungeon, the game instead became focused on learning through collaborative play. This change will influence future work. Regarding the rest of the study, geocamp provided an opportunity to not only create relationships between the research team and the school involved in the study but also to observe the children in a more 'natural' environment, gaining suggestions from the children themselves. The research team took part in activities all week such as field trips and touch rugby and this way, the children didn't see the team as a group that was testing them, but would approach us and be open about ideas and thoughts. At this opening stage, the children's ideas about designing and incorporating different elements into a game were not directed and showed little in the way of understanding the topic, as seen in papers by Khaled & Vasalou and Tan et al. [27, 55]. The interview process, however, allowed us to explore areas and topics of knowledge and culture that were unfamiliar to the researchers. Learning more of tikanga (customs and values of the Māori culture) as well as the idea of designing around the core competencies tied back to interviews being used to impart expert knowledge about the research field [7, 21, 26]. The previous relationship establishment with the participants also meant the semi-structured nature of the interviews allowed for more open discussions, further improvised questions into specific topics, and allowed for the participants to speak their own opinions of a matter that was important to them [14, 34, 38, 44, 46].

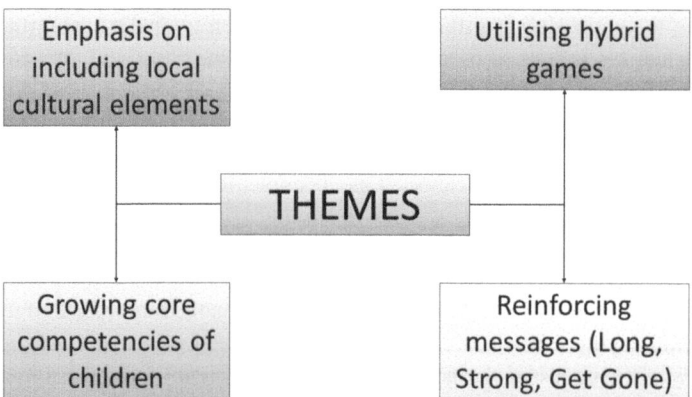

Fig. 4. A summary of the themes found during this study

The interviews also showed that it was more informative to design with the teachers than the children, as is seen in previous works. This reinforces that children should be brought into the design process after the product has been created [27]. During the user study, the children were more invested when playing the game than during the questionnaire. Here, observations provided more solidified answers about how the game was working than when the children were asked certain questions. Laughter, excited bouncing and smiling showed the game was engaging and fun [41], whilst remaining quiet during the questions and needing assistance from their teachers. As hinted at earlier, working with children also comes with challenges. Whilst observations are a good means to collect data more 'naturally', when asked specific questions the children would often become quiet and not prepared to answer. This is likely because, to them, a question felt more like a test, so were expected to get the 'right answer'. This often led to many clarifications needed with help from the teachers. As with previous work with kids, when engaging in discussions before the design process, children have many ideas that are not directed appropriately [27, 55]. Only after interviews with the teachers and experts were we able to work out what direction we needed to go with the game design. Studies using qualitative methods should find key themes to be recorded [7], several (see Fig. 4) which were seen throughout the study. There is a strong emphasis on constructing games which help to reinforce key messages, the children's core competencies, emphasise Māori culture and language (due to working with a Māori school) and using hybrid games (the combining of physical and digital games). These themes were seen throughout the study during observations, interviews and the user study, and should be considered in future work on this topic.

7 Conclusion

This study used exploratory qualitative research to construct and design a game for children in New Zealand. The prototype of *"5-Minute: Volcano"* was created using observations, interviews, and decisions that allowed the game to be made for a New Zealand context. The game worked well for the intended audience due to a combination of familiarity, engaging gameplay, and the collaborative nature of the game. When designing games for children, it is important to use observations in addition to interviews and questionnaires, so the children are relaxed and do not think they're being tested. Children who think it is a test will give you feedback they think the researcher wants instead of what they think. Teachers are thus a good middle ground when co-designing with children as they can understand the complex nature of the related topics, as well as know what the children need in their learning environment. Our work leads to the recommendation that when co-designing with children, it is better to involve the teachers from the start of the process and get their thoughts and understanding from the beginning. The children should be involved in the process once a prototype has been established and the topics are decided to aim their thoughts and ideas as seen in previous works. Based on this work, hybrid games, growth of core competencies, reinforcing messages and including elements of Te Reo Māori in a New Zealand context seemed to be the key themes seen. An inclusive design of this sort will benefit children and schools across the country in preparing for possible natural disasters.

7.1 Future Work

The full version of 5-Minute: Volcano was finished in 2023 based on results from the discussed user study. In 2024, we aim to look more into digital elements to add to the game, incorporating mini-games that focus on key questions around hazards and community resilience while using characters and aspects of 5-Minute: Volcano. This new game will continue to be co-designed with teachers from schools we work with, and later in the year, including the children in the design process. The upcoming game will focus on collaborative gameplay with hybrid elements that work within the context of New Zealand Schools. The 5-Minute: Volcano game will be further used and tested in a wider context to evaluate user experience and learning effects. Future work will also aim to include teachers, children and other stakeholders from across New Zealand and a methodology will be created that clearly shows how to incorporate these groups into the design process.

Acknowledgements. This project is supported by the New Zealand Ministry of Business, Innovation and Employment, Endeavour research programme Beneath the Waves, contract C05X2102. We also want to thank all the members of GNS, Te Kura O Te Paroa and all others associated with the study for their help, feedback, and ideas.

References

1. Disaster Master. https://www.ready.gov/kids/games/data/dm-english/
2. Earth Girl Volcano Tsunami Games. https://earthgirl2.com/
3. Stop Disasters! https://www.stopdisastersgame.org/#1540393340109-5d29849b-3c23
4. Auker, M.R., Sparks, R.S.J., Siebert, L., Crosweller, H.S., Ewert, J.: A statistical analysis of the global historical volcanic fatalities record. J. Appl. Volcanol. **2**(1), 2 (2013). https://doi.org/10.1186/2191-5040-2-2. https://appliedvolc.biomedcentral.com/articles/10.1186/2191-5040-2-2
5. Bogdan, R.C., Biklen, S.K.: Qualitative Research for Education: An Introduction to Theory and Methods, 2nd edn. Allyn & Bacon, Boston (1992)
6. Cabello, V.: Students understanding of earthquakes and tsunamis in high RiskAreas. Front. Earth Sci. **10**, 841251 (2022)
7. Creswell, J.W., Creswell, J.D.: Research Design: Qualitative, Quantitative, and Mixed Methods Approaches. Sage Publications (2017)
8. Dempsey, D., Cronin, S.J., Mei, S., Kempa-Liehr, A.W.: Automatic precursor recognition and real-time forecasting of sudden explosive volcanic eruptions at Whakaari, New Zealand. Nat. Commun. **11**(1), 1–8 (2020)
9. Dempsey, D., et al.: Evaluation of short-term probabilistic eruption forecasting at Whakaari, New Zealand. Bull. Volcanol. **84**(10), 91 (2022)
10. Dobran, F.: Vesuvius: education, security and prosperity. Elsevier (2006)
11. Dohaney, J., Brogt, E., Wilson, T.M., Kennedy, B.: Using role-play to improve students' confidence and perceptions of communication in a simulated volcanic crisis. In: Observing the Volcano World, pp. 691–714. Springer (2018)
12. Donovan, A.: Critical volcanology? Thinking holistically about risk and uncertainty. Bull. Volcanol. **81**(4), 1–20 (2019)
13. Facer, K.: Computer Games and Learning Why do we think it's worth talking about computer games and learning in the same breath? A discussion paper (2004)

14. Galletta, A.: Mastering the semi-structured interview and beyond: from research design to analysis and publication, vol. 18. NYU Press (2013)
15. Gampell, A., Gaillard, J., Parsons, M., Le Dé, L.: 'Serious' disaster video games: an innovative approach to teaching and learning about disasters and disaster risk reduction. J. Geogr. **119**(5), 159–170 (2020)
16. Gampell, A.V., Gaillard, J.: Stop disasters 2.0: video games as tools for disaster risk reduction. Int. J. Mass Emergencies Disasters **34**(2) (2016)
17. Hainey, T., Connolly, T.M., Boyle, E.A., Wilson, A., Razak, A.: A systematic literature review of games-based learning empirical evidence in primary education. Comput. Educ. **102**, 202–223 (2016)
18. Hanna, L., Risden, K., Alexander, K.: Guidelines for usability testing with children. Interactions **4**(5), 9–14 (1997)
19. Hawthorn, S., Jesus, R., Baptista, M.A.: Identification of knowledge gaps to inform a serious game for tsunami risk communication. In: 2021 14th International Conference on Human System Interaction (HSI), pp. 1–6 (2021). https://doi.org/10.1109/HSI52170.2021.9538748. ISSN: 2158-2254
20. Hawthorn, S., Jesus, R., Baptista, M.A.: A review of digital serious games for tsunami risk communication. Int. J. Serious Games **8**(2), 21–47 (2021). https://doi.org/10.17083/ijsg.v8i2.411. https://journal.seriousgamessociety.org/index.php/IJSG/article/view/411
21. Hopf, C.: Qualitative interviews: an overview. Companion Qual. Res. **203**(8), 100093 (2004)
22. Huizinga, J.: Homo Ludens: a study of the play-element in culture. Beacon Press (1955)
23. Hunter, D., McCallum, J., Howes, D.: Defining exploratory-descriptive qualitative (EDQ) research and considering its application to healthcare. J. Nursing Health Care **4**(1) (2019)
24. Iten, N., Petko, D.: Learning with serious games: Is fun playing the gamea predictor of learning success? Br. J. Educ. Technol. **47**(1), 151–163 (2016). https://doi.org/10.1111/bjet.12226. https://onlinelibrary.wiley.com/doi/abs/10.1111/bjet.12226. eprint: https://onlinelibrary.wiley.com/doi/pdf/10.1111/bjet.12226
25. Kaiser, L., Boersen, K.: Kura e Tai Aniwhaniwha (schools and tsunami): Bicultural and student-centred tsunami education in Aotearoa New Zealand. Aust. J. Emerg. Manag. **35**(2), 58–65 (2020)
26. Kallio, H., Pietilä, A.M., Johnson, M., Kangasniemi, M.: Systematic methodological review: developing a framework for a qualitative semi-structured interview guide. J. Adv. Nurs. **72**(12), 2954–2965 (2016)
27. Khaled, R., Vasalou, A.: Bridging serious games and participatory design. Int. J. Child-Comput. Interact. **2**(2), 93–100 (2014). https://doi.org/10.1016/j.ijcci.2014.03.001. https://www.sciencedirect.com/science/article/pii/S2212868914000063
28. Kilgour, G., et al.: Whakaari/White Island: a review of New Zealand's most active volcano. New Zealand J. Geol. Geophys. **64**(2–3), 273–295 (2021). https://doi.org/10.1080/00288306.2021.1918186
29. Kolb, D.: Experiential Learning: Experience as the Source of Learning and Development, vol. 1 (1984). Journal of Business Ethics
30. Mani, L., Cole, P.D., Stewart, I.: Using video games for volcanic hazard education and communication: an assessment of the method and preliminary results. Natural Hazards Earth Syst. Sci. **16**(7), 1673–1689 (2016)
31. Mitchell, T., Tanner, T., Haynes, K.: Children as agents of change for Disaster Risk Reduction: Lessons from El Salvador and the Philippines (2009)
32. Muñoz Cardona, J.E., Chandra, S., Rios Rincon, A., Wood, L.J., Dautenhahn, K.: Designing games for and with children. Co-design methodologies for playful activities using AR/VR and social agents. In: Interaction Design and Children, pp. 662–665. ACM, Athens, Greece (2021). https://doi.org/10.1145/3459990.3460517. https://dl.acm.org/doi/10.1145/3459990.3460517

33. Newman, J.P., et al.: Review of literature on decision support systems for natural hazard risk reduction: current status and future research directions. Environ. Model. Softw. **96**, 409 (2017)
34. World Health Organization: How to investigate the use of medicines by consumers. Technical report, World Health Organization (2004)
35. Paris, R.: Source mechanisms of volcanic tsunamis (2015). https://doi.org/10.1098/rsta.2014.0380. https://royalsocietypublishing.org/doi/epdf/10.1098/rsta.2014.0380
36. Pereira, G., Prada, R., Paiva, A.: Disaster prevention social awareness: the stop disasters! case study. In: 2014 6th International Conference on Games and Virtual Worlds for Serious Applications (VS-GAMES), pp. 1–8. IEEE (2014)
37. Pfefferbaum, B., Pfefferbaum, R.L., Van Horn, R.L.: Involving children in disaster risk reduction: the importance of participation. Eur. J. Psychotraumatol. **9**(sup2), 1425577 (2018)
38. Polit, D.F., Beck, C.T.: Nursing research: Generating and assessing evidence for nursing practice. Lippincott Williams & Wilkins (2008)
39. Polit, D.F., Beck, C.T.: Essentials of nursing research: Appraising evidence for nursing practice. Lippincott Williams & Wilkins (2010)
40. Preece, J., Rogers, Y., Sharp, H., Benyon, D., Holland, S., Carey, T.: Human computer interaction. Addison-Wesley Longman Ltd. (1994)
41. Read, J.C., MacFarlane, S., Casey, C.: Endurability, engagement and expectations: measuring children's fun. In: Interaction Design and Children, vol. 2, pp. 1–23. Shaker Publishing Eindhoven (2002)
42. Read, J., Sim, G., Gregory, A., Xu, D., Ode, J.: Children designing serious games. EAI Endorsed Trans. Game-Based Learn. **1**(1), e5 (2023). http://eudl.eu/doi/10.4108/trans.gbl.01-06.2013.e5
43. Reid-Searl, K., Happell, B.: Supervising nursing students administering medication: a perspective from registered nurses. J. Clin. Nurs. **21**(13–14), 1998–2005 (2012)
44. RJWF: Semi-structured Interviews. Robert Wood Johnson Foundation (2008). http://www.qualres.org/HomeSemi-3629.html
45. Ronan, K.R., Paton, D., Johnston, D.M., Houghton, B.F.: Managing societal uncertainty in volcanic hazards: a multidisciplinary approach. Disaster Prev. Manag. Int. J. (2000)
46. Rubin, H.J., Rubin, I.: Interviewing: The art of hearing data. Thousand Oaks, CA (2005)
47. Scaife, M., Rogers, Y., Aldrich, F., Davies, M.: Designing for or designing with? Informant design for interactive learning environments. In: Proceedings of the ACM SIGCHI Conference on Human Factors in Computing Systems, pp. 343–350 (1997)
48. Sharpe, J.: Learning to be practical: a guided learning approach to transform student community resilience when faced with natural hazard threats. In: Observing the Volcano World, pp. 715–731. Springer (2017)
49. Shaw, R., Kobayashi, K.S.H., Kobayashi, M.: Linking experience, education, perception and earthquake preparedness. Disaster Prev. Manag. Int. J. (2004)
50. Shaw, R., Takeuchi, Y., Ru Gwee, Q., Shiwaku, K.: Chapter 1 disaster education: an introduction. In: Shaw, R., Shiwaku, K., Takeuchi, Y. (eds.) Disaster Education, Community, Environment and Disaster Risk Management, vol. 7, pp. 1–22. Emerald Group Publishing Limited (2011). https://doi.org/10.1108/S2040-7262(2011)0000007007
51. Slingerland, G., Lukosch, S., Brazier, F.: Engaging children to co-create outdoor play activities for place-making. In: Proceedings of the 16th Participatory Design Conference 2020 - Participation(s) Otherwise - Volume 1, pp. 44–54. ACM, Manizales Colombia (2020). https://doi.org/10.1145/3385010.3385017. https://dl.acm.org/doi/10.1145/3385010.3385017
52. Steen, M., Manschot, M., De Koning, N.: Benefits of co-design in service design projects. Int. J. Des. **5**(2) (2011)
53. Stelzer, J.: The seriousness of play: Johan Huizinga's Homo Ludens and the demise of the play-element. Int. J. Play **12**(3), 337–348 (2023)

54. Taillandier, F., Adam, C.: Games ready to use: a serious game for teaching natural risk management. Simul. Gaming **49**(4), 441–470 (2018). https://doi.org/10.1177/1046878118770217
55. Tan, J.L., Goh, D.H.L., Ang, R.P., Huan, V.S.: Child-centered interaction in the design of a game for social skills intervention. Comput. Entertainment (CIE) (1), 1–17 (2011)
56. Tang, S., Hanneghan, M.: Introduction to Games-Based Learning, p. 17 (2009)
57. Teasdale, R., Selkin, P., Goodell, L.: Evaluation of student learning, self-efficacy, and perception of the value of geologic monitoring from Living on the Edge, an InTeGrate curriculum module. J. Geosci. Educ. **66**(3), 186–204 (2018)
58. UNISDR: United Nations International Strategy for Disaster Reduction, Hyogo Framework for Action 20052015: Building the Resilience of Nations and Communities to Disasters (2005)
59. UNISDR: United Nations International Strategy for Disaster Reduction, Sendai Framework for Disaster Risk Reduction 2015–2030 (2015)

Conflicted Courses: A Matrix Game for Course Design

Richard Durham[1] and Ruth Lemon[2](✉)

[1] University of Auckland, Auckland 1010, New Zealand
r.durham@auckland.ac.nz
[2] Technology Education New Zealand, TENZ, Auckland, New Zealand
ruth.lemon@tenz.org.nz

Abstract. Course and program design is a complex scenario with multiple stakeholders with different goals for the course or program, including learning outcomes, workload requirements, and space utilisation. Heads of Schools, for instance, must look at a course regarding how its learning outcomes relate to the rest of the program, workload requirements, space utilised, and so on. Meanwhile, the Teaching Assistant focuses on how long it will take to complete the marking. Matrix games simulate complex scenarios, such as designing a robust cybersecurity response policy, identifying possible paths of peace in conflicts, and recreating historical scenarios in education to understand the decision-making at the time better. *Conflicted Courses* is a matrix game designed around the scenario of course design in higher education. The primary learning objectives are for players to produce a skeleton of a potential course that considers the balance of stakeholder goals. Secondly, to critique stakeholders' goals in the game in relation to their real-life contexts. This game is intended for educational institution staff engaging in curriculum design. *Conflicted Courses* contributes to the field by introducing simulation and gaming to the course design domain using games as a design tool.

Keywords: Serious game · team collaboration · matrix game · higher education · curriculum design

1 Introduction

Matrix and seminar games have traditionally been used to elicit information in complex scenarios, discover background motivations, predict possible outcomes, and develop stakeholder trust [1]. We refer to Zagal, Rick and Hsi's [2] definition of participants when we define stakeholders as those who may benefit or suffer from the outcomes of a team's efforts. An explicit statement of goals and negotiating them, is a critical step towards collaboration. Course and programme design is a complex scenario with multiple stakeholders with different goals for the course or program, such as learning outcomes, workload requirements, and space utilisation. This complex scenario is fraught with stakeholders' overlapping goals. Games are often used in learning contexts as a way to shift ways of knowing, when aligning gameplay with learning outcomes [3]. Using matrix games while designing a curriculum makes the overlapping goals of the stakeholders explicit [4, 5]. Matrix games provide a framework for these complex discussions [6], servicing all stakeholders while moving towards the related common goal of a curriculum design.

Conflicted Courses is a novel matrix game designed around the course design scenario, involving multiple stakeholders with conflicting goals for the course and their purpose for involvement. The primary learning objectives are for players to produce a skeleton of a potential course that considers the balance of stakeholder goals and critiquing stakeholders' goals in the game in relation to their real-life contexts. Working in the tertiary sector, we saw a need that could be met through a game. We started with a matrix game focusing on a specific course in 2019 [7]. *Conflicted Courses* was iterated twice by 2024 [8, 9], and this paper represents a fourth iteration of the game.

This game is intended for educational institution staff engaging in curriculum design. *Conflicted Courses* aims to contribute to the field by introducing simulation and gaming to the course design domain using games as a design tool. This paper focuses on the current rules for the game and associated meta-play information. It draws on selected key literature in exploring how the game is novel.

2 Literature Review

We began with an analogy of education as the shifting playing field of a political game, as described by Scribner, Reyes, and Fusarelli [10]. The analogy illustrates how competing values create conflicts at all levels of school governance and in the political arenas where these institutions operate. This clash of values shapes a political game with winners and losers, where negotiation and compromise are necessary to address competing social imperatives. Building on this analogy, we selected literature that extends this perspective to course design in higher education, a domain directly relevant to our practice. In selecting our literature, we looked at course design methods, common problems and conflicts. Then, because we were framing this as a game, we looked at common game structures for working collaboratively in groups and common course design methodologies.

We focused on Wiggins and McTighe's Backwards Design methodology for course design because it is commonly used in course design within higher education [11].

For common game collaborative game structures, we identified a history of seminar games and their development into Matrix games as a discursive tool in serious contexts outside the use of militaries [12].

To focus more closely on the conflicts in course design in the higher education sector, we used the literature review of Chan et al. [13], who identified that while it is agreed that core generic competencies are valuable, challenges arise because of differing views on the purpose of a university and inconsistent terminology. They propose aligning teaching methods, curriculum, and student engagement to systematically teach core competencies, supporting students' success in tertiary education.

Fung's [14] focus is on the relationship between research and teaching in the higher education space and the connections that can be made between the two. Fung draws from a growing evidence base that students will benefit from opportunities to collaborate and to inquire collectively. The last component that we identified as significant in course design relates to what Russell identifies as "the curse of knowledge" [15], a challenge that lecturers face in course design because they need to think back to the time they did not yet know something and consider what contributed to their acquisition of this knowledge and what facilitated its acquisition. These were the key considerations for us in our game design.

Taking the role of an inexperienced educator or a stakeholder in course design who has a perspective different than their own can help understand the position of those other people [16–19]. The design process is often a structured conversation, with the goal of a functional course with aligned activities, assessment, and learning outcomes [20, 21]. Games are a rule-structured activity with a goal. This makes them perfectly copacetic with the task of course design. The added benefit of a game is the players being in a ludic state, which is when players agree to a suspension of belief and acceptance of an artificial goal for the sake of a game, allowing more playful, curious, exploratory, and divergent ways of thinking, which then converge again in the course of play to achieve the ludic goals. In the case of a learning game, it is desirable to have a high degree of ludic-goal and activity alignment with real-life external activities and goals [22].

Seminar games are discussion games moderated by an umpire, originally played as wargames used to engage experts with complex real-life situations to make predictions, draw out relevant knowledge from, and analyse the proposed decisions by the involved experts [12]. Price encourages developers to check their roles by adding emphasis - if the motivation is strong enough, emphasis will be required [23]! As Seminar games are primarily discussion-based, with some visual aids, they are cheap and easy to implement. They are used in some form in areas ranging from cybersecurity and disaster relief to climate change responses [1, 4, 16, 24–27]. By the end of the 1980s, the criticism of seminar games as just a "bunch of guys sitting around a table," or BOGSAT, was that it was too subjective and, with poor facilitation, often led to grousing sessions or experts trotting out their pet-talking points [28–30]. This led to the development of a style by Chris Engle called Matrix Games [31, 32].

The key development in the Matrix game style is the adjudication process: In response to a situation, a player proposes an action and desired result, along with a justifying reason or two on why that result is likely. Other players may add more justifications (pros), reasons why the action will fail, or the result is unlikely (cons). The action is then resolved with these in mind, often simply with a dice roll with the odds weighted by the balance of pros and cons [32].

Engle describes the concept of the "matrix" as the individuals' mental maps of the world. Through play, our understanding of this matrix evolves, shaped by our life experiences and knowledge. Each game explores, modifies, and expands our mental maps [33].

Matrix games, emerging from a rationalist perspective, serve as a practical verbal tool to gather and organise ideas. As such, they function well as a tool to generate possible futures based on choices in complex scenarios. The result and process leading to this can be analysed, but they should not be confused with quantitative simulations. The result is purely qualitative and is well suited for post-game discussion about the events that developed or how the motives of roles influenced their responses [6, 32].

Like many socio-political games, Matrix games include physical components to supplement the discussion. They focus player attention and feature tangible elements representing what the players can control by physically manipulating them. The physical components highlight parts of the mental models in play and are a resource to be leveraged when justifying actions. They are often on a map to illustrate their relation to each other. This physical point of attentional focus in a game helps maintain engagement in the task and frame players' decisions [34, 35].

Our findings are that Matrix-style seminar games are an appropriate game structure to facilitate collaborative activity in complex scenarios or conflict resolution. With this game, we are trying to produce a collaborative output that requires successful alignment with opposing or overlapping goals, a key difference from other seminar games, and an output from the activity different from other Matrix games. In our previous iteration, collaboration between players was too strong, as goals were different but complemented each other rather than creating tension. This iteration attempts to generate more inherent tension between the roles by having their goals overlap only partially with multiple other roles.

In the following sections, we overview the gameplay tested at the ISAGA 2024 conference and outline best practices before succinctly sharing the game's strengths in the conclusion.

3 Overview of the Game and Materials

You are designing a course in *Conflicted Courses,* but it's never as simple as that. Each player (or team) has a different **Role**, each role holding different priorities for the course and having power over different domains. Your job is to discuss and map the course as best you can, considering the conflicting priorities and abilities. In mapping the course, you'll leverage the role's **Power** (e.g., a Head of School allocating extra funding) while attempting to satisfy the role's diverse priorities. One participant will act as Facilitator, coordinating the game and moderating the group's decisions.

Materials

As the Facilitator, you should gather the following materials for play. These are the minimum required, though if you want to you can include any other tools/materials you wish. Background documents for the roles can either be created ahead of time by the Facilitator or done as part of a session.

- 2 Six-sided dice (2d6)
- 1 A1/Poster paper to be used as a map - whether a course map or a map of the school, community, etc., in which the scenario is set or both of the above
- Per team of 1–5 people

    - Blank A4/Letter paper for each team, pens/pencils for each player on the team
    - 4 tokens (such as glass beads) per team to represent their Power over their domains of responsibility.
    - Set of turn-order tokens numbered for the number of Teams you will have (e.g., If there are five teams, use tokens numbered 1–5).

- 1 pad of sticky notes per team.
- Any Role background documents the Facilitator has created ahead of time.

4 Setting up the Scenario

This can be done before play by the Facilitator, or the Facilitator can guide the playing group to create some details for the scenario. If your purpose for playing is generating ideas for a real course, the Facilitator should prepare scenario information ahead of time and present it to the players.

If creating a scenario as a group, fill in and read out the following using words from Table 1 below, or write your own list.

"We've gathered today to discuss [COURSE], which is strategically important to [ADMIN] because it will [IMPACT]. And to [other ADMIN] because it will [other IMPACT]. Our job is to satisfy those in a way that is okay for most people here. The [PRESCRIPTION] for the course follows."

Table 1. Setting the course.

List	Example
COURSE	– TTEC 100 – Teaching Technology – POLI 300 – Democracy or demoCRAZY – EDUC 100 – What is a duck, and can it quack?
ADMIN	– Accreditation Board/Regulatory/Industry – Vice Chancellor/President – Faculty Dean – Community Stakeholders
IMPACT	– Increase/retain student numbers – Reduce staff workload – Have better job prospects – Align our values
PRESCRIPTION	– TTEC 100 focuses on strategically integrating technology across construction, food and materials, biotechnology, and coding. Students explore innovative solutions to real-world problems through design-based interventions, emphasising stakeholder needs and sustainable technological practices – POLI 300 explores the complexities of global democratic systems and their strengths, weaknesses, and challenges. Students analyse political ideologies, institutions, and practices using interdisciplinary perspectives to understand democratic governance and its impact on societies – EDUC 100 delves into foundational education concepts, exploring diverse theories and methodologies. Students examine the essence of learning, cognition, and pedagogical approaches, questioning conventional wisdom and fostering critical thinking about the nature of knowledge acquisition and transmission

4.1 Setting the Scenario Context

The course doesn't happen in isolation. It will be delivered to imaginary students in a context. Part of the background documents prepared by the Facilitator should briefly outline the context in which the course will be taught, or players can determine these. For example, a scenario context could include background from these categories:

- **School history and geography** – Where is the school, in what kind of community, with what historical relationship to the present?
- **Economics of the school** – For budgets, institutional support, etc. How is the school funded?
- **Infrastructure** – Physical and tangible material. What facilities are available, and what facilities are lacking?
- **School politics** – Are there existing clashes of personalities or internal concerns apart from the established "Admin?"
- **Social dimension** – Who's taking the course? Who's encouraged? Who's excluded? Who cares?

Regarding the course, you can consider many details if you prepare beforehand. It is often better to be brief in this game context and let details be determined. However, if you are inclined to include details on the course beyond the prescription, consider the following:

- Prerequisite knowledge or courses/ where the course fits in the program
- Accreditation requirements/external outcomes from an industry body or graduate profile
- Technical space and practicum requirements
- Number of students needed to run the course/course costs
- Timetabling and assessment requirements

5 Setting up the Roles

After the scenario is established, break the players into teams. Each team represents a single role involved in developing the course for delivery. If the Facilitator prepared **Role Background** documents earlier, hand them out now. Or the teams can create them now to deepen their connection with the scenario. Either way, the process is similar:

1. Identify roles relevant to developing and delivering the course. Aim for roles that will have tension between their functional and personal goals and between the goals of other roles. Also, roles that overlap in what they have power over. It is helpful to draw a network diagram of these roles.
2. Each team is assigned a role to develop (or the Facilitator develops them as Background documents ahead of time).

For example, if playing with POLI300 - Democracy or DemoCRAZY, you might have a team representing the teacher, one for the Head of School, a Graduate Teaching Assistant, etc. Alternatively, if playing with TTEC 100 – Teaching Technology, you can choose to have only specialist teacher roles involved, such as a food technology teacher, a hard materials teacher, a biotechnology teacher, and a digital technologies teacher. The example below will use hierarchical and functional roles like Head of School, Teacher, Course Director, etc.

If creating a custom scenario during the game, the Facilitator should poll the players for possible Roles to determine the most appropriate ones as a group.

Example Roles: Teacher, Course Director, Head of School, Teaching Assistant (change for your context).

5.1 Establishing Role Goals

Roles will have **Goals** that are not known to the other teams. The Facilitator will pre-write each Role's Goals and include them in the Role Background document. Alternatively, each team can generate these after being assigned their Role and write them on their A4/Letter paper in titled sections. In either case, each Role should be differentiated enough that their goals cause conflict.

When thinking of goals, think about the Role as a person, with outside pressures and influences they'd consider when developing a course.

Goals are best written in a bulleted list of 3 to 4 strongly worded objectives the Role strives for, even if they aren't explicitly achievable. A rule of thumb for writing goals is adding an exclamation mark to the end to see if it sounds right. For example, a Teaching Assistant might have – "Stay employed!" as a Motivation, as opposed to "Agree to whatever is asked of you so you don't lose your job." The former is actionable while also being less prescriptive.

Some Goal examples are below:

- Teacher:
  - Use only the latest best practices!
  - Protect my family time!

- Teaching Assistant:
  - Minimise work outside of class!
  - Stay employed!

- Head of School:
  - Show I'm the big boss!
  - Get good value for money!
  - Get funding to expand the school!

- Course Director:
  - Keep It Simple, Stupid!
  - Improve the reputation of the programme!

5.2 Setting up Powers

Powers are the areas of responsibility that a Role has some control over. The Facilitator writes these so that there is some overlap between the Roles, but at different levels (e.g., a Teacher may determine activities for class but be overruled by the course director) or impacting the area differently (e.g., a Course Director may determine how much time is allocated for a Teaching Assistant to do marking, but the Teaching Assistant determines how the marking is done). *Note: This game mechanic has been introduced to this iteration.*

In this way, generating categories relevant to the scenario may be useful, and then considering how each Role has any Power to affect them. Each Role should consider 2–3 responsibility categories they control. For example, consider the categories below:

- **Relationship with the school community**
- **Economics of the school** – School budget, classroom spending, raising funds for the school, etc.
- **Infrastructure** – Physical and tangible materials. Facility usage, classroom resources, etc.
- **School politics and logistics** – Timetabling, work-loading, hiring and firing, setting teaching guidelines, etc.
- **Pedagogical and subject content** – Teaching activities, assessment types, timings, course outcomes, etc.

Example Powers for Example Roles:

- Head of School

  – Has control over the budget allocated to programmes and staff.
  – Sets school teaching guidelines and policy and liaises with Admin.

- Course Director

  – Control over timetabling of a course, including approving field trips, course meeting times, and assessment schedules.
  – Control course learning outcomes and delegate teaching, marking, and moderating responsibilities.

- Teacher

  – Determines the type and nature of the assessments in alignment with outcomes.
  – Determines the course syllabus, including content and activities.

- Teaching Assistant

  – Control over how course activities are delivered.
  – Helps determine the type and nature of assessment and marking.

Goals are kept within teams for now (they will be alluded to during play). Powers will become apparent during play.

Distribute Turn-Order Tokens. These determine the order teams will take turns during the second half of each Round. If there are four teams, the tokens are numbered 1 to 4. While setting up the Roles, the Facilitator gives each team a random Turn-order token. Teams may trade these during the Planning step of each round.

Teams might trade turn-order tokens because they will establish facts of the scenario during gameplay as they take actions. Each action they take will have more or less success based on the previously established facts. As a result, the order in which teams act could significantly impact whether the action they want to take is made moot or – if facts in their favour are established ahead of time – their action finds easy success. Put another way, going early in a round means you have more control over the narrative. However, going later in the round means you can leverage earlier decisions (though you may need to think more on your feet if your plan has been disrupted). Teams have another tool to control the narrative: Power tokens.

Distribute Power Tokens. The Facilitator also gives each team four Power tokens. These have a few uses:

- A team can give the Facilitator one to reroll the dice immediately after an action is resolved with a dice roll.
- A team can support a proposed action before a dice roll (including their own action) by giving one of their tokens to the Facilitator, justifying why the action will be successful in relation to their Power and background.
- A team can show their opposition to a proposed action before the dice roll by giving one of their tokens to the team taking action and justifying why the action would not be successful. For details on this, see the Gameplay section.
- Power tokens can also be traded between teams as a show of trust, exchange of power, or simply to bargain.
- The Facilitator will be able to redistribute some Power tokens to the teams during the game by declaring particular external events that impact the scenario. The more Power tokens they distribute, the more impactful the event the Facilitator should narrate.

5.3 Setting up the Scenario Map

A scenario map will represent the teaching environment, school, and/or community where the course will be taught. It could be a conceptual map representing course activities, assessments, and schedules. Functionally, it will accumulate decisions the roles have made that influence the ongoing scenario. If the Facilitator prepares Background documents ahead of time, they can also prepare the Scenario map. However, generating the scenario map with the players at the start of play will get them involved in co-creation early on and help cement the scenario in their minds.

The map should represent factors that perhaps aren't outlined in Role background documents, such as types of local businesses and demographic and environmental information, that will contribute to a successful course. For instance, if the distance to a local forest is a factor (e.g., for field trips and investigations), show the forest on the map. It is up to you what map is appropriate, and you may have more than one.

If generating the scenario as a group to start play, the maps can be quick sketches co-constructed with the role teams. In this case, each team contributes a portion of the map according to their role's background and responsibilities. For instance, a Head of School might offer up community sponsors to add to the map because community involvement is a factor in the success of the course, and budgetary concerns are the Head of School's Power. On a conceptual course map, the Teaching Assistant might suggest a section for technical lab times because scheduling is an important factor to consider.

An example procedure for map generation:

In turn order (as assigned during Setting up the Roles), each team suggests an addition to the map. They must state what factor they want added to the map, followed by any specific addition. If the map feels incomplete to the Facilitator after each role has added something, the Facilitator should add more until they feel it captures the scenario. For example:

- Scheduling is important; add the Time of Day to the course map.
- Student travel time is a factor; add the school zone to the map.
- The local natural environment is a factor in this course; add this forest and beach to the map.

6 Gameplay

Gameplay moves into a Rounds structure after setting up the Scenario, Roles, and Scenario Map.

The gameplay is five rounds, each with a Planning and Action step. The Planning step is strictly timed and is where the Facilitator announces the task for that Round, and then each team has time (~8 min) to plan an Action, visit other teams to debate, promise support, and trade power and turn-order tokens.

During the Action step, each team in turn-order proposes and resolves an Action. Once each team has resolved their Action, the Facilitator begins the next Round by announcing the next Round Task and starting the timer for the Planning step.

6.1 Round Task and Events

The Facilitator sets the Round Task. It is a short-term goal that may be set by an event the Facilitator presents or related to a stage in course development. If the Facilitator determines that the players met the Round Task (or mitigated an Event), they will award 1 Power token to each team. The Facilitator can reward an additional Power token to the team with the best contributions and 1 to the Role that raised the best opposition. "Best" is determined by the Facilitator.

To set the Round Task, the Facilitator can work through parts of course development, using models such as Backwards Design [11] or create an Event that responds to players' actions. See Table 2 for some example course development-related Round Tasks.

Table 2. Example course development Round Tasks

Round	Round Task
1	Determine a learning outcome essential to deliver the course content as per the course prescription
2	Determine key resources that could be used to introduce and teach one of the learning outcomes for the course
3	Determine a key activity that could be used to develop students' understanding of one of the learning outcomes for the course
4	Determine a key assessment task that could check students' understanding of one of the learning outcomes for the course
5	Fund the course - Do you have enough in the budget?

Creating Events as Round Task

Events are different from normal Round Tasks in that they happen at the start of a Round rather than acting as an objective to be completed. To create an Event as a Round Task, the Facilitator thinks of either a positive or negative external event that can impact the scenario or a complication that resulted from the player's earlier actions. As a rule of thumb, use Positive events when players struggle to progress the narrative or complete Round Tasks. Use Negative events or complicate matters when the players are too chummy, or the scenario seems too easy to resolve. Events can also be responsive to the scenario and actions of the players. For example, if players establish that some teaching activities rely on a large travel budget, the Facilitator might create an event that requires budget redirection. Some examples of unpredictable external forces are in Table 3 below.

Table 3. Example Events

Negative events	Positive events
New government requirement	New government subsidy
Critical staff leaving	Benefactor donation
Funding shortfall	School is highlighted in the news
Community protest	Regional competition or fair
Regional disaster	Criteria changed for international student visas

The Facilitator can assign a variable Power token reward for an Event based on how many Power tokens the teams have given the Facilitator to support their actions. Highly complicated events will have a higher Power token award at the end of the round if the players can respond to it to the satisfaction of the Facilitator. In this case, the Round Task reward is not 1 Power token but the value assigned by the Facilitator. How this is handled is up to the Facilitator, but here are a couple of principles to keep in mind:

- Highly complicating events come when the teams have been very supportive of each other and thus are running low on Power tokens. This is a way to create a problem that will be harder to resolve because they have a lower ability to support each other and a way to return Power tokens to them as a reward.
- Even if the teams fail to mitigate an event, the Facilitator may want to award the typical amount for a Round Task based on who had the "best" contribution and opposition.

6.2 Planning Step (Strictly Timed, 8 min)

Teams determine an action that advances their Goal and addresses the Round Task for the course. Actions will be easier if supported by established facts from earlier actions or if other Roles choose to support it in the Action step. Role-teams prepare an Action by writing down the desired result on a sticky note (see Action phrasing below).

During the Planning step time:

- Players may move freely between other teams and any central table with the scenario map. This is so they may coordinate, debate, and pledge support.
- Role teams may give Power tokens to other teams freely, but turn-order tokens must be exchanged with another turn-order token (so each Role team has a turn-order token).

6.3 Action Step (Approximately Timed, 2–5 min per Team)

When the Planning time is up, the Facilitator signals that players return to their team, and then the Action step begins. Begin with the team that has Turn-order token #1. Each team's turn follows the steps below. When each team has had their turn, the Facilitator can close the round by summarising events and begin the next round by setting the next Round Task.

Steps for a team's Action turn.

1. **Propose Action and Result**: A member of the current team verbally proposes their Action and states what the result would be if it is successful.
2. **Established support**: The current team may support their Action by drawing upon previously established facts or situations in the scenario. These facts should support why the action is more likely to have the successful result the team proposed. Each substantial supporting fact will add +1 to the resolution dice roll.
3. **Established opposition:** Any team may now point out previously established facts or situations that justify why the action will not have the intended result or otherwise fail. Each substantial opposing fact will subtract −1 from the dice roll.
4. **Raised support**: Back to support, any team (including the current team) may now give a Power token to the Facilitator and justify why the action will have the intended result, leveraging their role's background or powers. Again, each substantial raised support adds +1 to the dice roll.
5. **Raised opposition**: OR something in their role's background or powers that might lead to the proposed action failing. The first team raising opposition may even suggest an alternative result should the action fail. When raising opposition, that team wagers a Power token. If their result fails, this token will be given to the current proposing team. If the result is successful, the wagering team keeps it. Each substantial raised opposition will again subtract −1 from the dice roll.

6. **Roll the dice**: To determine if the action had the intended result or failed, the current team will roll two 6-sided dice (2d6) and add +1 for each substantial support and −1 for each substantial opposition. The action has the desired result if the roll is greater than 7. If it is 7 or lower, the result of the raised opposition happens or otherwise fails, and the Facilitator narrates the result. If any team does not like the dice roll, they can give the Facilitator a Power token to re-roll. Each team can only do this once per action resolution. The dice represent the many unknowns from complex scenarios like course design. Players can not, nor should they, account for every variable. And even the best-laid plans fail when encountering students for the first time. In this game context, players need to learn that they do not have ultimate control over how a course turns out, regardless of how much time they spend planning it.

Whatever the result (whether the intended one or an opposition's result), record it on a sticky note and place it on the scenario map in an appropriate place. If there isn't, place it off to the side. Alternatively, results can be recorded for all players to see on a whiteboard or in a shared digital space.

Posted results often change the situation by establishing a fact (e.g., a team securing funding for an activity, new technology for the classroom, or arranging a field trip to a local community site). These can be leveraged as support by future actions. If conflicting facts/results are established, remove the older one.

Action Phrasing. Actions should be kept simple and follow a general template of "We are going to [ACTION] so that [RESULT]." The facilitator and players must tightly regulate the scope of an action and its related result.

For instance, imagine a game simulating a 1-week period of a group designing the activities, assessments, and learning outcomes of a course in a small rural school. Having a player in a Head of School role propose an action of "We are going to fly to Silicon Valley and meet with Jeff Bezos so that we secure a billion dollar donation to our school" is far outside the realm of possible reality and not worth the group's time to arbitrate.

Instead, a Teacher role might propose, "We are going to negotiate with the local maker space so that students can have a field trip there to create prototypes of their project in week 10."

It may be helpful to include a list of words in the Background documents for each Role relevant to the kinds of actions they may take. For instance, a Head of School might "negotiate" with external people. With course mapping, you might have Teacher roles using language like creating an "Investigation" or "Production" activity or others from Laurillard's Learning Activity Type framework [36].

7 Game Ending

After five rounds or so (go as long as your time allows or until just before the players run out of energy), the Facilitator can lead a debrief discussion. This will help review the game's activities, allow time for reflection on why things turned out the way they did, and discuss their Role's goals.

Whatever your motive for playing, the Facilitator should facilitate a discussion highlighting those features. Matrix games for thorough analysis would include more tracking of the various support and opposition statements. This game is better suited for post-game discussion among the participants. Here are some example talking points:

- How were the students' needs considered, prioritised, or ignored?
- Was there a bias towards the goals of particular roles, or was balance maintained between the different roles? Why? How?
- Critique the Powers of the Roles in the game in relation to their real-life contexts.

8 Suggestions for Facilitation

As Facilitator, you set the game's purpose and ensure the game moves through the timed steps, ensure actions and results are reasonable, that support and opposition statements are substantial (and not frivolous), and create Round Tasks and Events. This is not an easy job, but like most things, it gets easier with experience. A few suggestions. First, on the schedule.

Conflicted Courses has timed rounds to keep pressure on planning and to force decisions - something that is sometimes avoided in real-life collaborative course design. This game can be run as a full or half-day session (6 or 3 h) or broken up into small sessions. Table 4 is an example 2-h "introductory" timeline for 4–20 players. It assumes the Facilitator has pre-made 4 Roles and all reference documentation.

Table 4. Example timeline for an Introductory 2-h session

Section	Timeline
Introduction. Scenario and Setting the Course	5 min
Team Roles. Teams review their assigned Role (1–5 players per Team for each of the 4 Roles)	5 min
Prepare Gameplay. Describe Round structure, scenario map, Power tokens and Action phrasing	10 min
Rounds. 8 min for the Planning step, and ~8–10 for the Action step ~2.5 min per Role)	90 min
Debrief. Discussion time (see *Game ending*)	10 min

Secondly, a suggestion on moderating actions and results and support and opposition statements is needed. You'll have your own feeling for what's sensible and in scope as an action for the game, but here are some guiding questions:

- Does the result feel proportionate to the action?
- Does the role have any Power related to their action?
- Is it a reasonable inference even if an established fact/situation isn't explicit?

Finally, remember that this is a game. Even if you're using a real course and hope to generate useful thoughts on a course, it is best to let players stay in a ludic mindset and prioritise the engagement of the players over arguing details or staying precisely on schedule.

9 Conclusion

Course design in the tertiary setting is often a high-stakes process. We adapted the Matrix Game format to keep the structure loose and draw out creativity. The collaborative nature of the game is inspired by Zagal, Rick and Hsi's work in recognising differing goals [2]. The Round structure leverages Backwards Design by focusing on the end outcome and working "backwards" to the activities aligned with the outcomes [11]. Language-using frameworks such as Laurillard's learning activity types scaffold the kinds of Actions teams might write.

The game is innovative in terms of the scenario. Conflicting Courses offers an opportunity to enjoy a process that is often rushed due to numerous urgent deadlines. In addition, course design meetings are generally unregulated by process, allowing those conflicting goals to fester. Applying a matrix game format to course design allows a structured debate around actions that contribute to the development of a course.

In the scenario of course design, the abstraction of the scenario to a matrix game was challenging because matrix games are usually about direct conflict and have better representations of physical space. In a course design scenario, the conflicts are over concepts, and the design often has logistical concerns that are less oriented around a scenario map. However, including a physical map in a course design scenario reminds the course designers that the course is taught to real people who live in a real place.

An issue that we had in early prototyping was that players collaborated too well and we did not need the structured conflict. A key tension we experienced lay in our discussions around how players could take action or whether they would be providing support for proposals. This is why we added the mechanism of the power tokens, to make explicit the exchange of providing support.

Going forward, there are potential directions for game development and research. Regarding game development, we now want to trial different educational scenarios to assess the degree of generalisability of this game. We also noted that in setting up the course scenario, we provided too much irrelevant or confusing detail for players. For the next iteration, we will work on reducing the prescriptiveness (e.g. offering specific course timetabling options) and streamlining the content so that the role groups' focus can be on the systems comprising a good course design (e.g. well-balanced workload, manageable budget, a timetable that fits the facilities, etc.).

In our test at ISAGA 2024, we tested the power token economy's success in eliciting explicit support or opposition to proposed actions. Something that worked well was players using the power tokens to take actions and increase their chances of success. This did work to create and resolve tension between the roles based on their goals. However, they did not exchange power tokens with each other or the role-order turn cards and instead focused their interactions on the course design.

However, their actions did not impact the underlying systems of the course design, as they were represented too prescriptively, which added to the irrelevant and confusing material. Future development will simplify the interactions between roles and the course design by aligning it with player interactions. That is, a role's action will increase or decrease stress on the underlying system, increasing or decreasing the chances of success for actions related to that system.

For example, a Course Director role might take action to increase the workload of a teaching assistant role. Or a Head of School passing a regulation that decreases stress on timetabling, making actions related to timetabling more likely to succeed.

Finally, in reflection, Zagal's lessons in collaborative game design [2] were very helpful and could frame a whole paper on how this game addresses the elements of collaborative games.

For future research, we did not focus on measuring the development of collaborative skills through the game, their transfer outside the game, or their application in matrix-style games more broadly. These areas represent potential avenues for further investigation. Since this game is in active development, future iterations and research could also explore the design outcomes or players' responses to a course-design-focused game structure, as opposed to traditional practices in higher education.

Disclosure of Interests. The authors have no competing interests to declare relevant to this article's content.

References

1. Callaghan, P., Fiadotau, M.: Using meaningful choices and uncertainty to increase player agency in a cybersecurity seminar game. In: Dondio, P., et al. (eds.) Games and Learning Alliance, pp. 23–32. Springer, Cham (2024). https://doi.org/10.1007/978-3-031-49065-1_3
2. Zagal, J.P., Rick, J., Hsi, I.: Collaborative games: lessons learned from board games. Simul. Gaming **37**, 24–40 (2006). https://doi.org/10.1177/1046878105282279
3. Ke, F.: Designing and integrating purposeful learning in game play: a systematic review. Educ. Technol. Res. Dev. **64**, 219–244 (2016). https://doi.org/10.1007/s11423-015-9418-1
4. Penney, D.: Playing a political game and playing for position: policy and curriculum development in health and physical education. Eur. Phys. Educ. Rev. **14**, 33–49 (2008). https://doi.org/10.1177/1356336X07085708
5. Wedig, T.: Getting the most from classroom simulations: strategies for maximizing learning outcomes. PS Polit. Sci. Polit. **43**, 547–555 (2010). https://doi.org/10.1017/S104909651000079X
6. Curry, J.: The utility of narrative matrix games. Nav. War Coll. Rev. **73**, 39–58 (2020)
7. Lemon, R.: Know-how and Know-that: Finding a balance with my Initial Teaching students. TENZ Conference: R.I.S.E. Reflect Innovate Shine Educate. Albany Senior High School, Auckland (2019)
8. Durham, R., Lemon, R.: Conflicted Courses: A matrix RPG for Technology and Hangarau course design in intermediate and lower secondary. TESAC 2024: Implementing Innovation and Thinking. Ōtautahi, University of Canterbury (2024)
9. Durham, R., Lemon, R.: Conflicted courses: a matrix RPG for course design. In: Zamboni, C., Farber, M., and Merchant, W. (eds.) Roll for Learning: Micro Tabletop Role-Playing Games to Use in the Classroom. ETC Press (in-print)
10. Scribner, J.D., Reyes, P., Fusarelli, L.D.: Educational politics and policy: and the game goes on. J. Educ. Policy **9**, 201–212 (1994). https://doi.org/10.1080/0268093940090516
11. Wiggins, G.P., McTighe, J.: Understanding by Design. Association for Supervision and Curriculum Development, Alexandria, VA (2005)
12. Mason, R.C.: Wargaming: its history and future. Int. J. Intell. Secur. Public Aff. **20**, 77–101 (2018). https://doi.org/10.1080/23800992.2018.1484238

13. Chan, C.K.Y., Fong, E.T.Y., Luk, L.Y.Y., Ho, R.: A review of literature on challenges in the development and implementation of generic competencies in higher education curriculum. Int. J. Educ. Dev. **57**, 1 (2017). https://doi.org/10.1016/j.ijedudev.2017.08.010
14. Fung, D.: A Connected Curriculum for Higher Education. UCL Press (2017). https://doi.org/10.14324/111.9781911576358
15. Russell, T.: Inspirations and challenges for innovation in teacher education. In: Goodnough, K., Galway, G., Badenhorst, C., and Kelly, R. (eds.) Inspiration and Innovation in Teaching and Teacher Education, pp. 171–184. Lexington Books, Lanham, Maryland (2013)
16. Barab, S., Gresalfi, M., Ingram-Goble, A.: Transformational play: using games to position person, content, and context. Educ. Res. **39**, 525–536 (2011). https://doi.org/10.3102/0013189X10386593
17. Bolstad, R.: Playing for peace: Complex role-play gaming in high school history A case study (2017). https://doi.org/10.13140/RG.2.2.31785.08806
18. Schwarz, J.O.: Business wargaming for teaching strategy making. Futures **51**, 59–66 (2013). https://doi.org/10.1016/j.futures.2013.06.002
19. Stover, W.J.: Teaching and learning empathy: an interactive, online diplomatic simulation of middle east conflict. J. Polit. Sci. Educ. **1**, 207–219 (2005). https://doi.org/10.1080/15512160590961801
20. Biggs, J.: Aligning Teaching for Constructing Learning (2003)
21. Lemon, R., Durham, R.: Conversations between a teacher and game designer: redesigning a teaching game about Māori–Pākehā histories. Set Res. Inf. Teach. 12–19 (2018). https://doi.org/10.18296/set.0113
22. Carvalho, M.B., et al.: An activity theory-based model for serious games analysis and conceptual design. Comput. Educ. **87**, 166–181 (2015). https://doi.org/10.1016/j.compedu.2015.03.023
23. Price, T.: Running matrix games. In: The Matrix Games Handbook: Professional Applications from Education to Analysis and Wargaming, pp. 27–50. The History of Wargaming Project (2019)
24. Barab, S., Pettyjohn, P., Gresalfi, M., Volk, C., Solomou, M.: Game-based curriculum and transformational play: designing to meaningfully positioning person, content, and context. Comput. Educ. **58**, 518–533 (2012). https://doi.org/10.1016/j.compedu.2011.08.001
25. Bartels, E.M., Chivvis, C.S., Grissom, A.R., Pettyjohn, S.L.: Conceptual Design for a Multiplayer Security Force Assistance Strategy Game. RAND Corporation (2019)
26. Baylouny, A.M.: Seeing other sides: nongame simulations and alternative perspectives of middle east conflict. J. Polit. Sci. Educ. **5**, 214–232 (2009). https://doi.org/10.1080/15512160903035658
27. Fiadotau, M., Tramonti, M., Brander, H., Callaghan, P.: BIG GAME: balancing player preferences and design considerations in a serious game about environmental issues. In: Kiili, K., Antti, K., de Rosa, F., Dindar, M., Kickmeier-Rust, M., Bellotti, F. (eds.) Games and Learning Alliance, pp. 329–334. Springer, Cham (2022). https://doi.org/10.1007/978-3-031-22124-8_34
28. Caffrey, M.: On Wargaming. Newport Pap. (2019)
29. Pettyjohn, S.: Connections 2016 - Strategic Wargaming. Connections UK professional Wargaming conference (2016)
30. Weuve, C., et al.: Wargame Pathologies. https://apps.dtic.mil/sti/pdfs/ADA596774.pdf. Accessed 10 May 2024
31. Curry, J., Perla, P., Engel, C. (eds.): The Matrix Games Handbook: Professional Applications from Education to Analysis and Wargaming. The History of Wargaming Project (2019)
32. Engle, C.: Matrix game rules. https://sites.google.com/view/free-engle-matrix-games/home

33. Engle, C.: Walking in the dark: an allegory of knowledge. In: The Matrix Games Handbook: Professional Applications from Education to Analysis and Wargaming, pp. 81–82. The History of Wargaming Project (2019)
34. Cutting, J., Deterding, S.: The task-attention theory of game learning: a theory and research agenda. Hum.-Comput. Interact. **39**, 1–31 (2022). https://doi.org/10.1080/07370024.2022.2047971
35. Wasser, B., Oberholtzer, J., Pettyjohn, S.L., Mackenzie, W.: Gaming Gray Zone Tactics: Design Considerations for a Structured Strategic Game. RAND Corporation (2019)
36. Laurillard, D.: Rethinking University Teaching: A Conversational Framework for the Effective Use of Learning Technologies. Routledge, London (2013). https://doi.org/10.4324/9781315012940

A Framework for Co-design of Edu Escape-Room Aimed at Exploring Cultural Identity

Weronika Szatkowska[1]( ), Małgorzata Ćwil[1], and Blanka Błaszczak-Rozenbaum[2]

[1] Koźmiński University, Warsaw, Poland
wszatkowska@kozminski.edu.pl
[2] Jagiellonian University, Kraków, Poland

Abstract. The paper gathers the current knowledge and trends in educational escape rooms and co-design practices, linking them to the discussion on the application of these two concepts in the context of participatory game design. It explores the benefits of applying an escape room experience to reflect on cultural identity while indicating the benefits of the application of co-design methodology to develop such an experience under inclusive conditions.

In this paper, we propose a framework to co-design educational escape rooms, based on the experience from the project *The Inheritor - the development of an edu escape room to explore cultural identities*. As an outcome, we explain pragmatically the main stages adapted from the co-design methodology enriched with game design elements. We explain the roles of the co-designers that emerged during the process and propose a framework to co-design escape room experiences with them. The area was particularly challenging due to references not only to the existing systems and connections but also to the past events and social relations that influenced the current perception of the "cultural self", which we aimed to address within this framework.

Keywords: Escape Room · Co-design · Culture Identity

1 Introduction

The trend to use escape rooms in the process of education has increased in recent years [1–6]. It is also visible in the increasing number of studies in this area. Escape rooms are emerging as a new type of playful, interactive, engaging learning activities [7, 8]. They are designed to help learners gain knowledge, develop new skills, boost motivation to study and collaboration between participants. In this paper we propose a framework to co-design edu escape rooms, based on the experience from the project *The Inheritor - development of an edu escape room to explore cultural identities*.

2 Escape Rooms in Education

2.1 Educational Escape Rooms

An escape room is an adventure interactive game in which players solve a series of puzzles, challenges and riddles using clues, hints, and strategy to complete the given objectives [9]. The elements that are often included in the escape rooms are: teamwork and time limitation [3]. In *The Inheritor* participants collect information from various (fake) historical personal items, i.e. letters, books, family photos and search for information about existing inheritors of the heritage belonging to Ukrainian-Polish businessmen who settled in the USA.

When the escape rooms are used in the process of learning, they become a teaching tool [10]. Many playful activities are included and thanks to that, a more immersive learning experience for the participants is created [11]. In *The Inheritor* participants interact with tape recordings, old photographs, hand-written letters, or newspapers. Escape rooms are based on social-constructivist approach, where participants build their knowledge based on real-time experiences while advancing through the provided challenges [12]. The strategy of learning-by-doing is used here. In *The Inheritor* it is the task given by the Unsolved Cases Agency to find out who is the inheritor, based on the diligent investigation of the memorabilia sent by the client. As the players - new members of the Agency - progress, they discover new hints and traces.

Escape rooms can be used as a form of experiential learning and problem-solving activity. Researchers investigate how participants engage in the challenges presented, examining aspects such as for example cognitive processes, teamwork dynamics, and the impact of time pressure on decision-making. In the educational escape rooms, sometimes the time limit is as short as 15 min, so that more students can have an opportunity to solve the puzzles, however usually the time limit is set as around 60 min [4]. In our case, it was 35 min for the experience and 30 min for the debriefing.

The scenarios and themes of escape rooms can vary widely, ranging from mystery and adventure to horror or science fiction. Escape rooms can be used in many different fields in education. For example, they are very commonly used in health, medical or pharmaceutical education [2, 13–23]. Other fields that include the usage of educational escape rooms are: natural sciences [24], mathematics and statistics [25, 26], chemistry [27, 28], computer sciences [29], cryptography [30], programming [31, 32], climate change [33], teamwork and communication [34, 35], language skills [36], manufacturing [37]. This type of learner-centered teaching method gained recently the interest of scholars also in the field of earthquake preparedness [38], cybersecurity [39], music [40], sex education [41] or cultural issues [42]. In our case, we searched for an engaging way to discuss complex cross-cultural issues, and evoke reflection on cultural identity, thus, we decided to develop a simulation game in the form of an escape room.

Educational escape rooms can be used at every level of education: from primary school kids [3, 24, 33], through high school [26, 32] and university students [28, 43, 44, 19, 45, 31, 20], up to professionals [13, 37, 10, 14], what was in line with our target group.

When it comes to different types of escape rooms, the majority of them have a physical form [ex. 4, 5, 24, 25], however in recent years also some digital/virtual [31,

46, 39, 28, 47] and hybrid ones were created [18]. Physical escape rooms can have different forms, the most popular ones being: escape the room [ex. 20] and breakout boxes [ex. 48, 49]. In the breakout boxes, the aim is not to escape from a place but rather to manage to open boxes that contain a treasure or to answer a mystery [11], which was the case of *The Inheritor*. Hybrid escape rooms offer both virtual [e.g., QR codes, social media platforms etc.] and physical [e.g., locks, boxes, etc.] objects [4]. In digital escape rooms, players use technology [ex. computers, phones, tablets, apps, VR, AR, QR codes] to open a series of digital locks or password-protected documents [5].

2.2 Reasons to Introduce Escape Rooms

The reasons why escape rooms are introduced in the process of education can be various. First, they enhance higher levels of students' engagement [30]. If designed correctly, they should boost participants' motivation to study, as they are in a state of flow [50]. According to Csikszentmihalyi's theory, to achieve flow, it is important to maintain the players in a total immersion state in which they are neither over-challenged nor under-challenged. The participants should face the challenges on the optimal level of complexity, to find the perfect trade-off between boredom and frustration [30]. The level of difficulty should differ between tasks and puzzles in escape rooms. Being stuck at the very first riddle can be discouraging for participants. The same applies to tasks that are too easy for the participants, even when the gameplay continues.

Second, educational escape rooms increase the level of participants' knowledge in the particular area of study [30, 43]. The students need to master the material in order to succeed in the escape room, which was important point to choose the form of escape room, not a typical board game. Moreover, the educational escape rooms can be introduced to increase the low pass rate during some of the classes [30]. If introduced properly, and with an adequate degree of difficulty, they improve analytical skills such as critical thinking [12], problem-solving [4], and creativity [51].

Third, escape rooms can be used to master communication and team-working skills [4, 11]. Most of the challenges are solved in the groups and proper collaboration is needed to succeed. Educational escape rooms create a chance to develop natural leadership behavior [5], which is important while working with high school students, the target group of *The Inheritor*.

In general, studies show that students enjoy participating in escape rooms, and, at the same time, consider them a valuable learning experience [18, 52, 55]. Escape rooms can produce high levels of enjoyment [23] and engagement [54]. Previous studies found that students prefer educational escape rooms over regular classroom experiences [44, 52]. They can provide a supplemental method for reviewing material [10].

3 Co-design in Escape Rooms

The search for effective learning tools raises questions about appropriate frameworks for the design process. Design itself, as a multifaceted and dynamic construct [55], permeates various domains, including games [i.e. 56, 57] and education [among many: 58, 59, 60]. It influences the creation and evolution of artifacts, systems, and experiences

[61]. Design can be conceptualized as a purposeful and iterative process, encompassing both problem identification and solution generation [62]. More broadly, it is a way to visualize a better future [63, 55] and search for ways to achieve it [61, 64, 65]. Within this framework, co-design emerges as a collaborative paradigm wherein individuals collectively contribute their knowledge, skills, and resources toward accomplishing a shared, and desired future outcome [66].

3.1 Application of Co-design

The statement *design is always co-design* emphasizes the inherently social nature of the design process [67]. Co-design is manifested through diverse approaches, spanning research-oriented methodologies like applied ethnography to design-oriented practices employing generative tools [68]. The emphasis on user involvement ranges from approaches where researchers and designers converge toward users, such as usability testing, to those where users actively engage with researchers and designers, i.e. participatory design. This inclusive approach ensures that collective creativity permeates all the design process [69].

Co-design represents a collective practice where participants engage in collaborative knowledge-sharing [66, 70, 61], combination of skills [i.e. 71], and resource pooling [70, 72] fostering a shared responsibility for design outcomes [73]. This cooperative approach not only facilitates the development and experimentation of innovative ideas related to a specific problem but also entails negotiations surrounding the evolution of these ideas [61]. Consequently, co-design activity transcends the act of designing - it becomes a process of producing new knowledge and shared understanding of the problem.

In contemporary contexts of complex social, political, environmental, educational, and technological challenges, co-design gains significance. The recognition that no single individual possesses the knowledge and skills required to comprehend and solve such multifaceted issues underscores the need for a collaborative approach [68]. Co-design, in this context, becomes an instrument for empowering individuals to actively participate and take control of their own lives and environments [65].

The convergence of diverse individuals, driven together by disparate agendas, needs, knowledge, and skills, characterizes the essence of co-design. Participants unite, overcoming or leveraging their differences, contributing to an exchange of perspectives that enrich the design process [67]. Therefore, the co-design process is not without its ethical dimensions. Ethical considerations become salient in participants' ability to articulate and share their experiences, discuss and negotiate roles and interests, and collectively aim at positive change [72].

Finally, co-design is recognized for effectively addressing complex, *wicked problems*, those that defy clear definition, and resist simple linear resolutions [74]. The existing challenges cannot be solved by individual actors - they require design thinking and collective actions. It draws attention of educators and simulation game designers to co-design or participatory design activities as a great contribution to existing challenges in the area of education.

3.2 Co-design in Simulation Games

Although applied widely in healthcare or public services, co-design still leaves us with questions regarding the process dynamics and the interplay between design elements and the learning experience in terms of simulation games and serious play. Here, we can benefit from rich works on a proximate term, participatory systems modeling, conducted by recognized academics in our field, including prof. Duke [i.e. 75], prof. Klabbers [i.e. 76], or prof. Geurts [i.e. 77]. Under this term, they framed a process actively involving various stakeholders - often representing conflicting views - driven by their experience and clearly defined goals. As a parallel, the iterative nature of co-design, "[…] involves finding as well as solving problems", thus the stakeholders influence the co-evolution of the solutions and framing the problems [62].

In co-design, users, traditionally considered consumers of designed products, experience a transformation within the co-design framework. They transition into co-designers, recognized as experts of their own experiences [66]. Researchers, in turn, assume the role of facilitators, easing users' expression of creativity. Professional designers contribute their expertise in the product under design, and these latter two roles often converge in learning contexts, emphasizing the integrated and synergistic nature of co-design within educational environments. In summary, co-design in games and education represents a collaborative, ethical, and transformative process that not only addresses the challenges of contemporary contexts but also redefines the roles of users, researchers, and designers within the educational landscape.

Summing up, co-design is a broad concept, covering various fields and disciplines. It is characterized by a specific mental discipline - design thinking - focused on an active, creative search for solutions, visualizing and developing tools to address existing challenges with those who experience them. Stakeholders play a central role in the process, however, their participation is facilitated and supported by facilitators, who support them in the non-linear strive for satisfying and ethical outcomes. In reality, the execution of co-design is diverse, so it works as an umbrella term for concepts like participatory game design or systems modeling, which makes those terms mutually informative. Thus, co-design makes space for more subject-specific design methodologies, including game design, which may be applied within this approach.

4 Methodological Assumptions and Principles for the Project

The Inheritor was developed as a non-commercial project for Salam Lab, a peace-promoting NGO. The goal was to explore the roots of various cultural identities of the inhabitants of Poland and reflect upon the cultural diversity with teenagers (15+). The client (NGO) required an ethical approach to the whole process, and the involvement of actors relevant for the stories: Ukrainian migrants, Ukrainian minority in Poland, Polish citizens, Catholics and Orthodox Catholics. Therefore, it required a grasp into the nuances of cultural identity. Since the beginning, we planned to engage actors representing distinct backgrounds. The game design process required a clear structure, comprehensible for the stakeholders. Thus, we adopted the triadic model of game design by Harteveld and Kortmann [78], further developed by Harteveld [79]. It matched the framework of the project due to focus on the particular elements:

reality: represent various existing cultural, historical, ethical and political complexities related to the identities of the actors involved and the stories of their relatives;
meaning: evoke a reflecting process on the meaning of identity, contribute to peace-making beyond borders, and understand of the origin of stereotypes.
play: engage in a playful way high school students and youth to delve into the complexities of cultural identity.

The above-mentioned elements informed further stages of scope definition, design, game-building, and testing (Fig. 1).

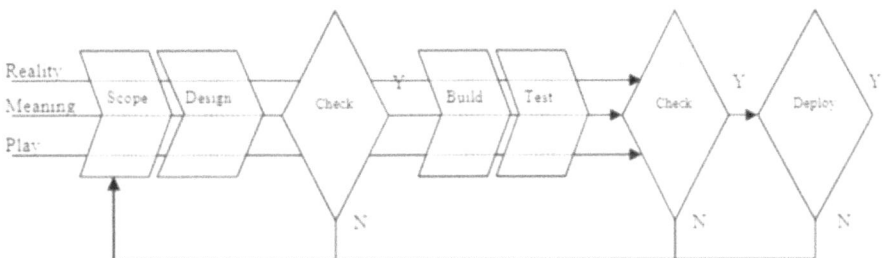

Fig. 1. Triadic Game Design development model [78].

Due to the benefits and inclusive assumptions of co-design, we decided to apply the Harteveld and Kortmann model, however, within a co-design framework. Specifically, we applied a model based on Barbera, Garcia, and Fuertes-Alpiste [80] stages of the co-design process. The stages consisted of the following stages (Fig. 2):

preparation to contextualize the problem, the relevant actors, safety and inclusivity prerequisites;
exploration with the focus on particular shades of the discussed problem, listing the most important cultural and historical threads;
envisionment as the debate on the form of the game, the expected ways of interaction and embodied design;
operationalisation to make physical prototype with the engaged actors who took various roles;
assessment and reflection, as a still on-going process to evaluate the effects of the developed tool.

Following the framework of Barbera, Garcia, and Fuertes-Alpiste [80] we divided the process into workshop-based stages and applied some of the proposed tools for co-design. Also, we ensured the active participation of stakeholders throughout the whole process.

Lastly, the client shared several technical requirements: the game was expected to be easily portable and possible to play at youth festivals, thus it could not be too complicated or facilitation-based. Also, it was planned to be used in high-school classes, so it should accommodate up to 30 players at once.

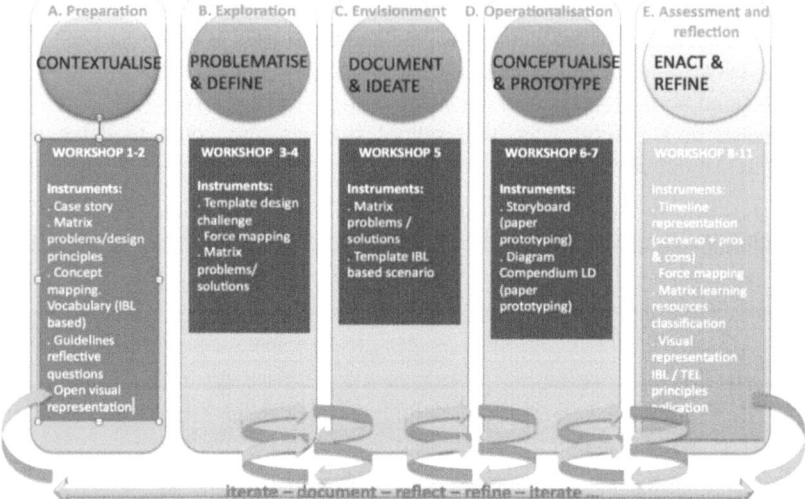

Fig. 2. Co-design process embedded in a design-based research framework [80].

5 The Co-design Process of *The Inheritor* Escape-Room

5.1 Preparation

In *The Inheritor* the preparation process was conducted online as the designer and the client team were located in distinct cities. The preliminary workshops aimed at establishing the meta goal for the game, prerequisites (i.e. technological limitations, target group, applicability), and setting a wider context of the project. It concerned the *meaning* of the tool, educational goals, and the feasible, *playful* game forms, to be co-designed further. The decision to apply co-design principles and develop an edu escape-room was made at that time as a consequence of the design thinking process. To support this process, we deployed open visual representations, deliberated on the case story, and shared reflective questions with the client.

5.2 Exploration

The exploration stage was based on the outcomes of the initial, online kick-off meeting. The on-site workshop was designed in line with the prerequisites, and aimed to delve into the *reality* represented in the game and its *meaning* for the players. The participants were volunteers of the organization of various national, ethnic, and spiritual backgrounds.

The actors together defined the relevant aspects of the past and the present, to be covered by the game story and mechanics, especially in terms of the existing stereotypes, and harmful discourses (Fig. 3). Importantly, at this point, the stakeholders could have impacted the *scope* of the game.

A Framework for Co-design of Edu Escape-Room Aimed   135

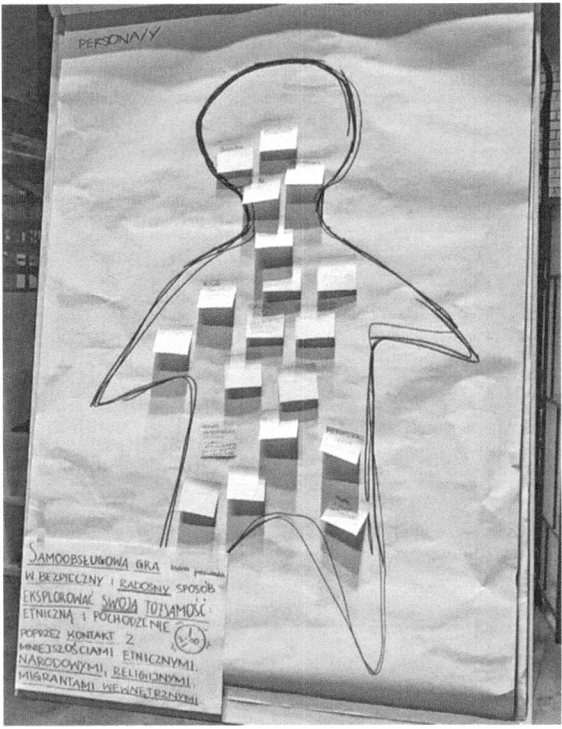

Fig. 3. Problem mapping and envisioning the tool.

5.3 Envisionment

In the second open workshop, participants connected the thematic threads into storyboards (see Fig. 4). They deliberated on what stories, personas and plot twists would reflect the complexity of identities of the inhabitants of Poland, Polish citizens and minorities' representatives. The actors shared their personal stories and commented on how they see it as part of the plot. Moreover, the NGO added threads derived from the research on the integration of Ukrainian minorities in Poland.

During the workshop participants come up with the rules for the game and media for interaction for the players (see Fig. 4). It was facilitated by a researcher/game designer who took care of the inclusive discussion and provided space for all the actors to share their ideas.

5.4 Operationalisation

This stage included a workshop and individual tasks performed by the stakeholders and managed by the NGO. It was the physical prototype building (see Fig. 5) stage as the previous workshops led to the development of a paper-based prototype and storyboards. This stage included several important roles for the stakeholders, which appeared naturally while sharing the tasks:

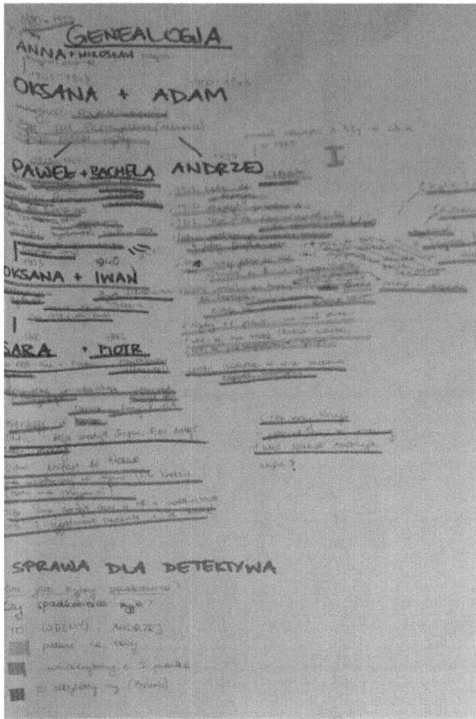

Fig. 4. The threads connected to the family tree of the protagonists with colors representing the clues types.

- **input providers**: suggest content for the materials, i.e. letters to relatives;
- **makers**: create the materials - graphically, manually, or purchase them, i.e. a book with Yiddish folklore poems, fake newspapers;
- **fact-checkers**: verify the information and the reality of the story course, and the quality of the materials;
- **legitimizer**: monitor the ethical, cultural or other implicit consequences of the combination of symbols, stories and meanings in the game.

Some of the roles were overlapping, for instance, fact-checkers or makers legitimized the elements of the game, while makers checked the information generated by input-providers. The iterative process of materials and content development ensured inclusive conditions for the participants, who, additionally, were encouraged to critically approach the game or suggest changes. This stage was supported by regular online calls, to monitor the progress and share reflections.

5.5 Assessment and Reflection

The last stage is still on-going (2024, January), as it includes iterative gameplay and improvements. After having finished the game prototype, we engaged non-engaged people to test the escape-room in three gameplay sessions, 6 testers each. The testers

A Framework for Co-design of Edu Escape-Room Aimed 137

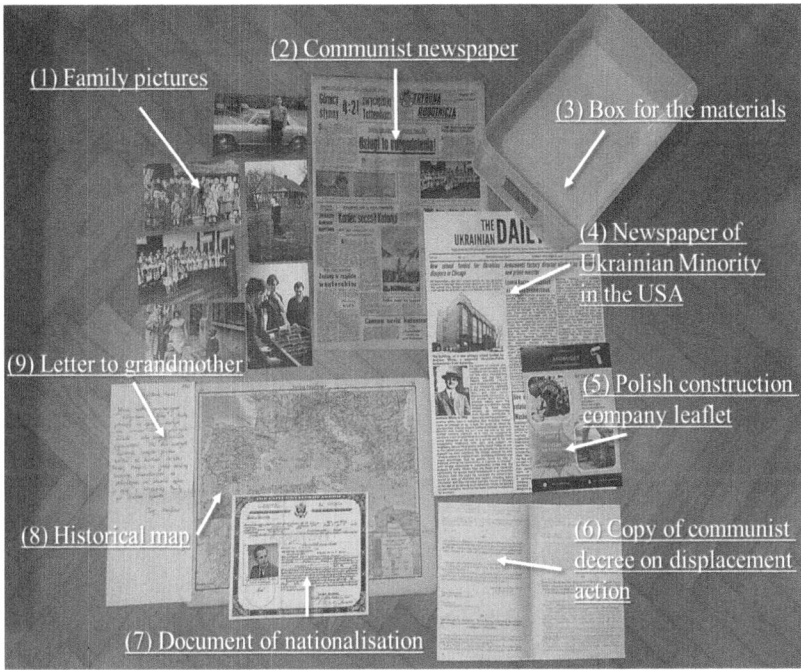

Fig. 5. Part of the edu escape-room materials co-created by the participants.

included representatives of different cultural backgrounds and indicated mostly small mistakes at the level of logic behind the story and the protagonists' rationales.

The initial testing sessions verified the elements from the Kortmann and Hartveld model:

- **reality**: are the narratives convincing? Is the setting realistic, including materials and personas?
- **meaning**: what is the meaning of the play? What reflections come to mind after the gameplay? Was it meaningful for the testers?
- **play**: is it an engaging and playful experience?

In the second iteration, the game was adjusted and played with 25 high school students, who highly appreciated this form of learning. Importantly, in the end, the game is always debriefed with the facilitator (Fig. 6).

The main focus was on the gameplay time and players' engagement as they represented the target group.

5.6 Challenges and Limitations

Although the process was very engaging and fruitful, we encountered some obstacles to be discussed further. Firstly, one of the significant challenges was the historical verification of the stories included in the game and fact-checking. In *The Inheritor*, there are various historical threads [II World War, human displacement, migration, communist

Fig. 6. Measurement board for 4 teams playing simultaneously, with division into three boxes of the escape-room.

era, Ukrainian war, conversions, etc.], thus, despite the memories of the participants, it was important to reach for the historical evidence or the knowledge of experts.

Ethical verification was another important issue as we faced a challenge to deal with culture bias and various, unexpected sensemaking outcomes of the players. The game was multicultural, and included elements in different languages [Polish, Ukrainian, Russian, English], and various symbols, hence we needed the perspectives of people with distinct backgrounds and a process empowering their voices. The management of this task was challenging, so, it was shared by NGO and researcher/co-designer. Importantly, it is still under investigation, despite a recent game release.

The co-design process and design thinking tools evoked generation of numerous excellent ideas. However, it was difficult to narrow down the scope and maintain it at a simple and comprehensible level. Although simplified, the game remained slightly too long.

Finally, one of the core challenges was the availability of stakeholders - due to the voluntary character of the project, some of the participants could not join or engage in part of the activities. It reflects one of the biggest disadvantages of the co-design process - it is significantly time and energy-consuming compared to the traditional game design process.

6 Conclusions

The edu escape-room *The Inheritor* is a successful example of a simulation game co-design project. To achieve this novel combination of simulation game design and edu escape-room, we took advantage of the triadic game design model and adapted the framework for co-design by Barbera, Garcia, and Fuertes-Alpiste [80]. These mutually informing approaches ensured a safe and clear process, engaging and comfortable for the actors involved.

In pragmatic terms, we adopted the structure and tools typical for the co-design process, nevertheless, the content of the sessions, their assumptions and the outcomes were driven by the Harteveld and Kortmann model, which was carefully monitored by the researcher/facilitator.

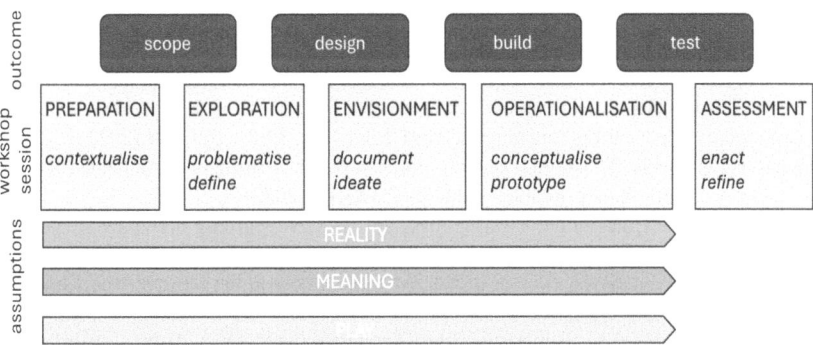

Fig. 7. The new model of simulation game co-design process based on Harteveld and Kortmann [78] and Barbera, Garcia, and Fuertes-Alpiste [80] and the project outcomes.

The participants, representatives or agents of the story threads, build the game model and participate in initial testing. They are free to suggest additional design stages, forms, or elements. Further tests and evaluations are executed with external participants. The manifestations of reality, meaning and play are deliberated among the co-design group and agreed on explicitly (Fig. 7). However, it is the role of the facilitator to monitor whether these elements are considered in the further stages. In this case, the role of facilitator, researcher, and game designer was played by one person, who took responsibility for the process structure. She paid attention to the focus of the project and the comprehensibility of the game elements, adapting the so-called helicopter view.

Feedback of game co-designers as well as from test groups [to be published in a wider study] shows that the co-design approach to game development led to a meaningful experience within an authentic insight into cultural identity. We recommend this approach for projects involving non-linear storytelling, interactive narratives or embodied design. It benefits from the inclusive approach embedded in co-design methods and stages, while addressing the challenges of game design. In the new model, the scope is co-designed with the client and relevant stakeholders, who also influence the design *per se*. It assures the innovative, synergic outcomes, as well as the development of rich, transboundary stories.

Acknowledgments. The study was conducted in partnership with Salam Lab.

Disclosure of Interests. Authors have no competing interests.

References

1. Díaz, D.A., Clapper, T.C.: Escape rooms: a novel strategy whose time has come. Simul. Gaming **52**(1), 3–6 (2021)
2. Kutzin, J.M.: Escape the room: Innovative approaches to interprofessional education. J. Nurs. Educ. **58**(8), 474–480 (2019)
3. Nicholson, S.: Peeking behind the locked door: a survey of escape room facilities (2015)
4. Nicholson, S.: Creating engaging escape rooms for the classroom. Child. Educ. **94**(1), 44–49 (2018)
5. Fotaris, P., Mastoras, T.: Escape rooms for learning: a systematic review. In: Proceedings of the European Conference on Games Based Learning, pp. 235–243 (2019)
6. Taraldsen, L.H., Haara, F.O., Lysne, M.S., Jensen, P.R., Jenssen, E.S.: A review on use of escape rooms in education–touching the void. Educ. Inq. **13**(2), 169–184 (2022)
7. Fotaris, P., Mastoras, T.: Room2Educ8: a framework for creating educational escape rooms based on design thinking principles. Educ. Sci. **12**, 768 (2022)
8. López-Pernas, S.: Educational escape rooms are effective learning activities across educational levels and contexts: a meta-analysis. IEEE Trans. Learn. Technol. (2023)
9. Kroski, E.: Escape rooms and other immersive experiences in the library. American Library Association (2018)
10. Anderson, M., Lioce, L., Robertson, J.M., Lopreiato, J.O., Díaz, D.A.: Toward defining healthcare simulation escape rooms. Simul. Gaming **52**(1), 7–17 (2021)
11. Grande-de-Prado, M., García-Martín, S., Baelo, R., Abella-García, V.: Edu-escape rooms. Encyclopedia **1**(1), 12–19 (2020)
12. Vygotsky, L.S., Cole, M.: Mind in society: development of higher psychological processes. Harvard University Press (1978)
13. Adams, V., Burger, S., Crawford, K., Setter, R.: Can you escape? Creating an escape room to facilitate active learning. J. Nurses Prof. Dev. **34**(2), E1–E5 (2018)
14. McLaughlin, J.L., Reed, J.A., Shiveley, J., Lee, S.: Escape room blueprint: central orientation contagion crisis. Simul. Gaming **52**(1), 24–30 (2021)
15. Spears, S., Díaz, G.M., Diaz, D.A.: A community pediatric camp escape room: an interactive approach to applying real-life critical thinking skills. Simul. Gaming **52**(1), 31–39 (2021)
16. Sanders, J.E., Kutzin, J., Strother, C.G.: Escape the simulation room. Simul. Gaming **52**(1), 62–71 (2021)
17. Friedrich, C., Teaford, H., Taubenheim, A., Boland, P., Sick, B.: Escaping the professional silo: an escape room implemented in an interprofessional education curriculum. J. Interprof. Care **33**(5), 573–575 (2019)
18. Hermanns, M., Deal, B., Hillhouse, S., Opella, J.B., Faigle, C., Campbell IV, R.H.: Using an "escape room" toolbox approach to enhance pharmacology education (2017)
19. Boysen-Osborn, M., Paradise, S., Suchard, J:. The toxiscape hunt: an escape room-scavenger hunt for toxicology education. J. Educ. Teach. Emerg. Med. **3**(1) (2018)
20. Aubeux, D., et al.: Educational gaming for dental students: design and assessment of a pilot endodontic-themed escape game. Eur. J. Dent. Educ. **24**(3), 449–457 (2020)
21. David, K., et al.: Twelve tips for creating an escape room activity for medical education. Med. Teach. **44**, 366–371 (2022)

22. Smith, M.M., Davis, R.G.: Can you escape? The pharmacology review virtual escape room. Simul. Gaming **52**(1), 79–87 (2021)
23. Valdes, B., Mckay, M., Sanko, J.S.: The impact of an escape room simulation to improve nursing teamwork, leadership and communication skills: a pilot project. Simul. Gaming **52**(1), 54–61 (2021)
24. Peleg, R., Yayon, M., Katchevich, D., Moria-Shipony, M., Blonder, R.: A lab-based chemical escape room: educational, mobile, and fun! J. Chem. Educ. **96**(5), 955–960 (2019)
25. Piñero Charlo, J.C.: Educational escape rooms as a tool for horizontal mathematization: learning process evidence. Educ. Sci. **10**(9), 213 (2020)
26. Veldkamp, A., Daemen, J., Teekens, S., Koelewijn, S., Knippels, M.C.P., van Joolingen, W.R.: Escape boxes: bringing escape room experience into the classroom. Br. J. Edu. Technol. **51**(4), 1220–1239 (2020)
27. Dietrich, N.: Escape classroom: the leblanc process—an educational "escape game." J. Chem. Educ. **95**(6), 996–999 (2018)
28. Elford, D., Lancaster, S.J., Jones, G.A.: Stereoisomers, not stereo enigmas: a stereochemistry escape activity incorporating augmented and immersive virtual reality. J. Chem. Educ. **98**, 1691–1704 (2021)
29. Borrego, C., Fernández, C., Blanes, I., Robles, S.: Room escape at class: escape games activities to facilitate the motivation and learning in computer science. J. Technol. Sci. Educ. **7**(2), 162–171 (2017)
30. Ho, A.M.: Unlocking ideas: using escape room puzzles in a cryptography classroom. Primus **28**(9), 835–847 (2018)
31. López-Pernas, S., Gordillo, A., Barra, E., Quemada, J.: Examining the use of an educational escape room for teaching programming in a higher education setting. IEEE Access **7**, 31723–31737 (2019)
32. López-Pernas, S., Gordillo, A., Barra, E., Quemada, J.: Comparing face-to-face and remote educational escape rooms for learning programming. IEEE Access **9**, 59270–59285 (2021)
33. Ouariachi, T., Wim, E.J.: Escape rooms as tools for climate change education: an exploration of initiatives. Environ. Educ. Res. **26**(8), 1193–1206 (2020)
34. Duncan, K.J.: Examining the effects of immersive game-based learning on student engagement and the development of collaboration, communication, creativity and critical thinking. TechTrends **64**(3), 514–524 (2020)
35. Craig, C., Ngondo, P.S., Devlin, M., Scharlach, J.: Escaping the routine: unlocking group intervention. Commun. Teach. **34**(1), 14–18 (2020)
36. Urbieta, A.S., Peñalver, E.A.: Escaping from the English classroom. Who will get out first? Aloma: revista de psicologia, ciències de l'educació i de l'esport Blanquerna **37**(2), 83–92 (2019)
37. Berthod, F., Bouchoud, L., Grossrieder, F., Falaschi, L., Senhaji, S., Bonnabry, P.: Learning good manufacturing practices in an escape room: validation of a new pedagogical tool. J. Oncol. Pharm. Pract. **26**(4), 853–860 (2020)
38. Novak, J., Lozos, J.C., Spear, S.E.: Development of an interactive escape room intervention to educate college students about earthquake preparedness. Nat. Hazard. Rev. **20**(1), 06018001 (2019)
39. Loffler, E., Schneider, B., Zanwar, T., Asprion, P. M.: Cysecescape 2.0 – a virtual escape room to raise cybersecurity awareness. Int. J. Serious Games **8**, 59–70 (2021)
40. Babazadeh, M., Botturi, L., Reggiani, G.: Let's jazz: a case study on teaching music with educational escape rooms. In: Proceedings of the 16th European Conference on Games Based Learning, ECGBL, Lisbon (2022)
41. von Kotzebue, L., Zumbach, J., Brandlmayr, A.: Digital escape rooms as game-based learning environments: a study in sex education. Multimodal Technol. Interact. **6**(2), 8 (2022)

42. Koenig, N., Denk, N., Wimmer, S., Prandstaetter, H.: Creating an escape room for cultural mediation: insights from "the archivist's dream". In: Proceedings of the 16th European Conference on Games Based Learning, ECGBL, Lisbon, Portugal (2022)
43. Sarage, D., O'Neill, B.J., Eaton, C.M.: There is no I in escape: using an escape room simulation to enhance teamwork and medication safety behaviors in nursing students. Simul. Gaming **52**(1), 40–53 (2021)
44. Walsh, B., Spence, M.: Leveraging escape room popularity to provide first-year students with an introduction to engineering information. In: Proceedings of the Canadian Engineering Education Association (CEEA) (2018)
45. Cain, J.: Exploratory implementation of a blended format escape room in a large enrollment pharmacy management class. Curr. Pharm. Teach. Learn. **11**(1), 44–50 (2019)
46. Guo, Y.R., Goh, D.H.L., Luyt, B.: Tertiary students' acceptance of a game to teach information literacy. Aslib J. Inf. Manag. **69**(1), 46–63 (2017)
47. Mystakidis, S., Christopoulos, A.: Teacher perceptions on virtual reality escape rooms for stem education. Information **13**(3), 136 (2022)
48. Moreno-Fuentes, E.: The "Breakout EDU" as a key tool for the gamification in the initial training of teachers. Edutec. Rev. Electrón. Tecnol. Educ. 66–79 (2019)
49. Schaffhauser, D.: Breakout! Gaming to learn. The Journal **44**(4), 6–11 (2021)
50. Csikszentmihalyi, M.: Flow. The Psychology of Optimal Experience. New York (Harper-Perennial) (1990)
51. Foster, T., Warwick, S.: Nostalgia, gamification and staff development–moving staff training away from didactic delivery. Res. Learn. Technol. **26** (2018)
52. Gómez-Urquiza, J. L., Gómez-Salgado, J., Albendín-García, L., Correa-Rodríguez, M., González-Jiménez, E., Cañadas-De la Fuente, G.A.: The impact on nursing students' opinions and motivation of using a "Nursing Escape Room" as a teaching game: a descriptive study. Nurse Educ. Today **72**, 73–76 (2019)
53. Eukel, H., Morrell, B.: Ensuring educational escape-room success: the process of designing, piloting, evaluating, redesigning, and re-evaluating educational escape rooms. Simul. Gaming **52**(1), 18–23 (2021)
54. Zhang, X.C., Diemer, G., Lee, H., Jaffe, R., Papanagnou, D.: Finding the 'QR' to patient safety: applying gamification to incorporate patient safety priorities through a simulated 'escape room' experience. Cureus **11**(2) (2019)
55. Erlhoff, M., Marshall, T.: DESIGN. In: Erlhoff, M., Marshall, T. (ed.) Design Dictionary: Perspectives on Design Terminology, Berlin, Boston: Birkhäuser, pp. 101–106 (2008)
56. Jacobs, G., Ip, B.: Establishing user requirements: incorporating gamer preferences into interactive games design. Des. Stud. **26**, 243–255 (2005)
57. Mitgutsch, K., Alvarado, N.: Purposeful by design? A serious game design assessment framework. In: Proceedings of the International Conference on the Foundations of Digital Games, pp. 121–128 (2012)
58. Koper, R., Olivier, B.: Representing the learning design of units of learning. J. Educ. Technol. Soc. **7**(3), 97–111 (2004)
59. Britain, S.: A review of learning design: concept, specifications and tools. A report for the JISC E-learning Pedagogy Programme (2006)
60. Gravemeijer, K., Cobb, P.: Design research from a learning design perspective. In: Educational Design Research, pp. 29–63. Routledge (2006)
61. Zamenopoulos, T., Alexiou, K.: Co-design as collaborative research (2018)
62. Lawson, B.: How Designers Think – The Design Process Demystified. University Press, Cambridge (2006)
63. Simon, H.A.: The science of design: creating the artificial. Des. Issues **4**(1/2), 79 (1988)
64. Brown, T.: Design thinking. Harv. Bus. Rev. **86**, 84–92 (2008)

65. Dorst, K.: Frame Innovation: Create New Thinking by Design. The MIT Press, Cambridge (2015)
66. Dodero, G., Melonio, A., Gennari, R.: Gamified co-design with cooperative learning. In: Proceedings of the Extended Abstracts of the 32nd Annual ACM Conference on Human Factors in Computing Systems - CHI EA 2014 (2014)
67. Bucciarelli, L.: Designing Engineers. MIT Press, Cambridge (1994)
68. Steen, M., Manschot, M., De Koning, N.: Benefits of co-design in service design projects. Int. J. Des. **5**(2) (2011)
69. Sanders, E.B.N., Stappers, P.J.: Co-creation and the new landscapes of design. CoDesign **4**(1), 5–18 (2008)
70. Moser, S.: Can science on transformation transform science? Lessons from co-design, current opinion. Environ. Sustain. **20**, 106–115 (2016)
71. Pirinen, A.: The barriers and enablers of co-design for services. Int. J. Des. **10**(3), 27–42 (2016)
72. David, S., Sabiescu, A.G., Cantoni, L.: Co-design with communities. A reflection on the literature. In: Proceedings of the 7th International Development Informatics Association Conference, Pretoria, pp. 152–166 (2013)
73. Goodyear-Smith, F., Jackson, C., Greenhalgh, T.: Co-design and implementation research: challenges and solutions for ethics committees. BMC Med. Ethics **16**(1), 1–5 (2015)
74. Steen, M.: Co-design as a process of joint inquiry and imagination. Des. Issues **29**(2), 16–28 (2013)
75. Duke, R.D.: Gaming: The future's language. SAGE Pubications (1974)
76. Klabbers, J.H.G.: The Magic Circle: Principles of Gaming & Simulation. Sense Publishers, Rotterdam (2006)
77. Duke, R.D., Geurts, J.: Policy Games for Strategic Management. Rozenberg Publishers, The Netherlands (2004)
78. Harteveld, C., Kortmann, R.: Triadic Game Design workshop. ISAGA Conference (2009)
79. Harteveld, C.: Triadic Game Design - Balancing Reality, Meaning and Play. Springer (2011)
80. Barbera, E., Garcia, I., Fuertes-Alpiste, M.: A Co-design process microanalysis: stages and facilitators of an inquiry-based and technology-enhanced learning scenario. Int. Rev. Res. Open Distrib. Learn. **18**(6) (2017)

Theory Informing Practice – Theorizing Good Facilitation Practice

Elyssebeth Leigh[1(✉)] and Laurie L. Levesque[2]

[1] University of Technology Sydney, Sydney, NSW 2007, Australia
`elyssebeth.leigh@icloud.com`
[2] Suffolk University, Boston, MA, USA

Abstract. While being a competent facilitator is accepted as a vital skill for effective use of simulations and games for learning, the theory behind good practice is less often examined critically. This paper considers theories underlying the *what* and *why* of enactment of facilitation, drawing on work from fields as diverse as adult learning, knowledge management, philosophy, physics and organisational behaviour. It explores relationships among these theories as presented in the book 'Facilitating Simulations' [13]. A framework for exploring connections - and gaps - between theory and practice is introduced to identify and strengthen connections between theoretical formulations of concepts and practical applications of resulting propositions.

Key concepts introduced, include mapping the learning journey from novice to expert, developing a preparedness mindset, clarifying underlying values and beliefs informing well-known modes of education, factors influencing curriculum design, and ways in which knowledge creation is modelled and managed. For facilitators who find they are already unconsciously enacting many of these precepts, becoming consciously aware can improve practice. Conversely newcomers to facilitation can find ideas for shaping behaviour to better accord with good practice requirements.

Keywords: Facilitation · Good practice · Theoretical underpinnings

1 Introduction

There is a growing body of knowledge about information and skills required by people wishing to employ *good practice* as facilitators of simulation and games. However, there is less attention paid to the theory underlying good facilitation practice, not necessarily because it does not exist, but because it is spread across a diverse collection of disciplines and the overriding intent of research has largely been on improving the quality of practice by seeking answers to the questions of 'what' and 'how' rather than 'why'. To address this gap, we have focused for the past few years on collating material for a framework drawing together the threads for a coherent and expanding network of theories to inform the use of good practices for facilitating simulations and games. This article reports on our current contribution to such a body of knowledge to help practitioners - both novices and experts - update their practice as simulations and games facilitators, and to guide researcher/theorists towards a better appreciation of how practices are being informed by their theories.

2   Working Within a 'Good Practice' Framework

The term *pedagogy* - whose generic meaning "comes from the Greek word paidagogos, a combination of 'paidos' (child) and 'agogos' (leader)" [20] - is often used to describe 'educational principles' in general, however this usage obscures the reality of differences in the interests and learning capabilities of younger and older human beings. Work on developing and naming adult learning principles has been evolving for two hundred years (and more!) such that today there is more awareness - and acceptance - that adults approach learning in ways that differ from those used to educate children. Consequently, the terms *andragogy* and *heutagogy* have emerged and are accepted as more valid and accurate terms for describing educational principles and practices relevant to working with adult learners [2].

Building on these two concepts we combine them with a 'good practice' framework as the beginning point for exploring theories informing facilitation as practice, skill, and capability. Applying concepts from the Cynefin domains of knowledge [18, 19], we consider that a '*good* practice' framework is preferable to a '*best* practice' one which can only be applied to highly contextualised situations whose features remain similar over time. In contrast, each facilitation context is unique, and learners' needs and goals are seldom the same, so the self-similarity of 'best practice' is rarely found in facilitation contexts. Further than this, immersion in simulation-based learning environments creates the potential for participants to be/become creators of their own unique knowledge. Thus, concepts of knowledge creation see for example Nonaka et al., [16] as a characteristic of simulations is a further cause for considering facilitation as an exercise of 'good practice' and not 'best practice'.

To date our work has resulted in publication of the book 'Facilitating Simulations' [13] as a contribution to Edward Elgar's *Teaching Methods in Business* series. To address the criteria for publication in that series we focused on three elements: a) a Conceptual and theoretical framework, b) Considerations of Context, and c) How to Prepare for Facilitation. Because of the anticipated needs of the intended audience (business and organisation behaviour academics mainly in the USA) the second and third elements are directed towards answering 'what' and 'how' questions that arise when academics consider engaging with more active teaching/learning strategies. The first component – providing readers with a conceptual and theoretical framework with which to build a 'good practice' teaching strategy – is the focus of this paper.

Facilitators are expected to operate effectively and efficiently in learning contexts requiring flexibility, adaptability, and contextual awareness. Practice is essential to achieving such competence, and work requirements usually leave little time for the luxury of thoughtful reflection. Conversely, time spent in careful research can provide insights and guidance to improve practice and assure practitioners of the quality of their work. However, the time lag required to complete such research means it is less often available in timely practice-oriented ways. This can mean that the distance between practitioner and researcher perspectives feels like an uncrossable chasm, while finding a way to bridge the gap can help all parties improve their respective contributions. We therefore introduce a 'third perspective' from which to examine possible means for improving communication between the perspectives of action (practice) and reflection/analysis (research).

2.1 Employing a Third Perspective

This paper – and the book it introduces – is intended to provide busy practitioners with essential theoretical research to inform and support their practice. The 'third perspective' presented below outlines a way to replace a didactic 'teaching' mindset with a learning-oriented approach combining a focus on practice (managing a simulation) with the curiosity of a researcher wanting to better understand the mechanics of the process as a whole.

In her 2004 doctoral dissertation [11] explored the very different perspectives of Practitioners (focused on practice) and Researchers (focused on theory) and concluded there is scope for a 'meeting of minds' in the shape of a third perspective. She identified this as a 'PractitionerResearcher' stance – which is often developed through life experiences, coupled with factors like curiosity and appreciation of complexity. Table 1 summarises the positions of Practitioner, Researcher and PractitionerResearcher in relation to five key educational concerns and interests.

Completion of that work led to a renewed focus on Practitioner interests and the urge to collect information about theoretical concepts and models continued to inform that practice. However, as is often the habit of good Practitioners, relevant theories and concepts continued to be taken up and applied where it suited identified learning needs but were less often considered in the manner of those having a Theorist orientation.

2.2 Facilitation as Practice and Doing

Using a competency-based approach, Kortman and Peters [10] established a well-grounded model for the practice of facilitation. They called the role 'unseen helmsman' to indicate the importance of unobtrusive facilitator behaviour during the use of simulations for learning. Their model of facilitator competencies (first proposed in 2017) included the following list of expected knowledges:

- Game-specific knowledge
- Procedural game facilitation knowledge
- Game session related knowledge
- Domain knowledge
- Knowledge about players
- Practical/logistic knowledge

Perhaps because this approach is based on competency concepts there is no accompanying list of theoretical concepts from such domains as education, philosophy, or human behaviour. This is not to criticise the model or the concepts underlying this vital work of defining the role and practice of facilitating simulations. Indeed, Kortman and Peters' work has been vital in prompting awareness of the complex set of expectations in regard to effective facilitation.

Table 1. Comparing Practitioner, Researcher and PractitionerResearcher concerns

Feature/concern	Practitioner	Researcher	PractitionerResearcher
Primary orientation	... *to complete work tasks* and achieve immediate goals; deems research to be useful only when directly relevant to practice	... *to identify questions worthy of investigation;* to develop insights into the results of practice; to create new knowledge and understanding of widest possible benefit	... *first to practice; then to research and achieve integration of the two* A broader perspective than a pure practitioner focus, and more practical than 'pure' research
Curiosity	... is driven by work needs, not by any *need to know* for its own sake	... is driven by *need to know* for its own sake, less concern for practical applications	... is simultaneously driven by work needs as much as the *need to know*. Believes each informs the other, values interconnectedness as essential to a unified approach to action
Questions	... are about how to act; unconcerned by potential for creating new knowledge	... are to generate new knowledge; less interested in applications of results derived from research	... are about how to *apply* new knowledge and the capacity to generate it from *within* practice
Method Purity and Degree of Verifiability	Driven by pragmatic needs, unconcerned by *objective* verifiability. Method's purity is less vital than quick access and application	Driven by a primary concern for ability to verify research methods or findings. Need to demonstrate that research methodology conforms to standards	Driven first by the pragmatic stance of practitioners in re-usability of knowledge. And then alert to benefits of research for justifying and supporting practice
Time frames	Aligned to fast returns on time/effort invested and immediate needs of client or employer. Less interested in long term	More interested in long time frames, completing complex projects, developing information about trends illustrating generalisable implications of research results	Addresses concurrent time frames: meeting immediate goals and appreciating benefit of research practice for mid-term improvements and long-term understanding and change

Each of the items in their list has its own set of supporting theories, which together create a large body of knowledge for busy practitioners to absorb and employ. These do not extend sufficiently to include consideration of relevant educational theories that underlie facilitation practices. This relative absence of attention to educational theory for informing good practice is the focus of our work.

3 Bridging the Gap

With this gap in mind, we begin our exploration and consider three approaches to shaping learning processes and link these to a method for choosing facilitator behaviour to suit specific learning contexts and goals. Employing andragogical and heutagogical concepts rather than pedagogical ones provides a starting point for exploring the educational concepts involved. Both terms shift attention to addressing what the learner understands about their needs rather than focusing on formal and external expectations about what is 'to be taught'.

Andragogy and heutagogy are terms relatively recent in origin while pedagogy has a much longer history. Andragogy was coined by the German educator Alexander Kapp in 1833 and developed by another German philosopher and adult educator Eugen Rosenstock-Huessy whose writing and work in the USA helped to popularize awareness of the need to think differently about adult educators. While the use of simulations and games for learning is clearly not confined to work with adult learners, appreciating adult learning principles is relevant to understanding theories underpinning facilitation skills development. This is particularly important because of the way they shift attention from the *content* to the *process* of learning. Malcolm Knowles is a well-known advocate of adult learning principles and in 1984 he summarised these principles as follows:

1. Adults need to be involved in the planning and evaluation of their instruction.
2. Experience (including mistakes) provides the basis for the learning activities.
3. Adults are most interested in learning subjects that have immediate relevance and impact to their job or personal life.

    Adult learning is problem-centered rather than content-oriented [3].

Attending to these principles enables facilitators to choose activities that will resonate with participants. Doing so also guides and shapes their behaviour towards other learners who are often their peers in terms of such things as age and life experiences.

Heutagogical concepts Kenyon & Haze [9] are a more recent addition to ways of understanding how to provide appropriate environments relevant to the needs and interests of 21st century learners. In terms of its effects when employed, heutagogy as an extension of andragogy increases the emphasis on the learner's role and responsibility in the learning process. Blaschke (2012 p61) represents the features of heutagogy and andragogy as a continuum as shown in Table 2.

Table 2. Heutagogy as a Continuum of Andragogy

Andragogy (self-directed learning)	Heutagogy (self-determined)
Single loop (practice)	Double-loop (reflection on experience)
Competency development	Capability development
Linear design and learning approach	Nonlinear design and learning approach
Instructor-learner directed	Learner-directed
Helping students to learn content	helping students understand how (process)

Theory Informing Practice – Theorizing Good Facilitation Practice   149

Each element in Balschke's table represents a separate and complex set of theoretical work about learning, some of which we have incorporated into our work, with some still awaiting further exploration and analysis. In effect the two conceptual frameworks of andragogy and heutagogy together completely reframe the educator's role and position facilitators of simulations and games in a space that is unfamiliar and may even be daunting for those more used to being a 'teacher' with ultimate control over choices about all things educational e.g., content to be memorized, process to be used while doing so.

The values underlying pedagogy, andragogy, and heutagogy [1, 5, 8] differ in some irreconcilable ways. Pedagogy positions the learner as 'less than' and 'un-informed' and regards the minds of learners as a kind of tabula rasa, i.e., a blank slate on which to write 'new' knowledge. Andragogy in contrast positions learners as self-motivated and autonomous individual who are able to choose what to 'write' on that slate and can do so with the educator as guide. Heutagogy takes that further and positions educators of adult as being managers of learning opportunities for self-managing learners (Table 3).

Table 3. Adapted version of John Heron's model of Facilitator Dimensions and Power Modes

		Ways of engaging		
	Power / Facilitation Dimensions	**Hierarchical** — Educator - thinks and acts on behalf of the group	**Cooperative** — Educator guides group towards self-direction	**Autonomous** — Educator does not do things for or to the group
	Planning - Relates to group's aims, and how to fulfil them.	Educator - makes all decisions	Educator - engages learners who contribute to decisions about methods and content.	Educator - is as resource. Learners decide on methods and content.
	Meaning - About making sense of an experience, knowing what to do and how to react.	Educator - tells the meaning and directs responses to content.	Learners - develop their own meanings. Educator guides talk about options.	Learners - derive personal meaning from experiences. Educator observes.
Factors to be managed	**Confronting** - raising awareness of a group's resistance to/avoidance of things it must deal with.	Educator - identifies presence of resistance/avoidance names it.	Educator - and/or learner may identify resistance/avoidance.	Anyone - can name resistance/avoidance behaviors and group finds ways to respond.
	Feeling - about managing feeling in a group.	Educator - has charge of emotional quotient throughout	Feelings - can be named by anyone and handling them is decided by mutual agreement	Feelings - are acknowledged and individuals name and address their own emotions.
	Structuring - what will be the form of experiences in a group and how will they be structured.	Educator - makes all decisions about how learning is structured	Decisions - on learning structures are carried out together	Group - is responsible for decisions on structuring learning.
	Valuing - about integrity; creating a supportive climate; staying in touch with true needs and interests.	Educator's values - determine the climate	Values - are named and decisions made after due consideration of all issues identified	No - one person has priority in shaping issues such as integrity.

In his work on the roles and tasks of the facilitator, John Heron (1999) chose to look at the respective behaviour and responsibilities of learners and educators using the two key dimensions of 'ways of engaging' and 'factors to be managed'. He locates ways of engaging with learners along a continuum from Hierarchical through Cooperative to Autonomous. From this perspective, hierarchical and pedagogical stances are similar since both position the learner as someone to whom an educator *does things,* i.e., by retaining control of all of the factors to be managed. Andragogy, in contrast, shifts power relationships by incorporating management of learning into a cooperative relationship, while heutagogy creates an environment where learners can employ autonomy as individuals and/or as a group.

Heron's perspective offers a framework for working out the *how* and *when* of managing interactions in educational contexts. Taking his insights into account means that both educators and learners are, or become aware of, current and approaching power shifts and are able to adjust their responses to align with emerging relationships among learning needs, capabilities, stages of group development and desired learning outcomes. Thus, he helps to explain 'why' facilitators do certain things – take specific actions – as the simulation process unfolds.

Expert facilitators of simulations and games for learning who begin as novices and persist in using the tools, despite encounters with hazards and failures, gain expertise through trial and error, use of reflective practice, and extensive preparation prior to using an activity. Novices, immersed in perceptions of primacy of their authority over the learning process may find themselves hesitant to begin, being fearful of the relative uncertainty of outcomes. Heron does not advocate for any one of the three modes as more/less valuable than any other, while advising novices and newcomers to become familiar with all three as potential strategies for supporting learners and then building expertise in choosing an approach that best suits their educational philosophy, the maturity of participants, along with identified/agreed learning goals and relevant contextual factors.

Thus, facilitators of simulations and games for learning who read this abbreviated version of his work should quickly see that, by choosing an activity without seeking participants' prior agreement, they are exercising hierarchical authority within the planning dimension. It is also possible to see how (and why) it can be important to delay decisions about modes of engagement in regard to Heron's other factors (e.g. 'meaning making', 'feelings', and 'valuing') until they and the participants are sufficiently immersed in the learning process. Being able to do so requires both thoughtful planning and flexible preparedness to shift one's stance and thinking to accord with participants' emerging understanding and evolving awareness of personal/group beliefs and insights.

Returning to the matter of bridging the gap between theory and practice, it is clear that understanding and applying the principles of andragogy and/or heutagogy using Heron's framework can provide practitioners with a flexible theoretical framework for informing and shaping their practice.

4 Developing a Preparedness Mindset

Designers of simulations and games for learning are at pains to specify the focus, and suitable conditions, for use of their designs. This means that no single activity will be suitable for all occasions. Heraclitus - as explored by von Oech [21] - first advised us of this by counselling that 'No man ever steps in the same river twice, for it's not the same river and he's not the same man.' In parallel, we propose that 'no two runs of a simulation or game are exactly the same, for this is not the same moment and these are not the same participants.' Drawing on research and practice in fields as diverse as healthcare and disaster management we propose that facilitators benefit from developing a *preparedness mindset* to achieve a flexible and responsive approach to choosing and using simulations or games in their educational practice. Key characteristics of such a mindset are:

1. An ongoing state of anticipation and readiness.
    There is no room for complacency when using simulations or games.
2. Proactively evaluate all aspects of the learners, the simulation, and the context of each simulation's deployment.
    Remember these will never be exactly the same.
3. Vigilance in anticipating how each enactment of a simulation will be unique in some ways and familiar in others.
    Being aware of simulation enactments as both 'the same' and 'different' can dramatically reduce the risk of unexpected disasters.

This kind of mindset takes time to develop, and novice facilitators can expect to make mistakes as they progress. Use of reflective practice, rehearsal, and conversations with peers and more expert facilitators are all ways of developing the necessary skills. The unwelcome alternative to a preparedness mindset can be the unexpected discovery that some unanticipated event has destabilised an activity's potential for creating a relevant learning experience.

It is important to note in this regard that individual examples of simulations and games for learning may be developed for a specific context and then adapted for use in quite different settings. This is not to suggest that an activity could become universally applicable but does suggest that the best activity for a desired learning outcome may be found in disciplinary settings that initially appear to be far removed from the actual learning context. An example of this is 'The Road Game' [15] which was first presented as an activity for helping young children understand the nature of political borders. It has since been employed successfully with adult members of organisational units needing to become collaborative after extended periods of competition. Although initially a primary school activity, it has had great success in adult learning contexts. Such crossing of contextual borders requires an alertness to the potential and flexibility of simulations and games and a willingness to look well beyond one's own familiar boundaries. Being ready and able to experiment, explore, and investigate is one trademark of an expert facilitator of simulations who has developed that necessary preparedness mindset.

5 Building Expertise – from Novice to Expert

This leads to our final theme in this paper – the development of facilitation expertise as a lifelong learning journey drawing on experiences, reflection, analysis, discussion and the unexpectedness of failures that teach. Anyone with experience of healthcare services will be aware of the expectations we have about the expertise of those attending to our needs. As nursing education became professionalized, Benner explored what happened as new students entered and progressed through their training. The four stages of performance improvement that she identified are summarised in our book thus:

1. moving *from* relying on abstract principles and rules, *to* use of past, concrete experiences – that is from knowing *about* to knowing *what*
2. expanding capability away *from* reliance on analytic, rule-based thinking *to* employment of intuitive (tacit) knowledge – that is, applying knowledge that is holistic rather than sequential
3. changing learners' view of a situation *from* perceiving it as a compilation of equally relevant bits to an increasingly complex whole, where only certain parts are relevant – in effect becoming able to think holistically
4. no longer being a detached observer standing outside the situation, instead being positively involved, and fully engaged in the situation – and thus able to see both the whole and its relevant parts [13].

In effect Benner was able to describe how nursing skills are built over time, through repetition, engaging with reflective practice and requiring commitment to the process beyond merely observing it. We contend that the same phases occur for those building facilitation expertise and further propose that, as Nonaka et al. [16] demonstrated, this is a knowledge creation and building process going well beyond mere absorption of information. Lived experiences contribute to the building of skills and knowledge and this inevitably involves engaging with failures as much as successes. Expert facilitators may not 'celebrate' their failures but will often talk about them as the moments when new insights and capabilities emerge.

This, in turn, emphasizes the value of storytelling as a skill building tool. In our book we employ a number of anecdotes provided by expert facilitators who are able to describe such moments and explain how they have contributed to an increase in awareness and capability in managing the complexity and challenges of the role. Expertise is a growing, shifting ever-changing proficiency and, as Sellman [17] notes in regard to nursing, experts can sometimes find themselves back in a novice state because of a change in their situation or role. Writing our book into existence was one such transition and we look forward to more as we continue our own journeys, while wishing readers success in their own and – above all – a willingness and capacity to embrace failures and challenges alongside their successes.

6 Future Explorations

We noted above that each pair of elements in Blaschke's table aligning andragogy and heutagogy represent a separate and complex set of theoretical work about adult learning, some of which we have incorporated into our work, while others await further exploration and analysis. For example, shifting an educational focus from reliance on linear design of learning strategies to employment of nonlinear learning approaches - as presaged in Duke's 1974 concept of multilogue [4] requires a good deal of effort and is likely to involve some serious shifts in understanding about the nature of adult learning and the design of appropriately relevant syllabus strategies. In this regard Leigh, Shepherd, Davies and Tipton [12] have proposed an approach for integrating simulation into syllabus design and this is to be further developed in the time ahead. Similarly, Heeswijk [6, 7] is conducting extensive research on the role of values and beliefs in enactment of the facilitator role which will – over time – become central to the wider array of knowledge about facilitations.

7 Conclusion

Facilitation is a fascinating process that can never occur in exactly the same way twice. In this article and our other work, we aim to provide theoretical support for the tasks involved as well as practical encouragement to take up the role and pursue it as a viable and essential contribution to supporting acquisition of effective learning skills. Neither theory nor practice alone creates expertise. The frequently joyous, sometimes challenging, experiences of active engagement with simulations and games for learning create the foundations for continuing development. Conversely, attention to theories which help explain specific results and outcomes provides sustenance and defence against objections based on ignorance or unawareness of the value of building learning on the twin foundations of practice and theory.

In 1945 Kurt [14] asserted that 'nothing is so practical as good theory'. We contend that the opposite is equally true, namely that 'nothing is so theoretical as good practice.' and both are equally vital for achieving a balance in emphasis when addressing skill development.

Disclosure of Interests. The authors have no competing interests to declare that are relevant to the content of this article.

References

1. ALA. Adult learning principles: What is andragogy? (2024). https://ala.asn.au
2. Blaschke, L.: Heutagogy and lifelong learning: a review of heutagogical practice and self-determined learning. Int. Rev. Res. Open Distrib. Learn. **13**(1), 56–71 (2012). https://doi.org/10.19173/irrodl.v13i1.1076
3. Culatta, R., Kearsley, G.: Andragogy (Malcolm Knowles) (2024). https://www.instructionaldesign.org/theories/andragogy/
4. Duke, R.: Gaming: the Futures Language. Sage Publications, New York (1974)
5. Farr, A., Kleinschmidt, T., Yarlagadda, P., Mengersen, K.: Wayfinding: a simple concept, a complex process. Transp. Rev. **32**(6), 715–743 (2012). https://www.brainyquote.com/quotes/heraclitus_107157
6. de Wijse-van Heeswijk, M.: Ethics and the simulation facilitator: taking your professional role seriously. Simul. Gaming **52**(3), 312–332 (2021)
7. Heron, J.: The Complete Facilitator's Handbook. Kogan Page, UK (1999)
8. Kearsley, G.: Andragogy (M. Knowles). The theory into practice database (2010)
9. Kenyon, C., Hase, S.: Moving from andragogy to heutagogy in vocational education. Paper presented at the Australian Vocational Education and Training Research Association Conference (4th, Adelaide, Australia, 28–30 March). ERIC Documents Adelaide (2001)
10. Kortman, R., Peters, V.: Becoming the unseen helmsman: game facilitator competencies for novice, experienced, and non-game facilitators. Simul. Gaming **52**(3), 255–272 (2021)
11. Leigh, E.: A Practitioner Researcher Perspective on Facilitating an Open, Infinite, Chaordic Simulation. (EdD). University of Technology Sydney. Sydney (2003). https://opus.lib.uts.edu.au/handle/2100/308
12. Leigh, E., Shepherd, I., Davies, A., Tipton, E.: A roadmap to simulation in education. In: Angelini, L., Muñiz, R. (eds.) Simulation for Participatorry Education: Virtual Exchange and Worldwide Collaboration. Springer Texts in Education, Switzerland (2023)

13. Leigh, E.E., Levesque, L.L.: Facilitating Simulations. Edward Elgar Publishing, Cheltenham (2024)
14. Lewin, K.: The research center for group dynamics at Massachusetts Institute of Technology. Sociometry **8**, 126–135 (1945)
15. Long, B.E., Freeman, R.E., Nyhan, P.A.: The Road Game. Paper presented at the Intercom #107, Simulations for a Global Perspective. Global Perspectives in Education, New York, NY (1985)
16. Nonaka, I., Toyama, R., Konno, N.: SECI, Ba and leadership: a unified model of dynamic knowledge creation. Long Range Plan. **33**, 5–34 (2000)
17. Sellman, D.: From expert to novice: Shocking transitions in nursing. Nurs. Philos. Int. J. Healthc. Professionals **19**(4), e12224 (2018)
18. Snowden, D.J., Boone, M.E.: A leader's framework for decision making. Harv. Bus. Rev. **85**, 68–76 (2007)
19. Snowden, D., Rancati, A.: Managing complexity (and chaos) in times of crisis. Joint Research Centre (2021). https://op.europa.eu/en/publication-detail/-/publication/712438d0-8c55-11eb-b85c-01aa75ed71a1/language-en
20. TopHat. Glossary: pedagogy (2024). https://tophat.com/glossary/p/pedagogy/
21. Von Oech, R.: Expect the unexpected or you won't find it: A creativity tool based on the ancient wisdom of Heraclitus. Berrett-Koehler, San Francisco (2002)

The Impact of Participants Motivation and Playfulness for the Facilitation of Simulation Games

Friedrich Trautwein[✉] [iD] and Tobias Alf [iD]

Centre for Management Simulation, Baden-Wuerttemberg Cooperative State University, Stuttgart, Germany
`friedrich.trautwein@dhbw-stuttgart.de`

Abstract. Motivation is often seen as a key factor for learning and due to their special approach playfulness might be of special importance for seminars using simulation games. Therefore this paper evaluates the impact of students' motivation and playfulness on learning and lecturing with simulation games using quantitative methods. Based on three different questionnaires on motivation, playfulness and teaching with simulation games data was gathered in three simulation game seminars (n = 49). In addition, the share price as in game success factor is used. Measuring key variables at four different times during a 3-day-simulation game seminar, a longitudinal study was conducted.

Key questions were how different components of motivation developed over the course of simulation game seminars and whether individual components of motivation influence the course and results of simulation game seminars. In addition, it was examined, whether the question on motivation within the inventory of the Centre for Management Simulation can be externally validated and whether participants' playfulness influence the simulation game seminars.

It is found that student motivation impacts teaching with simulation games in various ways while playfulness has no impact on the educational process of simulation game-based teaching.

Keywords: Simulation · Gaming · Management Simulation · Motivation · Playfulness

1 Introduction

According to evaluation model personal aspects of participants play a role in teaching and learning with simulation games next to many other aspects like game quality, facilitation, communication (Kriz & Hense, 2006). On the participants side this could be prior experience, knowledge, preferences, or motivation. The aim of this research is to spotlight two influencing aspects on teaching and learning with simulation games on the students' side: Motivation before and during gameplay on the one hand and the playfulness of students on the other hand.

Motivation is of central importance for learning with simulation games (Mayer et al., 2013). It is often assumed that simulation games are particularly motivating due to their nature. The reason for this could be that simulation games appeal to the participants' instinct to play, but also because competition with other participants and rival teams is seen as an incentive. Despite the great importance of motivation for the learning process, there are only limited empirical studies in the context of simulation games that focus on motivational aspects (see Knogler 2018 as an example, for an overview of research work see Zeiner-Fink et al. 2023 and Alf 2023). However, greater knowledge of the cause and effect of motivational aspects would be very important for the successful design of simulation game seminars. The aim of this exploratory survey is to see how motivational components contribute to simulation game classes and where and whether motivational aspects play a role in the course and outcome of simulation game seminars. In particular, the results should form a basis for more differentiated follow-up surveys.

In addition, it will be investigated, to which extent the question contained in the inventory of the Centre for Management Simulation (ZMS inventory) on motivation ("My interest in the simulation game at the beginning of the seminar was…") can be validated externally. To this end, it is to be investigated whether and, if so, with which dimensions of the questionnaire on current motivation (FAM) there is agreement.

Next to the aspect of motivation, this study examines the impact of the playfulness of a person on learning with simulation games. Playfulness is described as an individual's "predisposition to frame (or reframe) a situation in such a way as to provide oneself (and possibly others) with amusement, humor, and/or entertainment" (Barnett, 2007). It is therefore a person's ability to interpret (non-playful) situations and behave in a certain way that turns the situation into a playful one. It can be assumed that playful individuals tend to enjoy and learn with playful methods. However, play is described as a purposeless intrinsically motivated activity (Dörner et al. 2016; Kettler et al., 2019). Game on the other hand is an organized activity and characterized by rules and roles in which the players (or gamers) act (ibid.). So, there is an essential distinction between play (fullness) and gaming. The idea of this research is to explore whether the playfulness of a person influences the perception of (rule based) gaming with certain educational goals. Prior investigations (with weaker data and instruments) show no interaction between playfulness and learning with simulation games (Alf/Trautwein 2022).

Based on the objectives of the survey, four research questions arise:

- Research question 1: How do different components of motivation develop over the course of the simulation game seminar?
- Research question 2: What is the relationship between the individual components of motivation and the progress and results of simulation game seminars?
- Research question 3: What is the relationship between the motivation question in the ZMS inventory and the questions in the questionnaire on current motivation (FAM)?
- Research question 4: What impact does the participants' playfulness have on simulation game seminars?

This study is part of an evaluation project in which over 3,000 students have been surveyed in more than 200 simulation game seminars with over 30 different simulation games since May 2021. For this study, the motivation and playfulness of participants in a subsample of three simulation game seminars was recorded using specific questionnaires in addition to the ZMS inventory. The course of the game is also included in the study.

2 Methodology

This study includes data from 49 students from the Business Informatics and Business Administration-International Business degree programs who took part in three business simulation seminars between May 2022 and July 2022. The seminars each took place in blocks of three days at the Centre for Management Simulation at DHBW Stuttgart, with the third day of one seminar being held online. The participation at the seminars was obligatory and there was no grading. Answering the questionnaires was voluntary. All three management game seminars were led by the same highly experienced facilitator.

The TOPSIM Mastering General Management simulation game (see TOPSIM 2022), which is used as a standard simulation game at numerous universities and companies, was used in all three of the simulation game seminars evaluated. The task of the students in the TOPSIM Mastering General Management simulation game is to manage fictitious companies in teams of typically 3–5 students over a period of usually 6 financial years. The students have to make numerous business decisions of increasing difficulty in a dynamic environment and the companies are in competition with each other. The decision-making areas include marketing, human resources, research and development, purchasing, production, finance and accounting. The aim is to manage one's own company as successfully as possible and to have the highest share price, especially after the last game period.

The empirical survey is based on three survey instruments.

The ZMS inventory for the evaluation of simulation game based seminars is used to record key aspects of the use of the simulation games (cf. Trautwein/Alf 2023a). This involves collecting data on the students, cooperation in the small groups, the simulation game, the facilitators and the framework conditions of the simulation game. In addition, the success of simulation game seminars is recorded in terms of satisfaction and skills acquisition (overall assessment).

The questionnaire on current motivation (FAM) by Rheinberg, Vollmeyer, Burns (2019) was used to record motivation in a differentiated manner. This question inventory divides motivation into four categories: fear of failure (5 items), challenge (4 items), probability of success (4 items) and interest (5 items). The fear of failure scale describes the negative incentives that arise from the risk of failure, while the challenge scale expresses the extent to which students enjoy tackling the tasks. The probability of success scale shows how confident the students are that they will be able to cope with the tasks. The interest scale measures how relevant students consider the content of a seminar to be.

The short questionnaire on playfulness in adulthood (KVE) by Proyer (2014) is used to measure playfulness. The questionnaire uses 5 items to measure the speed of onset and intensity of playful experiences in everyday life combined with the frequency of playful activities.

All three inventories are based on a survey of the participants, with the ZMS inventory supplemented by a survey of the teachers using standardized questionnaires. In the case of the ZMS inventory, the data is predominantly recorded on a six-point Likert scale, which usually ranges from "does not apply at all" (1) to "fully applies" (6). Also the questions of the FAM and KVE were answered on six-point Likert scales, which ranges from "does not apply at all" (1) to "fully applies" (6). For all three survey instruments, detailed descriptions with a wide range of statistical data can be found in the sources provided. In addition to the questionnaires, the teams' share prices and the ranking of the share prices were surveyed. The share price as in game data is based on 12 different factors, e.g. profits, dividends, turnover, product quality, sustainability. Although luck plays a role in achieving a high share price, good calculations are the basis for reaching a high share price. Due to the fact that there is a huge number of decisions to be taken over the course of the seminar, luck certainly influences single results, but in the long run it is statistically very unlikely to make good decisions permanently based on luck.

The survey followed the following scheme: after the introduction to the simulation game and before the start of the group phases, the students' playfulness and motivation were assessed using the respective test inventories (time T1). Using a short questionnaire derived from the questionnaire on current motivation, which contains two questions from each scale, the current motivation was recorded again before the start of round 3 (time T2) and before the start of round 5 (two simulation game seminars) and round 6 (one simulation game seminar) (time T3). This provides information about the development of motivation over the course of the simulation game. At the end of the seminar, but before the evaluation of the last game round and the final debriefing, the ZMS inventory was used to collect comprehensive data on the key structural elements of the simulation game seminar (time T4). The questionnaires from the different points in time can be assigned to each other using a coding system requested from the students in each survey.

3 Results

The main results of the empirical survey are presented below. Table 1 provides an overview of the scales used for the evaluation. The scales labeled T1 to T3 are based on the questionnaire on current motivation, while the other scales are based on the ZMS inventory (time point T4).

As can be seen from the table, the response rates vary over the course of the seminar. Answering the questions was voluntary and obviously the compliance especially at T3 was lower compared to the beginning and the end of the seminar. A reason might be, that some students wanted to continue immediately with the next round without answering the questions in between. In addition, there were some drop outs during the seminar. All scales were answered on six-point Likert scales (see methodology).

Looking at the results at a glance, the sometimes moderate α values for the motivation scales are particularly striking. However, the low values are not entirely unexpected if the information in the test description is taken as a basis. For example, α values between $\alpha = 0.66$ and $\alpha = 0.90$ are reported for the German version of the FAM, sometimes even lower (cf. Rheinberg et al. 2019). Since the motivation scales only contained two items at T2 and T3, the even lower α-values are to be expected, but values below $\alpha = 0.5$ hardly allow a meaningful use (cf. on α-values Taber 2017, Trautwein 2004, p. 98). With the exception of the scale (Facilitator Competence), the scales of the ZMS inventory have at least satisfactory, in some cases very good internal consistencies.

Table 1. Results: Scales of Motivation and ZMS-Inventory

Scale	n	x	sd	α
T1_Fear Of Failure	49	2,44	1,07	0,80
T1_Challenge	49	3,73	0,92	0,67
T1_Probability Of Success	49	4,24	0,69	0,66
T1_Interest	49	3,49	0,81	0,64
T2_Fear Of Failure	38	2,50	1,14	0,58
T2_Challenge	38	3,78	1,13	0,41
T2_Probability Of Success	38	4,30	0,96	0,04
T2_Interest	38	4,03	1,17	0,60
T3_Fear Of Failure	25	2,36	1,12	0,55
T3_Challenge	25	4,06	1,15	0,55
T3_Probability Of Success	25	4,32	1,19	0,36
T3_Interest	25	4,18	1,05	0,64
T4 SG Comprehensibility	36	4,72	0,87	0,77
T4 SG Practical Relevance	36	4,44	0,83	0,76
T4 Facilitator Competence	36	5,63	,578	0,37
T4 Facilitator Communication	36	5,67	0,57	0,92
T4 Team Organisation	36	5,08	0,75	0,75
T4 Team Task Distribution	36	4,28	1,16	0,82
T4 Student Engagement	36	4,86	1,23	0,91
T4 Overall Assessment	36	4,44	1,12	0,95

3.1 Research Question 1: How Do Different Components of Motivation Develop Over the Course of the Simulation Game Seminar?

Figure 1 provides an overview of the development of the different components of motivation (mean values). Overall, a positive trend can be seen, particularly in the development of interest and, to a lesser extent, the development of challenge. A slight drop can be observed in the fear of failure curve, which means decreasing worries and is therefore positive. The probability of success curve runs largely parallel[1].

---

[1] If the scales at time point T1 (as at time points T2 and T3) were based on only two variables, there would be slight changes. For example, the development of the fear of failure would be even more positive, while that of the probability of success would tend to be slightly negative (fear of failure = 2.63, challenge = 3.59, probability of success = 4.36, interest = 3.70).

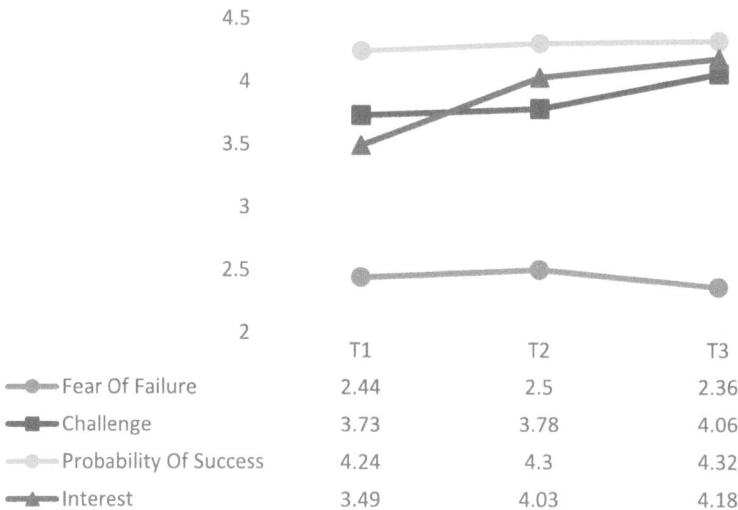

Fig. 1. Overview: Change of different aspects of motivation over time (mean values, scale: 1 to 6)

3.2 Research Question 2: What is the Relationship Between the Individual Components of Motivation and the Progress and Results of Simulation Game Seminars?

The four motivational components surveyed at the beginning (fear of failure, challenge, probability of success and interest) have hardly any influence on the game results at T2, T3 and T4. There is only a (weak) significant correlation for two of the 20 correlations examined here: those who have a positive attitude towards challenges occupy a better position at time T3 ($r = .307*$), those who rate the probability of success better have a lower share price at time T2 ($r = .322*$).

In addition, the extent to which the development of the share price and the rankings of the teams influence the different motivation components was investigated. It was found that at time T2, the current share price (announced before the survey) correlates highly significantly negatively with the expectation of failure at T2 with $r = -.430**$. A high share price therefore results in a lower failure orientation. A low share price, on the other hand, corresponds with a strong failure orientation ("I feel under pressure to do well in the task" and "When I think about the task, I am a little worried."). At time T3, there were no significant correlations between share price or team ranking and the different motivation values (but it has to be kept in mind that only 25 data sets were included in the analysis whereas 38 data sets were included at time T2.

In addition, the correlation between student motivation at the beginning of the seminar and the overall assessment (satisfaction and learning) was analysed. Table 2 shows that there are some strong and highly significant correlations between the motivation scales at time T1 and the overall evaluation of the seminar at time T4.

Table 2. Correlations between overall evaluation (ZMS inventory) and the four FAM scales.

	Correlation with Overall Assessment
T1_Fear Of Failure	n.s
T1_Challenge	.499**
T1_Probability Of Success	.603***
T1_Interest	.457**

3.3 Research Question 3: What is the Relationship Between the Motivation Question in the ZMS Inventory and the Questions in the Questionnaire on Current Motivation (FAM)?

In addition, the present survey was also used for a further external validation of the ZMS inventory. In the ZMS inventory, motivation is assessed with a question ("My interest in the course was…"), which is answered from "very low" to "very high" on a six-point Likert scale. Table 3 provides an overview of the correlations between the four dimensions of the questionnaire on current motivation and the motivation question from the ZMS inventory. It should be noted here that the FAM questions were answered at time T1, i.e. at the beginning of the business simulation seminar, while the ZMS inventory was answered at time T4.

Table 3. Correlation coefficients between ZMS "Motivation" and the four motivation scales of the FAM

	Correlation with Motivation (ZMS)
T1_Fear Of Failure	n.s
T1_Challenge	n.s
T1_Probability Of Success	.360*
T1_Interest	.341*

The ZMS question on motivation therefore reflects motivation in the dimensions of probability of success and interest. Exemplary questions for the probability of success are "I think I can cope with the difficulty of the task" and "I think anyone can do it." Interest is measured in the FAM with the following questions, among others: "I don't need a reward for tasks like this, I enjoy them just as much" or "In this task, I like the role of the scientist who discovers connections".

3.4 Research Question 4: What Impact Does the Participants' Playfulness Have on Simulation Game Seminars?

As playfulness is mapped using only one scale, the results are presented in detail in Table 4:

Table 4. Results of Playfulness

Scale Playfulness (α = .805)		x	sd
		3,95	0,96
1	I am a playful person	4,14	1,19
2	Good friends would say that I am a playful person	4,14	1,26
3	In my everyday-life I often do playful things	3,84	1,21
4	It only takes very few impulses for me to switch from a serious to a playful attitude	3,71	1,21
5	Sometimes I completely forget about the time around me when I'm playing a game and get completely absorbed in it	3,90	1,53

With a value of 0.805, the internal consistency of the scale can be described as good in accordance with scientific conventions (cf. Taber, 2018) and is within the expected range according to the test description (cf. Proyer 2014). The average score of 3.95 on the six-point Likert scale is in the medium range.

With regard to the research question, the result is clear. There is not even a single significant correlation with any of the four motivation scales or any of the scales of the ZMS inventory (SG Comprehensibility, SG Practical Relevance, Facilitator Competence, Facilitator Communication, Team Organisation, Team Task Distribution, Student Engagement, Overall Assessment). Based on the available data, the playfulness of the participants does not play a significant role in the course and outcome of the simulation game seminars - neither positively nor negatively.

The present study, based on a scientifically sound inventory of questions on participants' enjoyment of the game, thus confirms the findings obtained by Trautwein/Alf (2023a) in the development of the ZMS inventory. Here, the enjoyment of playing games was recorded with only one self-developed item ("I like to play strategy games (e.g. chess, Risk, Settlers of Catan)" (cf. Trautwein/Alf (2023a) and Alf/Trautwein (2022)). As this earlier survey also did not reveal any relevant impact associated with enjoyment of games, the item was not included in the final ZMS inventory.

4 Discussion

Based on the results of the survey, the following section discusses the key issues in relation to the four research questions, outlines limitations and provides some ideas for further research.

4.1 Research Question 1: How Do Different Components of Motivation Develop Over the Course of the Simulation Game Seminar?

An increase in the Challenge and Interest curves over the course of the seminar is to be considered desirable and positive, as this expresses that the students see themselves in a position to successfully complete the tasks, while at the same time their interest increases. Parallel, the fear of failure scale is trending downwards, which indicates a decreasing fear of failure. The overall positive development of the motivation scales is pleasing because TOPSIM Mastering General Management is a competitive simulation game in which there must inevitably be winners and losers in relative terms in referring to placement and share price. Obviously, the scenario with its new challenges in each round is designed in such a way that the students nevertheless increasingly perceive themselves as competent to master the tasks and the simulation game thus contributes to a positive development of self-efficacy expectations.

4.2 Research Question 2: What is the Relationship Between the Individual Components of Motivation and the Course and Results of Simulation Game Seminars?

Motivation was measured using four different components based on a scientifically evaluated inventory of questions. With regard to the influence of the motivation components on the course of the simulation game, only two significant correlations can be identified, one of which is contrary to expectations. A positive assessment of the probability of success therefore has a negative effect on the share price at time T2. A reason could be a self overestimation of the participants at the beginning. Another possibility would be that a positive assessment of the probability of success leads to riskier decisions leading to the contrary result. The second significant correlation between a positive attitude towards the challenge and good performance, on the other hand, is obvious.

Given that TOPSIM Mastering General Management is a team simulation game and not a single-player simulation game, it is not entirely surprising that the motivation of individual participants has hardly any effect on the course of the simulation game. Since the teams were put together randomly and therefore students with very different motivation profiles were represented in the different teams, the heterogeneous profiles within the teams, as far as can be seen from the available data of the study, mean that the motivation profiles of the individual team members have little, if any, effect on the course of the game.

On the other hand, it is rather surprising that, conversely, the course of the simulation game has hardly any effect on the various components of motivation. It could therefore be expected that participants whose team had a lower ranking or a below-average share price would be correspondingly less motivated, particularly in view of the fact that the survey at T2 and T3 took place immediately after the debriefing in the plenary session in which the game results were announced. However, there was only a highly significant correlation between the current share price and fear of failure, as expected.

As anticipated positive motivation values at the beginning (T1) have a positive effect on the evaluation of the simulation game seminars (T4). However, it is surprising that the correlations in between motivation values at the beginning and overall assessment are partly over r = 0.6*** (probability of success to overall assessment). In contrast, the (negative) expectation of failure has no significant influence on the overall assessment. At this point, the results show how important positive student motivation is for the overall assessment (combining learning success and satisfaction) with simulation game seminars.

4.3 Research Question 3: What is the Relationship Between the Motivation Question in the ZMS Inventory and the Questions in the Questionnaire on Current Motivation (FAM)?

The positive correlation between the ZMS inventory's question on motivation on the one hand and the "Interest" scale, which is aimed at a more general interest, and the success orientation scale of the questionnaire on current motivation on the other hand, illustrates that the ZMS inventory succeeds in validly recording the participants' motivation in these two forms with a single item. This is all the more remarkable as the ZMS inventory expects respondents to indicate their own motivation at the beginning of the seminar retrospectively at the end (T4), while the students answered the questionnaire on current motivation at the beginning (T1). Since recording motivation in the ZMS inventory right at the beginning of the seminar would massively increase the effort required to record it and thus also increase the threshold for using the questionnaire, a single point in time for recording is central to the success of the ZMS inventory. It is also important for the success of the ZMS inventory to keep it as short as possible in order to enable low-threshold use. By comparing the ZMS item on motivation with the questionnaire on current motivation, the ZMS inventory can be considered externally validated in terms of both content and time of collection.

4.4 Research Question 4: What Influence Does Participants' Playfulness Have on Simulation Game Seminars?

If we consider the importance of playfulness as a basic disposition of people for the course and success of simulation game seminars, no significant correlation can be found between playfulness and even a single dimension of the ZMS inventory. These findings may support the often described distinction between play (fullness) and gaming (Dörner et al., 2016). Further research should assess how students' relation to gaming effects learning with simulation games. The conclusion to be drawn from this result in combination with Alf/Trautwein (2022) for use at universities is that simulation games can be regarded as a fundamentally suitable teaching and learning method regardless of the playfulness of individual students.

4.5 Limitations and Further Research

The research design and the scope of the quantitative survey give rise to a number of limitations that need to be taken into account when interpreting the results.

With regard to the transferability of the results to other business simulation seminars in particular, it should be noted that the students surveyed were exclusively DHBW Stuttgart students from the Business Information Systems and Business Administration-International Business degree programs. A transfer to structurally similar degree programs at DHBW Stuttgart or other locations seems to be obvious, but not confirmed by the available data. In view of the specific framework conditions of studying at the Cooperative State University, it is also not clear from the sample whether the results can be transferred to students at other universities (or even participants in simulation game seminars outside the university sector). Particularly in view of the fact that participation in the business game seminars at the DHBW is compulsory and that the students have a different background than students at other universities due to the close integration of theory and practice, differences in motivational dimensions appear to be quite realistic. The results of the study are also limited to the TOPSIM Mastering General Management simulation game. The extent to which the results can be transferred to structurally different simulation games, for example in the areas of politics, change management or sustainability, remains to be seen.

In addition, the sample is relatively small with only 36 students who took part in the survey both at the beginning and at the end of the simulation game seminars. This makes it all the more important that some of the results are highly significant despite the small number of participants. However, in order to obtain more reliable results, it would be essential to increase the sample size in future studies. With regard to the results on motivation at time points T2 and T3 and thus the course of motivation, it should also be noted that the α-values are very low in some cases and that the scale on the probability of success in particular does not provide a reliable basis on which to base empirically sound decisions. Furthermore, it cannot be ruled out that the fluctuating number of survey participants may lead to distortions.

The present study is also primarily based on the students' self-perception. Even if the connection between self-perception and external perception is well documented scientifically (cf. Pfeiffer et al., 2015), it should be noted that student perception only represents a section of reality and is fraught with difficulties (cf. Spinath & Seifried, 2018). In view of the fundamental importance of this question, it was subjected to a more detailed analysis for the ZMS inventory in several studies. It was found that various indicators point to a good perception of the students. For example, the student assessment of satisfaction with the simulation game seminar correlates highly significantly with the assessment by the facilitators (cf. Trautwein/Alf 2023b). In addition, students perceive facilitators who conduct the simulation game very frequently and subjectively feel confident with the simulation game as significantly more competent than facilitators with less experience (cf. Trautwein/Alf 2023b).

In addition to the above mentioned ways of addressing the limitations of this study, future research should integrate qualitative data alongside quantitative metrics. This would make it possible to identify the reasons for the change in motivation and its impact on the course of the seminars.

Disclosure of Interests. The authors have no competing interests to declare that are relevant to the content of this article.

References

Alf, T.: Gelingensbedingungen von Planspiellehrveranstaltungen – Ein Systematic Literature Review. die hochschullehre **8**(33), 468–480 (2023). https://doi.org/10.3278/HSL2233W

Alf, T., Trautwein, F.: Zum Einfluss von Studierenden auf die Lehre mit Planspielen. In: Alf, T., Hahn, S., Zürn, B., Trautwein, F. (eds.) Planspiele - Erkenntnisse aus Praxis und Forschung. Norderstedt: Books on Demand (ZMS-Schriftenreihe), pp. 89–96 (2022)

Barnett, L.A.: The nature of playfulness in young adults. Pers. Individ. Differ. **43**(4), 949–958 (2007). https://doi.org/10.1016/j.paid.2007.02.018

Dörner, R., Göbel, S., Effelsberg, W., Wiemeiyer, J.: Serious Games. Foundations, Concepts and Practice, 1st ed. Springer, Cham (2016)

Kettler, C., Kauffeld, S.: Game-based Learning. In: Simone Kauffeld und Julius Othmer (eds.) Handbuch Innovative Lehre. Springer Fachmedien Wiesbaden, Wiesbaden, pp. 249–253 (2019). https://link.springer.com/content/pdf/10.1007%2F978-3-658-22797-5_18.pdf. Accessed 11 May 2024

Kriz, W.C., Hense, J.U.: Theory-oriented evaluation for the design of and research in gaming and simulation. Simul. Gaming **37**(2), 268–283 (2006). https://doi.org/10.1177/1046878106287950

Mayer, I., Warmelink, H., Bekebrede, G.: Learning in a game-based virtual environment: a comparative evaluation in higher education. Eur. J. Eng. Educ. **38**(1), 85–106 (2013). https://doi.org/10.1080/03043797.2012.742872

Pfeiffer, H., Rach, H., Rosanowitsch, S., Wörl, J., Schneider, M.: Lehrevaluation. In: Michael Schneider und Maida Mustafic (eds): Gute Hochschullehre: Eine evidenzbasierte Orientierungshilfe, pp. 153–184. Springer, Heidelberg (2015)

Proyer, R.T.: KVE. Kurzfragebogen zur Verspieltheit im Erwachsenenalter [Verfahrensdokumentation und Fragebogen]. In: Leibniz-Institut für Psychologie (ZPID) (eds.) Open Test Archive. Trier: ZPID (2014). https://doi.org/10.23668/psycharchives.6553

Rheinberg, F., Vollmeyer, R., Burns, B.D.: FAM. Ein Fragebogen zur Erfassung aktueller Motivation in Lern- und Leistungssituationen [Verfahrensdokumentation aus PSYNDEX Tests-Nr. 9004322 und Fragebogen]. In Leibniz-Zentrum für Psychologische Information und Dokumentation (ZPID) (eds.) Testarchiv. Trier: ZPID (2019). https://doi.org/10.23668/psycharchives.4486

Spinath, B., Seifried, E.: Was brauchen wir, um solide empirische Erkenntnisse über gute Hochschullehre zu erhalten? Zeitschrift für Hochschulentwicklung **13**(1), 153–169 (2018). https://zfhe.at/index.php/zfhe/issue/view/57

Taber, K.S.: The use of Cronbach's alpha when developing and reporting research instruments in science education. Res. Sci. Educ. **48**, 1273–1296 (2018). https://doi.org/10.1007/s11165-016-9602-2

Topsim: Mastering General Management (2022). https://www.topsim.com/wp-content/uploads/2022/05/KB_Mastering_General_Management.pdf

Trautwein, F.: Berufliche Handlungskompetenz als Studienziel. Sternenfels: Verlag Wissenschaft und Praxis (2004)

Trautwein, F., Alf, T.: Theory-based development of an inventory for the evaluation of simulation game lectures. In: Harteveld, C., Sutherland, S., Troiano, G., Lukosch, H., Meijer, S. (eds.) Simulation and Gaming for Social Impact. Proceedings of the 54th Conference of the International Simulation and Gaming Association, 3–21 (2023a)

Trautwein, F., Alf, T.: The role of facilitators for learning and satisfaction of students in simulation game courses. In: Becu, N. (eds.) Simulation and Gaming for Social and Environmental Transitions. Proceedings of the 54th Conference of the International Simulation and Gaming Association, pp. 158–167 (2023b)

Zeiner-Fink, S., Geithner, S., Bullinger-Hoffmann, A.C.: Lerneffekte und Akzeptanz von Planspielen: Ein systematischer Literatur-Review. In: Zeitschrift für Hochschulentwicklung, 18 (Sonderheft Planspiele), pp. 41–60 (2023)

Pratiti …Becoming Aware: Promoting Simulations and Games on a Global Platform

Jigyasu Dubey[1(✉)], Elyssebeth Leigh[2], Vinod Dumblekar[3], Anand Rajavat[1], and Upinder Dhar[1]

[1] Shri Vaishnav Vidyapeeth Vishwavidyalaya, Indore, India
jigyasudube@yahoo.co.in
[2] University of Technology Sydney, Ultimo, Australia
elyssebeth.leigh@icloud.com
[3] MANTIS, New Delhi, India

Abstract. Conferences and seminars have been the traditional way of sharing new ideas and expanding our connections within – and across – disciplines. Webinars are a comparatively new addition to the modes of communication and the series titled Pratiti…becoming aware has grown into a rich and valuable set of resources for simulationists around the world. This article describes the motives for beginning the series at a University in India, and reviews the feedback received from participants of 53 one-hour-long presentations on simulations and games between October 2020 and December 2023. It reports on the process of establishing the series, describes some of the challenges encountered, summarizes highlights of the webinars and identifies possible opportunities that may arise. The authors recommend that future webinars should cover topics of interest of university students, while inviting more female speakers and speakers from USA and Australasia.

Keywords: Experiences · Feedback · Learning · Themes · Webinar

1 Introduction

Shri Vaishnav Vidyapeeth Vishwavidyalaya (SVVV), Indore (India) was established in 2015 with the vision to be a leader in shaping a better future for mankind through quality education, training and research [1]. SVVV is promoted by a 140-year-old Shri Vaishnav group of trusts [2]. It pursues the mission to make a difference in sustaining the growth of global societies by developing socially responsible citizens. Value-based education being at the helm, SVVV promotes endurance, excellence, fairness, honesty and transparency as its core values. It consists of several constituent institutes to impart education in the disciplines of Agriculture, Architecture, Computer Applications, Engineering, Fine Arts, Forensic Science, Humanities and Arts, Journalism and Mass Communication, Law, Life Science, Management, Science and Social Sciences. SVVV has more than 8000 students studying in different disciplines [3].

1.1 International Simulation and Gaming Association (ISAGA)

Founded in the seventies, International Simulation and Gaming Association (ISAGA) is one of the oldest communities of people involved in the domain of simulations and games (S&G). Its members have a vast knowledge and tradition in developing and using simulation, gaming, and related methods. Today, the community brings together researchers and practitioners from the fields of management, social and environmental sciences, education, planning, and technical sciences. They study the design, facilitation, and debriefing methods as well as evaluation protocols of gaming/simulation. The aims of the ISAGA are to promote gaming simulation methods, including research, consulting, learning, and teaching methods, such as traditional business and management simulation games, policy exercises, computer simulations and computer-supported simulation games, role play, learning games, scenarios, dynamic case studies, experiential learning activities, business-theatre, etc. [4].

Dr Upinder Dhar and Dr. Vinod Dumblekar, co-authors of this study, attended the 50th Conference of ISAGA in Warsaw, Poland from August 26–30, 2019, where ISAGA invited SVVV to organize the 51st ISAGA Conference in India in 2020. Dr. Dhar accepted the invitation on behalf of SVVV and agreed to conduct the 51st Conference as the chairperson. He nominated Dr Jigyasu Dubey and Dr Vinod Dumblekar as the coordinators of the Conference and formed the organizing team in SVVV. The team designed the brochure and planned the promotion of the Conference.

1.2 Pratiti …Becoming Aware

At the start of the New Year 2020, the COVID-19 pandemic began to spread across the world [5, 6]. Chaos, confusion and uncertainty prevailed; governments and medical experts did not know how to respond to the situation. Several countries declared lockdown and directed their people to stay within their homes and restricted their outdoor movements and travel [7, 8]. Everyone was in fear and worried about the lives of their family members. People were prevented from leaving home for work or other needs. Under such difficult conditions of the first wave of COVID-19, ISAGA and SVVV postponed the Conference to September 2021 hoping that the world would return to normalcy by then, and renamed it as the 52nd Conference [9].

Offices, schools, businesses, streets, and transport were moving at a pace considerably slower than before [10]. Confronted with the humongous problem of marketing the conference in such difficult conditions, SVVV seized the initiative and used webi-nars as a precursor to the conference to promote the core theme of simulations and games to the world. The launch of the webinars turned out to be timely because the world was on the verge of learning new practices such as using online communication platforms due to COVID-19. The initiative was supported by ISAGA, and soon, SVVV conducted the first webinar in October 2020 [11].

The second wave of COVID-19 hit in March 2021 and people were back to their homes, again. SVVV proposed to organize the conference in an online format which was accepted by ISAGA [12, 13]. SVVV organized the 52nd annual ISAGA conference online from September 6–10, 2021 which attracted many papers and other contributions [14]. By that time, SVVV had conducted 28 webinars that were addressed by game designers, developers, practitioners, academicians and other professionals across the world [15]. The book of the 28 webinar presentations was titled *Pratiti …becoming aware* and released by the chief guest of the conference, Dr. Sivasailam Thiagarajan, during the inauguration [16].

1.3 Centre of Excellence in Simulation and Gaming (CoE_SG)

Spurred by the successful conference, SVVV announced the establishment of the Centre of Excellence in Simulation and Gaming (CoE_SG) during the valedictory session, thus became the first University in India to have a deep focus on S&G. The objectives of the CoE_SG are [17]:

(a) To carry and promote the research in the different aspects of the S&G.
(b) To popularize S&G as teaching pedagogy among the teaching fraternity.
(c) To conduct workshops, webinars, seminars and faculty development programs on different topics of S&G.
(d) To organize the gaming contest for the students.
(e) To organize the game play learning sessions for the students, teachers and executives.
(f) To spread awareness in society about the relevance of S&G in contemporary times.

The first major step of CoE_SG was to continue the webinar series of *Pratiti …becoming aware* after the conference. Subsequently, 25 webinars were organized between December 2021 and December 2023 [18, 19]. The CoE_SG coordinates with ISAGA and other such professional bodies to promote S&G globally. The National Education Policy (2020) (NEP) of India suggests using innovative pedagogy to make learning more engaging and fun [20]. In this light, CoE_SG proposes the use of educational S&G to enhance learning outcomes.

1.4 Rationale of the Study

The use of webinars to promote S&G, a multidisciplinary learning pedagogy, was risky. Therefore, to use them as a precursor for any international conference was a pioneering effort. The organizers wondered whether the series of webinars as innovative and persistent initiatives were appropriate. Would the outcomes of the series be justified by the elaborate planning and execution of the series by CoE_SG and the deployment of huge resources by SVVV? Would the webinars of *Pratiti …becoming aware* bring together academicians, students and practitioners in S&G from across the world?

1.5 Objectives of the Study

The study aims to analyse, assess and understand the processes, actions and outcomes of the webinar series called Pratiti …becoming aware. Therefore, it will explore the likely outcomes from webinar data in terms of the following objectives:

(a) To understand the themes of webinars.
(b) To identify the geographical distribution of the speakers.
(c) To understand the participant feedback.

(d) To identify the strengths and weaknesses of the process.
(e) To draw conclusions from the findings.
(f) To explore ideas for further research.
(g) To recommend actions for improvement.

2 Method

The study covers 53 webinars organized by SVVV from October 2020 to December 2023. The webinars were live streamed on the Internet using video conferencing software and on SVVV's YouTube channel with the facility to watch later.

2.1 Speakers

SVVV chose designers and developers in S&G, teachers, trainers, practitioners and educators in experiential learning and researchers with expertise, experience and reputation in S&G as Speakers. Most eligible candidates were affiliated with ISAGA as members. They were first invited by SVVV at least a month before the webinar day. Later, the dates were fixed with their consent, after receiving the profile and a summary of the presentation from each speaker.

2.2 Process

Each webinar lasted at least an hour during which speakers presented their S&G topics for about 45 min, and afterwards responded to the participants' queries for about 10 min, leaving time for introductions, concluding remarks and announcements by the organisers. The largest body of international presenters was expected to be from the European continent. Therefore, especially for their convenience, each webinar started at 3 pm IST on a Saturday, which also suited everyone whether at school or work during the week. A gap of 1–3 weeks between any two webinars was maintained.

On receipt of confirmation from the speaker, SVVV would block the calendar spot for the webinar. It then created a flyer in JPG format for every webinar to announce the event. It was then emailed to over 8,000 students, alumni and teachers in SVVV, over 3,000 corporate executives and over 1,000 academicians in the education fraternity, about a month before the webinar (Fig. 1).

The recipients registered for the webinar via online links and received the respective connectivity links from SVVV. To deepen the awareness and ensure their presence, SVVV emailed reminders to all recipients, whether registered or otherwise, at least two more times before every webinar. Registered recipients linked to the webinars via either the video conferencing software (for live participation) or SVVV's YouTube channel (for live participation and later viewing).

2.3 Participants

The Question & Answer (Q&A) sessions that followed every presentation were vigorous and elicited valid feedback responses from 67% (7,428) out of 11,130 registered

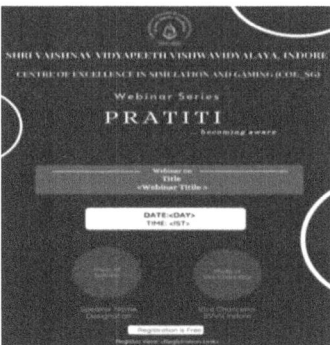

Fig. 1. Sample Flyer

participants (Fig. 2). Out of these responses, 3,023 (41%) were from females, 5,580 (75%) were from university students of whom 4,649 (83%) were from SVVV. Of the remainder, 1,585 were academicians such as teachers, 173 were research scholars, 80 were ISAGA members, and 10 were other viewers.

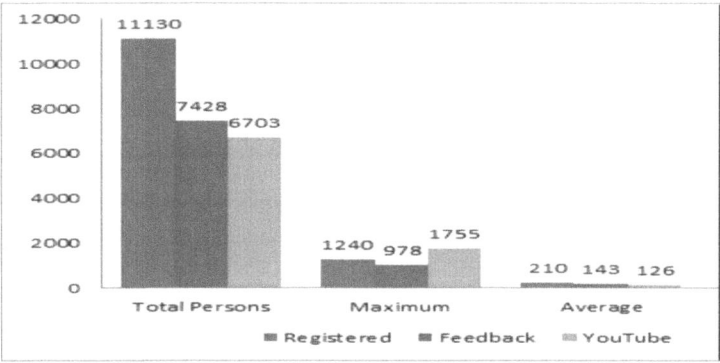

Fig. 2. Webinar participants

More participants (60% or 6,703 out of 11,130 registered) watched the sessions on YouTube than on the video conferencing software, perhaps due to their ease or familiarity with the former. The average number of registrations (210) per session and the maximum number of registrations (1,240) in a session attests to the popularity of the sessions.

2.4 Feedback

Participants conveyed their experiences about each webinar in a Feedback form (Appendix 1). A long document may have discouraged responses; hence, care was taken to create a short and simple form. It was made available online towards the end of every webinar to capture their experiences afresh.

3 Results

3.1 Themes

The webinars covered topics in design, development, facilitation and other practices, learning and research in S&G. They discussed S&G in environmental and sustainable development goals, serious games, 3D and online games, fidelity versus reality, mobility and urban planning, change and disaster management, road safety, cooperation and resilience. Most (45%) of the contents of the 53 webinars covered applications and use of S&G while a smaller proportion (32%) was devoted to fundamental theories (Fig. 3).

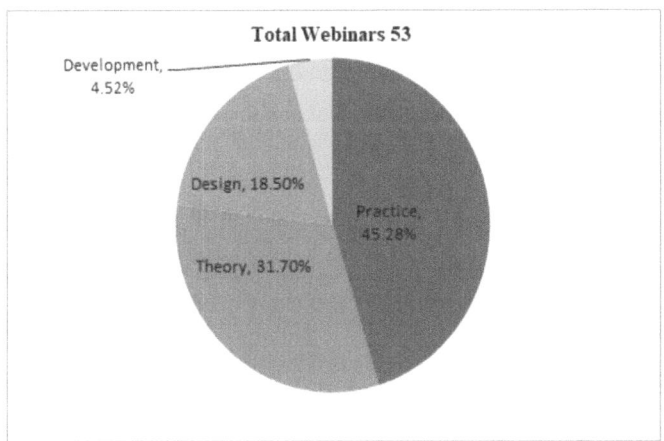

Fig. 3. Webinar themes

Speakers. The Netherlands was the most prominent contributing nation with speakers in 12 webinars (Fig. 4). India and Japan were close behind with nine and eight webinars, respectively. Amongst the other nations were Austria, Finland, France, Italy, Malaysia, New Zealand, Poland, Russia, Thailand, the UK and the USA.

The webinars had 45 speakers from 17 countries and four continents; some speakers spoke at more than one webinar. Twelve speakers (27%) were females and 23 (51%) were academicians (professors and other roles) while the others were consultants (e.g. game producers, suppliers and trainers).

Feedback. The responses to the statements in the feedback form were scored on a 5-point Likert scale, where 1 (least agreement) was the lowest value and 5 (most agreement) was the highest value of the response. They were collated and led to the following results as an evaluation of the webinar objectives, speakers and topics (Table 1):

The high means (all more than 4) of all statements suggest that the webinars generated satisfying knowledge experiences for the participants. The standard deviation (SD) of .80 for statement #4 pointed to the diversity of perceptions, just as in statement #5 (SD of .78).

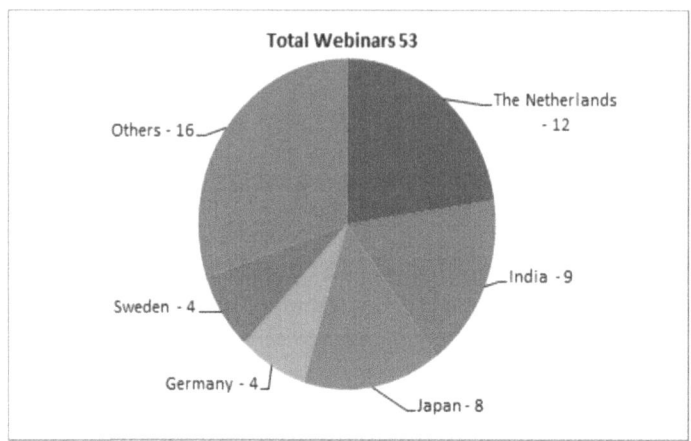

Fig. 4. Geographical locations of speakers

Table 1. Feedback from participant (n = 7428) responses

Statements	Mean	SD
1. Experts/Speakers have put good efforts in explaining things to make me understand the topic	4.41	.58
2. This webinar has increased my knowledge and skill in the discussed topic	4.32	.60
3. The webinar objectives were clearly stated	4.32	.62
4. As a result of this webinar, I gained knowledge applicable to my work	4.06	.80
5. How do you rate the quality of the speakers invited?	4.27	.78
6. Please indicate your satisfaction for the following aspects of the webinar	4.31	.61

Most feedback responders heard of the webinars from SVVV's emails (2,828 or 38%) and SVVV's Facebook announcements (1,921 or 26%) (Fig. 5).

Feedback, Open-Ended. Some entries in the comments/suggestions section of the participants' responses were extracted for the study and pooled together. Four distinct patterns of perceptions pointed to their pleasant experience, interest in simulations and gaming topics, utility value, and insightful suggestions for improvement of the webinar process, as seen below.

I. Satisfaction. 1. Again, an excellent webinar. The only reason I ranked it at 75% was because much of the content was already familiar to me due to my research. 2. Each webinar is mind-blowing. I would like to attend all webinars in this series. 3. Every webinar was wonderful; I am really glad that I got an opportunity to join this webinar, lot of information was presented in this webinar, and I enjoyed this. 4. I believe today's topic was a little complicated, so it would be better if more sessions were conducted on the same topic. 5. I liked the webinar very much. Obviously, the resource person was very good. 6. I would like to attend more webinars. 7. Very experienced speaker. Great

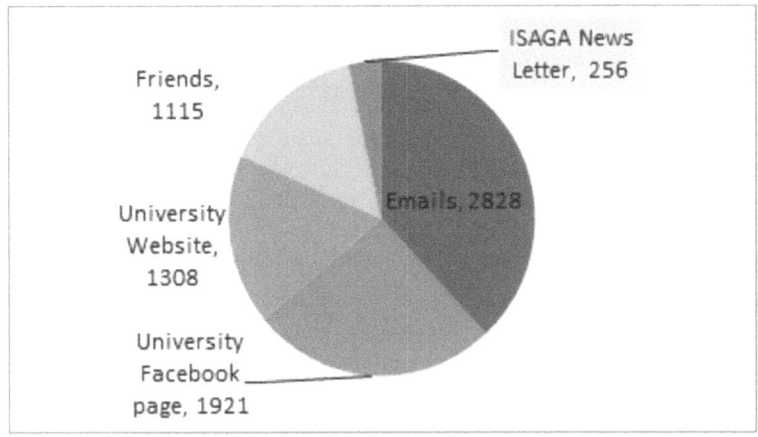

Fig. 5. Media source of responders (7,428)

use of simple examples explains the key concepts. 8. We are thankful for giving us this opportunity free of cost. Again, we are thankful to the team ISAGA 2021. 9. Topics are discussed in a lucid manner.

II. Gaming. *1. I'm interested in gaming development as a career opportunity; how to get started? 2. Joining this Webinar has helped me to understand better about gaming approach to education. 3. Thank you for an interesting tour through these ways of addressing waste management and disaster planning as well as providing insight into more general aspects of using simulation. 4. The disaster risk management-related serious games/simulations offer a rich social experience with players collaboratively solving a problem. With a capacity to reach diverse audiences (embracing adults, children, experts and communities) and realistically simulating disaster reality, serious games/simulations may assist Disaster Risk Management, especially in the realm of raising disaster risk awareness, identifying hazards, undertaking preventive actions, triggering empathy and perspective-taking.*

III. Usefulness. *1. Found this webinar interesting and there was a lot of new insight to learn. 2. Good and knowledgeable webinar. 3. The webinar was great and very knowledgeable for us. 4. It was an amazing experience, and I will be waiting for more such webinars regarding higher studies. 5. It's quite knowledgeable and enthusiastic. 6. Thank you for sharing. 7. Thank you very much. I feel privileged and honored to be able to attend this webinar which absolutely expanded my vision and showed a new possibility from a futuristic approach. 8. Thank you very much as these kinds of topics are not generally covered.*

IV. Suggestions. *1. The duration of the Webinar was too short; it should have been at least 5 days. 2. Let me know if there is training. If my schedule permits, I would be most interested. 3. Have webinars in the Hindi language. 4. I would like to know about future webinars in this series. 5. We can surely understand it but a slow pace will be more helpful. 6. Webinars should be more relatable for students. 7. More practical aspects can be included.*

Additional suggestions (111) were received in response to item #8 (*Are there any topics you'd like to see covered in future webinars?*) of the Feedback form (Appendix 1). From these suggestions, 32 statements were segregated into three categories, viz.,

- **Presentations for awareness** *(Serious games, game design based on theories, game theory applications, games to assist mentally disabled children in learning, gaming and multidisciplinary studies, story-telling simulation, game science, and dynamic simulation).*
- **Workshops for skilling** *(Simulations and games in flood management, women empowerment, management and marketing, SDGs, agriculture, on minds and for mental health, medicine, behavioural change and real-life challenges, design of cooperative games, game development, actual simulation activity, game project, best practices for using, developing and implementing S&G with several examples, facilitation of simulation and gaming, and skills and capabilities).*
- **Technology-based games** *(AI-based simulations and games and their applications, new technology in modern game design, and creation of infinite worlds in simulation games like Minecraft).*

4 Discussion

The 53 webinars in S&G from October 2020 to December 2023 were studied to understand them across three dimensions, viz., themes, feedback and process.

4.1 Themes

The webinars covered a wide variety of themes in both design and analytical sciences to create knowledge (about 55%) such as in serious games, participation and fidelity, and in the use of games (about 45%) such as in education, energy, policy and disaster management (Fig. 3). This range of S&G topics in the 'space' of barely 53 webinars was due to the contributions and perspectives from speakers of 17 countries (Fig. 4).

4.2 Feedback

Students comprised the bulk (about 75%) of the respondents (Fig. 2) who may not have understood the variety of conceptual and global topics (4.06 for statement #4, Table 1) covered in the presentations, despite their acknowledgement of increased knowledge from the webinars (4.32 for statement #2, Table 1).

The voluminous open-ended feedback of participants showed deep interest and included suggestions. Almost all participants sat engrossed throughout the webinars, their satisfaction showing in expressions like *excellent, mind blowing, wonderful* and *enjoyed* in their open-ended feedback for longer and more frequent sessions. Their enjoyment must be attributed to the breadth of themes and the presentation manner of the speakers, some of whom received praise as *very good resource person, lucid* and *very experienced speaker*. Another reason for their enhanced satisfaction was the novelty of the experience [21].

The interest in gaming themes such as career opportunity, risk management and gaming approach to education challenged their understanding but kept them engaged in a state of flow [22]. They found the content and discussions useful (*knowledgeable, insightful, amazing, futuristic* and *expanded my vision*).

Participants were direct and honest in reviewing their webinar experience and offered many suggestions. Some wanted longer and slower sessions, and training. Others wanted practical aspects, sessions in Hindi, and content tailored for students. The additional suggestions showed that participants were keen to be informed on S&G topics like serious games and game science and theory, to become skilled in S&G tasks such as development and facilitation in domains such as agriculture, medicine and tech-based games.

4.3 Process

The emails of SVVV got more attention (2,828) than its Facebook page (1,921) or website (1,308) (Fig. 5). They reached over 12,000 recipients which were far more than the number of connections on the Facebook page. This aggressive approach by SVVV also attracted more participants than its website because the emails addressed the recipient, directly and personally, in comparison to the general announcement on the website.

The length of an hour for each webinar was in line with global expectations and practices. The Q&A generated thoughtful questions that extracted more meaning out of the speakers. Before every webinar ended, quick impressions were sought from the participants (Appendix 1) before their experiences would become forgotten later.

4.4 Limitations of the Study

The feedback forms did not collect adequate demographic details of the participants such as age. Although webinars were conducted to suit the European and Asian continents, the timing may not have suited the Australasian and American continents due to which fewer speakers were received from the latter.

4.5 Implications for Research

The large number of participants (at least 210 per webinar, Fig. 2) is a huge opportunity for surveys. Researchers may designFig. Instruments for specific themes and variables (such as self-efficacy and player satisfaction) and administer them to collect data in such captive sessions. In future, conference organisers may design feedback forms to capture socio-demographic details of the participants such as age, gender, education, occupation and affiliation.

4.6 Recommendations for Practice

Countries such as the UK and the USA have a strong history of research and practices in S&G; therefore, future webinars may seek speakers from such countries. Webinars may cover under-represented themes such as e-sports, online games, storytelling, war games, game development and toys. Additionally, the feedback has unearthed many topics of interest such as serious games, game science and theory, AI-based games and business games which may be the topics of future webinars. Games for the development of theories, measurement of learning outcomes and organizational development need attention [23].

A large proportion (75%) of participants in the webinars was university students; future webinars must therefore address their curiosity and expectations with topics of their interests such as e-sports voiced in the feedback. Perhaps, webinars could ad-dress topics of students, academicians and other communities in separate sessions. Future webinars must seek out female speakers who were only 12 (27% of the total) in the study; their contributions are expected to be different and may attract a larger proportion than the 41% of the female audience during the study period.

Addressing the entire world and ensuring participation from every time zone is a huge challenge for any webinar organiser. Therefore, webinars in future may be con-ducted at other times of the day or week to suit speakers and participants from other parts of the globe. To serve its objectives, SVVV may reach out to other under-represented communities via collaborations with other S&G organisations such as DiGRA, IndSAGA, JASAG, NASAGA, SAGANET, SAGSAGA and SimAust.

5 Conclusion

The webinar is an effective process to collect and disseminate information, experiences and expertise on a large scale. It attracts a large number of interested participants whose feedback may facilitate the development of the domains of learning, education and S&G. Conference organizers may conduct webinars for speedy and low-cost promotion of events to global audiences. Webinars are a rich source of data for learning, practice, research and collaborations. Adversity (such as COVID-19) need not stop a project like an international conference. It could give rise to innovation such as webinars that became the driving force for SVVV's entry into the world of S&G. The pioneering initiative of SVVV could not have succeeded without the active participation of S&G experts and participants such as students and academicians and organisations such as ISAGA.

Appendix 1

Pratiti: Feedback Form

- Webinar Title: ……………
- Date: …………………..
- Speaker Name: ………………
- Speaker Designation: ………………………….
- Please Enter Your Valid Details: ………………
- Title: (Mr./Ms./Mrs./Dr./Prof.)
- Full Name:(in capital letters) …………………..
- Institute / Organization Name: ………………………………..

- Category: (ISAGA Member, S&G Professional, Academician, Research Scholar, Student)
- Contact (WhatsApp preferably):
- City: ……………………
- Country: ……………….

1. Experts/Speakers have put good efforts in explaining things to make me understand the topic.

    - Strongly Agree
    - Agree
    - Neutral
    - Disagree

2. This webinar has increased my knowledge and skill in the discussed topic.

    - Strongly Agree
    - Agree
    - Neutral
    - Disagree

3. The webinar objectives were clearly stated.

    - Strongly Agree
    - Agree
    - Neutral
    - Disagree

4. As a result of this webinar, I gained knowledge applicable to my work.

    - 100%
    - 75%
    - 50%
    - 25%
    - 0%

5. How do you rate the quality of speakers invited?

    - Excellent
    - Very Good
    - Good
    - Average
    - Poor

6. Please indicate your satisfaction for the following aspects of the webinar.

    - Strongly Satisfied
    - Satisfied
    - Neutral
    - Not satisfied

7. How did you hear about the webinar?

- Website
- News
- Social Media
- Friends
- Other

8. Are there any topics you'd like to see covered in future webinars?

   ----

9. Suggestion/Comment (If any)

References

1. Madhya Pradesh Act No.04 of 2015, The Madhya Pradesh Niji Vishwavidyalaya (Sthapana avam Sanchalan) Dwitya Sanshodhan Adhiniyam (2014). https://govtpressmp.nic.in/history-gazette-extra-2015.html
2. https://www.svvv.edu.in/
3. https://svg.vaishnavindore.com/
4. https://isaga.com/
5. CNN Editorial Research. Covid-19 Pandemic Timeline Fast Facts. https://edition.cnn.com/2021/08/09/health/covid-19-pandemic-timeline-fast-facts/index.html
6. Listings of WHO's response to COVID-19. https://www.who.int/news/item/29-06-2020-covidtimeline
7. The virus that shut down the world: 2020, a year like no other, UN News, Global Perspective Human Stories. https://news.un.org/en/story/2020/12/1080702
8. Dunford, D., Dale, B., Stylianou, N., Lowther, E., Ahmed, M., de la Torre Arenas, I.: Coronavirus: the world in lockdown in maps and charts. BBC News World (2020). https://www.bbc.com/news/world-52103747
9. ISAGA News Letter (2020). Accessed 30 Mar 2020
10. Saha, J., Chouhan, P.: Lockdown and unlock for the COVID-19 pandemic and associated residential mobility in India. Int. J. Infect. Dis. **104**, 382–389 (2021)
11. ISAGA News Letter (2020). Accessed 23 Oct 2020
12. ISAGA News Letter (2021). Accessed 24 Mar 2020
13. ISAGA News Letter (2021). Accessed 19 May 2021
14. Dumblekar, V., Dubey, J., Dhar, U.: Development of the player satisfaction scale - a factor analytic study. In: Dhar, U., Dubey, J., Dumblekar, V., Meijer, S., Lukosch, H. (eds.) Gaming, Simulation and Innovations: Challenges and Opportunities. ISAGA 2021. Lecture Notes in Computer Science, vol. 13219. Springer, Cham (2022). https://doi.org/10.1007/978-3-031-09959-5_13
15. Pratiti …becoming aware
16. Pratikriti, A.: Bi annual news letter of SVVV-Indore. In: Dhar, D. (ed.) January to June 2021 and Volume 6(1) July to December 2021, vol. 5, no. 2, pp. 21–23 (2021)
17. Minutes of First Meeting of the members of CoE_SG, SVVV, Indore
18. Pratiti 2022…becoming aware
19. Pratiti 2023…becoming aware (In process of publication)
20. Government of India. National Education Policy 2020 (2020). https://www.education.gov.in/sites/upload_files/mhrd/files/NEP_Final_English_0.pdf

21. Dumblekar, V., Antony, S.P., Dhar, U.: Openness to experience and player satisfaction in a simulation game. Simul. Gaming (2024). https://doi.org/10.1177/10468781241234131
22. Csikszentmihalyi, M.: Flow: the psychology of optimal experience. 1st Harper Perennial Modern Classics ed. Harper Perennial, New York (2008)
23. Kriz, W.: Types of gaming simulation applications. Simul. Gaming **48**(1), 3–7 (2017). https://doi.org/10.1177/104687811768

Analyzing Relationship to Nature Within a Game Frame
Proposal and Application of a Conceptual Framework and its Evaluation Method

Éléonore Sas and Nicolas Becu

LIENSs Laboratory, La Rochelle University, La Rochelle, France
eleonore.sas@gmail.fr, nicolas.becu@cnrs.fr

Abstract. The dualistic paradigm of human-nature relationship prevailing in Western societies, here referred to as classic modern Western (CMW) relationship to nature, has become a conceptual prison when faced with ecological crises. Simulation games can be useful artifacts for transforming a player's apprehension of such subject. Therefore, the research presented here is part of a thesis seeking to help one deconstruct its CMW relationship to nature by playing a simulation game. To achieve this, it is essential to be able to observe the presence and patterns of expression of the dimensions composing the CMW relationship within the game. However, to our knowledge, there is no such conceptual framework specific to games. Therefore, this paper aims to present for the first time a conceptual framework of the main dimensions of the CMW relationship, within a game frame, and to experience its evaluation method on players. The presented exploratory research crosses borders of scientific disciplines, spanning both human geography and design sciences, and drawing insights from other humanities. Starting with a multidisciplinary literature overview, this article describes the process and result of synthesizing the dimensions of the CMW relationship to nature. The conceptual framework obtained leads to a methodological approach, grounded in the case study *My Spot of Sea*, to observe these dimensions among players, considering design effects. Finally, results from applying this method to game sessions with middle school students are presented and discussed.

Keywords: Human-nature relationship · Design effect · Simulation Gaming

1 Introduction: Human Classic Modern Western Relationship to Nature and Simulation Games

The classic modern Western[1] (CMW) relationship of human to nature is one possible worldview, based mostly on a dualistic separation and hierarchy between Human and Nature. Supposedly born around the 17th century in Europe, this historically unique worldview has spread through modern societies, helped by contemporary globalization

---
[1] This term used throughout this paper is inspired by Berque's paradigm designation [1].

and capitalism contexts [2]. Today, it has become the most prevalent one. In fact, it is so dominant that it is easy to overlook as just one among many perspectives and to forget that the relationship to – what CMW humans commonly refers to as –*nature* is a social construct. The very use of this term is characteristic of this specific vision of the world(s). This way, the CMW worldview has become an unconscious conceptual prison [3] that prevent Westerners from dealing with ecological crises, when this same worldview has contributed to the current Anthropocene era. Therefore, this CMW relationship to others living beings would appear to be one of the main obstacles while facing the contemporary issues [4]. Simulation games as experiential learning devices seem to be a relevant means of addressing the diversity of aspects of such subject. The issue in this research, embedded in a broader thesis, addresses the possibility to use simulation game to enable players to *deconstruct* (understood as the concept of Derrida [5], who sees deconstruction as a process that involves successively unveil, reflect, and reconstruct) this relationship to nature.

Relationships of Humans to Nature. Several humanities disciplines tries to describe the classic modern Western (CMW) relationship for better conscientization [6, 7], or to show the hidden or unrecognized diversity of other possible ontologies [1, 8, 9]. Given that this literature is prolific and multidisciplinary, the authors of this paper attempted to realize a non-exhaustive overview of it, shortly presented here and then reused in Sect. 2.1 to create the conceptual framework. More precisely, because the work presented here is model based, this review focuses mostly on the macro scale literature of cultural worldviews, with a particular focus on the typologies proposed by Descola [6] and the environmental ethics.

According to the former, four major ontologies exist(ed), i.e., ways in which societies see themselves in relation to other living beings and assign them properties that will influence their mutual relationships. These ontologies differ according to two criteria named identification schemes: physicality (morphological or physiological characteristics) and interiority (internal characteristics, such as soul or consciousness). Cross-referencing these identification schemes reveals four possible pairings: totemism, analogism, animism, and naturalism. The latter corresponds to the CMW relationship to nature, which is dualistic and tends to divide and hierarchize living beings according to their interiority, presumed by those who share this ontology.

Similarly, authors of environmental ethics consider that this relationship placing humans at the center of things corresponds to anthropocentrism. This posture emphasizes the human exceptionalism and its separation from nature, and is rooted in Judeo-Christian, Greek and humanist traditions. It contrasts with biocentrism, which prioritizes life's intrinsic value, but is criticized for perpetuating human-nature distinction. To exceed that, ecocentrism attributes intrinsic value to biosphere entities [10]. Huybens [11] proposes to combine the antagonisms and contradictions of these postures via her concept of multicentrism (yet little used). Overall, ethical positions involve assigning diverse values to non-humans (but doesn't fully embrace the concept of plural attribution of values): instrumental, intrinsic, systemic, or relational [12].

While not exhaustive, this literature reveals the diversity and complexity of human relationships to nature that have existed and have been conceptualized. This paper focuses on the relationship of CMW to nature: for this reason, nature is understood here as their cultural production of all living other than humans and their environments.

Simulation Gaming. Our research aims to deconstruct the CMW relationship to nature through a game. In the context of this work, we want to emphasize certain aspects related to the gaming domain that influence relationships to nature and their observation.

Games are mainly based on models abstracted from reference systems of a perceived reality. This aspect aids in making complexity more apprehensible for players (participating or not in the modeling process). Games also organize reflexivity in a rather special way: the in-game experience and the debriefing [13]. This is one reason why games are seen as potentially transformative for players [14], and thus might help deconstruct worldviews. For example, games' ability to provoke reflexivity [15], while offering a secure space to explore possibilities [16], seems particularly appropriate.

In a similar way, games can help apprehend a complex system (such as worldviews), as well as the plurality of viewpoints and representations held by its designers or players. By manipulating the system represented within the game, players confront their own representations with those modeled and those of other participants [17]. This way, the game acts as an intermediary object [18]: it gathers, communicates and generates dialogue around the social and individual representations of a group, at a given moment, on a given system. A model-based game thus represents a compromise between the representations of the world used as input, whether these come from the designers (representation process) or from their prior investigative work (translation process).

Furthermore, games contain more or less free play [19], empowering players and enabling them to modify it. With free play, the model represented in the game can be rearranged to correspond more closely to the players' representations. Nevertheless, the obtained model often risks corresponding to an average of the main worldviews of players, failing to account for more marginal divergent voices [17]. In this sense, the authors postulate that simulation gaming can be seen as a magnifying mirror of a society's relationship to nature: it would convey it in a simplified, apprehensible artifact, enabling players to become aware of it, confront their own relationship with it and question it.

Moreover, like any technique, the game artifact and its facilitation carry inherent biases, termed *design effects*, influencing player behavior and thinking. Thus, games developed by designers within a CMW culture embody and project it (e.g., through anthropocentric values), shaping the games themselves through design effects that influence players. The modeling paradigm often used to develop a game (i.e. agent-based modeling [20]), while suitable for socio-ecosystem modeling [21], still maintains a degree of positivist ontology, limiting actors to one role in the game. Players, often unaware of these design effects, may unintentionally adopt the worldview embedded in the game. Debriefing becomes crucial to assess player consciousness of these effects. Furthermore, design effects can be intentional [22, 23] or unintentional [15]. The first option could enable using these game properties to make it a perfect opportunity to study worldviews (of players). However, the design effects related to designers' culture are often not examined by them and are unintentionally incorporated into the games.

Despite the various limitations discussed in the literature review, simulation games seem to be relevant for helping players to free, or at least, distance themselves from their conceptual prison. However, to determine whether a game actually has an impact on the players' classic modern Western (CMW) relationship to nature – and therefore, whether it can help them deconstructing it –, it is essential to be able to observe the presence and patterns of expression of this relationship within the game. But as describe in the literature, this CMW concept is not directly measurable and needs to be operationalized. This necessitates the development of a conceptual framework to facilitate its application in research. However, to our knowledge, there is no prior conceptual framework tailored for this purpose in the context of a game.

Therefore, the structure of this article deviates slightly from the traditional format. It first introduces for the first time a conceptual framework (Sect. 2) to characterize the CMW relationship to nature into key dimensions. Then it presents the game case study *My Spot of Sea* and the associated research questions and hypothesis (Sect. 3). Next, it displays the evaluation method designed, based both on the conceptual framework and the game studied (Sect. 4). This new evaluation method aims at observing these dimensions among participants interacting within the game frame. Subsequently, it shows (Sect. 5) and discusses (Sect. 6) the results of applying this method to middle school pupils. As this is exploratory research, the latter sections welcome both insights directly linked to the research questions and hypothesis, as well as inductive findings that enrich our understanding of the results.

2 Conceptual Framework: Key Dimensions of the Human Classic Modern Western Relationship to Nature

Before exploring the key dimensions of the CMW relationship to nature, it is important to acknowledge that the authors are themselves immerged in the same cultural worldview (although trying to take a critical attitude about it). Similarly, the conceptual framework was developed by a doctoral student which is herself rooted in human geography and design scientific fields, mainly from a French cultural perspective. In addition, the literature used to synthesize these dimensions comes from modern sciences, and the framework is applied according to a research objective and approach. Moreover, it is crucial to note that this study is grounded in the non-neutral context of gaming, shaping the conceptualization of this framework. Taking the game design effects into account implies being aware that the players' relationships to nature will not be evaluated independently, but rather through the game that influences the players.

2.1 Conceptual Synthesis of Literature

To assess the CMW relationship to nature it was necessary to isolate its principal dimensions. They were identified based on a review of multidisciplinary literature that includes those from Sect. 1 (i.e., mostly large typologies of relationships to nature), to which other references presented here have been added. In addition, the studied material includes archetypal personalities [24–28], but also recent investigations of social representations of nature in France [29] and concrete framework to evaluate current and attractive relationship to nature [30]. Moreover, literature on the history of the CMW ontology in Europe [31, 32] and its significations [33] were also consulted. The materials also includes papers describing others ontologies (and entanglements of ontologies), such as the analyses of other cultures [1] or the reflections on other paradigms [1, 7, 9]. Moreover, the themes of the experience of nature [34, 35] and connection to it [36, 37] were also considered.

Faced with the various possible readings of this multidisciplinary literature, and to respect this research constraints, we had to choose one perspective to synthesize it. This synthesis enabled us to characterize the CMW relationship to nature through ten dimensions, detailed in Table 1. These dimensions usually entangled are divided here for easier evaluation later. Other typologies would have been possible based on the same literature, but they would certainly express similar ideas with slight variations.

In our case, we chose four analysis criteria to identify those key dimensions from the literature: **1)** Transversality across the scientific fields addressing this relationship with nature (dimension identified: e.g., *Externalization* or *Instrumentalization*); **2)** Specificity of the prism of modern scientific environment (e.g., *Uniformity of reality* or *Objectification*); **3)** Observability enhanced by the easy identification of opposing dimensions in the literature (e.g., *Apathy* or *Prioritization*); and **4)** Specificity and applicability to the gaming context (e.g., *Individualism, Predictability* or *Categorization*). Several of these four criteria were also often combined to identify each dimension (e.g., *Apathy* met both the first and third criteria, while *Predictability* was identified through both the second and fourth criteria).

2.2 Conceptual Framework: Classic Modern Western Dimensions

The dimensions are presented in alphabetical order in the Table 1. For simplicity, each dimension is shortened in an acronym formed from its three first letters, which will be used in this paper.

In addition to these key dimensions and in order to account for the non-neutral game frame, we sought to identify the biases of the specific game studied in this paper (the game, *My Spot of Sea*, is presented in Sect. 3.1). These potential design effects were preidentified through an analysis of the game material and the archives of its conception, as well as inductive observations from game sessions in first and third person.

Each of the 24 design effects identified was then associated with the dimension it predominantly strengthens, even though it often influences multiple dimensions. For instance, the design choice to introduce lately in the game a board exclusively for humans, is a design effect connected to the EXT dimension. Even though those design effects are often specific to the studied game, the essence of most of these effects could be found in many board games. For example, it is common practice to visually categorize the elements of a game, as is the case in the game studied with the use of the same pictogram to represent individuals of the same species on the different tiles, which we identified as a design effect related to the CAT dimension.

Table 1. Synthetic description of the key dimensions composing the CMW relationship of humans to nature, as well as their acronym coding.

Apathy towards living beings (APA) – Relative emotional indifference and loss of affect towards other living beings and their interdependent living environment, adopting a detached stance

Categorization of living beings (CAT) – Spontaneous/conscious organization of entities of nature into distinct categories, often perceived as independent. This process may lead to the standardization of elements within a category, creating the impression that they are interchangeable and substitutable

Externalization of humans from nature (EXT) – Clear distinction between society and nature through a dualistic perspective. All living beings and their interdependent living environment are perceived as a unified whole (the natural realm) external to humans and their creations

Individualism anthropocentric (IND) – Autonomous and individualistic perception of humankind, distinct from other living beings and/or their interdependent living environment, considered as a whole

Instrumentalization of living beings (INS) – Use and management of nature to meet human needs. The valuation of nature is based on the material or physical benefits it can provide to the human species or its individual members (instrumental or utilitarian value)

Objectification (OBJ) – Other living beings are regarded as *things*, passive and devoid of any own intentions and capabilities. Without agency, these beings only react mechanically to humans or geo-climatic *stimuli*. They tend to be considered outside of their environments and interdependencies

Predictability of living beings and systems (PRE) – Living beings and their interdependent environment follow laws or always respond in the same way to the same conditions. Everything is governed, determined by sets of mechanical rules, making everything predictable. This leads to the impression that living beings can be manipulated and that modern science may one day explain everything

Prioritization of living beings (PRI) – Conscious or unconscious ranking of living beings or species based on value judgments, often resulting in a sense of human domination

Pure substance (SUB) – No spiritual aspect considered, as it is often taboo and devalued

Uniformity of reality (UNI) – Belief in one reality, as the fact that there is only one real world that is the same for everyone, despite different perspectives. The physical world exists in itself and is uniform: all components and living beings adhere to the same physical laws, measurable by modern sciences. Substances are valued and considered as preceding the relationships between them

---

3 Research Questions Relating to the Application of a Given Game

Our conceptual framework was applied to the study of how the relationship to nature is expressed through the application of an existing game, called *My Spot of Sea*. We first present the game, then the research questions and hypothesis associated.

3.1 Studied Game: *My Spot of Sea*[2]

This research focuses on the 4th version of the simulation game *My Spot of Sea* (*Mon Lopin de mer* in French), which was designed by IFREMER and LIENSs laboratories, in partnership with the association *Les Petits Débrouillards*, before the thesis in which this research is included. This collaborative board game was intended for education and awareness on littoral social-ecological systems and was integrated into school educational programs. However, it can also work independently and with older players. This game belongs to the category of games intended to address the issues and questions raised by ecological crises. Moreover, its purpose makes it characteristic of games seeking to represent other visions of nature: here, that of socio-ecosystems.

The game can be played by 2 to 4 groups, each consisting of 3 to 10 players. It is composed of two main steps that have the same duration. The first step consists of the free construction of the group's spot of sea, using the hexagonal tiles available on the boards and selected solely based on the group's wishes. Rules representing the interdependencies of the socio-ecosystems built are then gradually added. The second step adds a city-board next to the spot. Players then choose amongst cards which of this city's human inhabitants' daily needs they wish to solve, while respecting the spot's life gauge. All the game's components mentioned can be seen on Fig. 1.

Fig. 1. Game session, featuring all the game's components: tiles, boards, cards, and life gauge.

As shown in Fig. 2, these steps are subdivided in sub-steps of varying durations. Moreover, the session includes both intermediate and final debriefings. These debriefings serve as guided opportunities for the players to engage in thoughtful discussions, reflecting on the events that happened in the game and considering their connections to real-life elements. This way, even if debriefings are shorter than other parts of the game, they are presumed crucial moments for the result analysis.

---

[2] More details on the game can be found here: https://www.ifremer.fr/fr/la-mediation-scientifique-l-ifremer/nos-offres-pedagogiques/monlopindemer.

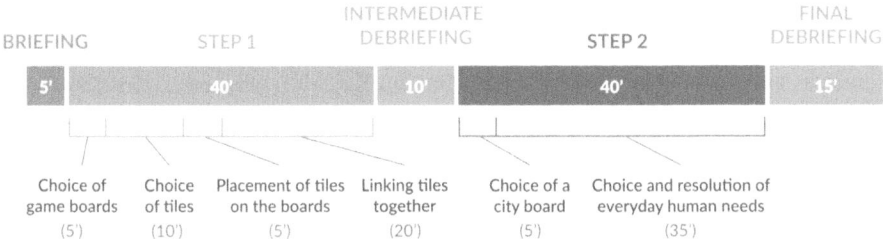

Fig. 2. Schematic distribution of the durations (in minutes) of the main and sub-steps of the game.

3.2 Research Questions and Hypotheses

Applying the conceptual framework to the studied case of *My Spot of Sea* raises two main sub-questions. First, are all the key dimensions of the CMW relationship to nature observable in *My Spot of Sea*, a game conceived by CMW designers? Simultaneously, which aspects of this game influence players' reflexivity and/or opposition to these dimensions expressed by players? Four hypotheses follow these questions:

1. *My Spot of Sea* – a game conceived in a CMW culture without the benefit of hindsight – reveals mostly CMW dimensions through positively weighted verbatims[3].
2. Because relationship to nature is something mostly unconscious, data from the game session – where players are immersed and less cautious of their speeches – is more insightful than the data collected from the debriefing part.
3. *My Spot of Sea* having been partially conceived to reveal players' attachments to coastline socio-ecosystems, the Apathy is the dimension for which players express the most opposition (negatively weighted verbatim) or reflexivity (debriefing part).
4. The ways in which the dimensions are expressed by players within the game (temporally and qualitatively) reveals the likely impacts of design effects on it.

4 Material and Method

To answer our questions, we defined indicators to evaluate the dimensions of relationship to nature presented in our conceptual framework, we runed two game sessions and collected and analyzed the players' speech and playing activities.

4.1 Method: Analyzing Classic Modern Western Dimensions with Indicators

The assumption that the conceptual dimensions would appear in the studied game seemed to lead to a rather deductive form of research method. We created an analysis grid with indicators to observe the presence (quantitatively) and expression patterns (qualitatively) of those dimensions in the players and facilitators discussions and game actions. Each dimension was measured with several indicators of different types (e.g., focused on behaviors or language elements), which enabled to cross-check them. These indicators were weighted positively or negatively, according to whether they indicated the presence

---

[3] The term verbatim refers to a word-for-word reproduction of the players' oral expressions.

of the dimension or, on the contrary, the presence of an opposite dimension (e.g., internalization versus EXT). In addition to this deductive coding via indicators, unanticipated elements could be noted inductively during coding.

4.2 Materials: Two Game Sessions

Two kinds of experiments were conducted, complementing each other: 1) full game-sessions and 2) shorter sessions with redesigned parts of the game (closer to practice-based research in design field). The analysis grid was used in both cases. However, only the first kind of experiment and its results are presented and discussed below.

Two sessions of tests in full game-sessions were conducted and facilitated by the same person, with middle school students of La Rochelle, a port city in the Western France. The first session was conducted with 11 last-year pupils (i.e. aged 14 to 15), divided between 8 girls and 3 boys, at a middle school named here A[4]. This school is located in a working-class district and some of the teenagers were not originally French speakers. This class was following the "Introduction to the Sea" option to take an exam focused on sea issues and jobs, in addition to their regular degree. Three groups of 3–4 pupils played in a single two-hour session.

The second session took place in a class of 28 first-year pupils (i.e. aged 11 to 12), divided between 16 girls and 12 boys, at the middle school B, in the city center. The session was divided into two one-hour sessions, set a week apart. Each time, the same three groups of 9–10 teenagers were playing together. Moreover, the results from a previously conducted game-session at the same B middle school with last-year pupils were also considered in this study (we'll refer to it as Pre-test here). However, this session didn't include the step 2 of the game. Finally, in all three cases teachers remained throughout the sessions, regularly interacting with the groups of players.

4.3 Data Collection and Analysis

Voice recordings were placed on the tables for subsequent analysis of players exchanges. After the sessions, the players' verbatims recorded were transcribed manually and partially. They were also manually encoded in the speech analysis software Sonal with tags referring to the indicators of CMW dimensions. During the game, video recordings – with cameras at each table focused on the game board and players' arms – along with external observation (from one observer) were also documented. These last types of data were primary used to complement to the analysis of the audio files.

This verbatim analysis focused on three main points: the quantitative distribution of verbatims through the game's sub-steps, their weighting (positive or negative) and the identification of qualitative expression patterns. For this last part, the verbatims noted were the most representative and/or those highlighting specific salient points.

---

[4] The middle schools' names are anonymized here.

5 Results

5.1 Overview: The Dimensions in *My Spot of Sea*

Analysis of the game results shows that the majority of the CMW dimensions appears through positively weighted verbatims, confirming the overall presence of a CMW relationship to nature. However, two of all these dimensions are absent or almost (SUB and EXT, with respectively 0 and 4 verbatim occurrences) and three others are barely visible (IND with 17 occurrences, PRE with 17 and UNI with 19). The CMW relationship is therefore mostly appearing through the other dimensions: APA (181 occurrences), INS (140), CAT (96), OBJ (78), and PRI (43). These dimensions are distributed throughout the sub-steps of the game (see Fig. 3, not considering the Pre-test because of their absence of step 1). Overall, the dimensions are mostly expressed in the first step of the game (with a clear majority of APA and INS in their respective sub-steps), as compared to step 2. Thus, these results suggest that the first step of the game is the most relevant for making players express their relationship to nature.

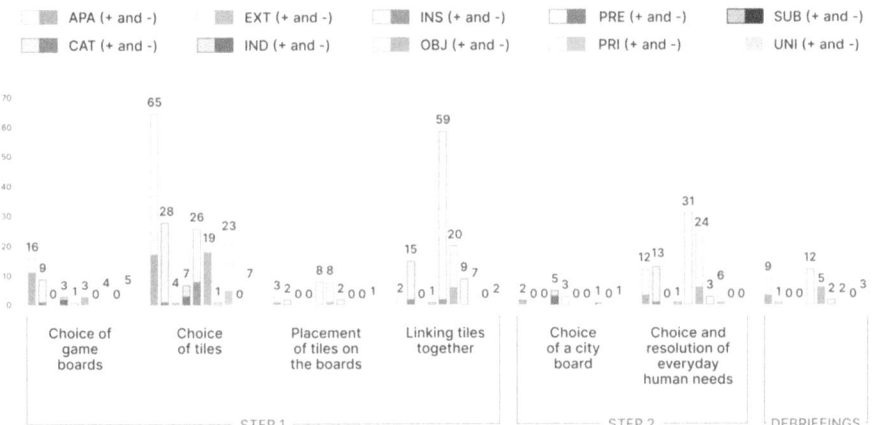

Fig. 3. Distribution of verbatim occurrences according to the game's sub-steps and the dimensions of the CMW relationship to nature, without considering the Pre-test data. (The data labels above each vertical bar represent the total number of occurrences of this dimension in this game sub-step. Within the same dimension, negatively weighted occurrences appear as a full color fill).

Within the game, the players express very little opposition to the dimensions of the CMW (meaning that their representation are aligned with CMW). This is confirmed by four types of results: 1) throughout the game, a minority of negatively weighted verbatims is observed; 2) even when adding the Pre-test data, only 35% of the verbatims are coded negatively; 3) these verbatims are also often occurring in only one of the case studies, suggesting group effects; 4) furthermore, they seem to diminish in number as the game goes on (and especially after the *Choice of tiles* sub-step). The only moments where there is a majority within a dimension are in *Choice of game boards* (with APA) and in *Choice of tiles* (with OBJ), i.e., the two first sub-steps of the game, corresponding to the freest play moments. These results suggest that the game does not encourage players to express oppositions to the CMW. Another interpretation is that the game's sub-steps have an impact (i.e., a design effect?) on the expressions of the dimensions.

Regarding the debriefing, it could have been expected to be one of the most reflexive parts of the game, where the players most express reflexivity and/or oppositions to the CMW to nature. However, little oppositions are observed (27% of the de briefing verbatims are negatively weighted). On top of that, the entire debriefing only includes 49 occurrences, which seems little compared other sub-steps like *Choice of game boards*, containing 43 occurrences but being three times shorter. The only two notable aspects here are that: 1) INS and APA are quantitatively the most present dimensions, and 2) OBJ is mainly present through negatively weighted verbatims (but through little quantity as well). Apart from that, these results illustrate that the observation of the debriefing shows quantitatively little data compared to the one of the in-game. The qualitative analysis confirms the limited relevance of debriefing analysis compared to the in-game.

5.2 Key Dimensions Detailed: Apathy, Instrumentalization and Categorization

In this section we analyze more specifically some results of the three most prominent dimensions: APA, INS and CAT. Other dimensions are not further detailed here.

Apathy (APA). In the beginning of the game, analysis of the verbatims shows that there is a high proportion of empathic expressions (APA negatively weighted verbatims) from players (particularly in *Choice of tiles*). This aligns with the initial design intention of revealing players' attachments to socio-ecosystems through the step 1. This can be attributed to the following fact: as rules (i.e., constraints) are deployed incrementally and progressively, the start of the game contains the freest play and seems to have a beneficial impact on the expression of negatively weighted APA verbatims.

Nevertheless, APA appears mainly through positively weighted verbatims throughout the game. These are expressed mostly through rational arguments, focusing often on the quantification and the optimization of the tiles. This last point seems to be a consequence of an intentionally developed design effect: stress players and make them realize the limited place available in our terrestrial livability zone [7] by representing it with a limited number of tile-locations on game boards and a specific balance of the associated mechanic. Overall, these results suggest that the game falls short in encouraging players to express opposition to APA once *Choice of tiles* is over. However, 40% of the APA verbatims are tagged negatively throughout the entirety of the game. This last data shows that APA is the dimension for which players express the most opposition, even if these expressions are mostly gathered at the start of the game.

Throughout the game, the boards become almost invisible (despite drawing a lot of emotional comments at the start of the game, mostly on aesthetic aspects). This way, at the beginning, players place the tiles on the boards depending on what they both represent. But, as the game progresses, the board is forgotten in favor of inter-tile links (e.g., a whale may end up on the sand). This may be due to design effects occurring: opaque tiles hiding the board, and incremental rules nudging players to focus only on the tiles. This way, this result reveals the likely impacts of design effects on APA here.

After the sub-step *Linking tiles together*, the expressions of the player's emotions tend to diminish (both positive and negative). One pattern is observed: players focus more on gaming elements than on what they represent. This tendency is reversed in the debriefing, where players start talking again about the content represented on the tiles. This last result shows that the debriefing helps players regain meaning on their play. However, the debriefing represents only 12% of the APA occurrences. This is very little data to analyze compared to the in-game. Thus, for the overall aim underlying this study, the observation of APA seems to be more relevant in the step 1 of the game (and, more precisely in the first two sub-steps) than in the step 2 or the debriefing.

nstrumentalization (INS). This dimension appears as one of the most preeminent CMW dimensions expressed in the game, considering its quantity and its proportion of positively weighted verbatims. More precisely, INS is particularly present in the sub-steps *Linking tiles together* and, for half less, in *Choice and resolution of everyday human needs*. This result seems to show that these two sub-steps encourage the expression of positive INS. In both cases, the usefulness of the tiles is rather expressed by the identification of concrete tile placement issues linked to game mechanics than by the meanings of these links. Moreover, INS arguments are manifested mostly by utilitarian (and often OBJ) vocabulary and arguments about the value of living beings. This set of outcomes could be explained by the fact that the game mechanics of these two sub-steps no longer require considering the tiles for themselves, but rather relatively to external things (like other tiles or human needs).

On another note, the expression patterns of positive INS varies throughout the game: players transit from words as "need" (step 1 and debriefing) to "service" or "uselessness" for someone/something (step 2). These results may be explained by the fact that the game nudges players to move from mainly inter-tile relationships (step 1) to more explicit human needs (step 2). Thus, freer play of the beginning (with many negative APA) seems to be progressively replaced by mechanics favoring anthropocentrism.

Another pattern is that INS appears mostly around tile choices moments, leading to two reactions: putting the most complex tile because it's supposed to be useful in the near future; or selecting the less complex tiles because it should require less effort to keep them alive later. Moreover, the recurrent expression "it's useless" is systematically used in arguments aimed at removing a tile from the game board. These two results may be caused by the same combined design effects: restraining space on the boards and representing linearly the tile links, through instrumentalist and trophic values.

These same tile choice moments are also the time when utilitarian (positive INS) and less numerous intrinsic values (negative INS) often debated. In these cases, the former usually wins. The carriers of intrinsic value often seem to be heard only with an external mediation (i.e., the teachers or the facilitator). This result seems to show that facilitation favorizes negative INS expressions. However, the teachers and the facilitator also often tend to reinforce the tile substitutability bias (to choose tiles with less complex links) when trying to help stuck players. In this way, external help both favors negative INS to be respected and reinforce other positive INS. Thus, the facilitator role in deconstructing the CMW relationship is still ambiguous in this version of the game.

Little opposition to INS is occurring in the game (7% of INS verbatims). The rare negative verbatims are gathered in the freest play sub-step, *Choice of tiles*. This may be because in this sub-step players are proposed to build their ideal spot of sea. Facing this only rule, players often react by minimizing as much as possible the presence of humans, which they interpret as negative (especially *via* the idea of pollution). Players often explicitly assume that the game, or the facilitator, expects them to create a "good" and rather ecological environment. Conversely, some groups interpret the instructions differently, assuming that the hidden aim of the game is to achieve a balance taking the most predictable human needs into account from the beginning. But even in this second case, the notions of "good nature" and "nature useful to humans" (depending on the players' posture) remain very present. These results show that, even though free play enables players to express more opposition to INS (although groups react differently), it also does not remove INS way of thinking. This permanent INS view could be attributed to the gaming context, which may encourage players thinking strategically.

In addition, the absence of negative INS in the debriefing, despite its prevalence here, suggests that the game currently does not foster opposition to it. Consequently, the analysis of the debriefing data offers limited insight compared to the in-game one.

Categorization (CAT). CAT emerges as one of the most present CMW dimensions expressed in the game, both in terms of frequency and its high proportion of positive CAT (92% of the verbatims are positive). Moreover, CAT is twice more visible in the step 1 (mainly in *Choice of tiles*) than in the step 2. This result may be explained by the players' needing to make sense of the multitude of tiles presented at the same time, whereas this would be less necessary after, as the tiles are already known.

At the opposite, there is not many oppositions about CAT: negatively weighted verbatims are rare and almost gathered in one study case (suggesting group effects), and there is no sub-step with a consequent proportion of negative CAT (as for APA and INS). Moreover, negatively weighted CAT are completely absent from the debriefing (where CAT is missing anyway). This finding indicates not just a lack of opposition towards CAT, but also its almost invisibility during the supposed reflexive debriefing. Nevertheless, this analysis is to be mitigated by the fact that the current debriefing does not include any elements questioning CAT (i.e., even less than in APA and INS cases).

On another note, CAT data is particularly fruitful for identifying relating patterns and design effects, detailed here through four main examples. The first one (**1**) is about the design effect of coloring tile edges. This design effect is visible throughout the game, especially in *Choice of tiles* where players tend to both preferably organize their tiles by edge color, and refer to them by their color property. Besides, this color design effect is visible throughout the game (in players choices of tiles, in their own interpretation of colors…). Another pattern (**2**) concerns the selection of one tile rather than another, mostly through INS values. This way, in *Linking tiles together* and *Choice and resolution of everyday human needs*, INS is mainly expressed by selecting a few representative tiles from a larger category, either premade or implicit. Indeed, these sub-steps choice often imply less tiles than previously, which could explain the more precise choice of *representative* tiles at this point. This behavior could be encouraged by the design effect of representing different possibilities to fill the needs of one tile on the same graphical level (with an "or" proposition and a similar visual). Moreover, the arguments used to choose one representative tile are often imbued with INS vocabulary and values (and some Prioritization). A third example (3) relates to the category types made by players. Throughout the game is that players tend to categorize sets of tiles using two ways: from one tile to a larger ensemble, or the opposite. Among the most frequent categories through the game, we found "animals" (most of the time not including the human, and thus being related to an Externalization phenomena), but also "fish". This last result could be explained by the theme of the game (the sea, which is commonly and culturally associated with these species), or by the difference of visual representation on the tiles. Indeed, the last exampled pattern presented here (**4**) concerns the fact that these categories seem to be reinforced by a specific design effect: using similar pictograms and name labels for representing the members of a same species. In fact, the presence of two tiles representing different fish (although associated with different *needs*) often troubles the players, who tend to question each other or the facilitator on the subject. This result shows that the players expect fish to be a single species in the game, and thus that they unconsciously perceive CAT as a norm to be respected.

Overall, these four results can be interpreted as the fact that CAT seems to be a dimension very inherent to game boards, and that particular care must therefore be taken when using a game to deconstruct CMW relationship to nature.

6 Discussion and Perspectives

6.1 Key Findings

Sub-questions (see Sect. 3.2) Answers. Concerning the **first sub-question**, the key dimensions of the CMW relationship to nature are indeed observable in the game, except for SUB. This absence could be explained by the context of the experimentations, in middle school, where the taboo of the spirituality is particularly crystalized[5] [38] (even if generally spread in the French society, and even more in modern sciences). However, not all dimensions are equally present in the game. Only APA and INS are particularly salient, followed, for the most observable, by CAT, OBJ and PRI. The results of the other ones are too small for meaningful analysis. This way, it seems that both the conceptual framework and its evaluation method proposed in this paper, when applied to the specific game *My Spot of Sea*, enable observing mostly APA, INS, CAT, OBJ and PRI among the dimensions of the CMW relationship to nature.

Concerning the **second sub-question**, the results of this study enable to identify some aspects of the game on the reflexivity and the opposition to the CMW dimensions. First, the supposed reflexive moment of the debriefing doesn't seem to enable players to express many oppositions and/or thinking about CMW relationship to nature, in its current form. Hence, the game and debriefing format could be reworked to enhance reflexivity following the recommendations made in the literature [39, 40], but this is outside the scope of our research, which focuses on the game's current format. Secondly, the main aspects of the game influencing player's expression of the CMW dimension are design effects, distributed through the game: e.g., graphically representing different individuals within a species on tiles, as in the example of fish tiles (which design effect could explained by a *Gestalt* perception effect [41]). Whatever the case, the results enable more identifying potential design effects that seem to reinforce CMW dimensions than design effects that seem to help players to oppose them and/or think about them. Indeed,

---

[5] It is also historically grounded in the French context of the Ferry laws in 1881, abolishing religion teaching and wearing of symbols in school.

the oppositions to CMW dimensions are mainly gathered in the *Choice of tiles* sub-step, where the rules to constrain the players' actions allows the maximum free play [19]. It would then seem that the rules and mechanics added afterwards do not encourage players to maintain this type of reaction and perhaps even push them towards positive weightings that reinforce the dimensions. Overall, the current version of the game doesn't seem to help players deconstruct their CMW relationship to nature.

Hypotheses Answers. Concerning the **first hypothesis**, the game reveals mostly CMW dimensions through positively weighted verbatims. Indeed, most of the visible dimensions, including those with the least data, contains very little proportion of negatively weighted verbatims, exception made of APA. More specifically, the CMW dimensions all appear mainly in step 1 of the game. This inductive finding shows that this step seems to be the more relevant for our overall aim.

This last result seems to validate our **third hypothesis**: the APA dimension is the dimension for which players express the most opposition or reflexivity. Indeed, in terms of quantity, APA is the dimension with the most oppositions through the game and the most reflexivity. However, the OBJ dimension seem to be qualitatively better on these issues: it holds a greater proportion of negatively weighted verbatims both in the debriefing and in the game sub-step where APA is majoritarian. Thus, it should be interesting to analyze more precisely the relation between negative APA and negative OBJ to see whether or not the two are impacted by the same aspects of the game.

The results also validate our **second hypothesis**: concerning our subject, the analysis of the data collected during the in-game is more insightful than the data collected from the debriefing. Consequently, the players and the facilitator do not speak about the CMW dimensions spontaneously here. Moreover, the rare positive mentions of it are mostly not reflexive and are rarely compensated by opposed reactions. Thus, the debriefing seems to offer few results that are relevant compared to other sub-steps in the game, despite its reflective purpose that we assumed would bring out much more data [13]. Furthermore, this seems linked to another inducted overall finding: the current version of the game explores more the concrete, functional relationships of players with nature than their representations of it. Then, the players' representations emerge (and are analyzed here) mostly when they are confronted with constraints and/or diverging opinions during the game. However, the debriefing is more structured around individual responses and thus elude these confrontations of opinions. This could be one reason for the limited representations (and thus dimensions) of nature in the debriefing.

Overall, the results validate our **fourth hypothesis** about the influence of design effects on the players' expressions of the CMW dimensions in the game. Indeed, many design effects about this subject are observed. The results show that they are not explicitly identified or questioned by players, proving that players are either unconscious of them or do not consider them as sufficiently important to be discussed [15]. Nevertheless, some pre-identified design effects are not much observed with our method (e.g., the impact on EXT of the addition of a board specific to humans in the step 2 of the game) while not anticipated ones (e.g., the design effect negatively impacting APA with fish representations) are made visible with this same method. This way, design effect identified could be used for further improvement of the game (as it has been done in design rhetoric previous works [22]): by reducing them as much as possible, or by using and reinforcing them if they are negatively impacting the dimensions (e.g., using the same representing logic than the one in these fish tiles).

However, the analysis can't offer explanations about the precise impact of the design effects on the dimensions. This highlights limits in the method used, even if it was not aiming to be centered on design effects but only on considering these biases.

6.2 Limitations and Perspectives

Method Limitations. The method used to evaluate the CMW dimensions includes several limitations. First, it is mainly based on discourse analysis when the corporal experience (and, thus, non-verbal behaviors) could have been also considered. Similarly, so far it focuses only on the game session, excluding contextual analysis. The grid of indicators also contains some indicators imprecisions, not detailed here, but the authors hope that this exploratory study will help them improve it. Moreover, and as already mentioned, the conceptual framework used is very specific and is situated at a macro scale when other graduations and typologies could have been used. The deductive and partial transcription approaches also limit the insights of this study. Furthermore, as the game is multiplayer and collaborative, two scales of relationships to nature could appear – at the individual or group scale – but this method doesn't really distinguish them both: and perhaps are they inseparable in the game context?

Perspectives. For the next phase of this research, the analysis grid will be improved, and the method enhanced with complementary approaches (i.e., preliminary and post questionary to situate players before and after the game on the dimensions studied). More generally, *My Spot of Sea* will be transformed following the model of Derrida's deconstruction process [5] and then assessed again with this new version of the method. Due to the results of this first phase of the thesis, we will focus the design of the game and its assessment only on the four prominent dimensions: APA, INS, CAT and OBJ (non-detailed in this paper). Similarly, only the first step of the game and its debriefing will be re-used in the new version of the game as they were the most relevant here. Finally, the new version of the game aims to be played (and evaluated) on adult publics.

More generally, the CMW relationship to nature conceptual framework raises questions in the era of transitions. This work intends to be a first exploration on how to deconstruct this worldview through a game. It is to be regarded in the same way as other efforts addressing the deconstruction of nature relationships (such as the French examples of Zoepolis design collective which co-designs with and for all living beings[6], as well as the third edition of the Science-Fiction Committee, working on interspecies communication through an exploratory biology-and-art approach[7]). Within this range of initiatives, we find the distinctive use of a game particularly intriguing and perhaps less disconcerting for common participants than other forms of sensory experiences (e.g. exploring the feeding behavior of barnacles through movement improvisation [42]). Others can seize on this work to hybridize it with other experiences.

---

[6] Website: https://www.zoepolis.com.
[7] Website: https://ite.sorbonne-universite.fr/de-la-science-aux-actes/le-comite-de-science-fiction.

References

1. Berque, A.: Poetics of The Earth: natural history and human history. Routledge, Abingon (2020)
2. Latour, B.: We Have Never Been Modern. Harvard Univ. Press, Cambridge (1994)
3. Descola, P., Pignocchi, A.: Les alternatives existent (2022)
4. Barnosky, A.D., et al.: Has the Earth's sixth mass extinction already arrived? Nature **471**, 51–57 (2011)
5. Derrida, J.: Deconstruction in a Nutshell: A Conversation with Jacques Derrida. Fordham University Press, New York (2021)
6. Descola, P.: Beyond Nature and Culture. The University of Chicago Press, Chicago (2014)
7. Latour: Down to earth: politics in the new climatic regime. Polity Press, Cambridge (2018)
8. Escobar, A.: Thinking-feeling with the Earth. In: Knowledges born in the struggle. pp. 41–57. Routledge, Abingdon (2019)
9. Haraway, D.J.: Staying with the trouble: making kin in the Chthulucene (2016)
10. Leopold, A.: A Sand County Almanac. Oxford University Press, London (1968)
11. Huybens, N.: Comprendre les aspects éthiques et symboliques de la controverse socio-environnementale sur la forêt boréale du Québec. VertigO (2011)
12. Pascual, U.: Why do we need a more pluralistic approach to valuing biodiversity? Biodiversity Revisited is an initiative of the Luc Hoffmann Institute. In: collaboration with WWF, Fu-ture Earth, ETH Zürich Department of Environmental Systems Science, University of Cambridge Conservation Research Institute, and the Centre for Biodiversity and Environment Research at University College London, vol. 126 (2019)
13. Crookall, D.: Serious games, debriefing, and simulation/gaming as a discipline. Simul. Gaming **41**, 898–920 (2010)
14. Klabbers, J.H.G.: The saga of ISAGA. Simul. Gaming **40**, 30–47 (2009)
15. Monfort, A., Becu, N., Amalric, M.: Feedback on a "Territory-Responsive" participatory simulation on coastal flooding risk applied to two case studies in France. In: Harteveld, C., Sutherland, S., Troiano, G., Lukosch, H., Meijer, S. (eds.) Simulation and Gaming for Social Impact, pp. 99–120. Springer International Publishing, Cham (2023)
16. Brougère, G.: Jouer/apprendre. Economica (2005)
17. Étienne, M. (ed.): Companion modelling: a participatory approach to support sustainable development. Springer, Dordrecht (2014)
18. Vinck, D.: Intermediate objects in the scientific cooperation network. Contribution to include these objects in social dynamics. Revue française de sociologie **40**, 385 (1999)
19. Klabbers, J.H.G.: The Magic Circle: Principles of Gaming & Simulation: Third and Revised Edition. Brill (2009)
20. Ferber, J., Gutknecht, O.: A meta-model for the analysis and design of organizations in multi-agent systems. In: Proceedings International Conference on Multi Agent Systems (Cat. No. 98EX160), pp. 128–135. IEEE (1998)
21. Becu, N., Frascaria-Lacoste, N., Latune, J.: Distributed asymmetric simulation - enhancing participatory simulation using the concept of habitus. In: Kriz, W.C., Eiselen, T., and Manahl, W. (eds.) 45th Conference of the ISAGA, pp. 75–85. Berstelmann, Austria (2014)
22. Schneller, A.: Design rhetoric: studying the effects of designed objects. Nat. Cult. **10**, 333–356 (2015)
23. Vial, S.: Court traité du Design. Presses universitaires de France, Paris (2015)
24. Bang, M., Medin, D.L., Atran, S.: Cultural mosaics and mental models of nature. Proc. Natl. Acad. Sci. **104**, 13868–13874 (2007)
25. Braito, M.T., Böck, K., Flint, C., Muhar, A., Muhar, S., Penker, M.: Human-nature relationships and linkages to environmental behaviour. Environ. Values **26**, 365–389 (2017)

26. Flint, C.G., Kunze, I., Muhar, A., Yoshida, Y., Penker, M.: Exploring empirical typologies of human–nature relationships and linkages to the ecosystem services concept. Landsc. Urban Plan. **120**, 208–217 (2013)
27. Kellert, S.R., Wilson, E.O.: The Biophilia Hypothesis. Island Press (1993)
28. Muradian, R., Pascual, U.: A typology of elementary forms of human-nature relations. Curr. Opin. Environ. Sustainabil. **35**, 8–14 (2018)
29. Ducarme, F., Pautard, E.: Une nature en quête de sens: état des lieux des représentations sociales de la nature dans la France contemporaine. La Revue du CGDD (2021)
30. Muhar, A., et al.: A model integrating social-cultural concepts of nature into frameworks of interaction between social and natural systems. J. Environ. Planning Manag. **61**, 756–777 (2018)
31. Chanvallon, S.: Anthropologie des relations de l'Homme à la Nature : la Nature vécue entre peur destructrice et communion intime (2009)
32. Wulf, A.: The Invention of Nature: The Adventures of Alexander von Humboldt, the lost hero of Science. John Murray, London (2016)
33. Maris, V.: La part sauvage du monde. Seuil, Paris (2018)
34. Fleury, C., Prevot, A.: Le Souci de la nature. CNRS (2017)
35. Soga, M., Gaston, K.J.: Extinction of experience: the loss of human–nature interactions. Front. Ecol. Environ. **14**, 94–101 (2016)
36. Rahmani, L., Haasova, S., Czellar, S., Clergue, V., Martin, C.: How often do you think about your relationship with nature? the measurement of environmental identity salience and its relationship with proenvironmental behaviors. Front. Psychol. **13** (2022)
37. Schultz, P.W.: Inclusion with Nature: The Psychology of Human-Nature Relations. In: Schmuck, P., Schultz, W.P. (eds.) Psychology of Sustainable Development, pp. 61–78. Springer, Boston (2002)
38. Béraud, C., Massignon, B., Mathieu, S.: French students, religion and school: the ideal of Laïcité at stake with religious diversity, pp. 51–80 (2008)
39. Whitton, N., Moseley, A.: Deconstructing engagement: rethinking involvement in learning. Simul. Gaming **45**, 433–449 (2014)
40. Crookall, D.: Engaging (in) gameplay and (in) debriefing. Simul. Gaming **45**, 416–427 (2014)
41. Wertheimer, M.: Laws of organization in perceptual forms. Psycologische Forschung. **4**, 301–350 (1923)
42. Metcalfe, D.: Multispecies Design (2015)

Extraordinarily Large-Scale Gaming for the Youth

Ryoju Hamada[1] and Tomomi Kaneko[2]

[1] National Institute of Technology, Asahikawa College, 2-2-1-6 Syunkoudai, Asahikawa 0718142, Hokkaido, Japan
hamada@edu.asahikawa-nct.ac.jp
[2] National Institute of Technology, Tomakomai College, Nishikioka 443, Tomakomai 059127, Hokkaido, Japan

Abstract. Gaming simulation is considered a "miniature garden" of a complex society. Most gaming simulation researchers have yet to learn how to gather thousands of participants. As a member of the UNESCO Creative Cities Network, Asahikawa City in Hokkaido, Japan, hosted a whole-city learning event called the Machinaka Campus (MCAN, "City Center Campus" in English) in 2022 and 2023. The event is aimed at providing an opportunity to present inquiry-based learning to Japanese students. The authors invited students who wanted to demonstrate their works, and 36 exhibitions were subsequently organized. The authors printed and delivered 27,000 leaflets to all pupils in the city and hosted a stamp rally with the exhibitors on a pedestrian-only road in the city center. In total, 63,000 people participated in the learning event. Some derivative movements emerged from MCAN beyond the authors' control. MCAN may be a rare example of extraordinarily large-scale gaming that had once been considered impossible.

Keywords: UNESCO Creative Cities Network · Asahikawa · Machinaka-Campus · autonomy · Large-scale · Gaming

1 Introduction

Real life is real life, and gaming is simply gaming. The goals of gaming have always been simpler than real-world goals. In resolving social issues, the use of gaming at a real-life scale turns gaming into a political platform. In real politics, direct democracy is not always effective because it involves too many stakeholders and too many complexities. The authors might find a breakthrough against the premise that we provide on gaming.

Asahikawa, the second largest city in the Hokkaido region, Japan, designed an interactive learning opportunity called the "Asahikawa City Center Campus (MCAN)," which attracted 63,000 people in 2022 and 68,000 people in 2023. They were not required to participate in the event, but they decided on their own to attend, and eventually had great fun. Twenty-five organizations set up 36 tents on a 1 km pedestrian street in 2022 and 2023. These organizations displayed, demonstrated, and shared their experiences in their daily work on inquiry-based learning that contribute to Sustainable Development Goals

(SDGs), urban development, or design. MCAN was announced to all pupils (G1–G12, 33,000 in 2023) across all schools in the city through paper leaflets. The authors prepared a "Stamp Rally" for children to encourage them to learn something new from adults.

Moreover, the authors encouraged students to work in their tents and to visit, join, and learn collaboratively. Circulation occurred between the students, and some were still active. Consequently, the authors could say that MCAN is the first large-scale gaming platform that they have seen. This article reports on a rare trial of an extraordinarily large-scale gaming case, focusing on its facts and specifications.

2 Literature Review

Large-scale physical games are difficult to develop. If a game aims to resolve problems that really exist, it often fails to express a solution. Aiming to overcome this puzzle, Duke [1] argued that gaming is a new type of communication:

…The individual needs to be part of the processes affecting his life, but is currently devoid of effective means to join the dialogue about potential change. This situation has grown more urgent because the problems of today are more complex, involving systems and interactive subsystems that go beyond normal human ken…..; there is a growing personal urgency because the solutions pursued today constitute a more pervasive intrusion in the individual's life. (Duke, p. 24).

His story continues to the famous idea called "gestalt communication." Duke obviously did not consider that involving all facts in gaming simulations is possible. Greenblat [2] also introduced her definition of "simulation" at the beginning of her book:

A simulation is an operating model of central features or elements of a real proposed system, process, or environment. (Greenblat, p. 14).

Gaming simulation researchers have followed these ideas, ultimately creating a "miniature garden" based on their findings, theories, models, or teaching objectives.

This development has a practical reason as well. If we challenge ourselves to develop extremely large-scale gaming, the task would be difficult for university researchers. It is also costly, time consuming, and difficult for participants and facilitators. Therefore, few researchers have attempted to resolve social problems by building large-scale gaming simulations.

3 Backgrounds

3.1 Origin: UCCN Approval

On October 31, 2019, Asahikawa City was approved to join the UNESCO Creative City Network (UCCN) in the design category. The UCCN is an organization that shares the best urban planning practices by utilizing the power of culture while maintaining sustainable city development. It comprises seven categories: literature, music, film, craft and folk art, design, media art, and gastronomy. Approximately 300 cities were nominated, and 49 cities were nominated under the design category. The furniture industry has fostered a design culture in Asahikawa. Today, Asahikawa City must extend the UCCN or its design aspect to other industries horizontally and to younger generations vertically. As members of the academic sector, the authors were asked to propose an event for the youth under the design category called the Asahikawa Design Week (ADW).

3.2 Design: Set of Diverse Ideas

Design is a common word that even kids know, but its meaning is complex. Long ago, the word referred to a product's shape, color, and sometimes its function. However, design was extended to the business field around the year 2000. Many derivative ideas have emerged, and they include "design management" and "design thinking." Design is considered as a significant way to improve business. Design targets are not limited to products but also extend to opportunity design, communication design, career design, and so on. To be sustainable, a city must use the power of design in diverse ways. In other words, design has no fixed direction. A similar story might apply to the SDGs. The SDGs are extensive ideas that can be applied to most people's work. Thus, the same story arises; no reliable direction is available. Therefore, realizing sustainable city development by using the power of design is extremely tough.

3.3 Inquiry-Based Learning

The authors found that many students are struggling with SDG studies in Japanese high schools. In 2012, Japan's Ministry of Education promoted active learning. Inquiry-based learning was introduced to all high schools in 2018. Students form groups, establish hypotheses, and prove them in real society. Table 1 shows the results of a questionnaire administered to high school teachers instructing inquiry-based learning. We note that the topic is familiar to students and is easy to understand.

However, inquiry-based learning has received many complaints from students. Although they spend much time on this program (6–8 credits), it does not appear in university admission. In most cases, the final evaluation is restricted within the school, which means that a student's work is not subject to competition with the work of students from different schools.

Table 1. Major Topics of Inquiry-based Learning*

Topics	% (n = 1,597)
Social, Regional Issue	58.0
Career Design	53.8
Global Social Problem	29.4
Literary, History, Culture, Art	26.2
Science, Mathematics	23.2
Business Issue	11.3
Others	2.6

* Bennese (2021) [3]

3.4 The Origin of the Project

The authors considered that if we provide an opportunity to appeal their inquiry-based learning results to the public, including all high schools in the city and across many generations, we can complete the city's request: "Vertical idea sharing over generations." Accordingly, we developed the project "Asahikawa Machinaka Campus" (MCAN, where machinaka means "city center" in Japanese) and proposed it to city officers. They appreciated our idea, and it was included in the big design event called the ADW.

The authors visited all high schools (14), universities (4), and public research institutes (3) in Asahikawa and interviewed participants in the fields of design, city, or SDGs. The authors confirmed that at least one team in all the schools conducted research on SDGs, design, or the city.

3.5 Challenges

Despite SDGs learnings are common, we faced many challenges to develop the new learning opportunity.

Never Seen Such a Gaming. All schools have an experience of inquiry-based learning presentation individually. However, no one can imagine such presentations gather on the street, hence, few people recognized the effectiveness of MCAN project. The authors spent a long time explaining our ideas.

Estimation of Time, Labor, and Cost. The authors did not have any idea for the volume of the event, how much resources we need. The authors walked around the city to seek the sponsor companies, but explanations were so difficult.

No Future Image. At the beginning of the project, even the authors could not believe such large-scale gaming is able to carry out. While MCAN is growing, we recognized similarity gradually and tried to include ideas of Simulation Gaming.

4 Methods

4.1 Dates

The authors and their teams hosted MCAN twice, as listed in Table 2. MCAN was a two-day program. Most exhibitions lasted for two days, whereas others were held within a day. Unless otherwise stated, the subsequent descriptions are based on the facts and data obtained in MCAN2022 because the authors lacked essential data for 2023.

Table 2. MCAN Schedules

MCAN2022	Saturday, June 17–Sunday, June 18	10:00–16:00
MCAN2023	Saturday, June 18–Sunday, June 19	10:00–16:00

4.2 Exhibitions

Considering the UCCN policy in design, we called for specific tenants, as shown in Table 2. The theme was not restricted; instead, free ideas and expressions were welcomed. Table 3 illustrates the organizations and their themes. In the exhibitions, high school, university, and college students presented their inquiry-based learning results to children. To teach the children, the presenters studied diligently to understand what they had learned before the event. Elementary school students did not come to the city center alone; they were accompanied by their guardians who also sought new knowledge. Table 3 lists the number of exhibitions that were conducted. As some high schools or universities hosted more than two exhibitions, the numbers of organizations and tenants differed.

4.3 Mapping

Kaimono Koen Dori (Shopping Street Avenue) is an 11 m-wide former national road that stretches 1 km north of Asahikawa Station and is a pedestrian-only zone. Figure 1 shows tents lined up along the street while Fig. 2 shows a map of MCAN.

A unique characteristic of MCAN is its straight layout. As participants could see all tenants in their view, they are encouraged to traverse the venue within their own time. As shown in the venue map in Fig. 2, tents with similar themes were gathered together. The 1 km stretch was divided into four zones (red, yellow, orange, and green). Children could gain differently colored stamps at stamp stands, indicated as stars in the map. They could then exchange four stamps with stationery items or other goods. The authors did not set a specific entrance for the venue. Kaimono Koen Dori was divided into 14 blocks. Map and stamp sheets were available anywhere. People could conveniently enter and join MCAN from anywhere in the venue and enjoy the exhibitions. Participants could freely enter and leave the event.

Table 3. MCAN 2022 Exhibitions*

No	Organization	No. of Tenants	No	Organization	No. of Tenants
1	National Institute of Technology, Asahikawa College	3	14	Japan Chamber International Asahikawa	1
2	Asahikawa Engineering HS	2	15	Asahikawa Information Industry Cooperative	1
3	Asahikawa North HS	8	16	Asahikawa Creative City Promotion Society	1

(*continued*)

Table 3. (*continued*)

No	Organization	No. of Tenants	No	Organization	No. of Tenants
4	Asahikawa West HS	1	17	Hokkaido College of Northern Forestry	1
5	Asahikawa Special Education HS	1	18	Asahikawa UV Eguchi Seminar	1
6	Asahikawa Agriculture HS	1	19	Asahikawa UNESCO association	1
7	Asahikawa UV HS	1	20	Kamui Taisetsu Barrier Free Research Center	1
8	Asahikawa Ryukoku HS	1	21	Asahikawa Para Sports Association	1
9	Asahikawa Tosei HS	1	22	Girl Scout Association of Asahikawa	1
10	Asahikawa Vocational HS	1	23	Hokkaido UV of Education, Design Seminar	1
11	Asahikawa Medical UV AYASHIP	1	24	Hokkaido UV of Science	2
12	Hokkaido Architecture Research Center	1	25	Asahikawa Green Promotion Association	1
13	Hokkaido Forestry Research Center	1		TOTAL	36

* HS – High School, UV – University; the organization names without English equivalents were translated by the authors.

4.4 Silent Environment for Learning

As MCAN is a learning opportunity, our team allotted sufficient space in each block. We used a large tent (5.6 m × 2.0 m × 1.8 m) to operate the workshop. To keep the environment quiet, we avoided certain features that would attract large crowds, such as TV personalities, music, dance performances, large vehicles, or food. Consequently, we were able to create the quietest, most unique atmosphere among all street events (Figs. 3 and 4).

 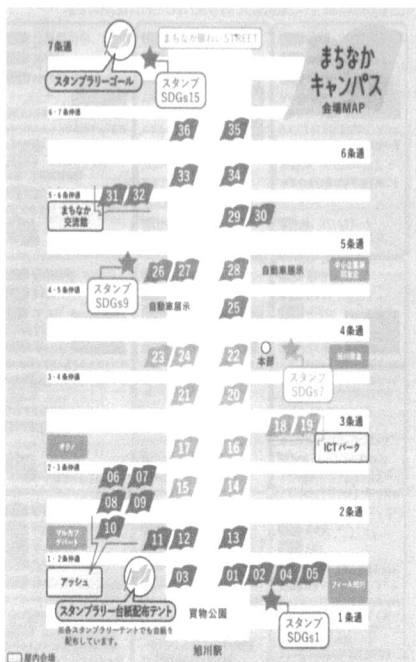

Fig. 1. MCAN Venue Layout

4.5 Characteristics of MCAN as a Gaming Platform

From the perspective of gaming, MCAN has the following features.

Responding to a Wide Variety of Learning Needs. MCAN covers all 17 SDGs Goals. For example, participants interested in the environment could visit the exhibits on waste issues.

No Compulsion. Anyone could participate in MCAN. Only those interested in this kind of learning or event would participate, thereby increasing motivation.

Learning Through Gaming Makes Learners Happy. Children recognize MCAN as a game in which they receive prizes. Fig. X illustrates an example. All children visited seven exhibitions (10, 11, 15, 20, 21, 22, and 23) in three different zones and received stationery as prizes.

Interaction Among Participants. Inquiry learning was initially limited to each school. At MCAN, participants met old friends by participating in workshops, experiments, or demonstrations. By doing so, they learned from one other and stimulated their curiosity.

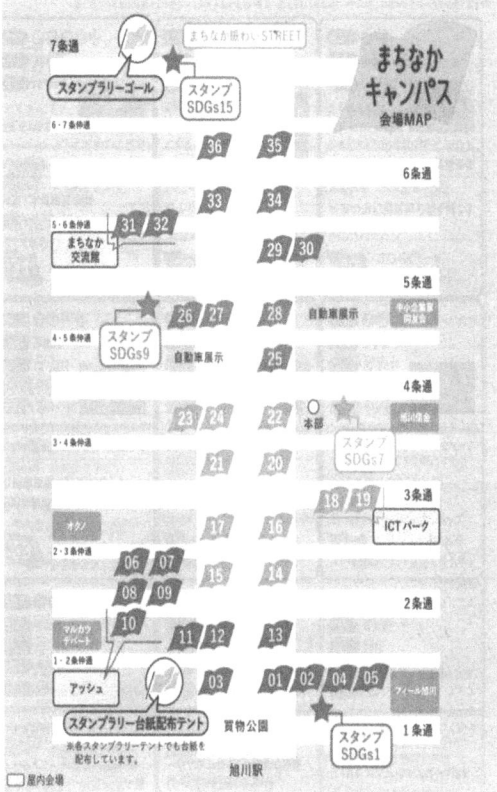

Fig. 2. Map of MCAN2022

5 Operations

5.1 Schedule

The authors spent almost a year developing the idea and formed the Organizing Committee (OC) in February 2022. After the launch of the OC, the authors worked diligently for four months. Table 4 presents the schedule at first glance.

5.2 Exhibitions

All expected organizations attended. The number of exhibitions increased in 2023, as Table 5 shows.

Figure 5 shows the typical scenes that we found in MCAN.

5.3 Student Committee

In 2022, OC officers and nine volunteer students from the Technology College managed all processes. Six students remained for the 2023 project. A Student Committee was formed to conduct the next project.

Fig. 3. Leaflet

6 Results

6.1 Number of Participants

In 2022, Asahikawa City officers estimated the number of participants to be 63,000. In 2023, this number increased to 68,000. Given that it was the first run and given the city's population (325,000), the event was undoubtedly impressive. It shows that people welcome open learning events on the streets.

6.2 Results of Participant Questionnaire

The authors asked the young stamp rally participants to answer questionnaires. A total of 411 questionnaires were collected; after excluding those from participants aged under 5 years and over 19 years, 303 questionnaires were retained, with the average age of the remaining respondents being 10.6 years. The participants comprised 202 elementary school students and younger, 46 junior high school students, and 24 high school students (excluding those who did not complete the questionnaire). Of the respondents, 157 were male, 140 were female, and 6 did not respond.

Fig. 4. Stamp Rally Sheet

Table 4. Major Activities' Dates for MCAN2022

Month	Description
January to March	Call for tenants, co-organizers, and sponsors
April	Finalize the exhibition title, along with a short description, related number of SDGs, and web materials
May	Print leaflets (27,000), posters (200), stamp rally sheets, flags, and signs Renew social media web pages (Instagram, Twitter) Secure permission for road usage
June	June 6: Send leaflets to all schools in the city June 7–8: Last briefing session June 16: Physical preparation June 17–18: MCAN2022
September	Awarding Ceremony

How Did they Know About MCAN? Table 6 shows the sources of MCAN recognition. As the targets (young children) did not have communication devices, the paper leaflet

Table 5. Number of Exhibitions

	High School	University, College	Others	Tenants	Total Exhibitions	Student No
MCAN2022	10	4	11	25	36	541
MCAN2023	9	7	13	36	55	581

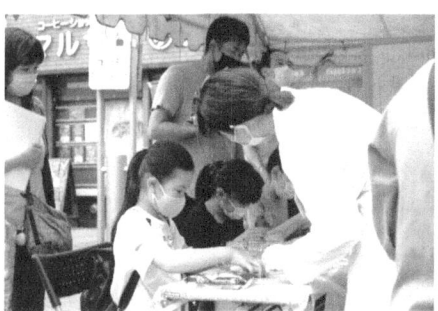

Fig. 5. Exhibitions in MCAN2022: Kids accompanied by parents

provided via the school was very effective. Meanwhile, internet-based promotions did not work well. An analog method is sometimes appropriate.

With Whom Did they Come? As shown in Table 7, 232 participants came with their families, 76 participated with their friends, and only 5 attended the event alone. Among elementary school students, 194 (83.6%) were accompanied by family members. Among junior high and high school students, 33 were accompanied by family members while 33 were accompanied by friends.

What Style of Exhibition Did they Like? Table 8 shows the results of the questions on what was enjoyable among the exhibitions. The most popular ones were those that visitors could participate in by moving their hands.

Understanding of SDGs, Design, and Creative City. Table 9 presents the results of the question on changes in interest in SDGs, design, and UNESCO Creative Cities. The sum of the top two responses, "Significantly Raised" and "Raised," was over 85% for

Table 6. How did kids learn about MCAN2022?

Media	No	%
Leaflet	232	71.8%
Friends	29	9.0%
Poster	10	3.1%
Newspaper (Advertisement)	9	2.8%
Asahikawa City's News	9	2.8%
Newspaper (Article)	6	1.9%
SNS	5	1.5%
Webpage	1	0.3%
Others	22	6.8%
Total	323	100.0%

Table 7. With whom did kids attend MCAN2022?

	No	%
Alone	5	1.6%
Family	232	71.8%
Friend	76	23.5%
N/A	10	3.1%
Total	323	100.0%

Table 8. Attractiveness Comparison in MCAN2022

Content	No	%
Experience	247	58.1%
Lecture	26	6.1%
Experiment	71	16.7%
Poster	36	8.5%
Sales	24	5.6%
Other	21	4.9%
Total	425	100.0%

SDGs and Design and 70% for UNESCO Creative Cities. Hence, the responses matched the learning objectives of MCAN.

Table 9. Participants' understanding of SDGs, design, or UCCN after attending MCAN2022

	SDGs		Design		UCCN	
Significantly Raised	155	51.2%	167	55.1%	127	41.9%
Raised	110	36.3%	91	30.0%	84	27.7%
No Change	32	10.6%	38	12.5%	82	27.1%
Not Raised	3	1.0%	3	1.0%	6	2.0%

Very Positive Image. Those who did not find MCAN to be enjoyable would not return for the next event. Table 10 clearly shows that the young participants enjoyed MCAN2022, with 95.7% of them responding positively. Therefore, the authors can say that an enjoyable "place to learn" was created for the children.

6.3 Stories Afterward

The authors identified two episodes from MCAN2022. The event seems like develop the new research motivations.

Asahikawa West High School's Case. The school demonstrated the idea of baking sweet foods, including sake lees. The audience appreciated this idea. The sake company decided to engage in collaborative research with the school. The sake company and the students sold their snacks in the autumn of 2022 at the gastronomy events in Kaimono Koen Dori.

Asahikawa Jistugyo Highschool's Case. The school exhibited sweet products in collaboration with a company specializing in sweet snacks. The audience members also supported their ideas. They conducted collaborative research and sold sweet items in MCAN2023.

Table 10. Children's impressions on MCAN2022

Answer	No	%
Very Fun	214	70.6%
Fun	76	25.1%
Useful	57	18.8%
Bored	1	0.3%
N/A	2	0.7%

7 Discussions

The high schools and universities that attended MCAN2022 learned who their audience was, how to create attraction for their studies, and how to talk to the children and parents. Therefore, the quality of exhibitions significantly improved even with the exhibits having the same themes as those in 2022.

7.1 Sustainable MCAN

Not only for their research targets but also for future children, students, teachers, schools, and many stakeholders, the team must continue the new type of learning festival on the streets. If MCAN did not exist, we could not discuss the possibility of extraordinarily large-scale gaming. To realize such an impressive possibility, the authors must sustain the event; then, more surveys can be conducted. The authors could manage such a huge event, but we must encourage more people to participate.

7.2 Improvement of Data Collection

At the beginning of the project, the authors did not know whether MCAN would be a large-scale event. We prepared an appropriate questionnaire as if we were designing a game in a classroom. However, the management of 63,000 festival participants left us with no margin to pay attention to the survey. The data analysis for 2023 failed, except for some parts; therefore, the authors excluded those incomplete datasets. The authors aim to avoid such loss of opportunity.

As mentioned in Sect. 6.3, more new studies could be conducted on MCAN2022 or 2023. If we can see that learning is becoming autonomous, then it proves that a new, self-motivated learning culture is spreading in the city.

7.3 Seeking Availability in Other Cities

We can easily imagine that Asahikawa had an excellent opportunity to change by joining UCCN. The appropriate keyword "design" had been provided for MCAN. Some may doubt whether MCAN will remain an occasional gaming venue that will only be available in Asahikawa. However, citizens' ideas about urban design, citizen empowerment, and civic pride are common topics in all cities worldwide. Hence, the authors wish that readers accept the limitations of this research and find useful ideas from Asahikawa's invention.

Acknowledgments. The research on MCAN was supported by the following foundation and research subsidies. The authors express their deepest gratitude to those who funded this study as shown below.

1) Foundation for the Fusion of Science and Technology (FOST): Supporting ISGC and its related Simulation and Gaming Research (2022–2023 FY).

2) Japan Association of Simulation and Gaming (JASAG): Financial support for our work via the following special interest groups (SIGs): Gaming Technology Transfer SIG, and Boad Game in Region SIG.

References

Duke, R.: Gaming: the future's language. In: WBV, Reprinted Version for ISAGA2014 (2014)
Greenblat, C.S.: Designing Games and Simulations: An Illustrated Handbook. SAGE (1988)
Benesse Corporation: Survey on high school learning guidance (2021) https://berd.benesse.jp/shotouchutou/research/detail1.php?id=5695. Accessed 25 Oct 2023

How Does Evaluating the Effects of a Participatory Simulation Raise Questions About the Design Intentions of Participatory Processes that May Involve Simulation/Gaming?

Amélie Monfort(✉)

UMR LIENSs 7266, La Rochelle University, 2, rue Olympe de Gouges,
17000 La Rochelle, France
amelie.monfort@gmail.com

Abstract. Simulation/gaming approaches, such as participatory simulation, are commonly developed and used to support social and ecological transitions. However, the growing interest in these methods is accompanied by challenges related to evaluating and demonstrating tangible effects for potential change. Assessments often lack objective evidence and primarily rely on empirical observations. When evaluations are conducted, they tend to focus on the design itself and frequently reveal limited effects in terms of effectiveness, which are often short-term and centered on knowledge acquisition–falling short of the broader ambitions attributed to simulation/gaming. Many studies attempt to explain these outcomes in relation to the design of these methods and/or by using analytical frameworks involving numerous process and contextual variables. In this contribution, aimed at presenting ongoing research reflections that intersect literature on the evaluation of simulation/gaming and citizen participation, we explore a hypothesis centered on the design intentions of the process. This reflection is based on an analysis of the limited effects of a participatory simulation on coastal flooding risk (LittoSIM-GEN). We observe effects that are primarily short-term and focused on cognitive dimensions, which do not fully align with the initial goals of the participatory simulation. The lack of (re)definition of design intentions–concerning objectives, target audience, status and key concepts of the process–emerges as a particularly promising avenue for further exploration in our future research on the evaluation of participatory processes, such as simulation/gaming practices, aimed at supporting socio-ecological transition.

Keywords: Simulation/Gaming · Participatory Simulation · Evaluation · Learning Effects · Design Intentions · Participation

1 Introduction

Simulation/gaming (S/G) approaches are commonly developed and used to support social and ecological transitions by fostering changes, particularly in behavior. The field of S/G encompasses various practices such as serious games, companion modelling, or participatory simulation (PS) [1]. These processes invite participants to engage in an abstraction of their reality in relation to issues such as environmental management. S/G practices are hybrid, resulting from the interaction between gaming, modeling and simulation of complex systems, as well as participatory approaches enabling shared control of actions among all involved stakeholders [2]. Generally, these practices pursue two main objectives: the educational aspect for learning and empowering participants, and supporting collective action within territorial projects or conflicts of use, for example.

However, a major limitation persists regarding the demonstration of the real impact of S/G for potential change. Studies on the subject are typically limited in number, lack objective evidence, and are predominantly empirical [3–6]. In a recent study involving over a hundred games related to agriculture, environment, food, and territories, Dernat and al. [7] emphasize that "the evaluation is weak for the games identified, and it seems challenging to highlight the real impact of games". Evaluating effects is not a major step in the process of designing and implementing S/G for designers, although this issue is recognized as crucial by practitioners, as evidenced by the ISAGA summer school in 2022 on the theme of "Evaluation and Research in games", and the organization in 2022 of the GAMAE conference in France exclusively dedicated to the question of the impact of games [8]. An overall analysis of the contributions to the conference reveals, however, that evaluating effects is often a challenging aspect to grasp and implement for S/G designers. Evaluations are still in preliminary stages and under development (reflection on objectives and evaluation methods, or how to handle data). Dernat and al. [7] mention various reasons related to a lack of time or interest, or a lack of anticipation during game creation, which, in any case, "show an absence of real reflection from the outset on the game's effects".

When evaluations are conducted, studies often focus on three aspects. The first one is on assessing the game design (e.g., understanding of rules, interface, animation) to enhance it, assuming that the quality of results depends on specific configurations of the artifact [2]. Some studies, for example, examine the affordances of S/G in relation to their effects on individuals, primarily aiming to enhance understanding of the system by promoting visualization, exploration, or shared envisioning of a desirable future [9]. The second aspect revolves around the evaluation of players' engagement in the activity, which is assessed through factors like *flow* [10, 11], motivation, and satisfaction [12]. Finally, evaluation studies often focus on assessing the effectiveness of S/G by measuring the learning outcomes achieved by individuals, based on the assumption that acquiring new knowledge through gameplay can translate into real-life practices, thus promoting a change in behavior [13]. Boyle and al. [14] show and regret that most S/G are used to support knowledge acquisition and validate the achievement of educational objectives. Evaluations aiming to demonstrate the effectiveness of S/G for skill acquisition and long-term behavior change, beyond playful circumstances, are less common or inconclusive [2, 14–16]. Therefore, the majority of observed effects are limited to short-term outcomes and measured through subjective means [3], including quantitative questionnaires and comparisons of responses before and after the S/G. This method has the advantage of obtaining a clear and immediate insight into spontaneous responses and engaging participants in reflection on what they have understood and retained from the experience [17]. However, the spontaneity of responses does not systematically guarantee objectivity, and results based on declarations must always be interpreted with caution [18], especially considering the growing interest in S/G for learning and behavior change.

Another element to consider in evaluating the effects concerns the difficulty, or even impossibility, of determining a causal link between the observed effect and participation in the S/G, particularly for long-term effects. This objective may even be deemed vain if the evaluation of the S/G is too detached from its application environment (territorial history, political context, relationships between actors, representations, etc.), given the complexity of current systems and the multifactorial dimension of change processes. Some works, such as those by Etienne [19] propose methods for evaluating the medium and long-term effects of S/G on behaviors, practices, and organizations by adapting Kirkpatrick's evaluation model originally designed for training. However, this approach still implies a straightforward causality by linking an observed effect to participation in the S/G.

Some of these limitations encountered in the evaluation of S/G are similarly observed in research examining the effects of citizen participation processes, which are defined as "the set of mechanisms through which citizens participate in the production of public action" [20]. Several decades of research on the evaluation of citizen participation processes have led to the development of a robust knowledge base on the effects of participation. It is valuable to draw upon this knowledge here to shed light on the issue of evaluating S/G. Authors emphasize the "anxious pursuit of effects" [21] of participation that would be limited across dimensions as varied as actors, groups, and decision-making [22, 23]. The same issues of identifying causal links are highlighted by political science researchers who caution against the risk of the autonomy of participatory processes from their public action context. They thus suggest not considering participation as the sole explanatory variable for potential change [20, 24], but strongly advocate for taking into account the territorial specificities of the study areas in evaluating the effects of any applied process, and for examining the origins and functioning of the participatory process.

Two hypotheses emerge to explain the various limitations in observing and evaluating the effects. The first hypothesis concerns the type of analysis methods employed to study the outcomes of the S/G. Other approaches, differing from the dominant perspective centered on learning effects, seem relevant for understanding the dynamics of a process. This may involve valuing the playful experience itself by examining aspects such as the roles or attitudes of the participants during the game [25–27]. It is also possible to highlight the conditions in which the process is deployed and on its uses in territories [20, 25, 28].

The second hypothesis, which we will delve into further here, questions the link between the objectives of S/G and their learning effects. Considering that the literature has extensively demonstrated the learning potential of S/G [2, 13, 29], it seems unlikely to dispute the existence of this link theoretically. The problem might, therefore, be practical, occurring during the design and/or implementation of the S/G. Research on citizen participation highlights the tension between objectives and effects in participatory processes, emphasizing the importance to distinguish between these two aspects, which do not necessarily overlap in evaluations [28]. This issue underscores the need to clarify the objectives of such processes, whose stakes might be overshadowed by an excessive focus on procedural elements [30]. In other words, there is a prevalent tendency to attribute the effects of participation to procedural characteristics–methods understood in their most technical, practical, and standardized dimensions–rather than engaging in deeper reflection on the objectives of the process or its integration with ongoing dynamics [28]. A similar parallel can be drawn in S/G research, where studies on design often attempt to infer the quality of effects from artifact configurations, such as examining the influence of model realism or the level of computerization [2, 31–33]. While the definition of objectives is indeed addressed in S/G evaluations, it is predominantly treated through analytical frameworks that focus on process design and contextual factors, incorporating the influence of numerous variables [e.g., 28, 29]. Some authors advocate for a more specific and precise examination of objectives. For instance, Mazeaud [22] raises questions about who the participants are (e.g., policy-makers or "ordinary citizens") and how they influence decisions, to better understand the potential effect of S/G on democratic socio-ecological transitions. Speelman and Rodela [3] propose a conceptual framework that articulates the objectives of S/G with the various stages and challenges of the issue-attention cycle. Finally, drawing from my doctoral research, I came to a similar perspective [25], aiming to link the development of objectives to the different stages of behavior change in social psychology [36].

For all of these reasons, the question of objectives–hereafter referred to as "design intention" to encompass a broader scope, including elements such as the target audience–emerges as a relevant assumption to explore in understanding the limited learning effects of S/G. It offers additional insights related to other hypotheses on artifact design and paves the way for broader reflection applicable to other participatory processes, beyond S/G, aimed at supporting social and ecological transitions. The paper builds on the findings of a previous study on the learning effects of a participatory simulation conducted during a doctoral research project carried out from 2019 to 2023 [25]. It provides a retrospective critical analysis of these results, examining how they prompt consideration of the design intentions in S/G. The next section briefly introduces the case study of the participatory simulation "LittoSIM-GEN" and outlines the methodology used to evaluate its learning effects on individuals. The primary findings on learning effects will then be summarized and discussed in relation to a specific hypothesis regarding the design intentions of the process.

2 A Participatory Simulation to Learn About Managing Coastal Flooding Risk

Here, we will mobilize the evaluation of the effects of a PS called "LittoSIM-GEN", which is implemented during half-day participatory workshops involving about ten policy-makers and administrative actors. The objective is to manage the risk of coastal flooding in a territory [37] by developing an adaptation strategy through various management solutions, including hard defense measures (construction of dikes), land use planning, or strategic retreat of assets from areas at risk. Participants must collectively formulate and implement this strategy on the scale of all the municipalities comprising the territory.

These objectives address significant challenges related to supporting coastal territories in their adaptation to climate change. In France, local stakeholders have been urged for several years to prioritize strategies considered more integrated. This approach relies on alternative solutions to hard defense, deemed more suitable for the increasing vulnerability of societies, and on regulatory changes that have altered the geographical scale of risk management. The learning and capacity-building objectives for participants primarily involve cognitive aspects (learning about risk, strategies, anticipation in the face of uncertainty, interdependencies), relational aspects (understanding others' perspectives and roles), and collaborative aspects (interactions between actors, coordination), as per the classification of learning by Becu [2]. These objectives aim to contribute to evolving the social reception of risk management by actors [38], i.e., their relationships with risk, which are founded and determined by a plurality of individual, sociotechnical and institutional factors [39]. These factors may include levels of information and knowledge, social representations, risk awareness, opinions, legitimacy and trust in institutions responsible for adaptation, as well as conditions for adaptation funding. Social reception, which is also influenced by external factors, is therefore a deeply rooted process, closely tied to individual subjectivity.

LittoSIM-GEN was deployed in several coastal territories in metropolitan France by researchers and locally established partners, forming the 'designer team' of the PS. The deployment occurred in two phases: a first phase in 2017 on the island of Oléron with the pilot version, and a second phase from 2019 to early 2022 in six coastal areas with a generic version capable of adapting to a variety of contexts [40]. Our focus will specifically be on this second phase of 12 workshops involving 121 participants, evenly distributed between policy-makers (mainly mayors and deputies) and administrative actors (from local authorities or other local structures).

This process underwent a significant evaluation protocol aimed at studying various dimensions, which are further detailed in another publication [25]. They are related to the use of the PS by local partners through project monitoring in the territories, participants' experiences during the game, and their subsequent learning effects. Here, our main emphasis will be on a summary of the primary findings regarding the individual learning effects of the PS. The cognitive, relational, and collaborative learning effects were assessed through a quantitative and qualitative survey.

The quantitative survey was based on questionnaires administered during each workshop, just before the game session and after the debriefing, which marks the final phase of the workshop. The aim was to assess the learning effects of S/G on the participants, and in particular the effects as perceived and reported by them. The qualitative survey relied on the debriefings at the end of each workshop and on *post*-workshop interviews with few participants one month after the workshop. The aim of this approach was to capture the spontaneous perception of the effects by the participants, without the framing imposed by the questionnaire, and to try to identify a certain permanence of these effects.

The response rate to the questionnaires was 89%. Due to the diversity of possible response cases (e.g., before, after, collected or not), the results rely on three samples of responses: $n = 96$, $n = 107$, or $n = 109$ respondents out of the $N = 121$ surveyed.

The qualitative results, on the other hand, are based on a set of 12 debriefings and 34 *post*-workshop interviews.

3 A Summary of the Limited Effects of LittoSIM-GEN on the Social Reception of Coastal Flooding Risk Management

The quantitative analysis reveals that participants consider effects related to the systemic and complex nature of coastal flooding risk to be particularly significant. They state that they have gained a profound understanding of the consequences of their decisions and the multiple interactions among various components of the risk (e.g., geographical, hydraulic, social). The PS has facilitated a better grasp of the quantity of information, issues, and management strategies available for handling the risk, considering the advantages and disadvantages of each.

Furthermore, the qualitative study highlights that the effects on representations of coastal flooding risk and management strategies, particularly hard defense, are frequently mentioned by participants. The PS helps them grasp the magnitude of the phenomenon, reducing optimism bias [41, 42], a cognitive tendency to underestimate one's own exposure to risk. It also induces a change in perspective among actors regarding their own practices, even sparking a desire to deepen their knowledge on the subject after the workshop. The PS also contributes to raising awareness of the limitations of a strategy based on building dikes, but it does not offer a practical solution to overcome this dependence.

Finally, participants identify various levers for the adaptation of coastal territories through participatory simulation. These levers refer to modes of governance, encompassing all processes and actors (political or non-political) involved in the political management of a society [43], particularly in favor of coastal adaptation [44]. Participants express the need to collaborate with other societal actors, such as scientists and civil society. They also emphasize the importance of utilizing specific management instruments and methods, such as models and simulations of weather-climate phenomena and management scenarios, the participation of "ordinary citizens" in decision-making, and the necessity for cooperation and territorial solidarity in the face of interdependence effects induced by the risk.

All these results indicate that LittoSIM-GEN had an impact on the individual and sociotechnical dimensions of social reception, affecting the level of knowledge about the territorial system, opinions on risk management options, and social representations of risk. The effects also influence the institutional dimension of social reception by questioning, for example, the involvement of citizens in adaptation processes and the coordination of actions. However, participants less emphasize the relational and collaborative effects concerning the development of knowledge and skills about others and for collective work.

Ultimately, it appears that these effects of LittoSIM-GEN are short-term, imprecise as to their nature, and mostly focused on the cognitive dimension of the PS' initial objectives. Indeed, there is no vision on the long-term persistence of the observed effects or the potential influence of these new knowledge on the practices and behaviors of workshop participants. Moreover, we favor the term "effect" rather than "learning", as initially considered, to more accurately describe the various forms of outcomes seen among participants. In this sense, the effects described can represent the development of new knowledge and skills, awareness, or the reinforcement of acquired knowledge. This approach aims to be as close as possible to the participants' experience and perceptions of what the PS has provided them.

Consequently, it is difficult to firmly conclude that the PS has made a fine and deep-rooted contribution to modifying the social reception of actors regarding coastal flooding risk management.

4 Discussing the Role of the PS' Design Intentions on Its Limited Effects

4.1 Study Limits: From Evaluation Protocol to Process Deployment Conditions

The results regarding learning effects do not fully meet the ambitions attributed to the process in the context of supporting social and environmental transitions. These findings are partially lit by limitations pertaining the evaluation protocol. Specifically, the methods employed (questionnaires and interviews) rely mainly on declarative mode, and no other on-site investigation method was implemented to observe effects at the individual level. Additionally, the timing of the study was relatively short, conducted at the end of the process, and thus did not consider the examination of long-term effects. These limitations are partly due to the significant number of study sites at the time of the survey (six) and other theoretical and methodological choices made regarding the evaluation.

It appeared more relevant to evaluate and value participants' experience during the game by studying their attitudes toward the PS, as well as the use of the PS by local partners involved in deploying LittoSIM-GEN workshops in the territories. Indeed, the workshops were not part of a long-term support process with participants, which could involve regular meetings structured by new workshops or under different conditions than the game. The deployment of a PS can be relatively punctual, as was the case with LittoSIM-GEN, ranging from half a day to a full day, and sometimes only occurring once per territory. Furthermore, the practice of PS mainly focuses on the simulation activity, i.e., the played exploration of the model by local actors, unlike companion modelling approaches that systematically integrate a significant phase of model co-construction with actors. These deployment conditions pose a limitation to be considered in the analysis, alongside the degree of definition regarding the PS' intentions by the designer team, which will be further examined in the subsequent discussion sections using two examples.

4.2 Process Objectives and Selection of the Participants

The limited effects of LittoSIM-GEN concerning the relational and collaborative dimensions of learning raises questions about the objective of coordination and the participant selection of the PS when implemented in new contexts. As a reminder, one of the objectives was to support collective action by fostering coordination and territorial solidarity among actors within the same management area in the face of a risk of coastal flooding, which ignores administrative boundaries. This objective was central from the initial deployment phase with the co-constructed pilot version deployed in 2017 with local actors from the island of Oléron. It aligned fully with the political context of the time regarding the transfer of the responsibility for managing the risk of coastal flooding ('GEMAPI') from the State to municipalities and intermunicipal authorities. The aim was to support the actors on the island in taking on this responsibility. In the broader context of decentralization in France, GEMAPI has contributed to altering power dynamics between the State and local authorities, as well as their modes of operation in terms of organization, exchanges, and coherence of the local policies for which they are in charge.

This coordination objective was maintained for the second deployment phase related to LittoSIM-GEN (2019–2021), despite two major differences. Firstly, the political circumstances regarding GEMAPI were different between the two deployments due to the changing nature of this public policy issue [45]. Territories were more or differently prepared during the second deployment, as the competence had been officially mandatory since 2018, and some had even taken it on in anticipation as early as 2016, as permitted by the law. Secondly, the groups of participants were also noticeably different. During the first deployment phase, there was a relatively strong correspondence between the policy-makers and administrative actors of risk management actually working together in the field and the participants in the workshops, facilitated in particular by the island context. However, we demonstrated that this coherence of actors in both "reality" and the game was not systematic in the workshops of the second deployment phase, with much more pronounced discrepancies [25]. Given these conditions, what are the possible coordination effects for participants? It necessarily modifies the potential influence of the PS deployed in very contrasting territorial conditions. Nevertheless, neither the initial objective of promoting coordination among risk management actors in the same territory nor the precise composition of participant groups were deeply questioned at the beginning or during the multi-site deployments by the researchers and local partners. Yet the definition of process objectives and the selection of participants are two factors that significantly influence the course and the outcomes of participatory processes [34, 35, 46–48]. Therefore, it appears essential to consider forcefully the territorial specificities inherent in any deployment by collectively (re)debating the question of objectives and target audience, especially when the process is deployed in multiple contexts necessarily different from its conception or when a process is designed based on the foundation of another.

4.3 Definition of Process Status and Key Concepts

The weakness of effects linked to their lack of precision can, in turn, be explained by the ambiguity observed in defining the status of the process and keywords for the objectives, whether as an awareness, learning, or even training process for coastal risk management. One of the PS' designers explains: "I think one of the debates that we [the scientific designers] had a lot, maybe we had it afterward, we didn't have it right at the beginning [because] we didn't measure all of this, but when it came time to write the project, […] it was about asking ourselves, what are we doing? Are we facilitating learning, are we raising awareness? And that wasn't so clear at the beginning" (interview, designer of the PS, 12/02/2021 [our translation]). The ambiguity, sometimes the back-and-forths in the use of different terms, and even differences among the designers in describing the PS' objectives have appeared repeatedly in the designers' discourse, whether in interviews, project development, or presenting it to participants during workshops.

This is particularly evident with the absence of discussions within the team of designers about the definition of the term "learning", which was ultimately the chosen approach for evaluating "what [LittoSIM-GEN] does [to participants]" (interview, designer of the PS, 12/02/2021 [our translation]). The objective of evaluating the effects from this perspective has revealed relatively different conceptions among the involved researchers on the project on one hand, and among the scientific communities on the other hand. A brief study of publications on the analysis of learning in S/G reveals the diversity of associated definitions. Learning can be described as "an acquisition of knowledge for effective action" [49], a "relatively durable change in behavior" [8 citing 9], what the participant retains and which can lead to potential change [2], "changes in practices in single or double loop" [52] for practitioners of companion modelling [53], or the acquisition of knowledge and skills within the game, without necessarily implying the ability to mobilize them outside the gaming experience [54]. Significant nuances emerge among all these approaches to learning –coming from cognitive psychology, political science, and education sciences– that nonetheless rely on the same evaluation methodologies, even though their underlying assumptions are different. At what point is an element truly learned, acquired? Is it when the intention of change is expressed? When an effective change, such as behavior change, is observed? Is learning only learning if it persists over time? What is the temporal horizon associated with "sustainable" learning? Faced with such diversity and its implications for the implementation of a process, it appears important to really question and debate what the term "learning" concretely means for each stakeholder involved in the design and deployment of an educational process. For example, do designers of S/G and local actors share the same conception of the relationship between learning, behavior change and action? Through this specific case, the issue of appropriation (from information to co-construction) of the participatory process in every dimension, by all stakeholders (e.g., researchers, local actors, participants), is highlighted.

5 Conclusion and Perspectives for Future Research

S/G approaches are increasingly used to explore social and environmental issues, particularly in the context of facilitating transitions. However, it remains challenging to comprehensively assess their effectiveness in moving towards transition. After examining the short-term, primarily cognitive learning effects of LittoSIM-GEN and their divergence from the initial objectives of the process, we explored how the lack of (re)defining the design intentions–regarding here objectives, target audience, status and key concepts of the process–might have influenced these outcomes.

Based on these findings, we hypothesize that the generally limited impacts of S/G stem from a lack of discussion and appropriation of design intentions by all the stakeholders involved. We extend this hypothesis more broadly to the evaluation of all participatory processes developed with the aim of contributing to socio-ecological transition. What are the objectives? For whom? What effects is it intended to have in relation to the significant challenges of the transition it seeks to influence (e.g., is it "merely" an educational issue)?

To explore these hypotheses, our future research on evaluation will analyze the design intentions behind a variety of participatory processes aimed at socio-ecological transition, potentially including S/G. We also aim to assess how evaluation work might benefit designers by encouraging reflective thinking on why and how they define and then implement the intentions underlying their processes.

At the time of writing this paper, we first sought to characterize the diversity of participatory processes aimed at supporting transitions that we are focusing on. To do so, we have identified, thanks to this reflexive work on LittoSIM-GEN and the literature, recurring questions and criteria related to design intentions to clarify and understand the participatory design of these processes: What are the objectives? Who are the participants? What are the modes of participation proposed? And what methodologies and tools are employed to facilitate this participation? Next, as part of an evaluation approach that we will carry out with the designers of various participatory processes aimed at supporting transitions in France, we will examine the intended objectives and desired outcomes, as well as the implementation of these processes. This will provide insights into the hypothesis that design intentions may or may not have been sufficiently developed or discussed among the stakeholders involved. It will also allow us to question whether the evaluation process generates reflective effects on the relevance and/or effectiveness of the processes for their designers.

We believe this work will contribute to a better understanding of the design and evaluation of participatory processes, including participatory simulation. Additionally, we stress that clarifying design intentions should not overshadow the "surprises" that may arise from these experiences, as they can stimulate and renew research questions in the field.

References

1. Becu, N., Crookall, D.: Companion modelling and participatory simulation: a glimpse. In: European Geoscience on Union Conference (2020)
2. Becu, N.: Les courants d'influence et la pratique de la simulation participative : contours, design et contributions aux changements sociétaux et organisationnels dans les territoires. La Rochelle Université (2020)
3. Speelman, E., Rodela, R.: Impact assessment of serious games: a conceptual proposal. In: Becu, N. (ed.) Simulation and Gaming for Social and Environmental Transitions, pp. 656–659 (2023)
4. Connolly, T.M., Boyle, E.A., MacArthur, E., Hainey, T., Boyle, J.M.: A systematic literature review of empirical evidence on computer games and serious games. Comput. Educ. **59**, 661–686 (2012). https://doi.org/10.1016/J.COMPEDU.2012.03.004
5. Hainey, T., Connolly, T.M., Boyle, E.A., Wilson, A., Razak, A.: A systematic literature review of games-based learning empirical evidence in primary education. Comput. Educ. **102**, 202–223 (2016). https://doi.org/10.1016/j.compedu.2016.09.001
6. Gris, G., Bengtson, C.: Assessment measures in game-based learning research: a systematic review. Int. J. Serious Games. **8**, 3–26 (2021). https://doi.org/10.17083/ijsg.v8i1.383
7. Dernat, S., Martel, G., Johany, F., Revalo, A., Gesbert, M.T.: Serious games as innovations for sustainable agri-environmental and food transitions in the territories. A French study. (2023). https://doi.org/10.21494/ISTE.OP.2023.0974

8. Dernat, S., Grillot, M., Guerrier, F., Martel, G., Salliou, N., Terrier-Gesbert, M.: Actes des 1eres journées GAMAE (2022)
9. Ditzler, L., et al.: Affordances of agricultural systems analysis tools: a review and framework to enhance tool design and implementation. Agric. Syst. **164**, 20–30 (2018). https://doi.org/10.1016/J.AGSY.2018.03.006
10. Csikszentmihalyi, M.: Flow and the foundations of positive psychology: the collected works of Mihaly Csikszentmihalyi. flow found. Posit. Psychol. Collect. Work. Mihaly Csikszentmihalyi. 1–298 (2014). https://doi.org/10.1007/978-94-017-9088-8/COVER
11. Hookham, G., Nesbitt, K.: A systematic review of the definition and measurement of engagement in serious games. In: ACM International Conference on Proceeding Series (2019). https://doi.org/10.1145/3290688.3290747
12. Steiner, C.M., et al.: Evaluation of serious games: a holistic approach. In: Proceedings of ICERI2015 Conference, Seville, 16–18 November 2015, p. 10 (2015). https://doi.org/10.13140/RG.2.1.3761.8002
13. Mayer, I.S.: The gaming of policy and the politics of gaming: a review. Simul. Gaming **40**, 825–862 (2009). https://doi.org/10.1177/1046878109346456
14. Boyle, E.A., et al.: An update to the systematic literature review of empirical evidence of the impacts and outcomes of computer games and serious games. Comput. Educ. **94**, 178–192 (2016). https://doi.org/10.1016/j.compedu.2015.11.003
15. Flood, S., Cradock-Henry, N.A., Blackett, P., Edwards, P.: Adaptive and interactive climate futures: systematic review of "serious games" for engagement and decision-making. Environ. Res. Lett. **13** (2018). https://doi.org/10.1088/1748-9326/aac1c6
16. Mayer, I., Bekebrede, G., Warmelink, H., Zhou, Q.: A brief methodology for researching and evaluating serious games and game- based learning. Psychol. Pedagog. Assess. Serious Games. 357–393 (2013). https://doi.org/10.4018/978-1-4666-4773-2.CH017
17. Michelin, Y., Dernat, S., Blache, N.: Jeux de plateau pour l'agriculture et le paysage. Editions Quae (2023)
18. Régnier, C.: L'évaluation des structures expérimentales innovantes. Diversité **169**, 203–208 (2012)
19. Etienne, R.: Accompagner des agriculteurs à l'aide d'une combinaison de jeux sérieux : quelles contributions aux changements de pratiques ? (2024). https://pastel.hal.science/tel-04532244
20. Mazeaud, A., Sa Vilas Boas, M.-H., Berthomé, G.-E.-K.: Penser les effets de la participation sur l'action publique à partir de ses impensés. Participations **2**, 5–29 (2012). https://doi.org/10.3917/parti.002.0005
21. Blondiaux, L., Fourniau, J.-M.: An overview of research on public participation in democracy: a lot of fuss about nothing? Participations **1**, 8–35 (2011). https://doi.org/10.3917/PARTI.001.0008
22. Mazeaud, A.: Serious games and democratic socio-ecological transitions: a critical look from political science. In: The 54th edition of the International Simulation and Gaming Conference (2023). https://videos.univ-lr.fr/video/2859-keynote-by-alice-mazeaud/
23. Dispositifis participatifs. Politix **75**, 3–9 (2006). https://doi.org/10.3917/POX.075.0003
24. Seguin, L.: Les apprentissages de la participation. Regards croisés sur un dispositif institué et une mobilisation contestataire (2016)
25. Monfort, A.: Réception sociale des modes de gestion du risque de submersion marine : une approche d'évaluation de la simulation participative appliquée aux littoraux français métropolitains (2023). https://theses.hal.science/tel-04338318
26. Daré, W.: Comportements des acteurs dans le jeu et dans la réalité : indépendance ou correspondance ? Analyse sociologique de l'utilisation de jeux de rôles en aide à la concertation. Thesis, p. 401 (2005)

27. Goutx, D.: La ludicité des simulations de crises : ce qui se joue au coeur d'une crise simulée (2022)
28. Gourgues, G.: Les politiques de démocratie participative. Presses universitaires de Grenoble (2013)
29. den Haan, R.J., van der Voort, M.C.: On evaluating social learning outcomes of serious games to collaboratively address sustainability problems: a literature review. Sustain **10**, 4529 (2018). https://doi.org/10.3390/SU10124529
30. Mazeaud, A.: Dix ans à chercher la démocratie locale, et maintenant ? Pour un dialogue entre politiques publiques et démocratie participative. In: Communication aux Journées doctorales sur la participation et la démocratie participative, GIS « Participation du public, décision, démocratie participative ». ENS Lyon (2009)
31. Amalric, M., et al.: Sensibiliser au risque de submersion marine par le jeu ou faut-il qu'un jeu soit spatialement réaliste pour être efficace? Sci. du jeu. (2017). https://doi.org/10.4000/sdj.859
32. Le Page, C.: Simulation multi-agent interactive : engager les populations locales dans la modélisation des socio-écosystèmes pour stimuler l'apprentissage social (2017). https://www.researchgate.net/publication/315491740_Simulation_multi-agent_interactive_engager_des_populations_locales_dans_la_modelisation_des_socio-ecosystemes_pour_stimuler_l'apprentissage_social
33. Becu, N.: Usability of computerized gaming simulation for experiential learning. In: Software Usability, p. 19. IntechOpen (2021). https://doi.org/10.5772/intechopen.97303ï
34. Hassenforder, E., Smajgl, A., Ward, J.: Towards understanding participatory processes: framework, application and results. J. Environ. Manag. **157**, 84–95 (2015). https://doi.org/10.1016/j.jenvman.2015.04.012
35. Rowe, G., Frewer, L.J.: Public participation methods: a framework for evaluation. Sci. Technol. Hum. Values. **25**, 3–29 (2000). https://doi.org/10.1177/016224390002500101
36. Prochaska, J., DiClemente, C.: Stages of change in the modification of problem behaviors. In: Hersen, M., Eisler, R.M., Miller, P.M. (eds.) Progress on Behavior Modification, pp. 184–214. Sycamore (1992)
37. Becu, N., et al.: Participatory simulation of coastal flooding: building social learning on prevention measures with decision-makers (2016)
38. Amalric, M., Becu, N.: The social reception of coastal risk management: an insight through the prism of participatory simulation. Rev. Int. psychosociologie Gest. des Comport. Organ. **XXVII**, 63–89 (2021). https://doi.org/10.3917/RIPS1.069.0063
39. Rey-Valette, H., et al.: Acceptabilité sociale des mesures d'adaptation au changement climatique en zones côtières : une revue de dix enquêtes menées en France métropolitaine. VertigO **19** (2019). https://doi.org/10.4000/vertigo.26537
40. Becu, N., et al.: Applying a descriptive participatory simulation to specific case studies: adaptation of LittoSIM coastal flooding management simulation. iEMSs. 10 (2020)
41. Peretti-Watel, P.: La société du risque. La Découverte (2010). https://doi.org/10.3917/DEC.PERET.2010.01
42. Rey-Valette, H., Rulleau, B.: Gouvernance des politiques de relocalisation face au risque de montée du niveau de la mer, vol. 7 (2016). http://journals.openedition.org/developpementdurable. https://doi.org/10.4000/DEVELOPPEMENTDURABLE.11282
43. Lévy, J., Lussault, M.: Dictionnaire de la géographie et de l'espace des sociétés (2013)
44. Rocle, N., et al.: Paving the way to coastal adaptation pathways: an interdisciplinary approach based on territorial archetypes. Environ. Sci. Policy **110**, 34–45 (2020). https://doi.org/10.1016/J.ENVSCI.2020.05.003
45. Laronde-Clérac, C., Mazeaud, A., Michelot, A.: Les risques naturels en zones côtières. Xynthia : enjeux politiques, questionnements juridiques. Presses universitaires de Rennes, Rennes (2015)

46. Claeys-Mekdade, C.: Qu'est-ce qu'une "population concernée"? L'exemple camarguais. Géocarrefour. **76**, 217–223 (2001). https://doi.org/10.3406/geoca.2001.2559
47. Fung, A.: Varieties of participation in complex governance. Source Public Adm. Rev. **66**, 66–75 (2006)
48. Barnaud, C., van Paassen, A.: Equity, power games, and legitimacy: dilemmas of participatory natural resource management. Ecol. Soc. **18** (2013). https://doi.org/10.5751/ES-05459-180221
49. Daré, W., et al.: Apprentissage des interdépendances et des dynamiques. In: La modélisation d'accompagnement. Une démarche participative en appui au développement durable, pp. 223–250 (2010)
50. Lapijover, A.: Révéler la dimension socio-politique des interactions entre pêcheries et petits cétacés dans le golfe de Gascogne (2018)
51. Heclo, H.: Modern Social Politics in Britain and Sweden: From Relief to Income Maintenance. Yale University Press (1974). https://doi.org/10.1177/003232927600600110
52. Argyris, C., Schön, D.: Organizational Learning II: A Theory, Method and Practice. Addison-Wesley, Mass (1996)
53. Etienne, M. ed: La modélisation d'accompagnement : Une démarche participative en appui au développement durable. Editions Quae, Versailles (2010)
54. Sanchez, É., Romero, M.: Apprendre en jouant. Retz (2020)

Digital Veggie Mart Game for Nutritional Education and Sustainable Food Supply Chain

Mizuho Sato[1(✉)] and Hajime Mizuyama[2]

[1] Tokyo University of Agriculture, 1-1-1 Sakuragaoka, Setagaya-ku 156-8502, Tokyo, Japan
ms207184@nodai.ac.jp
[2] Aoyama Gakuin University, 5-10-1 Fuchinobe, Chuo-ku, Sagamihara 252-5258, Japan

Abstract. In 2015, the UN General Assembly unanimously adopted the Sustainable Development Goals (SDGs). Target 12.3 states the following: "By 2030, halve per capita global food waste at the retail and consumer levels and reduce food losses along production and supply chains, including post-harvest losses." To create a sustainable society, reducing food waste and disposal throughout the Food Supply Chain (FSC) is necessary. Reducing the loss of vegetables and fruits is essential because they account for a significant proportion of losses and waste at each stage of distribution, retail, and consumption. In contrast, increasing the intake of vegetables and fruits is crucial for health. However, increasing vegetable intake is often challenging, and without proper utilization, vegetables can be wasted. Therefore, this study designed a digital game based on the vegetable supply chain to enhance consumer health awareness, increase vegetable intake, and develop a sustainable food supply chain.

Keywords: Sustainability · Food Supply Chain · Nutrition · Food Waste · Game Design

1 Introduction

This paper aims to investigate the potential of educational games in addressing the pressing issues of promoting healthier dietary habits and reducing food waste. Given the increasing importance of sustainable food practices, there is a growing need for innovative approaches to engage individuals in making healthier food choices and minimizing food waste. Despite the potential of educational games in this context, there is a lack of comprehensive research on existing games focusing on dietary nutrition and food waste reduction. Therefore, this study not only explores existing educational games but also proposes and designs a digital version of the Veggie Mart Game. By examining the design and features of the Veggie Mart Game and discussing its potential impact on player behavior, this research aims to provide practical insights into the role of educational games in facilitating incremental changes towards sustainable food practices at the individual level.

1.1 Importance of Sustainable Food Systems and Educational Games

In 2015, the UN General Assembly unanimously adopted the Sustainable Development Goals (SDGs). These goals, with a deadline of 2030, aim to achieve a sustainable, diverse, and inclusive society, consisting of 17 goals and 169 targets [1]. Target 12.3 states: "By 2030, halve per capita global food waste at the retail and consumer levels and reduce food losses along production and supply chains, including post-harvest losses." To create a sustainable society, reducing food waste and disposal throughout the Food Supply Chain (FSC) is necessary. Additionally, addressing Target 12.3 could contribute to the achievement of other goals. For example, redirecting food that normally would be wasted to people experiencing poverty or hunger can contribute to the attainment of SDGs such as "1. No Poverty" and "2. Zero Hunger." Moreover, the world population is projected to reach 9 billion by 2050, underscoring the need to utilize food efficiently for future food security [2].

Reducing the loss of vegetables and fruits is important, as they account for a significant proportion of losses and waste at each stage of distribution, retail, and consumption [3]. In the distribution stage, difficulties exist in maintaining uniform temperatures; in the retail stage, balancing supply and demand is challenging; and in the consumption stage, difficulties in utilizing products without waste result in numerous cases of disposal. Therefore, it is necessary to develop technologies such as establishing a cold chain at the distribution stage, improving demand forecasting, price determination, and sales methods at the retail stage, and effectively managing the entire process from purchase to cooking and storage at the consumption stage to utilize ingredients efficiently. Enhancing consumer awareness, knowledge, and skills is essential for effectively implementing measures in the downstream stages of the supply chain, such as retail and consumption.

As mentioned above, vegetables and fruits are difficult to handle and prone to loss and waste. However, they are recommended for consumption because of their high content of essential minerals and vitamins, which are necessary for health. People who consume large amounts of low-starch vegetables and fruits have been reported to have a lower risk of weight gain and obesity [4]. Obesity is linked to diabetes, cancer, and heart disease, making it important to increase the intake of vegetables and fruits to maintain a healthy lifestyle. Consequently, in Australia, the recommended daily intake is 375 g of vegetables and 150 g of fruits, whereas in the United States, it is recommended to consume 375 g of vegetables and 300 g of fruits per day [4, 5]. In Japan, the recommended daily intake is set at 350 g of vegetables and 200 g of fruits [6]. However, with an abundance of easily consumable processed foods, dietary intake tends to be imbalanced, with vegetables and fruits often being insufficiently consumed. Consequently, in Japan, many individuals fail to reach the recommended vegetable intake levels. The reasons for this include inaccurate awareness of one's vegetable intake and the perception of consuming sufficient vegetables despite not meeting the actual requirements [7, 8].

Efforts to increase vegetable intake have been implemented in Japan through educational institutions, companies, and other entities; however, reaching the target of 350 g remains challenging. For example, a study examining the impact of a nutrition education program combining seminars by registered dietitians and the provision of vegetable drinks as environmental support for vegetable intake immediately and at the stage of behavioral change among workers demonstrated that, without subsequent continuous intervention by mediators, there was no increase in vegetable intake. Therefore, nutrition education programs alone may not readily lead to behavioral changes [9]. Additionally, studies aimed at promoting increased vegetable intake among middle-aged adults emphasize the importance of promoting overall meal balance, such as encouraging the consumption of main dishes, side dishes, and soups twice or more per day, and are not limited to supporting vegetable intake alone [10]. Specifically, conveying the means of vegetable consumption is crucial. Furthermore, early childhood food education significantly influences future dietary habits and is essential. In a study focusing on developing food education tools to increase vegetable intake among toddlers and mothers, food education classes were conducted, and participants were provided with "I ate vegetables" sheets to stick stickers on when consuming vegetables, demonstrating an increase in vegetable intake using stickers on the sheets, indicating the effectiveness of gamification mechanisms [11].

In another study regarding food waste at the consumption stage, consumer segmentation was conducted to propose reduction methods tailored to each segment [12]. This study revealed that consumers with cooking skills tend to generate less food waste, regardless of their awareness of waste reduction. Therefore, acquiring practical skills is crucial in addition to raising awareness about waste reduction. Furthermore, Aschemann-Witzel et al. suggested that consumer behaviors aimed at reducing food waste are promoted by attitudes toward the environment, a tendency to save, and favorable social norms among families and peers [13]. Family influence plays a significant role in food waste, and everyday eating behaviors impact food waste. Therefore, visualization of such circumstances can be effective.

As stated above, merely providing nutritional education to promote vegetable consumption is challenging. Similarly, cooking skills are essential for promoting food waste reduction. Hansmann et al. divided students into two groups: one attended lecture on the current impact of food selection behaviors on future environmental and economic factors, and the other participated in game-based classes covering the same content. They investigated the differences in subsequent shopping behavior between the two groups. The results indicated that students who participated in game-based classes tended to exhibit more environmentally conscious behaviors when purchasing food than those who attended lectures. Therefore, by implementing games, it is possible to visualize the current situation and acquire practical skills to take action toward a desirable future society. Consequently, for the construction of sustainable food supply chains, games are effective in enabling players to learn the skills for actions they should take (such as increasing vegetable intake while reducing food waste) [14].

1.2 Existing Games for Dietary Nutrition and Food Waste Reduction

The Food and Agriculture Organization of the United Nations (FAO) has proposed educational programs to raise awareness among the youth regarding food waste issues. These programs consist of materials tailored for different age groups. They explain methods for cultivating habits that reduce food waste. For instance, using a board game with cards illustrating behaviors such as cutting out the rotten part of an apple to reduce waste, the program imparts knowledge on waste reduction actions to consumers. Additionally, organizations such as the World Wide Fund for Nature (WWF) conduct quizzes on their websites regarding food waste, all of which aim to provide consumers with knowledge to reduce waste [15, 16].

Furthermore, simulation games have been developed based on fruit supply chains, in which players engage in simulations that consider profits and food waste while selling produced fruits to consumers. These simulations focus on how to sell the produced fruit efficiently without wastage [17]. The Beer Distribution Game (Beer Game) is well-known in supply chain gaming [18]. While real-world beer has expiration dates, the Beer Game serves as a tool for learning the importance of information sharing and overall supply chain management without incorporating expiration dates. Therefore, a version of the Beer Game was developed with expiration dates (where deliveries cannot proceed after a certain deadline) to visualize the specific impacts of food supply chains. Additionally, Japanese business practices (1/3 rule) were incorporated into a simulation game called the Milky Chain Game, designed for the milk supply chain. The game was conducted with university students to demonstrate the effectiveness of the educational impact [19].

In addition, games focusing on nutrition education and changes in eating behaviors have been developed. These games are primarily used in schools. Their purpose is to impart nutritional knowledge and promote changes in eating behaviors. They combine game elements that stimulate changes in eating behavior and the psychological aspects of dietary intake. All aim to impart nutritional knowledge and raise health awareness. These games are designed to make learning about nutrition enjoyable for children and do not incorporate a supply chain perspective [20].

As mentioned above, games related to food waste encompass two main categories: (1) games where players learn about food waste and its mitigation strategies, and (2) games focusing on waste generated by the structure of the supply chain. Additionally, games concerning nutrition education and eating behaviors include (3) games designed to promote transformation towards nutritional education and healthy eating habits. However, to address food waste issues and encourage healthy eating behaviors among consumers, it is essential to consider the entire food supply chain. This is because downstream consumer behavior influences each actor within the supply chain and affects upstream producers. Therefore, consumers need to consider how their actions impact the food supply chain and what behaviors contribute to a sustainable food supply chain while adopting healthy eating habits. Consequently, games that encompass elements of categories (1) to (3) are necessary but are not currently widely available.

1.3 Developing the Digital Veggie Mart Game

Consequently, we developed the "Veggie Mart Game," focusing on the nutritional component of vitamin C in food, aiming to promote vegetable intake while considering food waste reduction [21]. The Veggie Mart Game is an analog board game featuring seven types of vegetables. Players assume the roles of both the supermarket manager (referred to as the "Supermarket") and consumers (specifically, the cooking representatives of a three-person family).

The objective of a supermarket is to sell vegetables to consumers and generate profit. Vegetable deliveries and purchase prices fluctuate depending on the weather conditions. Further, vegetables have expiration dates that require supermarket players to sell before they expire. Therefore, they need to devise sales strategies (such as portioning vegetables, offering vegetable baskets, or providing discounts) to minimize waste at retail level. Additionally, effective communication with consumers during sales is essential.

Consumers aim to consume as much vitamin C (VC) as possible, focusing on the dinner menu to compete for the highest VC intake from the vegetables consumed. Scores were calculated by multiplying the total VC intake by the number of vegetables consumed, thereby incentivizing the players to consume more vegetables. However, failure to utilize vegetables effectively results in waste generation at consumer level. Through this game, the importance of cooking skills in food waste reduction at this level was also emphasized.

Surveys conducted after playing the analog Veggie Mart Game demonstrated its effectiveness in raising awareness about food waste, emphasizing the importance of recipe variety for food waste reduction, and enhancing nutritional knowledge (such as variations in VC content and intake due to cooking alterations), as partially reported in [21].

However, in real life, ingredients and nutrients are diverse. Thus, incorporating nutrients, such as minerals, vitamins other than VC, and proteins into the game is preferable. However, as the original Veggie Mart Game is an analog game, players are responsible for tallying their scores and, therefore, can engage in the game with only limited ingredients (vegetables) and nutrients (VC). Therefore, this study digitalized the Veggie Mart Game to cover various ingredients and nutrients, so that consumer players can easily learn a variety of skills through playing the game.

2 Skills Required of Household Cooks

To discuss the skills required of household cooks, everyday food purchasing and cooking behaviors were delineated into four steps: (1) before shopping, (2) while shopping, (3) while cooking and eating, and (4) after cooking and eating for storage. These steps were further categorized into three sustainability dimensions: Environmental, Economic, and Social. Under the Environmental dimension, the focus was on "Food Waste." The Economic dimension pertained to "Food Expenses," while the Social dimension related to "Health." Concerning "Health," intrinsic factors encompass "Nutrition (Table 1)."

Table 1. Skills required of household cooks.

	Environmental (Food waste)	Economic (Food expenses)	Social (Health: Nutrition)
(1) Before shopping		1. Confirmation of contents in the refrigerator 2. Confirmation of items outside the refrigerator 3. Confirmation of food consumption and expiration dates in and outside the refrigerator 4. Creation of a shopping list	1. Confirmation of contents in the refrigerator 2. Confirmation of items outside the refrigerator 3. Creation of a shopping list **4. Acquire nutritional knowledge**
(2) While shopping		1. Deciding whether to purchase dis-counted, large quantity foods, products with a recent expiration date 2. Whether to purchase high-quality items but expensive 3. Whether purchases are made systematically	1. Deciding whether to purchase discounted, large quantity foods, products with a recent expiration date 2. Whether to purchase high-quality items but expensive 3. Whether purchases are made systematically **4. Checking nutritional labels before making a purchase**
(3) While cooking and eating		1. Whether to use ingredients efficiently 2. Whether to utilize leftover ingredients 3. Whether to store leftover dishes 4. Whether to serve leftover dishes on another day 5. To avoid leaving food uneaten	1. Whether to use ingredients efficiently 2. Whether to utilize leftover ingredients 3. To avoid leaving food uneaten **4. A nutritious and delicious meal with a balanced diet**
(4) After cooking and eating for storage		1. Checking the available storage capacity within the household for preservation purposes 2. Understanding the meaning of consumption and expiration dates accurately 3. Ensuring precise temperature management within the refrigerator 4. Judging disposal based on factors like appearance, taste, and aroma	1. Understanding the meaning of consumption and expiration dates accurately 2. Ensuring precise temperature management within the refrigerator **3. Learning the proper methods to preserve vegetables**

2.1 Before Shopping

Before shopping, checking refrigerators and food storage shelves helps prevent over-buying or purchasing the same items repeatedly. Overbuying or redundant purchases can lead to items expiring before use, resulting in waste and unnecessary expenses. Additionally, by inspecting food at home and creating a list of ingredients needed for today's menus, shopping has become more efficient. Therefore, acquiring nutritional knowledge is also important.

2.2 While Shopping

When shopping, choices such as selecting discounted items in large quantities or products with short expiration dates, as well as adhering to shopping lists, are crucial for reducing food waste and expenses. Additionally, checking nutritional labels is important for maintaining health.

2.3 While Cooking and Eating

The ability to use ingredients efficiently and repurpose leftover food during cooking is crucial for reducing food waste and controlling food expenses. In addition, it is important to consume a variety of ingredients from a balanced dietary perspective. Furthermore, skills such as minimizing leftovers and repurposing excess dishes on other days are significant.

2.4 After Cooking and Eating for Storage

When cooking and storing food after consumption, it is important to ensure the available storage capacity within the household, to have a clear understanding of expiration dates, and to maintain accurate temperature control in the refrigerator.

3 Digital Veggie Mart Game

3.1 Game Outline

The Digital Veggie Mart Game to be designed and proposed in this paper expands upon the original analog Veggie Mart Game [21]. The flow of materials and money in the game is shown in Fig. 1. The vegetables used in the game are the same as before and consist of seven types (tomato, carrot, onion, cucumber, cabbage, lettuce, and spinach). The game is structured into rounds, encompassing steps 1 to 4 within one round (one day), and the game is played for a total of 30 rounds (30 days).

In the digitalized version, particular emphasis is placed on the perspective of "health," as described in Sect. 2. Specifically, in previous analog version of the Veggie Mart Game, nutritional knowledge was limited to vitamin C; however, in the Digital Veggie Mart Game, other nutrients are also factored into the game's scoring system. Accordingly, the objectives of both players (supermarkets and consumers) remained the same as those in the original Veggie Mart Game, with consumer success determined not only by vitamin C intake but also by overall nutritional balance.

Digital Veggie Mart Game for Nutritional Education and Sustainable Food

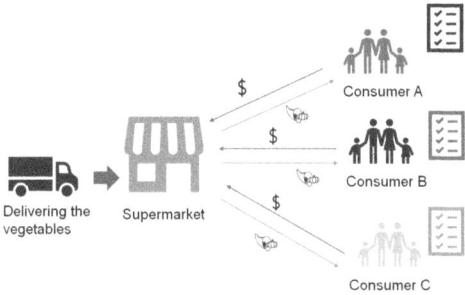

Fig. 1. The flow materials and money in the Digital Veggie Mart Game.

Fig. 2. The steps of the Digital Veggie Mart Game. (Colour figure online)

3.2 Game Flow

The progression follows the steps outlined below: The content added to the digital version is indicated in red text (Fig. 2).

Step 1. Pre-purchase: Consumers receive special offers and other information daily from supermarkets. Consumers review this information to decide on dinner recipes. Nutrient content can vary depending on the cooking method used. In the previous Veggie Mart Game, the cooking variations in vitamin C were listed on cards; however, in the digital version, the cooking variation rate of nutrients is calculated automatically. Additionally, supermarkets determine selling prices and methods based on the current procurement status.

Step 2. Purchase: Consumers purchase ingredients to create a well-balanced meal while keeping food costs low. Supermarkets consider consumers' purchasing trends when deciding on sales methods.

Step 3. Cooking and Eating: Cooking is performed using ingredients purchased from digital recipe cards. If leftover ingredients are present, players can create their own recipes. Events may occur during this step, and players must execute them. In addition, the meal balance is assessed. Supermarkets place orders with the suppliers in the next round.

Step 4. Score Confirmation: While it is important to replenish energy while providing food, it is also essential to consume a balanced meal. This includes adequate intake of proteins, fats, carbohydrates (sugars), minerals, vitamins, and other nutrients tailored to each individual's needs. Consumption of various foods in balanced proportions is necessary to obtain these nutrients. In the digital version, consumers who previously focused solely on calculating vitamin C intake are now prompted to consider other essential nutrients. Similarly, supermarkets are tasked with calculating revenue and managing waste disposal.

3.3 Incorporated Features

In Step 1, consumer players can verify their knowledge of the nutrients present in foods. Additionally, in Step 3's score calculation, they have the option to compute the nutrients contained in the foods themselves. However, performing nutrient calculations in every round can be burdensome for players. Therefore, players are initially required to manually calculate nutrients for a few rounds, after which computers take over to perform automatic calculations for the remaining rounds.

Furthermore, a newly introduced assessment function for meal balance is addressed in Step 3, where players' menus are revealed for evaluation. For instance, if the main dish is steak and the soup is miso soup, participants collectively assess whether the menu appears "appealing" or "not appealing."

In the original Veggie Mart Game, discussions during the debriefing typically revolved around optimizing the entire supply chain by deliberating on strategies to reduce food waste at both consumer and retail levels. Here, the participants often consider the intricate interplay between consumer behaviours and supermarkets' sales strategies, and how this interaction impacts food waste at the retail level. This discourse is facilitated by the opportunity for players to experience both the roles of the supermarket and the consumer, or at least by ensuring that the group includes members who have assumed the role of the supermarket.

In the proposed digital version, although there is a heightened emphasis on nutrients (and waste) at the consumer level, this discussion opportunity remains available. While the role of the supermarket can be automated and performed by a computer, the option for a human player to assume this role still exists, ensuring that the richness of the debriefing discussions is maintained.

4 Conclusions

In conclusion, this study has proposed and designed a digital game centered on the vegetable supply chain with the aim of enhancing consumers' health awareness, increasing vegetable intake, and fostering the development of a sustainable food supply chain. The game targets a broad range of age groups and is designed to facilitate visualizing daily vegetable intake requirements and developing skills for effective vegetable utilization.

Through the implementation of this game, it is anticipated that individuals will not only increase their vegetable consumption but also enhance their understanding of nutrition through engagement in nutritional calculations for vegetable-based dishes.

Furthermore, post-game reflections will enable participants to analyze vegetable scores, supermarket sales, and waste situations, fostering considerations for actions contributing to a more sustainable food supply chain.

Moving forward, future research will focus on testing the effectiveness of the proposed game through experimental studies. Additionally, further development and refinement of the game will be explored to maximize its impact on promoting healthy eating habits and sustainability practices among consumers.

Acknowledgments. This research was supported by the Foundation for the Fusion of Japan, Science, and Technology.

References

1. United Nations: resolution adopted by the general assembly on 25 September (2015)
2. Food and agriculture organization of the United Nations: state of food and agriculture 2019: moving forward on food loss and waste reduction (2019)
3. Food and agriculture organization of the United Nations: global food losses and food waste (2011)
4. World cancer research fund/American institute for cancer research: diet, nutrition, physical activity, and cancer: A global perspective (2018)
5. Aune, D., et al.: Fruit and vegetable intake and the risk of cardio-vascular disease, total cancer and all-cause mortality-a systematic review and dose-response meta-analysis of prospective studies. Int. J. Epidemiol. **46**(3), 1029–1056 (2017)
6. Ministry of health, labor, and welfare: health Japan 21, 3rd edn. (2024)
7. Ministry of health, labor and welfare: report on the national health and nutrition survey of 2017. https://www.mhlw.go.jp/content/000451755.pdf. Accessed 07 Feb 2024
8. Schatzer, M., Rust, P., Elmadfa, I.: Fruit and vegetable intake in Austrian adults: intake frequency, serving size, reasons for and barriers to consumption, and potential for in-creasing consumption. Public Health Nutr. **13**(4), 480–487 (2009)
9. Nobuta, Y., Maeda, Y., Sone, T., Eto, K.: Effects of a nutrition education program on vegetable intake behaviour among workers. Japan. J. Nutr. Diet. **78**(5), 210–222 (2020)
10. Ozawa, K., Takemi, Y., Eto, K., Iwama, N.: Association of vegetable intake with dietary behaviours, attitudes, knowledge, and social support among the middle-aged Japanese population. Japan. J. Public Health **65**(10), 589–601 (2018)
11. Sogabe, N., Miyamoto, Y., Otsuki, Y., Shinohara, Y., Inoue, K.: Dietary education classes and an educational tool promoting vegetable intake among children. J. Integr. Study Dietary Habits **10**(4), 289–296 (2016)
12. Sato, M., Mizuyama, H.: Devising food waste reduction measures through consumer segmentation: Based on the association between food-related lifestyle and food waste behaviour. J. Japan. Soc. Shokuiku **16**(4), 157–173 (2022)
13. Aschemann-Witzel, J., et al.: Key characteristics and success factors of supply chain initiatives tackling consumer-related food waste - a multiple case study. J. Clean. Prod. **155**(2), 33–45 (2017)
14. Hansmann, R., Scholz, R.W., Francke, C.-J.A.C., Weymann, M.: Enhancing environmental awareness: ecological and economic effects of food consumption. J. Simul. Gaming **36**(3), 364–382 (2005)
15. Food and agriculture organization of the United Nations: teaching guides for children and young students. https://www.fao.org/3/CA1475EN/ca1475en.pdf. Accessed 11 Feb 2024

16. World wide fund for nature: take the food waste quiz. https://www.worldwildlife.org/pages/take-the-food-waste-quiz. Accessed 11 Feb 2024
17. Alessandro, S., Paolo, R., Patrizia, B., Remigio, B.: Simulation game to match production and demand of fresh fruit market. In: 12th International Technology, Education and Development Conference, pp.834–838 (2018)
18. Forrester, J.W.: Industrial dynamics: a major breakthrough for decision makers. Harv. Bus. Rev. **36**(4), 37–66 (1958)
19. Sato, M., Manago, T., Mizuyama, H.: Milky chain game: a pedagogical game for food supply chain management. IFIP Adv. Inf. Commun. Technol. **690**, 347–362 (2023)
20. Baranowski, T., Ryan, C., Hoyos-Cespedes, A., Shirong Lu, A.: Nutrition education and dietary behavior change games: a scoping review. Game Health J. **8**(3), 153–176 (2019)
21. Sato, M., Mizuyama, H., Nakano, M.: Game design aimed at reducing the amount of vegetable waste at the consumption stage in Japan. In: The International Simulation and Gaming Association Congress Proceedings, pp. 554–567 (2019)

How Entrepreneurs Learn About Artificial Intelligence by Using an Analogue Card Game

Maria Freese[1(✉)], Birgit Zürn[2], and Helmut Wittenzellner[3]

[1] Otto von Guericke University Magdeburg, Universitätsplatz 2, 39106 Magdeburg, Germany
maria.freese@ovgu.de

[2] Centre for Management Simulation, Baden-Wuerttemberg Cooperative State University Stuttgart, Paulinenstr. 50, 70178 Stuttgart, Germany
birgit.zuern@dhbw-stuttgart.de

[3] Stuttgart Media University, Nobelstr. 10, 70569 Stuttgart, Germany
helmut.wittenzellner@hdm-stuttgart.de

Abstract. In order to effectively handle the challenges of our time, it is crucial that entrepreneurship education promotes the development of competencies that enable entrepreneurs to cope with artificial intelligence. One effective approach to achieve this is through the use of serious games. This article presents an overview of different types of serious games and their potential benefits for learning about artificial intelligence. It then focuses on 'Cards for Entrepreneurship', an analogue serious game which aims to stimulate the creative and critical thinking of entrepreneurs in relation to artificial intelligence by letting them actively think about challenges and opportunities. As part of a workshop, participants, engaged in both a rapid prototyping and a game play phase, were developing and playing 'Cards for Entrepreneurship'. This approach was evaluated with a pre- and post-questionnaire, which revealed that the participants experienced an increase in their familiarity with artificial intelligence. Also, during the workshop a high level of flow, serious fun, and productive dialogues were observed. Future research should address the question of the extent to which artificial intelligence literacy can be developed in this context.

Keywords: Artificial Intelligence · Card Game · Entrepreneurship Education · Mindset Nudging · Serious Game

1 Introduction

Entrepreneurs are essential in today's highly-dynamic and changing world as drivers of innovation, economic growth, and job creation. Their ability to identify opportunities, take calculated risks, and adapt to change is crucial for addressing the evolving needs of today's society.

1.1 Entrepreneurship Education

Entrepreneurship education plays a crucial role in fostering a mindset that encourages innovation, risk-taking, and adaptability. Entrepreneurship education can be defined as "[…] the process of providing individuals with the ability to recognize commercial opportunities and the insight, self-esteem, knowledge and skills to act on them" [1, p. 16]. This definition demonstrates clear overlaps with the domains of economics and social sciences, which aim to promote a wide range of necessary skills, entrepreneurial attitudes, and competencies among entrepreneurs [2]. This wide range of skills, attitudes and competencies calls for a holistic approach in education, encompassing decision-making know-how (e.g., start-up knowledge and business planning), operational approaches (e.g., financial literacy), and leadership and managerial skills. In a modern and ever-evolving world of business, entrepreneurial skills represent a form of human capital assets that serve as a key indicator in achieving organizational goals [3]. This is particularly relevant in a VUCA (volatile, uncertain, complex, ambiguous) environment, where being VUCA means the ability to adopt, transform, and change by implementing entrepreneurial thinking within the corporate mindset. Future entrepreneurs equipped with 21st century and even future skills play a vital role in supporting organizations to outperform their counterparts both in terms of competitiveness and sustainability performance [4]. Entrepreneurship education should address these 21st century and future skills, such as digital (e.g., data literacy) and non-digital key qualifications (e.g., creativity and problem-solving techniques). Consequently, entrepreneurship education equips future entrepreneurs with the requisite mindset, digital and life skills, learning competencies, and knowledge needed to navigate the challenges of today's volatile, uncertain, complex and ambiguous world, fostering innovation, economic development, and personal growth. Regardless of whether individuals choose to start their own businesses or contribute as intrapreneurs within existing organizations, the entrepreneurial mindset is a valuable asset in various aspects of life and work.

1.2 Role of Artificial Intelligence in Entrepreneurship Education

The European Commission has identified the up- or re-skilling of employees as a key priority in order to equip them with the skills required to navigate the current social challenges [5]. The Organization for Economic Co-operation and Development [OECD] has classified skills into three categories, namely cognitive, social/emotional and practical/physical skills, which are considered to be highly relevant for the future [6]. In particular, this latter category plays a significant role in the context of increasing digitalization and technologies based on artificial intelligence (AI). The OECD addresses this topic, among others, in the context of Human-AI Interaction. [7] has already conducted research in the field of AI literacy, addressing the question of which competencies are necessary to be able to critically evaluate AI. [6] also emphasizes critical thinking as well as creativity and stresses out that 1) these encompass aspects of all the above-mentioned three classes and 2) these are prerequisites for work. Recent studies have demonstrated that the appropriate use of AI can bring high benefit for students. For instance, the use of ChatGPT for developing a Business Model Canvas has been shown to be a fruitful approach. Nevertheless, the necessity for enhanced training on the effective use of AI tools within an educational context has been emphasized [8]. [9] argue that entrepreneurship educators should adapt to the growing use of generative AI in various domains. Educators should instruct students on the critical and reflective thinking necessary to navigate the opportunities and challenges of generative AI, as well as how to apply it in their entrepreneurial projects. All of this shows the need to deal with this topic in education. As serious games have already proven to be an adequate and innovative tool for acquiring skills [e.g., 10], we will deal with it in the next section.

1.3 Serious Games in Entrepreneurship Education

Entrepreneurship education refers primarily to learning moments at universities and universities of applied sciences with the aim of educating students as future entrepreneurs. In this context, serious games represent an adequate and innovative learning tool, as they enable active learning through trial and error [11]. In such serious gaming environments, it is possible to make mistakes that would be almost impossible in reality due to safety aspects, risk assessments or ethical considerations. Based on their analysis, [12] call for further use of serious games as a teaching method in entrepreneurship education, and [13] state that games offer significant benefits and added value for entrepreneurship educational processes.

In serious entrepreneurship games, students can experience the role of an entrepreneur in a single or team mode and experience the challenges of running a fast-growing start-up [14]. These games teach students how to 1) build a founding team, 2) scale and grow a company, and 3) find approaches to adapt product-market fit. Typically, teams are tasked with managing entrepreneurial finances, learning to negotiate with potential business partners, selling their services and products to customers, and pitching to investors and stakeholders. In general, there are three types of serious gaming and simulations relevant in the field of entrepreneurship education: analogue, digital, and hybrid games. Firstly, serious games that do not use any form of technology (analogue games) offer a low-threshold training tool for a broader range of educators, trainers, and facilitators in entrepreneurship education, particularly with regard to didactic elements of design thinking, business models or team compositions [15, 16]. Secondly, business simulation games in the form of digital games (e.g., computer-based) are used to simulate business scenarios and provide players with the opportunity to make decisions that affect the success or failure of a business. These games can also help to enhance players' skills in finance, marketing, sales, and management [17]. Additionally, virtual reality or augmented reality offer an immersive experience that allows players to experience business scenarios in a realistic environment [18]. Thirdly, hybrid games are designed to exploit the benefits of both analogue and digital serious games and simulations [15]. Each of these types has advantages and challenges and must (a) be chosen well in advance of the course and (b) be thoroughly debriefed at the end of the game (and even during), taking into account learning objectives and resources.

This paper focuses on the development and testing of an analogue game. Analogue games are particularly suited to fostering social interaction and emotional responses [19–21]. These aspects, which were also highlighted at the beginning of this publication, are of enormous relevance for the future and must therefore also be included in education. Serious games also contribute significantly to entrepreneurship education by providing an interactive, safe, and engaging learning environment. Such games facilitate the development of skills, the cultivation of an entrepreneurial mindset, and experiential learning, thereby preparing individuals for the challenges and opportunities in the dynamic world of entrepreneurship.

1.4 Research Question

The development of 21st century and future skills plays a crucial role in the field of entrepreneurship education. As indicated, AI inevitably finds its way into entrepreneurship education [9]. One of the central aspects is the development of "[…] students['] critical and reflective thinking […]" and "[…] assessment of practical and technical entrepreneurial skills, to support student's effective utilization of generative artificial intelligence" [9, p. 229]. Before the development of skills, such as critical thinking in relation to AI and creativity, can be comprehensively assessed, it is necessary to get familiar with AI first. That is why the present paper examines the extent to which an analogue serious game can support the process of becoming familiar with AI. To be able to answer this question, we developed the serious game 'Cards for Entrepreneurship', which is explained in the next section.

2 Cards for Entrepreneurship

The aim of the serious game Cards for Entrepreneurship is to let entrepreneurs think more deeply about risks and measures to mitigate these risks (or prevent them from arising) in the field of entrepreneurship and thus, to create awareness of and foster knowledge on topics around entrepreneurship by discussing risks and measures of one or more appropriate scenarios. The game is designed for a diverse group of entrepreneurs with different levels of experience.

The frame game approach was used for the development of Cards for Entrepreneurships. This means that, building on the serious game Cards for Biosafety[1] [22], specific game mechanisms were transferred to the field of entrepreneurship.

For this purpose, 24 students (Bachelor, 2nd study year) of the international study program Media Management & Engineering at Stuttgart Media University were first asked to identify risks and associated measures in relation to the following scenario: "An SME (approx. 50 employees) is about to enter the AI market." The results were made available in anonymized form.

In a second step, we analyzed the risks and measures and screened them using predefined criteria. For example, the content should not contain any judgements or explanations and the texts on the cards in general should be short and easy to understand.

The content was then transferred to Adobe Creative Cloud and a selection of cards was printed. This created a solid basis for the serious game Cards for Entrepreneurship. This preliminary development was considered necessary because it was not known to what extent sufficient content could be developed during the actual workshop. However, in order to enable a functioning game play, a conscious decision was made to have a minimum number of cards pre-produced. The general description of the game play does not differ from those already described in [22] or [23]; only the application context is different.

---

[1] Cards for Biosafety got inspired by the entertainment game Cards against Humanity (LLC, https://www.cardsagainsthumanity.com).

3 Methods

At an international entrepreneurship education conference in 2023, we gave a workshop that combined both a rapid prototyping approach with the actual playing of Cards for Entrepreneurship.

3.1 Participants

The workshop itself was attended by 25 participants including four people who participated in the first development phase (identification of risks and measures). We received fully completed pre- and post-questionnaires from eight participants, which forms the basis for this further analysis as part of this publication (female = 2, 6 = male). Of the eight participants, five belonged to age category 21 to 29 years, one to age category 30 to 39 years, and two to age category 40 to 49 years. Four of the participants were Bachelor students, one Master student, one lecturer, one founder, and one consultant.

3.2 Procedure

The workshop lasted about 50 min and consisted of the following parts:

1. Participants first joined one of three groups of tables, each with a maximum of 8 places. They then read a declaration of consent and signed it if they agreed to it.
2. This was followed by a short warm-up game that playfully illustrated the influence that perspective has on our perception in order to introduce the topic directly and invite participants to position themselves openly in relation to the workshop topic.
3. In the following, a pre-questionnaire was distributed to measure the familiarity with AI.
4. After this, the rapid prototyping phase began.
    a. The scenario within the Cards for Entrepreneurship game was read out loud by one of the participants and was defined as follows: "An SME (approx. 50 employees) is about to enter the market of AI." A rough briefing is seen as a means for flexible interpretation of the scenario and leaves room for creativity towards the participants. The idea here is to let the participants work with a scenario that is specific enough to stimulate their thoughts, but open enough to give room to creativity. Expected interpretations of this briefing are focusing on diverse options, such as for the specific perspective, the maturity level of technological innovation or the implementation of a new technological methodology replacing existing established organizational processes.
    b. After the scenario was introduced, the participants were given a maximum of 7 min to brainstorm risks that came to mind in relation to the scenario, regardless of any perspective. The participants wrote the risks on blank cards (see Fig. 1), with one risk being written down on each card, whereby teams of two (i.e., usually four teams at each group table) always completed this task together. The only requirements on our part were that the risks should be formulated as generally as possible and as briefly as necessary.

c. The same teams then had the task of considering at least two measures per identified risk to minimize this risk. They also had a maximum of 7 min time to do this with the same instructions in mind.
5. All the cards were shuffled and the pre-developed cards were added to the newly developed cards. After each player or team of two per group received five randomly selected risk cards, the game began.
6. The game play was followed by a debriefing to reflect on the workshop. During this, we reflected on the approach and discussed the identified key risks and corresponding measures related to the chosen subject as well as the insights gained by the participants.
7. Due to the limited time available for the workshop, a sheet with the QR code for the post-questionnaire was handed out to the participants as they left the workshop with the request to complete the questionnaire.

Fig. 1. Rapid Prototyping process.

Due to the small sample size, the results are evaluated purely descriptively.

4 Results

4.1 Game Experience

First of all, we asked the participants what they thought of the combination of an analogue game with a non-analogue topic. Participants stated that it was a very good experience because even in a very short time it was possible to think about an "[…] almost infinite number of solutions […]". They had great fun and they found it interesting. It seemed to be no problem at all to apply an analogue methodology to a non-analogue topic.

4.2 Familiarity with Artificial Intelligence

Participants were asked before and after the workshop to what extent they were familiar with AI. Answers were given on a 5-point Likert scale from very unfamiliar to very familiar. It was also possible to give no answer. Figure 2 shows that the participants were already quite familiar with AI before the workshop. However, there was an increase in the mean value in the post-measurement ($M_{post} = 3.88$; $SD_{post} = .35$) compared to the pre-measurement ($M_{pre} = 3.75$; $SD_{pre} = .71$).

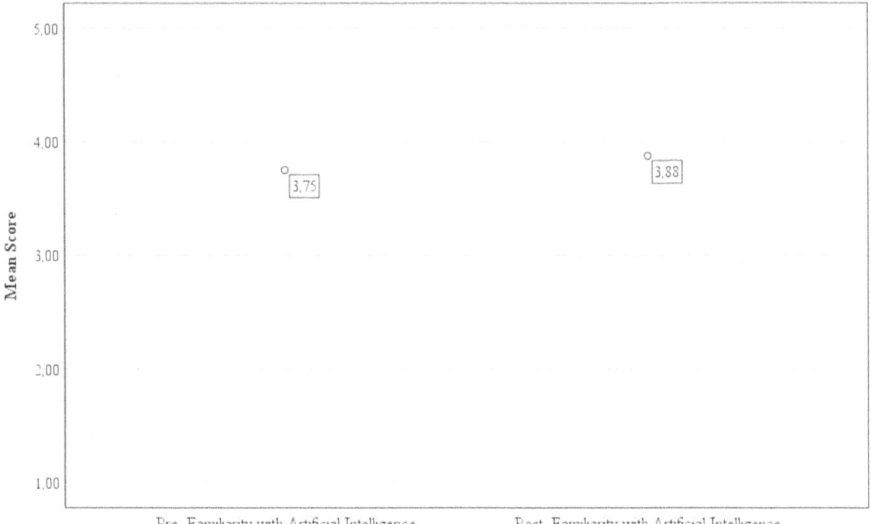

Fig. 2. Familiarity with artificial intelligence before and after the workshop.

4.3 Participants' Feedback

The questionnaire also asked for general feedback. Here we have received feedback concluding that "Having fun with AI helps to make it less frightening". This is also confirmed by the fact that the majority of participants agreed with the statement that serious games can help to reduce fears when dealing with AI ($M = 3.38$, $SD = 1.19$). Answers were provided on a 5-point Likert scale ranging from 1 (strongly disagree) to 5 (strongly agree).

4.4 Observations

The workshop was supported by three facilitators who also acted as observers. The most significant observations were discussed after the workshop.

Time. The initial part of the workshop involved a rapid prototyping approach, which is also frequently used in design thinking. According to the participants, the time constraints given in the workshop did not present a challenge. In the subsequent debriefing, they emphasized the step-by-step approach, which helped to mitigate any potential to get overwhelmed. This was a central component of the learning booster.

Flow. A crucial aspect of the design of a successful game is the concept of flow [24], which refers to the balance between the player's skills and the challenges presented during the game play. During the workshop, it became visible that the participants engaged in extensive discussions related to the topic of content. Despite the fact that not all of the participants knew each other at the beginning, the set-up facilitated a safe environment for discussing this subject matter.

Serious Fun. The role of serious fun for learning success has already been discussed in previous publications [23]. The following setting has also shown that humor stimulates valuable discussions. For example, one participant wrote "alien" on a card as a risk. This does not seem realistic, but by reflecting on this during the debriefing, it is possible to transpose the alien into the real every day or working environment of the participants and give the alien a real face.

Facilitator. As previously stated, three facilitators supervised the workshop, with each facilitator assigned to a table of eight participants. This also influenced the development and play phase of the game. Facilitator-related biases and their outcome of the workshop should always be taken into account. Implementing checklists and standardized protocols can help to minimize the occurrence of such biases. Such protocols may include information about the corresponding phase (e.g., briefing), the responsible person (e.g., facilitator, observer) and the associated tasks (e.g., introduction of game rules) with an estimated time per task. Nevertheless, each of the three facilitators independently perceived a positive atmosphere throughout the entire process, despite the considerable time constraints.

5 Discussion and Future Research

Given the role of AI in entrepreneurship education, the objective of the present article is to find out to which an analogue serious game can enhance the familiarity of entrepreneurship educators with this topic. To this end, a pre- and post-questionnaire were distributed as part of a workshop setting, with the aim of assessing the participants' familiarity with AI. Although the participants were already relatively familiar with AI, it became evident that the development and play of Cards for Entrepreneurship had facilitated further familiarity with AI, even in a short period of time (less than an hour). In order to be able to make generalizable statements, further research with a larger sample size is necessary. The participants also emphasized that the game can help overcome fear of AI. The original objective of the game was to reduce fear of using and implementing AI. The next step is to determine the extent to which this type of game contributes to the acquisition of AI literacy in education [25] and other application domains.

The high drop-out rate resulting from the given time slot must be discussed. As there was no time to complete the post-questionnaire during the actual workshop, the QR code with a link to the questionnaire was given to each participant. Although this was done in a personal talk, it did not have much added value considering the fact that only eight out of 24 participants completed both questionnaires. In future, the time and content of the workshop will have to be adjusted accordingly. The combination of a purely non-analogue theme with an analogue game was accepted by all participants, as in the age of AI it was considered very valuable to have something in one's hands.

Cards for Entrepreneurship is an example that makes use of a special game mechanism. Cards for Biosafety (Freese et al., 2022) inspired by Cards against Humanity[1] functions as a frame game and was transferred to the application area of entrepreneurship education in this case. Future research should continue to address this topic. Additionally, future research could consider more in-depth content analysis to identify what was actually learnt.

Acknowledgments. We are grateful to the students of Stuttgart Media University for their valuable input during the development phase as well as all workshop attendees for their insightful discussions and useful feedback.

Disclosure of Interests. The authors have no competing interests to declare that are relevant to the content of this article.

References

1. Jones, C., English, J.: A contemporary approach to entrepreneurship education. Educ. Train. **46**(8/9), 416–423 (2004)
2. Mayer, I., Kortman, R., Wenzler, I., Wetter, A., Spaans, J.: Game-based entrepreneurship education: identifying enterprising personality, Motivation and intentions amongst engineering students. J. Entrepreneurship Educ. **17**(2), 217–244 (2014)
3. Krieger, A., Stuetzer, M., Obschonka, M., Salmela-Aro, K.: The growth of entrepreneurial human capital: origins and development of skill variety. Small Bus. Econ. **59**, 645–664 (2022)
4. Ghafar, A.: Convergence between 21st century skills and entrepreneurship education in higher education institutes. Int. J. High. Educ. **9**(1), 218–229 (2020)
5. European Commission, Directorate-General for Research and Innovation, Renda, A., Schwaag Serger, S., Tataj, D.: Industry 5.0, a transformative vision for Europe – Governing systemic transformations towards a sustainable industry, Publications Office of the European Union (2022). https://data.europa.eu/doi/https://doi.org/10.2777/17322
6. Organization for Economic Co-operation and Development: The Future of Education and Skills: Education 2030. Position paper (2018). http://www.oecd.org/education/2030/E2030%20Position%20Paper%20(05.04.2018).pdf
7. Long, D., Magerko, B.: What is AI literacy? competencies and design considerations. In Proceedings of the 2020 CHI Conference on Human Factors in Computing Systems (CHI '20), pp. 1–16. Association for Computing Machinery, New York (2020)
8. Vecchiarini, M., Somià, T.: Redefining entrepreneurship education in the age of artificial intelligence: an explorative analysis. Intl. J. Manage. Educ. **21**(3), 100879 (2023)
9. Bell, R., Bell, H.: Entrepreneurship education in the era of generative artificial intelligence. Entrepreneurship Educ. **6**, 229–244 (2023)
10. Wouters, P., van der Spek, E. D., van Oostendorp, H.: Current practices in serious game research: a review from a learning outcomes perspective. In: Connolly, T., Stansfield, M., Boyle, L. (eds) Games-Based Learning Advancements for Multi-Sensory Human Computer Interfaces: Techniques and Effective Practices, pp. 232–250. IGI Global (2009)

11. Bellotti, F., et al.: Designing a course for stimulating entrepreneurship in higher education through serious games. Procedia Comput. Sci. **15**, 174–186 (2012)
12. Huebscher, J., Lendner, C.: Effects of entrepreneurship simulation game seminars on entrepreneurs' and students' learning. J. Small Bus. Entrepreneurship **23**, 543–554 (2010)
13. Fox, J., Pittaway, L., Uzuegbunam, I.: Simulations in entrepreneurship education: serious games and learning through play. Entrepreneurship Educ. Pedagogy **1**(1), 61–89 (2018)
14. Almeida, F.: Experience with entrepreneurship learning using serious games. Cypriot J. Educ. Sci. **12**(2), 69–80 (2017)
15. Kriz, W.C., Wittenzellner, H., Auchter, E., Schmidt, H.: SysTeamsGames – three games for management simulation. Dev. Bus. Simul. Exp. Learn. **39**, 333 (2012)
16. Wittenzellner, H., Schmidt, H., Kriz, W.C.: (2016): Strategy4Innovators - Training without software? The revised concept of the board game SysTeamsRybi. Dev. Bus. Simul. Exp. Learn. **43**, 322 (2016)
17. Beranič, T., Heričko, M.: The impact of serious games in economic and business education: a case of erp business simulation. Sustainability **14**(2), 683 (2022)
18. Yang, Q., Zhang, Y., Lin, Y.: Study on the influence mechanism of virtual simulation game learning experience on student engagement and entrepreneurial skill development. Front. Psychol. **12**, 772157 (2022)
19. Fang, Y.-M., Chen, K.-M., Huang, Y.-J.: Emotional reactions of different interface formats: comparing digital and traditional board games. Adv. Mech. Eng. **8**(3), 1–8 (2016)
20. Portelli, J.-L., Khaled, R.: Spectrum: exploring the effects of player experience on game design. In: Proceedings of 1st International Joint Conference of DiGRA and FDG, p. 9 (2016)
21. Freese, M., Schier, S., Mühlhausen, T.: Computer - oder Brettspiel? Entwicklungen am Beispiel des Planspieles D-CITE [Computer-based or board game? Developments using the example of the serious game D-CITE]. In: Hühn, C., Schwägele, S., Zürn, B., Bartschat, D., Trautwein, F. (eds.) Planspiele – Interaktion gestalten – Über die Vielfalt der Methode, ZMS-Schriftenreihe, 10, Norderstedt: Book on Demand GmbH (2017). ISBN: 978-3-7528-6192-1
22. Freese, M., Tiemersma, S., Verbraeck, A.: Risk management can actually be fun – using the serious cards for biosafety game to stimulate proper discussions about biosafety. In: Proceedings of the 52nd International Simulation and Gaming Association's Conference, Indore, 06–10 September 2021 (2021)
23. Freese, M., Bekebrede, G.: About dinosaurs in laboratories - evaluation of the serious game cards for biosafety. In: Harteveld, C., Sutherland, S., Troiano, G., Lukosch, H., Meijer, S. (eds.) Simulation and Gaming for Social Impact. ISAGA 2022. Lecture Notes in Computer Science, vol. 13622. Springer, Cham (2023). https://doi.org/10.1007/978-3-031-37171-4_4
24. Csikszentmihalyi, M.: Beyond Boredom and Anxiety: Experiencing Flow in Work and Play. Jossey-Bass, San Francisco (1975)
25. Laupichler, M.C., Aster, A., Haverkamp, N., Raupach, T.: Development of the "Scale for the assessment of non-experts' AI literacy" – an exploratory factor analysis. Comput. Hum. Behav. Rep. **12**, 100338 (2023)

The Impact of Simulation Games on the Success of Simulation Game Courses

Friedrich Trautwein(✉) 📵 and Tobias Alf 📵

Centre for Management Simulation, Baden-Wuerttemberg Cooperative State University,
Stuttgart, Germany
friedrich.trautwein@dhbw-stuttgart.de

Abstract. Whereas the majority of empirical studies in the field of simulation and gaming are based on one specific simulation game, this study includes a broad range of mostly business-related simulation games. Looking across the border of a single simulation game this article analysis, what are general aspects of simulation games that have an impact on the success of simulation game courses.

To do this, we evaluated courses that were taught with 33 different simulation games and collected feedback from more than 3,100 participants.

On the one hand, the study shows good values for the comprehensibility of simulation games, on the other hand, the practical relevance is rated lower. As both aspects are crucial for the success of simulation game courses, more emphasis should especially be given to illustrate the practical relevance of simulation games. In addition, the study shows, that there are several significant differences between computer-based and haptic simulation games. Nevertheless, the differences are of no practical importance with respect to satisfaction and learning.

The study also shows that, overall, the difficulty of the simulation games and the way in which they are facilitated is appropriate for the participants: While the difficulty is exactly right for about 80% of the participants, it is rather too low or too high for about 10% of the participants.

Keywords: Simulation · Gaming · Management Simulation · Board-Game · Computer-Based Game

1 Introduction

Simulation games have been an important part of the degree programmes at many universities for a long time (cf. Eckardt et al. 2024; Meßner et al., 2018; Muno, 2020; Zuern et al. 2023) and are widely used in other contexts as well. As a complex teaching-learning arrangement, simulation games place different demands on both students and teachers than traditional courses. They enable students often in groups to engage in action-orientated learning in a fault-tolerant, realistic learning environment. The students take on roles and act within a simulated learning environment according to predefined rules (cf. Klabbers 2018, p. 219).

An important instrument, both for the quality assurance of individual simulation game courses as well as for the further development of the simulation game method, is the evaluation of simulation games, which is too rarely carried out systematically (cf. Zeiner-Fink et al. 2023, p. 43). Here, simulation game courses pose special challenges due to their complexity. In addition to the aspects that are also relevant to traditional courses (students, teachers, framework conditions) the actual simulation game represents an essential aspect of teaching and learning in simulation game courses.

To date, there has been a lack of scientifically sound, evidence-based data on the contribution of simulation games to learning success in simulation game courses. A major limitation of almost all empirical studies is that the data is based on only one specific simulation game. In the extensive literature review of Zeiner-Fink (cf. 2022, appendix A) only five out of 133 studies included were based on more than one simulation game. Thus most studies hardly allow to draw empirically based conclusions, which part of learning and satisfaction is based on a simulation game itself or other aspects.

Against this background, this large-scale research project is across borders of one specific simulation game based on data from 33 different simulation games and over 3,100 participants. There is no comparable study known to the authors of this article, that has a comparable empirical basis. Consequently, the major aim of this article is to shed light on the impact of simulation games on the success of simulation game courses. Due to the fact that on the one hand specific aspects of simulation games are not part in the usual course evaluations questionnaires (cf. Rindermann 2009 as an example), and on the other hand questionnaires for one specific simulation game are not applicable to a wide range of different simulation games, the Centre for Management Simulation (ZMS) has developed the ZMS inventory for the evaluation of simulation game based courses on a theoretical model (see Fig. 1, cf. Trautwein/Alf 2023a).

Based on the objectives of this study, two research questions arise:

- **Research Question 1:** Which impacts have different aspects of simulations games (comprehensibility, practical relevance, difficulty, type of game) on participants' Satisfaction and Learning?
- **Research Question 2:** What is the relationship between simulation games and other aspects (facilitator, team, students, general conditions) of simulation game courses?

Whereas RQ1 refers to the relationship between simulation games (marked grey in Fig. 1) and Satisfaction and Learning, RQ2 refers to the relationship between simulation games and all other aspects of the theoretical model.

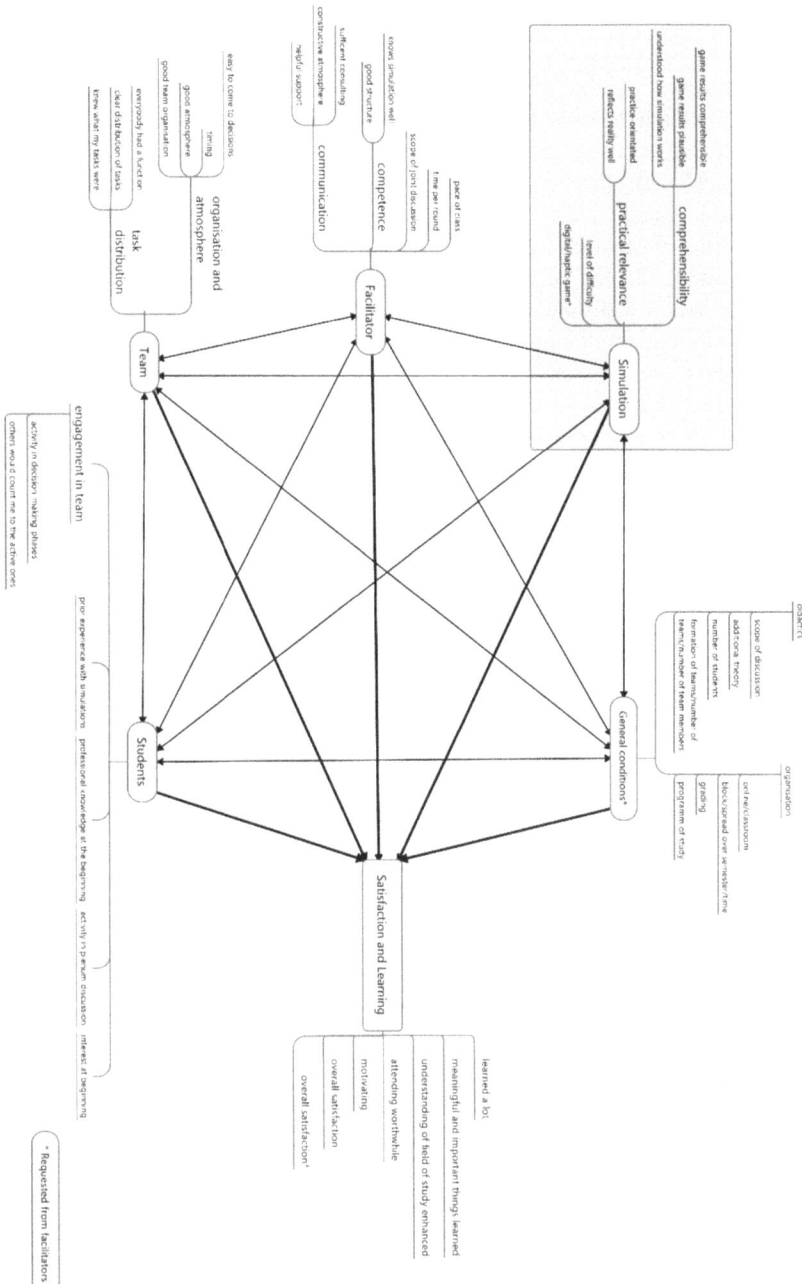

Fig. 1. Theoretical model of the study

2 Methodology

The study is based on the ZMS inventory for the evaluation of simulation game based courses which records key aspects of the use of the simulation games (cf. Trautwein/Alf 2023a). This involves collecting data on the students, cooperation in the small groups/teams, the simulation game, the facilitators and the general conditions of the simulation game courses. In addition, the success of simulation game courses is recorded in terms of satisfaction and learning (overall assessment).

The data was collected between May 2021 and March 2023. Based on the ZMS inventory, a total of 3,133 students were surveyed in over 200 simulation game courses, in which 33 different simulation games were used (cf. Trautwein/Alf 2024). The questionnaire for the students essentially consists of 27 Likert-scaled items. All questions are answered on a six-point Likert scale, which (apart from the question on overall satisfaction) ranges from "strongly disagree" (score = 1) to "strongly agree" (score = 6). The questionnaire was typically filled towards the end of the simulation game lectures, but not totally at the end to ensure a high response rate. It takes about five minutes. The facilitators mainly answer questions about the organisational framework (general conditions) of the simulation game course (the questionnaires are available online at https://zms.dhbw-stuttgart.de/en/research/research-projects/). All simulation game courses were held at the ZMS of the Cooperative State University (DHBW) Stuttgart.

The simulation games analysed in this study cover a wide range of topics (Table 1, for detailed information about the simulation games look at https://zms.dhbw-stuttgart.de/en/the-zms/our-simulation-games/) and cover, besides classical corporate business themes, also topics such as sustainability and change management. Of the 33 simulation games analysed, 13 are primarily haptic simulation games (1.404 participants) and 19 are primarily computer-based (digital) simulation games (1.711 participants); one simulation game is partly haptic and partly computer-based (18 participants). All simulation game courses included in the study were block courses meaning that students spend one to three days only working with the simulation game. Facilitators were present for the students for the entire duration of the class. Table 1 shows the simulation games used in this study and the number of students participating in courses based on the simulation games (for more details on the simulation games see https://zms.dhbw-stuttgart.de/en/the-zms/our-simulation-games/).

The analysis of the empirical data is carried out with SPSS version 28. The evaluation of the results follows scientific conventions (cf. Trautwein/Alf 2023b). Depending on the probability of error (p), we report the results on the .05 significance level (*), on the .01 significance level (**) or on the .001 significance level (***). Correlations (r) are designated as weak (r < |.30|), medium (|.30| < = r < |.50|) and strong (r > = |.50|). For the Cronbach's α, values above 0.8 are considered (very) good and from 0.6 to 0.8 as satisfactory (cf. on α-values Trautwein 2004, p. 98, Taber 2017). With regard to the effect size d, we follow the suggestions of Cohen (1988, 25) and speak at .2 or .3 of a small effect, around .5 of a medium effect and from .8 of a large effect.

Table 1. Simulation games in the study with participants and kind of game.

SG Name	Number of participants	Percent (%)	Digital = 1 Haptic = 2
Agile MemoGame Development	195	6,2	1
Beergame	18	0,6	1/2
BTI Factory	222	7,1	2
BTI Global Strategy	179	5,7	2
BTI Hospital Akut	92	2,9	2
BTI Logistic	29	0,9	2
BTI Store Manager	77	2,5	2
CAPSIM-Core	108	3,4	1
coludo-Industry	153	4,9	2
Fishing Game	109	3,5	2
Fountains	27	0,9	2
Grid	36	1,1	2
HR-Management	26	0,8	1
Inchaing - The Fresh Connection	19	0,6	1
IT-Service-Management	14	0,4	1
Mission Team Development	16	0,5	2
Management Simulation Day -Game	66	2,1	1
Oekonomikus Insurance	83	2,6	2
ProCom Medieval Market	9	0,3	2
riva SysTeamsChange	372	11,9	2
Serious Games.Studio	31	1,0	1
TOPSIM Applied Economics	30	1,0	1
TOPSIM BD Fitness	22	0,7	1
TOPSIM Easy Management	230	7,3	1
TOPSIM General Management	621	19,8	1
TOPSIM Going Global	10	0,3	1
TOPSIM Hospital Management	55	1,8	1
TOPSIM Immo Makler	24	0,8	1
TOPSIM Insurance	58	1,9	1
TOPSIM Logistics	101	3,2	1

(*continued*)

Table 1. (*continued*)

SG Name	Number of participants	Percent (%)	Digital = 1 Haptic = 2
TOPSIM Manufacturing Managem	15	0,5	1
TOPSIM Scale Up	15	0,5	1
TOPSIM Universal Banking	71	2,3	1
Total	3,133	100	

3 Results

Based on the theoretical model (see Fig. 1) of the empirical survey, the following scales were built (see Table 2). Looking at the results at a glance, the scales of the ZMS inventory have mostly good internal consistencies, especially keeping in mind the small number of items in most scales.

Table 2. Scales of the ZMS-Inventory

Scale Name (Number of Items)	x	sd	α
SG Comprehensibility (3)	4,84	0,94	0,83
SG Practical Relevance (2)	4,29	1,07	0,85
Facilitator Competence (2)	5,34	0,88	0,78
Facilitator Communication (3)	5,33	0,87	0,85
Team Organisation + Atmosphere (4)	5,13	0,83	0,83
Team Task Distribution (3)	4,60	1,21	0,82
Student Engagement (2)	5,06	1,01	0,79
Satisfaction and Learning (6)	4,49	1,12	0,94

To analyse the success of simulation games on simulation game courses, the results of the directly related scales are given in detail. Table 3 shows the results for Satisfaction and Learning outcomes.

The results for the simulation games on which the courses are based are given in Table 4 (Simulation Game Comprehensibility) and Table 5 (Simulation Game Practical Relevance). With a mean value of $x = 4,84$ the Comprehensibility of games is quite high, the result for the Practical Relevance is far lower with just $x = 4,29$.

Table 6 shows the correlations between SG Comprehensibility and SG Practical Relevance and the other scales of the model. It can be seen that there are small correlations between the two simulation game scales and Team scales as well as the student Engagement. Small correlations exist to the two facilitator related scales and strong correlations towards the Satisfaction and Learning.

Table 3. Results on Satisfaction and Learning in Simulation Game Courses

Scale for Satisfaction and Learning (α = .94)		x	sd
		4,49	1,12
SL1	I learned a lot in the simulation game	4,40	1,22
SL2	I learned something meaningful and important in this seminar	4,57	1,24
SL3	My understanding of my field of study has been enhanced by the seminar	4,25	1,38
SL4	All in all, attending the seminar was worth it for me	4,63	1,35
SL5	I found the simulation game very motivating	4,28	1,37
SL6	How satisfied are you with the seminar overall?	4,79	1,14

Table 4. Results on Simulation Game Comprehensibility

Scale for SG Comprehensibility (α = .83)		x	sd
		4,84	0,94
C1	The results of the simulation are very comprehensible	4,69	1,12
C2	The results of the simulation are plausible	4,70	1,09
C3	I understood how the simulation works	5,14	1,03

Table 5. Results on Simulation Game Practical Relevance

Scale for SG Practical Relevance (α = .85)		x	sd
		4,29	1,07
PR1	The simulation has a close practical orientation	4,42	1,16
PR2	The simulation game is a good representation of reality	4,16	1,12

Table 7 differentiates between digital and haptic simulation games. On the one hand haptic simulation games are rated better with regard to SG Comprehensibility as well as the Team Factors, on the other hand Facilitator Competence and Communication as well as Satisfaction and Learning are better rated if digital games are used. With regard to SG Practical Relevance as well as to Student Engagement no significant differences can be seen. According to Cohen's d the effects are more or less small or practically irrelevant.

Table 6. Correlation coefficients between SG Comprehensibility and SG Practical Relevance and other scales

Correlation matrix	SG Comprehensibility	SG Practical Relevance
Facilitator Competence	.34***	.33***
Facilitator Communication	.36***	.35***
Team Org. + Atmosphere	.25***	.17***
Team Task Distribution	.24***	.13***
Student Engagement	.24***	.16***
Satisfaction and Learning	.50***	.59***

Table 7. Influence of different types of simulation games (digital/haptic)

Constructs	Digital x	Haptic x	Δx	Cohen's d
SG Comprehensibility	4,70	5,01	0,31***	0,41
SG Practical Relevance	4,31	4,26	n.s	0,03
Facilitator Competence	5,47	5,18	0,29***	0,33
Facilitator Communication	5,43	5,22	0,21***	0,25
Team Orga. + Athmosphere	5,08	5,19	0,11***	0,12
Team Task Distribution	4,51	4,70	0,19***	0,16
Student Engagement	5,09	5,03	n.s	0,02
Satisfaction and Learning	4,53	4,42	0,11**	0,03

Table 8 shows differences depending on the subjective measurement of the difficulty of the simulation game by the participants. If a difference is significant, it is shown in the last column, L*R therefore means that the difference between a "Too Low" and "Right" is significant. For 2.487 of the participants the difficulty was exactly right, 275 answered that the difficulty of the simulation game was rather too low and for 329 participants the difficulty was rather too high (42 are missing values).

4 Discussion

Based on the results of the survey, the following section discusses the research questions.

Research Question 1: Which impacts have different aspects of simulations games (comprehensibility, practical relevance, difficulty, type of game) on participants' Satisfaction and Learning?

With an average of x = 4,49 (Table 3) on a six-point Likert scale, satisfaction and learning are perceived as quite good by the participants. This result seems to be acceptable, nevertheless at the same time it should be a motivation to further improve the simulation game courses.

Table 8. Influence of subjective measurement of difficulty

Scale	Difficulty of SG			Significance
	rather too low (L)	exactly right (R)	rather too high (H)	
SG Comprehensibility	5,06	4,94	3,91	L*H, R*H
SG Practical Relevance	3,76	4,39	3,96	L*R, L*H, R*H
Facilitator Competence	5,07	5,40	5,24	L*R, L*H, R*H
Facilitator Communication	5,08	5,40	5,12	L*R, R*H
Team Orga. + Athmosphere	5,16	5,17	4,80	L*H, R*H
Team Task Distribution	4,67	4,66	4,06	L*H, R*H
Student Engagement	5,09	5,13	4,54	L*H, R*H
Satisfaction and Learning	3,72	4,66	3,83	L*R, R*H

Table 6 shows strong correlations between Simulation Game Comprehensibility as well as Simulation Game Practical Relevance and Satisfaction and Learning. Therefore, both aspects of simulation games are very important for the success of simulation game courses. While the comprehensibility of simulation games is already quite high with an average of $x = 4,84$ (Table 4), the equivalent value for the practical relevance is $x = 4,29$ (Table 5). Choosing simulation games and facilitating them it is therefore especially important to keep the practical relevance for the participants in mind. Especially within briefings, in between-debriefings and the final debriefing facilitators should illustrate where the simulation game is helpful for the participants.

In addition, it is very important for the success of simulation game courses, that the subjective difficulty of the simulation game is neither too low nor too high (see Table 8). With a value of $x = 4,66$ participants rate their satisfaction and learning much higher if the difficulty is exactly right compared to those, for whom the difficulty is rather too low or too high. The fit between competencies of the participants and the difficulty of the simulation game therefore is very important for the success of simulation game courses. Overall, most students feel comfortable with the difficulty (2.487 out of 3,133). Only for roughly 10% of the students the difficulty of the simulation game is rather to too low or too high. Therefore, it can be stated, that the choice of the simulation games as well as the way they are facilitated fits most participants. Due to the fact, that depending on the previous knowledge of the students it is impossible to adjust the difficulty to every single participant this seems to be a (very) good result.

With an average of x = 4,53 Satisfaction and Learning for digital simulation games is rated slightly but nevertheless significantly better than for haptic games (x = 4,42) (Table 7). Based on Cohen's d this difference is practically irrelevant and might be the result of haptic simulation games used in online settings, where they perform significantly worse than digital simulation games (cf. Alf/Trautwein 2023).

Research Question 2: What is the relationship between simulation games and other aspects (facilitator, team, students, general conditions) of simulation game courses?

Besides the influence on satisfaction and learning, simulation games are also related to several other aspects of simulation game courses.

First of all, there are correlations between the two simulation game scales and the two facilitator scales on a medium level (Table 6). This means that either facilitators influence the perception of the simulation game or the other way round. Both directions seem to be possible. On the one hand a good simulation game might influence how facilitators are seen by the students, on the other hand a good facilitator might (hopefully) influence e.g. the comprehensibility of simulation games by making helpful debriefings. To a lesser extent (small correlation) simulation games are also related to the two team scales indicating that based on which game is used, team organization and atmosphere as well as task distribution within teams are more or less supported by simulation games.

In addition, the type of simulation game influences different aspects of simulation game courses (Table 7). While there is no significant difference in the perception of the practical relevance, haptic games are significantly better understood than digital simulation games. This difference, with Cohen's d of 0,41, is the highest of all in this study, indicates that facilitators are especially challenged to help students playing computer-based games to understand what they do and what implications e.g. their decisions have. The type of simulation game also influences the perception of the facilitators. Digital simulation games result in a better evaluation of facilitators competence and communication by the participants. The reason remains speculative based on the data of this study: Maybe the higher complexity of digital simulation games leads participants to attribute a higher competence to facilitators.

Another aspect of simulation games is the subjective measurement of their difficulty. Based on the data (Table 8) it can be assumed, that student engagement is much lower (x = 4, 54) if the difficulty is rather too high compared to x = 5,12 (if the difficulty is exactly right) or x = 5,09 (if the difficulty is rather too low). Therefore, facilitators should especially pay attention not to overstrain students or at least to think about how to deal with possible frustrations to avoid a decreasing engagement. Of course, it is also thinkable that students being demotivated from the beginning do not actively participate and therefore perceive the simulation game as rather too difficult.

Different to almost all empirical studies (cf. Zeiner-Fink 2022), this study is based on a broad basis of 33 different simulation games. Therefore, it allows a more general understanding of the impacts of simulation games on the success of simulation game classes than it is possible with data based on only one specific simulation game. Whereas staying within the borders of a single simulation game doesn't allow to measure the effects simulation games have in general on the success of simulation game classes, this study gives insights into the relevance of simulation games themselves.

Interpreting the results, some limitations have to be kept in mind due to research design and the scope of the quantitative survey (cf. Trautwein/Alf 2024).

The ZMS inventory is based on a survey of both students and facilitators. The focus is on the perception of the students. There are a number of reasons in favour of this approach (cf. Trautwein/Alf 2023a). For example, self-perception is more differentiated than the perception of others, it guides action and numerous studies have shown that students have a high level of judgement (Cronan et al. 2012; Pfeiffer et al. 2015). In view of the fundamental importance of this question, it was subjected to a more detailed analysis for the ZMS inventory in several studies. It was found that various indicators point to a good perception of the students. For example, the student assessment of satisfaction with the simulation game course correlates highly significant with the assessment by the facilitators (cf. Trautwein/Alf 2023b). In addition, students perceive facilitators who conduct the simulation game very frequently and subjectively feel confident with the simulation game as significantly more competent than facilitators with less experience (cf. Trautwein/Alf 2023b). Furthermore, results of a sophisticated mixed method study with another questionnaire (MEEGA +, cf. Petri et al 2018) as well as several qualitative instruments also underline the quality of the students' self assessment in the ZMS inventory (cf. Alf et al 2023). Nevertheless, when interpreting the results, it should be noted that they are largely based on the subjective perception of students and therefore only represent a section of reality and is fraught with difficulties (cf. Spinath & Seifried, 2018), as it is almost impossible to objectively record the very complex learning success even with complex research designs in small samples.

Another aspect is that the data were collected exclusively from courses conducted at DHBW Stuttgart (cf. Alf/Trautwein 2023). Due to the specific composition of the student body and the very close integration of theory and practice in studies at DHBW, the results cannot necessarily be transferred to simulation game courses at other types of higher education institutions. In addition, there is another institutional aspect: At the ZMS, where the data collection took place, knowledge about simulation-based teaching is institutionally bundled and a large proportion of faculty at the ZMS have been active in game-based teaching for years. Furthermore, the spatial equipment is optimized for the facilitation of simulation games. Although data is now also available from simulation game courses at other locations and from other universities, these are still of little significance in quantitative terms and were not included in this study. Due to the special circumstances of simulation game courses at the ZMS, the question must remain open as to whether the results can be transferred without restriction to simulation game courses in other contexts.

Further research should assess whether the results are valid for simulation game courses in other faculties, other universities or even outside universities. In addition, it would be very interesting to see if the results can be transferred to simulation games with completely different contexts, e.g. political simulation games.

Disclosure of Interests. The authors have no competing interests to declare that are relevant to the content of this article.

References

Alf, T., de Wijse-van Heeswijk, M., Trautwein, F.: The role of reflection in learning with simulation games – a multi-method quasi experimental research. Simul. Gaming (2023). https://doi.org/10.1177/10468781231194896

Alf, T., Trautwein, F.: Transition from face-to-face to online teaching. In: Becu, N. (ed.): Simulation and Gaming for social and environmental transitions, proceedings 54th ISAGA Conference, pp. 319–328 (2023)

Cronan, T.P., Leger, P.-M., Robert, J., Babin, G., Charland, P.: Comparing objective measures and perceptions of cognitive learning in an ERP simulation game: a research note. Simul. Gaming **43**(4), 461–480 (2012)

Eckardt, H.G., Zürn, B., Trautwein, F.: Einsatz von (Unternehmens-)Planspielen in der betriebs- und volkswirtschaftlichen Hochschullehre – Ergebnisse einer empirischen Erhebung. In: Alf, T; Hahn, S., Fischer, I., Zürn, B., Trautwein, F. (eds.): Planspiele – interdisziplinär vernetzt (ZMS-Schriftenreihe, 14), pp. 58–77 (2024)

Klabbers, J.H.G.: On the architecture of game science. Simul. Gaming **49**(3), 207–245 (2018). https://doi.org/10.1177/1046878118762534

Meßner, M.T., Schedelik, M., Engartner, T.: Handbuch Planspiele in der sozialwissenschaftlichen Hochschullehre. Wochenschau Verlag (2018). https://ebookcentral.proquest.com/lib/gbv/detail.action?docID=5438493

Muno, W.: Planspiele und Politiksimulationen in der Hochschullehre. Wochenschau Verlag, Kleine Reihe Hochschuldidaktik Politik (2020)

Rindermann, H.: Lehrevaluation. Einführung und Überblick zu Forschung und Praxis der Lehrveranstaltungsevaluation an Hochschulen mit einem Beitrag zur Evaluation computerbasierten Unterrichts. 2., leicht korrigierte Auflage. Landau: Verlag Empirische Pädagogik (Psychologie, 42) (2009)

Petri, G., Gresse von Wangenheim, C., Borgatto, A.F.: MEEGA+: A method for the evaluation of educational games for computing education. Brazil: Universidade Federal De Santa Catarina (2018)

Peiffer, H., Rach, H., Rosanowitsch, S., Wörl, J., Schneider, M.: Lehrevaluation. In: Schneider, M., Mustafić, M. (eds.) Gute Hochschullehre: Eine evidenzbasierte Orientierungshilfe, pp. 153–184. Springer, Heidelberg (2015). https://doi.org/10.1007/978-3-662-45062-8_7

Spinath, B., Seifried, E.: Was brauchen wir, um solide empirische Erkenntnisse über gute Hochschullehre zu erhalten? Zeitschrift für Hochschulentwicklung, **13**(1), 153–169 (2018). https://zfhe.at/index.php/zfhe/issue/view/57

Taber, K.S.: The use of Cronbach's alpha when developing and reporting research instruments in science education. Res. Sci. Educ. **48**, 1273–1296 (2018). https://doi.org/10.1007/s11165-016-9602-2

Trautwein, C.: Unternehmensplanspiele im industriebetrieblichen Hochschulstudium. Analyse von Kompetenzerwerb, Motivation und Zufriedenheit am Beispiel des Unternehmensplanspiels TOPSIM - General Management II. Wiesbaden: Gabler Verlag (2011)

Trautwein, F., Alf, T.: Online-Planspielveranstaltungen – ein Zukunftsmodell? In: #dual (in print) (2024)

Trautwein, F., Alf, T.: Theory-based development of an inventory for the evaluation of simulation game lectures. In: Harteveld, C., Sutherland, S., Troiano, G., Lukosch, H., Meijer, S. (eds.): Simulation and Gaming for Social Impact. Proceedings of the 54th Conference of the International Simulation and Gaming Association, pp. 3–21 (2023a)

Trautwein, F., Alf, T.: The role of facilitators for learning and satisfaction of students in simulation game courses. In: Becu, N. (eds.): Simulation and Gaming for Social and Environmental Transitions. Proceedings of the 54th Conference of the International Simulation and Gaming Association, pp. 158–167 (2023b)

Trautwein, F.: Berufliche Handlungskompetenz als Studienziel. Verlag Wissenschaft und Praxis, Sternenfels (2004)

Zeiner-Fink, S.: Konzeption und Evaluation eines Planspiels unter Besonderer Betrachtung von Lerneffekten und Planspielakzeptanz. Universitätsverlag Chemnitz (2022)

Zeiner-Fink, S., Geithner, S., Bullinger-Hoffmann, A.C.: Lerneffekte und Akzeptanz von Planspielen: Ein systematischer Literatur-Review. In: Zeitschrift für Hochschulentwicklung, 18 (Sonderheft Planspiele), pp. 41–60 (2023)

Zürn, B., Trautwein, F., Freese, M.: Empfehlungen zur curricularen Integration von Planspielen in Wirtschaftsstudiengänge. Zeitschrift für Hochschulentwicklung **18**, 167–185 (2023). https://doi.org/10.21240/zfhe/SH-PS/10

Feedback and Biofeedback Procedure and Results, Based on the Gearshfit Engine

Błażej Podgórski[1,2](✉) ⓘ, Marcin Wardaszko[1] ⓘ, and Piotr Wątrucki[2]

[1] Kozminski University, 57 Jagiellonska Street, Warsaw, Poland
bpodgorski@kozminski.edu.pl
[2] ECC Games S.A., Warsaw, Poland

Abstract. The main objective of this project was to develop an innovative vehicle behavior engine within a dynamic global gaming environment. This engine, once created, will serve as a versatile tool, enabling any development team utilizing the Unreal engine to craft advanced games centered around motorization. The primary focus of this research was the diversification of testing groups based on gender and experience for finding difference between different game engine. Additionally, three distinct scenarios were created to identify differences in biofeedback measures.

Keywords: Biofeedback · Computer Games Engine

1 Introduction

Over the past few years, video games have emerged as a predominant form of entertainment and a vital aspect of social and leisure activities (Griffiths and Hunt, 1995). Market Research Future projects a staggering valuation of nearly 14 trillion dollars for the industry by the year 2030. The surge in both user base and anticipated profits reflects the substantial growth experienced in the realm of video games. With a profound impact on younger generations, video games have seamlessly integrated into their daily lives, with gamers dedicating considerable time and effort to playing (Gentile and Anderson, 2003; Lenhart et al., 2005). Particularly noteworthy is the significance of video games for individuals without a driving license, as racing games provide them with a platform to engage in competitive experiences and gain insights into car mechanics.

The primary objective of this project was to develop an innovative vehicle behavior engine within a dynamic global gaming environment. This engine, once created, will serve as a versatile tool, enabling any development team utilizing the Unreal engine to craft advanced games centered around motorization. The development of the engine encompasses various aspects, including (1) suspension physics, focusing on overload parameters, (2) tire physics, incorporating pressure adjustments (Garatti and Bittanti, 2009; Pacejka, 2012), (3) brake behavior and performance, derived from telemetry results involving brake pedal pressure, brake fluid pressure, speed, and distance (Langhof et al., 2016), (4) drive ratio, involving measurements of gear ratio, acceleration, and overloads

(G parameter measurement), (5) engine parameters, such as water and oil temperature, acceleration, and torque (Li et al., 2016), (6) adhesion parameters on specific surfaces, including slip parameters resulting from loss of adhesion (Abe, 2015), and (7) GPS position in relation to the track (Balkwill, 2018).

2 Research Methodology

The use of electroencephalography (EEG) in experimental research methodologies focusing on gamers has gained traction due to its ability to provide real-time insights into the neurophysiological processes underlying gaming experiences. EEG offers a higher temporal resolution compared to other neuroimaging techniques, such as fMRI, making it particularly suitable for capturing the dynamic brain activity associated with fast-paced gaming environments (Kim et al., 2019). This capability allows researchers to analyze cognitive functions and emotional responses during gameplay, thereby enhancing our understanding of the effects of video gaming on the brain.

In the context of action video games, studies have demonstrated that gameplay can lead to significant changes in brain dynamics. For instance, Bejjanki et al. illustrated that action video game play can facilitate the development of improved perceptual templates, which are crucial for processing visual information efficiently (Bejjanki et al., 2014). This finding suggests that gamers may experience enhanced visual processing capabilities, potentially due to the increased feed-forward connectivity in visual processing networks induced by gaming. Furthermore, Malik et al. and Bakaoukas et al. both reported on the dynamic brain activity observed during gameplay, emphasizing the importance of high-resolution EEG in capturing these changes (Malik et al., 2012; Bakaoukas et al., 2015). These studies collectively highlight the potential of EEG to elucidate the neural mechanisms that underpin the cognitive advantages associated with gaming.

Moreover, the relationship between gaming and emotional responses has been a focal point of EEG research. For example, Kosinski et al. utilized EEG to analyze emotional changes during gameplay, linking specific game elements to players' emotional states (Kosinski et al., 2018). This approach underscores the utility of EEG in understanding how different aspects of game design can elicit varied emotional responses, which can be critical for developers aiming to create engaging gaming experiences. Additionally, Granato et al. explored the physiological data of players in virtual reality racing games, further demonstrating the capacity of EEG to provide insights into the emotional landscape of gamers (Granato et al., 2020). Such studies indicate that EEG can serve as a valuable tool for both psychological research and game design.

The implications of EEG findings extend beyond cognitive and emotional responses; they also encompass behavioral outcomes. Research by Cain et al. revealed that action video game experience can reduce the cognitive cost associated with task switching, suggesting that gamers may exhibit more efficient cognitive control (Cain et al., 2012). This efficiency is likely linked to the neurophysiological changes observed in EEG studies, where gamers show different brain activity patterns compared to non-gamers. Furthermore, the work of Maclin et al. supports this notion by demonstrating that video game practice can enhance attentional resource allocation, as evidenced by changes in electrophysiological indices (Maclin et al., 2011). These findings collectively suggest that the cognitive benefits of gaming may be rooted in measurable changes in brain activity, as captured by EEG.

In terms of methodology, the integration of EEG with other physiological measures, such as galvanic skin response and heart rate variability, has been proposed to provide a more comprehensive understanding of gamers' experiences (Derbali & Frasson, 2010). This multimodal approach can enrich the data collected during experiments, allowing researchers to correlate physiological responses with cognitive and emotional states more effectively. For instance, Derbali and Frasson highlighted the significance of using electrophysiological measures to predict players' motivational states during gameplay, indicating that a combination of EEG and other measures can yield deeper insights into the gaming experience (Derbali & Frasson, 2010).

The application of EEG in gaming research also raises important considerations regarding player demographics and individual differences. Studies have shown that factors such as gender can influence gaming experiences and outcomes, with male players often dominating action-oriented game research (Cain et al., 2012). This bias necessitates a more inclusive approach in future studies to ensure that findings are representative of the broader gaming population. Additionally, the expertise level of players has been shown to affect their cognitive processing during gameplay, as indicated by research that classified players based on their EEG signals (Anwar et al., 2017; Hafeez et al., 2021). Understanding these individual differences is crucial for tailoring gaming experiences and optimizing game design. Thus, the potential for EEG to provide feedback in game design is significant. Research has indicated that EEG data can be utilized to manipulate player interest levels and enhance engagement (Chan et al., 2012). By analyzing brainwave patterns associated with varying levels of interest, developers can create more immersive and captivating gaming experiences. This application of EEG not only benefits game designers but also contributes to the growing field of affective computing, where emotional responses are leveraged to improve user experiences (Smedt & Menschaert, 2012). The integration of EEG into game design processes represents a promising avenue for future research and development.

In this paper, we present the results of perception tests and share our perspective on the most effective methodology for this type of research and testing.

The research employed a quasi-experimental method (Creswell, 2012). It was conducted across three groups of research facilities. The first group comprised drivers with rally licenses, the second group included professional players, and the third group involved casual players, totaling no less than 30 participants in each wave of research. The research took the form of collecting biofeedback data and administering surveys covering demographic information, game usage, and game engine perception.

Aim of the study was to establish difference to the response to the different game engines with regards to the different groups of users. Thus we have formulated two hypotheses for this study:

Hypothesis I: There will be significant differences in response to the different game engines among the type of users.

Hypothesis II: Second game engine will have stronger preference among different user groups.

The hypotheses testing and validation is based upon data provided by participants in the questionnaires and gathered with biofeedback.

3 Research Procedure and Experimental Setup

The first step was group diversification base on sex and type of user. Base on this approach, the research results are more universal because we address the important issue of specific expectations for a given group.Biofeedback data collection adhered to principles established by the Association for Applied Psychophysiology and Biofeedback (AAPB). The collected data encompassed heart rate (EEG), breathing rate, skin sweating (skin conductance), and facial expressions. Specialized equipment and licensed software were utilized for this purpose.

Equipment:
The tests were conducted using the following equipment:

3. car driving simulators equipped with a steering wheel, pedals, gearbox, and computer setup.

2 games or versions of one game with pre-designed research scenarios. The first game featured a standard driving scenario on a track using a conventional game engine (without AI/ML). The second scenario involved driving a racing car on a track powered by a GearShift-based vehicle physics engine.

- One video with audio depicting the experience of driving a sports car.
- 3 sets of sensors for measuring and collecting data on the subject's body parameters.
- A license for software responsible for collecting and processing data from biofeedback sensors.

The research procedure ensured the safety of research facilities and the quality of data, emphasizing measurement stability. Each participant underwent the same procedure and retained the right to discontinue the study at any time, with their data excluded from the final analysis.

1. People were recruited remotely due to Covid restrictions. During the recruitment process, participants answered basic demographic questions and provided information about their video game usage patterns. They were briefed on the study's purpose and procedures. Upon confirming participation, appointments were scheduled for specific examination times and dates.
2. Upon arrival at the site, study participants completed and signed a consent form for the use of research data in compliance with GDPR. They received additional information about the study's purpose and procedures and had the opportunity to ask questions. Following consent completion, the research facility assigned a unique number to anonymize the data.
3. Participants proceeded to a technician who installed and calibrated the biofeedback sensors.
4. Participants engaged in three research scenarios:
a. In the first scenario, participants watched a video of driving a sports car with accompanying music for 4–6 min. This aimed to establish a baseline and reference point for further data.

b. The second scenario involved participants driving a sports car in simulated conditions based on a standard game engine for 5 min.
c. The third scenario required participants to drive a sports car in simulated conditions based on the GearShift game engine for another 5 min.

4 Research Results

Within the project scope, tests assessing the perception and immersion of vehicle behavior will be conducted utilizing the engine prototype across diverse target groups, including professional drivers, professional gamers, and casual gamers. Two entities submitted inquiries to the competitiveness database. Subsequent waves of experiments involved measurements using heart rate monitors, Hexoskin biofeedback shirts, and an EEG device. These tests were complemented by surveys and interviews.

Table 1. Outlines the sizes of individual subgroups tested in two waves of experiments

	Cohort 1		*Cohort 2*	
	Men	*Women*	*Men*	*Women*
Total Records	122490		74654	
No of particpiants	25	5	26	12
Standard participants	8	2	10	6
Professional drivers	4	1	4	1
Players	13	2	12	5

Table 1 illustrates the fundamental demographic characteristics of the participants within each study group. Adhering to the initial research assumptions, the groups were intentionally varied in both gender composition and professional background. Gender diversity ranged from 13% to 38.7% for females, and professional diversity varied from 16% to 38%. This deliberate stratification enhances the potential generalizability of the findings. However, it is crucial to acknowledge that the group sizes are relatively modest. Consequently, the initial set of findings discussed will be derived from the entire population and subsequently presented in Table 2.

As revealed by the research findings, the game featuring an integrated physics engine developed within the ambit of the Gearshift project garnered heightened popularity among players. Furthermore, the acquired results demonstrated statistical significance, substantiated by both Chi-square and Cramer's tests. A noteworthy proportion, specifically 50 out of 70 respondents, asserted the existence of noteworthy distinctions between the two games. It is pertinent to note that the evaluated parameters encompassed happiness, concentration, satisfaction, and focus. While the biofeedback outcomes were considered in conjunction with satisfaction surveys, these aspects will be expounded upon in subsequent publications. Additionally, it is imperative to underscore the formidable challenge encountered in harmonizing results across individual devices. Future endeavors should allocate heightened attention to refining this type of analysis.

Table 2. Which version of the game did you like more overall?

		No difference	Second	First	Total
Round	1	1	17	13	31
	2	3	33	3	39
Total		4	50	16	70

Chi-Square Tests

	Value	df	Asymptotic Significance (2-sided)
Pearson Chi-Square	11,607[a]	2	,003
Likelihood Ratio	12,080	2	,002
N of Valid Cases	70		

a. 2 cells (33,3%) have expected count less than 5. The minimum expected count is 1,77

Symmetric Measures

		Value	Approximate Significance
Nominal by Nominal	Phi	,407	,003
	Cramer's V	,407	,003
N of Valid Cases		70	

5 Conclusion

The primary focus of this research was the diversification of testing groups based on gender and experience. Additionally, three distinct scenarios were created to identify differences in biofeedback measures. A noteworthy finding was the similarity in results between biofeedback jackets and wrist heart rate monitors, suggesting the consideration of choosing one option in future research. Survey results aligned with EEG data, emphasizing its importance. Statistical tests confirmed significant preferences for the game with an integrated physics engine. The study evaluated parameters such as happiness, concentration, and satisfaction, with detailed biofeedback outcomes to be elaborated in subsequent publications.

Acknowledgments. The authors acknowledge the financial support of the National Research and Development (Narodowe Centrum Badań i Rozwoju) (Poland) under Grant No. POIR.01.02.00–00.0052/19, entitled " Gearshift project—an AI-driven engine for vehi-cle behavior and map generation for games based on Unreal Engine."

References

Abe, M.: Vehicle Handling Dynamics (2015)
Balkwill, J.: Performance Vehicle Dynamics (2018)

Borji, A.: Pros and cons of GAN evaluation measures. Comput. Vis. Image Underst. **179**, 4165 (2019)

Chung, J.: Gated recurrent neural networks on sequence modeling (2014)

Du, F., Zhang, J., Hu, J., Fei, R.: Discriminative multi-modal deep generative models. Knowl.-Based Syst. **173**, 7482 (2019)

Garatti, S., Bittanti, S.: Parameter estimation in the Pacejka's tyre model through the TS method. IFAC Proc. **42**, 13041309 (2009)

Gentile, D., Anderson, C.: Violent video games: The newest media violence hazard, D.A. Gentile (Ed.), Media violence and children: A complete guide for parents and professionals, Praeger, Westport, CT (2003), pp. 131–152 (2003)

Glaser, J.I., Benjamin, A.S., Farhoodi, R., Kording, K.P.: The roles of supervised machine learning in systems neuroscience. Prog. Neurobiol. **175**, 12637 (2019)

Goodfellow, I., Bengio, Y., Courville, A.: Deep Learning. MIT press, Cambridge (2016)

Goodfellow, I., et al.: Generative adversarial nets. In: Advances in Neural Information Processing Systems (2014)

Graves, A., Mohamed, A., Hinton, G.: Speech recognition with deep recurrent neural networks. In: 2013 IEEE International Conference on Acoustics, Speech and Signal Processing, pp. 6645–6649 (2013)

Griffiths, M., Hunt, N.: Computer game playing in adolescence: prevalence and demographic indicators. J. Commun. Appl. Soc. Psychol. **5**(3), 189–193 (1995)

Johnson, J., Alahi, A., Fei-Fei, L.: Perceptual losses for real-time style transfer and super-resolution. In: European Conference on Computer Vision, Springer (2016)

Langhof, N., Rabenstein, M., Rosenlcher, J., Hackenschmidt, R., Krenkel, W., Rieg, F.: Full-ceramic brake systems for high performance friction applications. J. Eur. Ceram. Soc. **36**, 3823–3832 (2016)

Ledig, C., et al.: Photo-realistic single image super-resolution using a generative adversarial network, pp. 4681–4690

Lenhart, A., Madden, M., Hitlin, P.: Teens and technology: youth are leading the transition to a fully wired and mobile nation. Pew Internet and American Life Project

Li, X., Zou, C., Qi, A.: Experimental study on the thermo-physical properties of car engine coolant (water/ethylene glycol mixture type) based SiC nanofluids. Int. Commun. Heat Mass Transfer **77**, 159–164 (2016)

Mohamed, A., Dahl, G.E., Hinton, G.: Acoustic modeling using deep belief networks. IEEE Trans. Audio Speech Lang. Process. **20**, 14–22 (2012)

Networks. In: 2015 IEEE International Conference on Acoustics, Speech and Signal Processing (ICASSP), pp. 4580–4584

ONVOLUTIONAL 1–16;

Sainath, T.N., Vinyals, O., Senior, A., Sak, H.: Convolutional, Long Short-Term Memory, fully connected Deep Neural (2015)

Pacejka, H.: Tire and Vehicle Dynamics (2012)

Pauwelussen, J.: Essentials of Vehicle Dynamics (2015)

Anwar, S., Saeed, S., Majid, M., Usman, S., Mehmood, C., Liu, W.: A game player expertise level classification system using electroencephalography (EEG). Appl. Sci. **8**(1), 18 (2017). https://doi.org/10.3390/app8010018

Bakaoukas, A., Coada, F., Liarokapis, F.: Examining brain activity while playing computer games. J. Multimodal User Interfaces **10**(1), 13–29 (2015). https://doi.org/10.1007/s12193-015-0205-4

Bejjanki, V., et al.: Action video game play facilitates the development of better perceptual templates. Proc. Natl. Acad. Sci. **111**(47), 16961–16966 (2014). https://doi.org/10.1073/pnas.1417056111

Cain, M., Landau, A., Shimamura, A.: Action video game experience reduces the cost of switching tasks. Atten. Percept. Psychophys. **74**(4), 641–647 (2012). https://doi.org/10.3758/s13414-012-0284-1

Chan, K., Mikami, K., Kondo, K.: From brain waves to game design: a study on analyzing and manipulating player interest levels. J. Soc. Art Sci. **11**(3), 59–68 (2012). https://doi.org/10.3756/artsci.11.59

Derbali, L., Frasson, C.: Prediction of players motivational states using electrophysiological measures during serious game play (2010).https://doi.org/10.1109/icalt.2010.143

Granato, M., Gadia, D., Maggiorini, D., Ripamonti, L.: An empirical study of players' emotions in vr racing games based on a dataset of physiological data. Multimedia Tools Appl. **79**(45–46), 33657–33686 (2020). https://doi.org/10.1007/s11042-019-08585-y

Hafeez, T., Saeed, S., Arsalan, A., Anwar, S., Ashraf, M., Alsubhi, K.: EEG in game user analysis: a framework for expertise classification during gameplay (2021).https://doi.org/10.1101/2021.01.29.428766

Kim, J., et al.: Diminished frontal theta activity during gaming in young adults with internet gaming disorder. Front. Neurosci. **13**, 1183 (2019). https://doi.org/10.3389/fnins.2019.01183

Kosinski, J., Szklanny, K., Wieczorkowska, A., Wichrowski, M.: An analysis of game-related emotions using emotiv EPOC, vol. 15, pp. 913–917 (2018). https://doi.org/10.15439/2018f296

Maclin, E., et al.: Learning to multitask: effects of video game practice on electrophysiological indices of attention and resource allocation. Psychophysiology **48**(9), 1173–1183 (2011). https://doi.org/10.1111/j.1469-8986.2011.01189.x

Malik, A., Pauzi, A., Osman, D., Khairuddin, R.: Disparity in brain dynamics for video games played on small and large displays (2012).https://doi.org/10.1109/shuser.2012.6268785

Smedt, T., Menschaert, L.: Valence: affective visualisation using EEG. Digital Creativity **23**(3–4), 272–277 (2012). https://doi.org/10.1080/14626268.2012.719240

Simulating Complex Adaptive Software System Technical Debt

David Gould(✉) ⓘ, Tim French ⓘ, and Melinda Hodkiewicz ⓘ

University of Western Australia, Crawley, WA, Australia
`dave.gould@research.uwa.edu`

Abstract. Long term impacts of shortcuts and compromises taken during software development are described by the metaphor Technical Debt (TD). TD is an emerging business issue in modern interdependent software systems. Our focus is on personnel involved in managing complex adaptive software systems used in automated Remote Operations Centers (ROC's) responsible for operating industrial equipment more than 1200 km away in the Australian outback. Recognizing and managing TD in these complex adaptive software systems is challenging. This paper builds on advances Serious Games have made toward improving situational awareness, applying these lessons to TD. The prototype Serious Game TD-Sim is tested with employees working in a ROC. Thematic analysis is used to assess pre- and post-game impacts on situational awareness of TD and this is triangulated with in-game information trails. A baseline efficacy of improved TD awareness is established, sufficient to warrant further game development. Results also identify areas for improving future game design. This study is unique, applying a Serious Game to build awareness of TD in complex adaptive software systems, something yet to be covered by traditional TD research.

Keywords: Serious Games · Technical Debt · Simulation

1 Introduction

TD describes the long-term impacts of shortcuts and compromises taken during the software development lifecycle [1]. It is a critical issue for the software development industry [2] with wider implications for industries in general, because all software systems have some form of TD [3]. The current impact of TD on global Gross Domestic Product is estimated to be at least $3 trillion USD [4].

Integrated interdependent software systems are being used to enable centralized control of remote industrial operations [5, 6]. TD within these complex adaptive systems requires management as these systems are critical to the operation of each ROC and for nationally and commercially important resources produced at these remote sites.

Understanding TD in complex adaptive systems requires situational awareness [7, 8]. Attaining such awareness is challenging for three reasons. Firstly, TD is invisible to all but software developers involved in its creation and maintenance [3]. Secondly, ROC decision makers being users, as opposed to developers, of software systems are

© The Author(s) 2025
H. Lukosch et al. (Eds.): ISAGA 2024, LNCS 15420, pp. 270–284, 2025.
https://doi.org/10.1007/978-3-031-86555-8_20

unlikely to hold software development expertise [9]. Finally, current TD research is mostly focused on the software development industry [1], limiting TD management guidance for decision makers in industries that do not develop software as their primary economic objective.

Serious Games (SG's) with demonstrated efficacy in increasing stakeholder awareness of issues previously invisible to them [8, 10] offer a means of addressing this challenge. SG's are yet to be applied to TD within industrial complex adaptive software system environments. In this study we address this research gap by applying a prototype SG, TD-Sim, designed to improve situational awareness of TD in a simulated supply chain. The study is conducted at a ROC run by a global iron ore mining company. Questions addressed in this study are as follows.

(RQ1) *What impact playing a serious game has on participants' understanding of technical debt?*

(RQ2) *What impact playing a serious game has on participants' experience of technical debt?*

(RQ3) How participants' prior knowledge of software development impacts (RQ1) and (RQ2)?

2 Literature Review

When software developers compromise maintainability to meet delivery deadlines they create TD [11]. Willingly accumulated, TD can speed up product functionality deployment by as much as three times [12]. Unmanaged TD can cause "unexpectedly large cost overruns, severe quality issues, inability to add new features and even lead to a crisis point when a huge, costly refactoring or the replacement of the entire (software) system needs to be undertaken" [13, p.13]. TD requires managing to optimize benefits and minimize disadvantages [12].

Complex systems that embody self-organization, adaptation and feedback mechanisms from which gestalt behaviors emerge are known as Complex Adaptive Systems (CAS) [8]. Integrated interdependent software systems embody CAS characteristics through interactions between technological elements, human decision makers and interdependent systems [14]. CAS decision makers, through their decisions shape CAS components as a function of the mental models they maintain [8]. Mental models are a central concept of situational awareness [7].

To improve TD decision making in complex adaptive software system environments, improved decision maker situational awareness is necessary. SG's are a well-researched means of understanding complexity and addressing situational awareness within CAS [8, 15]. For instance, SG's have been used to improve decision making through awareness in infrastructure and commercial port operations [8, 10].

As a pedagogical tool, SG simulations enable integration of knowledge across scientific disciplines [16]. A SG simulation could therefore provide participants without a background in software development, the experience of managing TD through simulation. Improving situation awareness whilst affording exposure to TD cross-disciplines, suggests SG's can address issues related to attaining TD awareness in complex adaptive software systems.

SG's, game-based learning and gamification are all concepts sharing the idea of "using positive gameful experiences" to achieve serious outcomes such as education or behavioral change [17, p.2]. "Gameful experiences" are applied to a wide range of software engineering topics [18] however only two gamification and one SG study exist at the time of writing that address TD / TD awareness. Only one of 103 gamification studies [19] focused on the gamification of a TD management tool used by software developers to motivate better TD management practices. The study was conducted within a national government agency [20]. Gamification is also applied in an educational context (as opposed to business sector) by [21] to improve TD awareness and subsequently TD management. The study design of [21] was unclear if gamification or use of TD identifying tools drove improvements in awareness.

A board game has been trialed to import the concept of TD to students in software engineering [22]. In this SG TD is created when simulated software development lifecycle steps (moves on the board) are bypassed to expedite game progress. TD is visualized by assigning players a "TD card" that results in loss of game points at game end. The intent of the study is to make software engineering students aware of the TD they create.

SG's are a plausible research tool for improving decision making within complex adaptive software system environments. Yet, immaturity of gamification based research in software development in a business environment, lack of empirical studies and the need for more research to clarify specific strengths and weaknesses of gamification elements has been noted by [19, 23]. A research gap exists regarding SG's being used to improve system users' awareness of TD in industrial contexts in general but specifically for users without a software engineering background.

3 TD-Sim

3.1 Design

A mid-game view of TD-Sim is shown in Fig. 1. TD-Sim is an electronic game written in the Python language using the PyGame package. It is a single player game hosted on a stand-alone laptop. To enhance the applicability of TD-Sim to mining and other industries in the future, the game is modeled on a generalized supply chain. In the following description italics relate to design elements in Fig. 1.

In TD-Sim players move randomly created red *Spanners* or yellow *Cogs* from a *Factory* to either *Warehouse* or *Dispatch* locations. Randomly created Green *Waste* needs to be moved to the *Waste* location. The game objective is to make in-game cash, *Turn $*, by dispatching products, whilst meeting each turn's *Objective* within six minutes of game play. Turns start when products are produced and finish when a dispatch occurs. Multiple turns can occur per game.

At the start of the game all created products take over 10 seconds to move from the *Factory* to the *Warehouse* or *Dispatch*. Players must wait until one move is completed before the next can start. The result is that it can take up to half a minute before cash can be made in early turns. This makes the game initially inefficient. At random intervals throughout each turn players are presented options to upgrade the game and if TD exists pay down (reduce) TD. Upgrading enables players to progress up a level.

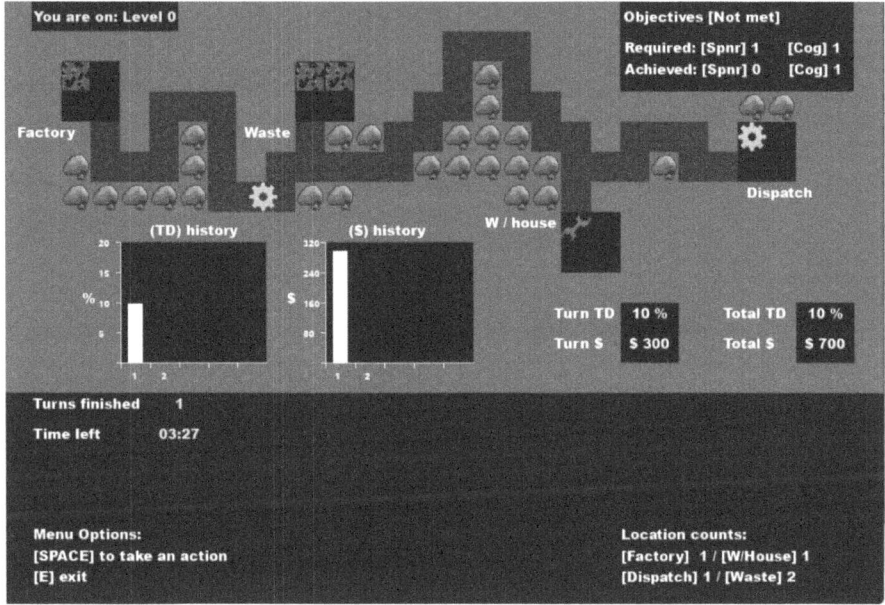

Fig. 1. TD-Sim mid-game showing Waste, Spanner and Cog movements

Each level increases product speed, faster product movement equates to more product dispatches increasing game efficiency. Upgrades incur TD. The more cash spent per upgrade the less TD incurred, reflecting real-world software development practice were doing things sustainably first time is more costly [24]. TD items created, whilst fictitious from a game perspective, are actual TD types reported by [25]. TD items are presented in a non-technical manner to enhance real-world game connection. TD in TD-Sim is modeled as a percentage (%TD), abstracted in a similar manner to other work [22]. The real-world analogy of %TD is the percentage of lines of "must-fix structural problems" within an application [26, p.51]. Connecting game-world TD to real-world TD enhances TD-Sim's transfer effect so that TD awareness gained perpetuates beyond game play [27].

3.2 Mechanics

TD-Sim is based on and informed by the causal loop model of ROC TD drivers developed by [14]. Three drivers of ROC TD are used in this study. Drivers are chosen as a pragmatic balance between development effort and what are considered by the researchers to be the minimum drivers needed to elucidate an experience TD management. Table 1 shows the ROC TD drivers used and the game mechanic they inform.

TD is created in-game by player actions, players experience TD as a supply chain phenomenon that they have accountability for creating. This embodies the *Developing software in house* driver. TD creation is modelled as an in-game system upgrade. Users are provided the experience of initiating a project from which TD is created which encapsulates *Projects created to manage Technical Debt*.

Table 1. TD Drivers and TD-Sim inclusion rationale, adapted from [14]

TD Driver	Game Mechanic Rationale
Developing software in house	Provide players a method to tangibly create TD connected to real-word TD creation
Projects created to manage Technical Debt	In game options to create new TD items or remove created items
Competition for project resourcing	Above certain % TD levels TD has consequences that impact game performance creating tension between creating TD and removing it

TD management is modeled on *Competition for project resourcing*. Contention between increasing the number of dispatched products per turn whilst generating TD and suffering from impacts from increasing levels of TD presents players with competing options. Players can spend their cash resources on either increasing TD or paying it down. TD-Sim is designed to encourage players to experiment with the impacts of varying TD levels by balancing rewards and penalties through competing resource allocation (cash), this experience is in essence managing TD [12].

4 Experiments

4.1 Methodology

The method used in this study is shown in Fig. 2. Pre- and post-test assessment are commonly used in SG validation [28]. Validation instruments and experimental methods used in TD gamification studies include a mixture of multiple-choice questionnaires, Likert scale questionnaires and interviews [22, 29], also used herein.

Game design elements, load and simulation are kept constant between game sessions. The only changing parameter between game sessions is participants, such that game

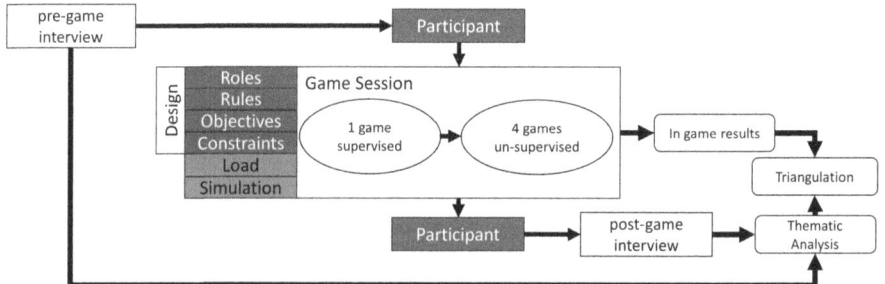

Fig. 2. Study methodology showing game play sequence, pre- and post-game interviews, in game result collection, thematic analysis and results triangulation. Game design elements (blue), game load and simulation parameters (orange) are kept constant with only participants (green) changing from one game session to the next. (Color figure online)

validation resembles a controlled trial [30]. To improve game "understandability" an initial supervised game is played. Game understandability is necessary for serious games to achieve their educational goals [31, p.114]. Each game session is then completed by participants playing four games in succession un-supervised.

4.2 Data Collection and Case Study

Each participant undertakes a pre-game brief and a post-game debrief. Briefings consist of participants reading a 1-page TD summary explaining key TD terms, definitions and concepts, followed by a survey. Survey questions are open-ended in accordance with accepted qualitative research design principles [32]. Participants are free to refer to the TD summary throughout their game session. Standardizing participant TD knowledge as a research precursor has been used prior [33]. In this study this is intended to ensure all participants, regardless of prior TD experience, have access to the same TD terms, definitions and concepts.

Survey questions are repeated in debrief interviews. Additionally, questions aimed at elucidating participant self-reflections and *learnings* gained from playing TD-Sim, are included in-line with the essential role debrief sessions play in SG research [34]. Analysis of survey and *learnings* is made using thematic analysis, a qualitative research technique applicable to the software engineering discipline [35].

Electronic SG's enable data to be collected during a game enabling detailed and reliable information capture [28]. Collecting, storing and transforming observable gameplay actions into quantitative data is a form of in-game assessment referred to as information trails [36]. In TD-Sim all menu choices and all game outcomes, such as TD outages, are captured to enable information trail development. These are triangulated with thematic analysis data to inform answers to research questions as per Fig. 2.

Participants are drawn from a single organization case operating a ROC based in Perth, Western Australia. Volunteers from the organization's graduate, and recent-graduate (alumni) employee pool are used. Participants are all employees with a science, technology, engineering or mathematics qualification and employed within departments that have an operational connection to the ROC. Alumni have less than two years post-graduate employment with the company, meaning all participants have less than two years exposure to industrial TD. Half of the cohort have a background in software engineering training (and some TD knowledge) and half have no formal software training (minimal to no prior TD knowledge).

4.3 Measuring TD Awareness

Bloom's taxonomy of educational objectives has been interpreted and applied by Kelly to assessing software engineering learning outcomes [37]. Research questions in this study are based on "understanding" and "experiencing" TD, verbs that map to Kelly's knowledge and comprehension cognitive objectives. By assessing changes in TD knowledge and comprehension across game sessions, changes in TD cognition and thus situational awareness can be measured. Table 2 presents the TD knowledge and comprehension definitions used, informed by [3]. To aid readability **cognitive objectives** are in bold font.

Table 2. TD Cognitive Objective Definitions

	Cognitive Objective	Definition
K	Potential TD	Debt not affected by a future evolution
K	Actual TD	Debt affected by a future evolution
K	Benefit Example	Benefits of potential TD
K	Suffering example	Detrimental aspects of TD
C	Creation	Introduction of technical debt as workarounds / shortcuts taken during the SDLC$^+$
C	Awareness	Symptoms of debt are realized
C	Tipping point	Actual debt is greater than Potential debt
C	Remediation	Removal of debt from the system
C	Getting value examples	Reduced delivery times / development savings
C	Suffering examples	Actual debt
C	Time sensitive	Debt matters as time flows and systems evolve
C	Evolutionary stages	Created > Awareness > Tipping point > Remediation

SDLC$^+$ = Software Development Life Cycle
K = Knowledge / **C** = Comprehension
Definition and cognitive objectives are abstracted from [3]

5 Results

Seventeen participants volunteered, each completing brief and debriefing sessions. Of the participants, eight self-rated themselves as having no knowledge of TD, five moderate and four extensive knowledge, approximating a balance of 50% participants with and without some level of prior TD knowledge. In the post-game five-point Likert scale responses, eighty-eight percent of participants agreed / strongly agreed that the game was played at a comfortable pace. Similarly, seventy-five percent of participants agreed / strongly agreed the game was easy to play.

5.1 Surveys

Survey results are shown in Fig. 3. Pre-game, cognitive objectives **Creation** and **Time sensitive** scored equally highest, **Awareness** scored highest post-game. None of the cognitive objectives were identified by all participants, shown as both pre- and post-game shaded areas being below the total number of participants.

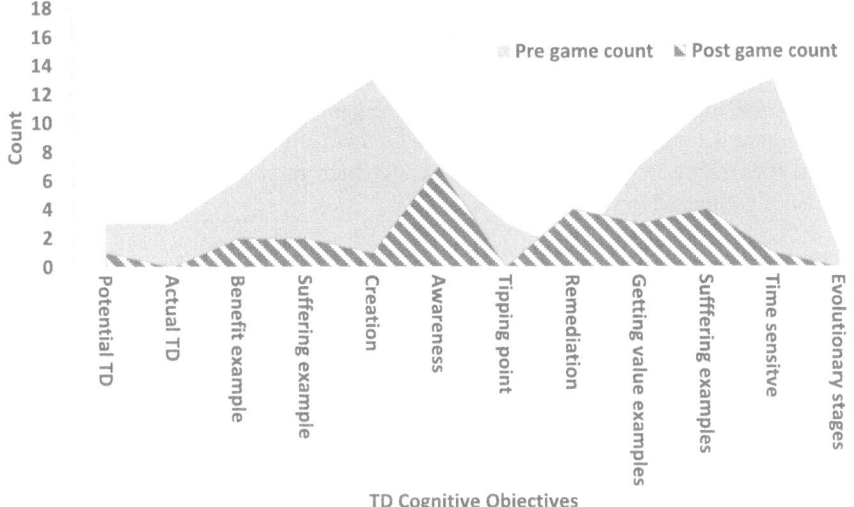

Fig. 3. Survey results for pre- / post-game cognitive objectives. Yellow shaded areas are pre-game counts of identified cognitive objectives, blue stripped shaded areas post-game counts. (Color figure online)

5.2 Thematic Analysis from Interviews

Eight parent themes are identified from analysis of TD learnings. Themes identified are as follows in italics: *Actual TD, Potential TD, Creation, Evolution, Tipping point, TD Impacts, Cost Benefit* and *Management*. Five parent themes (italics) share similarity with a cognitive objective (bold font); *Actual TD* ⇔ **Actual TD**, *Potential TD* ⇔ **Potential TD**, *Creation* ⇔ **Creating**, *Evolution* ⇔ **Evolution**, *Tipping point* ⇔ **Tipping point**.

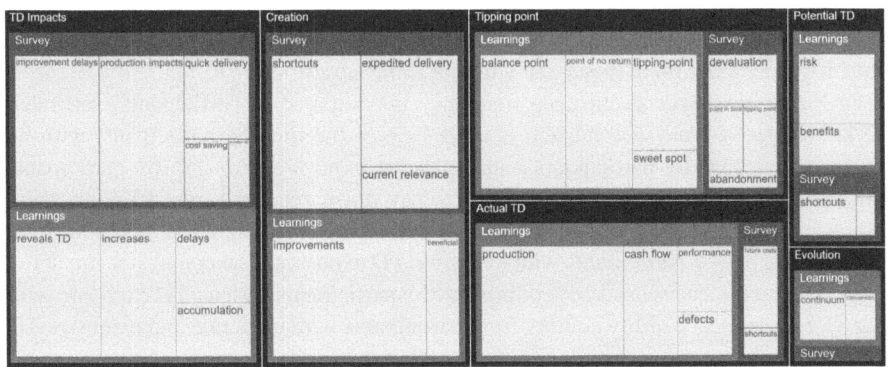

Fig. 4. Comparison of Learnings and Pre-game child themes. Themes are defined by a black border, labeled according to learnings theme names. Child themes are shown within each, the size of each child theme box reflecting the number of references from interviews; the bigger the box the more frequently a theme is accounted for by participants.

278   D. Gould et al.

TD Impacts shares similarity with cognitive objectives **Benefit example** and **Suffering example**.

Further thematic analysis is performed on surveys. Treating each survey cognitive objective as a theme yields 20 child themes; 17 pre-game, 7 post-game, with 4 common to both. Figure 4 compares post-game learnings themes to survey pre-game themes. Learnings themes are in general supported by a greater number, and different types of child themes compared to survey themes.

5.3 Information Trails

Each participant plays 4 games yielding 68 game trails. Each trail consists of one or more sequence/s. A sequence is defined as all in-game actions taken between one TD increase and the next TD increase. Out of 128 counted sequences, four unique sequences are identified. Table 3 shows each unique sequence, their contributing steps, a descriptor, the number of occurrences, and an ID to aid discussion.

Table 3. Unique Sequences, Descriptors and Frequency

ID	Steps	Descriptor	Frequency
1	create	(C)	10
2	create => impact	(C => I)	78
3	Create => pay down	(C => P)	18
4	Create => impact => pay down	(C =>I => P)	22

Sequence 1 is a single-create TD event. In sequence 2, TD is created followed by a TD impact such as a system outage, loss of a level or creation of a defect. In sequence 3, TD is created followed directly by a player paying down TD. Sequence 4 is where TD is created followed by an impact followed by paying down TD. Each of these unique sequences can occur more than once within a game's trail.

In Fig. 5, sequence occurrence frequency is compared to participants' self-rated TD knowledge. Create => impact, is used 49% of the time by participants with no TD exposure, 23% by participants with moderate exposure and 28% by participants with extensive exposure. For the create => pay down sequence over 65% of utility is by participants with no self-rated TD exposure, 26% by participants with moderate exposure and 8% by participants with extensive TD exposure. The create => impact => pay down sequence is used 18% of the time by participants with no TD exposure with over 81% of sequence utility coming from participants with moderate and extensive TD exposure.

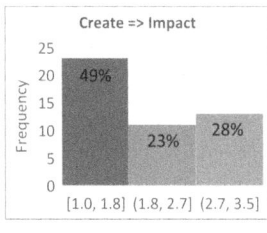 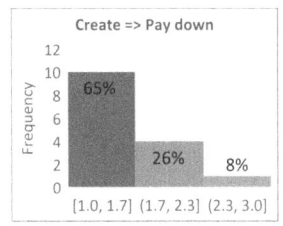 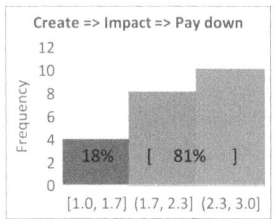

Fig. 5. Frequency of Self rated TD exposure comparing trail sequences 'create => impact (C => I)', 'create => pay down (C => P)', and 'create ⇒ impact ⇒ pay down (C => I => P)'

6 Discussion

6.1 Thematic Analysis

Differences between pre-game and post-game results in Fig. 3 are partly accounted for by the research methodology used. For instance, each participant is given a 1-page TD summary to read prior to a pre-game survey. Use of the summary page is left up to participant discretion when completing a post-game survey. The result is a disproportionate use of provided information between pre-game and post-game surveys. Further, participants are requested to answer their post-game survey based on game playing experience. This further exacerbates potential information disparities. Participants support this view, participant 5 provides a pre-game response aligned to the TD summary explaining a TD Benefit Example as "hitting a deadline is more important than producing a really quality finalized software". Post-game TD Benefit Example becomes "producing money from low capital". The latter is a reference to game-play economics not available in the TD summary.

Six post-game learnings parent themes share similarities with one or more pre-game surveys, however the number and types of child themes underlying parent themes differs between post-game learnings and pre-game surveys. For instance, the *Tipping point* parent theme for post-game learnings has *balance point, point of no return, sweet spot*, and *tipping point* as child themes. For pre-game survey **Tipping point** child themes are *devaluation, point in time, tipping point* and *abandonment*. The only common child theme is tipping point, suggesting nuances exist between pre-game and post-game responses.

Such nuances are exposed in the richness of language participants use to describe post-game learnings, not present in pre-game surveys. Participant 12 recants pre-game a **Tipping point** to be the "point of no return". Post-game *Tipping point* becomes "a sweet spot between optimization of system in terms of purchasing improvements and the instability that would cause". The latter is a lived experience informed by playing TD-Sim, the former a definition provided in the TD summary.

Evidence also exists of TD awareness moving from a pre-game abstract concept toward understanding obtained from playing TD-Sim. Participant 10 self-rated themselves as having no prior TD knowledge. Their pre-game account of **Actual TD** is "you are not gaining anything out of what you are doing and instead you're, yep losing". Post-game *Actual TD* becomes "technical debt would be things that are slowing production down", a direct reference to TD-Sim's reward-penalty mechanics. Participant 10 also shares that TD is "like it's a kind of necessary evil…and like be strategic about the way that you are going to incur it". This reflection of TD is not available in the TD summary, implying TD-Sim has provided an awareness of TD not previously present.

6.2 Game Trail Insights

Acquiring TD is nonnegotiable if players intend to improve game performance through upgrading, paying down TD is a choice. Through this lens, paying down TD equates to players managing TD of their own volition. Combining frequencies of game trails (C => P) and (C => I => P) suggests 31% of game time is spent managing TD. This is encouraging, implying current game mechanics provide a viable simulation of TD management.

Figure 5 shows participants with no prior TD knowledge increase TD at almost twice the frequency they pay TD down. For this cohort paying down TD is a relatively expensive undertaking, as participant 8 shares "when I tried to fix and pay off the technical debt it was also quite expensive". This cohort therefore is avoiding TD management. The implication here is that game mechanics are imbalanced, there is not enough reward to promote TD management. Improving this aspect of the game could improve the 31% game time spent managing TD.

Participants with moderate TD knowledge tend to manage TD by paying it down only after an impact, (C => I => P). It appears that those with prior TD exposure, through software engineering expertise, are comfortable with software, and by extension electronic game-playing. This cohort is potentially able to quickly work out how the game works, leaving more game time to experiment. Participant 15 reflected "the last game I was just like let's see what happens…just to sort of compare and contrast what the strategy was". This suggests more game time and more game sessions are necessary for players with no prior TD knowledge. This would allow all participants to reach a point where they can experiment with TD management before game play ends.

6.3 Findings

Participants agreed / strongly agreed that the game was both easy to play and played at an agreeable pace. For RQ1 (*What impact playing a serious game has on participants' understanding of technical debt?*) playing TD-Sim results in TD awareness changing from a view informed by the TD summary sheet to an unconstrained view gleaned through game play. Evidenced by participant responses, a **Tipping point** pre-game is "a point of no return" which post- game becomes a "sweet spot between optimization… And… Instability". Change in awareness is taken as a proxy for a change in understanding as per Sect. 4.3.

For RQ2 (*What impact playing a game has on participants' experience of technical debt?*), the experience of TD moves from an abstract concept toward a personalized lived experience based on creating, benefiting from, suffering from, and managing TD. For example, TD is described post-game as "things that are slowing production down".

Game trails combined with participants' self-rated prior knowledge of TD inform RQ3 (*How participants' prior knowledge of software development impacts (RQ1) and (RQ2)?*). Participants with less prior exposure potentially take longer to learn the game, thereby limiting their capacity to experiment with managing TD. Prior knowledge impacts participants' ability to experientially learn TD management, which in turn potentially limits TD understanding and experience.

6.4 Validity

There is no guarantee that all participants understand all interview questions equally. Those without a prior TD background may have been at a disadvantage comprehending and answering TD questions. This can exacerbate the differences observed between cohorts. Use of the TD summary pre-game is intended to help address this.

Perception and comprehension are personal phenomena, making measurement between participants challenging. Future work to increase sample size aims to address this.

Learnings thematic analysis follows an inductive grounded theory approach, themes are found from coding techniques. Conversely, survey thematic analysis started with themes to which child themes were coded, a deductive process where codes may have been found because they were looked for. Future research methodologies may be better served using grounded theory in both instances.

7 Conclusion

In this research a SG simulation of TD is developed and validated. Thematic analysis indicates TD-Sim improves participants' awareness of TD. Insight into the utility of TD-Sim for participants with and without a prior background in TD is gleaned through analysis of in-game trails.

This is an original contribution to SG's research by extending the use of SG's to situational awareness in industrial complex adaptive software systems. A novel SG research methodology is employed by triangulating thematic analysis and in-game trails. This methodology enables insights into the efficacy and utility of a SG to be assessed. An additional benefit of this approach is that opportunities to improve game performance are identified, a feature other SG researchers may find of benefit.

Future work on TD-Sim is to improve the areas identified, incorporate remaining causal loop TD drivers, and to verify further use cases of interdependent integrated software systems.

Disclosure of Interests. David Gould is a full-time employee of the case study. This research, however, is not funded by the case study. As such all opinions and conclusions drawn are those of the authors alone. To the extent that this publication draws on information provided by the study participants, it should not be assumed that any views expressed herein are also necessarily those of such participants.

References

1. Besker, T., Martini, A., Bosch, J.: Software developer productivity loss due to technical debt—a replication and extension study examining developers' development work. J. Syst. Softw. **156**, 41–61 (2019)
2. Nord, R.L., Ozkaya, I., Kruchten, P., Gonzalez-Rojas, M.: In search of a metric for managing architectural technical debt. In: 2012 Joint Working IEEE/IFIP Conference on Software Architecture and European Conference on Software Architecture, pp. 91–100. IEEE (2012)
3. Kruchten, P., Nord, R., Ozkaya, I.: Managing Technical Debt: Reducing Friction in Software Development. Adson-Wesley Professional, Boston (2019)
4. Omeyer, A.: The Cost of Technical Debt (2020). https://www.stepsize.com/blog/cost-of-technical-debt
5. Lakshmanan, V., Roy, R., Gorain, B.: Case study: digital disruption in the mining industry. In: Innovations and Breakthroughs in the Gold and Silver Industries, pp. 199–241. Springer (2019)
6. The Digital Mine (2022). https://minerals.org.au/wp-content/uploads/2022/12/The-Digital-Mine-2022.pdf. Accessed 14 Oct 2023
7. Endsley, M.R.: Toward a theory of situation awareness in dynamic systems. Hum. Factors **37**(1), 32–64 (1995)
8. Bekebrede, G., Lo, J., Lukosch, H.: Understanding complex systems through mental models and shared experiences: a case study. Simul. Gaming **46**(5), 536–562 (2015)
9. Australian_Jobs_2021 (2021). https://www.nationalskillscommission.gov.au/reports/Australian-jobs-2021/jobs-industry/mining. Accessed 14 Oct 2023
10. Wehrle, R., Wiens, M., Schultmann, F.: Application of collaborative serious gaming for the elicitation of expert knowledge and towards creating situation awareness in the field of infrastructure resilience. Int. J. Disaster Risk Reduction **67**, 102665 (2022)
11. Seaman, C., et al.: Using technical debt data in decision making: potential decision approaches. In: 2012 Third International Workshop on Managing Technical Debt (MTD), pp. 45–48. IEEE (2012)
12. Ramasubbu, N., Kemerer, C.F., Woodard, C.J.: Managing technical debt: insights from recent empirical evidence. IEEE Softw. **32**(2), 22–25 (2015)
13. Besker, T., Martini, A., Bosch, J.: The pricey bill of technical debt: when and by whom will it be paid? In: 2017 IEEE International Conference on Software Maintenance and Evolution (ICSME), pp. 13–23. IEEE (2017)
14. Gould, D., French, T., Hodkiewicz, M.: Understanding technical debt in remote operations centers. In: 26th World Mining Congress, pp. 123–132. 26–29 June 2023, Brisbane, Australia (2023). https://wmc2023.org/proceedings
15. Lukosch, H.K., Bekebrede, G., Kurapati, S., Lukosch, S.G.: A scientific foundation of simulation games for the analysis and design of complex systems. Simul. Gaming **49**(3), 279–314 (2018). https://doi.org/10.1177/1046878118768858. https://journals.sagepub.com/doi/abs/10.1177/1046878118768858
16. Kriz, W.C.: Creating effective learning environments and learning organizations through gaming simulation design. Simul. Gaming **34**(4), 495–511 (2003)
17. Krath, J., Schürmann, L., Von Korflesch, H.F.: Revealing the theoretical basis of gamification: a systematic review and analysis of theory in research on gamification, serious games and game-based learning. Comput. Hum. Behav. **125**, 106963 (2021)
18. Bucchiarone, A., Cooper, K.M., Lin, D., Melcer, E.F., Sung, K.: Games and software engineering: Engineering fun, inspiration, and motivation. ACM SIGSOFT Softw. Eng. Notes **48**(1), 85–89 (2023)

19. de Paula Porto, D., de Jesus, G.M., Ferrari, F.C., Fabbri, S.C.P.F.: Initiatives and challenges of using gamification in software engineering: a systematic mapping. J. Syst. Softw. **173**, 110870 (2021)
20. Foucault, M., Blanc, X., Storey, M.A., Falleri, J.R., Teyton, C.: Gamification: a game changer for managing technical debt? a design study. arXiv preprint arXiv:1802.02693 (2018)
21. Crespo, Y., Lopez-Nozal, C., Marticorena-Sanchez, R., Gonzalo-Tasis, M., Piattini, M.: The role of awareness and gamification on technical debt management. Inf. Softw. Technol. **150**, 106946 (2022)
22. Ganesh, L.: Board game as a tool to teach software engineering concept–technical debt. In: 2014 IEEE Sixth International Conference on Technology for Education, pp. 44–47. IEEE (2014)
23. Alhammad, M.M., Moreno, A.M.: Gamification in software engineering education: a systematic mapping. J. Syst. Softw. **141**, 131–150 (2018)
24. Cunningham, W.: The WyCash portfolio management system. ACM SIGPLAN OOPS Messenger **4**(2), 29–30 (1992)
25. Rios, N., de Mendonca Neto, M.G., Spınola, R.O.: A tertiary study on technical debt: types, management strategies, research trends, and base information for practitioners. Inf. Softw. Technol. **102**, 117–145 (2018)
26. Curtis, B., Sappidi, J., Szynkarski, A.: Estimating the size, cost, and types of technical debt. In: 2012 Third International Workshop on Managing Technical Debt (MTD). pp. 49–53. IEEE (2012)
27. Siriaraya, P., Visch, V., Vermeeren, A., Bas, M.: A cookbook method for persuasive game design. Int. J. Serious Games **5**(1), 37–71 (2018)
28. Bellotti, F., Kapralos, B., Lee, K., Moreno-Ger, P., Berta, R.: Assessment in and of serious games: an overview. Adv. Hum. Comput. Interact. **2013** (2013)
29. de Almeida Souza, M.R., Constantino, K.F., Veado, L.F., Figueiredo, E.M.L.: Gamification in software engineering education: an empirical study. In: 2017 IEEE 30th Conference on Software Engineering Education and Training (CSEE&T), pp. 276–284. IEEE (2017)
30. van der Kooij, K., Hoogendoorn, E., Spijkerman, R., Visch, V.: Validation of games for behavioral change: connecting the playful and serious. Int. J. Serious Games **2**(3), 63–75 (2015)
31. Abdellatif, A.J., McCollum, B., McMullan, P.: Serious games: quality characteristics evaluation framework and case study. In: IEEE Integrated STEM Education Conference (ISEC), pp. 112–119. IEEE (2018). https://doi.org/10.1109/ISECon.2018.8340460
32. Creswell, J.W., Poth, C.N.: Qualitative Inquiry and Research Design: Choosing Among Five Approaches. Sage Publications, Thousand Oaks (2016)
33. Tonin, G.S., Goldman, A., Seaman, C., Pina, D.: Effects of technical debt aware- ness: a classroom study. In: Agile Processes in Software Engineering and Extreme Programming: 18th International Conference, XP 2017, Cologne, Germany, May 22–26, 2017, Proceedings 18, pp. 84–100. Springer (2017)
34. van den Hoogen, J., Lo, J., Meijer, S.: Debriefing in gaming simulation for research: Opening the black box of the non-trivial machine to assess validity and reliability. In: Proceedings of the Winter Simulation Conference 2014, pp. 3505–3516. IEEE (2014)
35. Seaman, C.: Qualitative methods in empirical studies of software engineering. IEEE Trans. Software Eng. **25**(4), 557–572 (1999)

36. Loh, C.S., Anantachai, A., Byun, J., Lenox, J.: Assessing what players learned in serious games: in situ data collection, information trails, and quantitative analysis. In: 10th International Conference on Computer Games: AI, Animation, Mobile, Educational & Serious Games (CGAMES 2007), pp. 25–28 (2007)
37. Kelly, T., Buckley, J.: A context-aware analysis scheme for bloom's taxonomy. In: 14th IEEE International Conference on Program Comprehension (ICPC 2006), pp. 275–284. IEEE (2006)

Open Access This chapter is licensed under the terms of the Creative Commons Attribution 4.0 International License (http://creativecommons.org/licenses/by/4.0/), which permits use, sharing, adaptation, distribution and reproduction in any medium or format, as long as you give appropriate credit to the original author(s) and the source, provide a link to the Creative Commons license and indicate if changes were made.

The images or other third party material in this chapter are included in the chapter's Creative Commons license, unless indicated otherwise in a credit line to the material. If material is not included in the chapter's Creative Commons license and your intended use is not permitted by statutory regulation or exceeds the permitted use, you will need to obtain permission directly from the copyright holder.

Author Index

A
Agrawal, Shruti 81
Alf, Tobias 155, 249

B
Becu, Nicolas 182
Błaszczak-Rozenbaum, Blanka 128

C
Ćwil, Małgorzata 69, 128

D
Dalvi, Girish 81
Dhar, Upinder 168
Dubey, Jigyasu 168
Dumblekar, Vinod 168
Durham, Richard 110

F
Freese, Maria 239
French, Tim 270

G
Gould, David 270

H
Hamada, Ryoju 200
Hodkiewicz, Melinda 270
Hoermann, Simon 96

K
Kaneko, Tomomi 200
Kennedy, Ben 96
Kikkawa, Toshiko 1
Kriz, Willy Christian 1
Kutay, Cat 19

L
Leigh, Elyssebeth 19, 144, 168
Lemon, Ruth 110
Levesque, Laurie L. 144
Linegar, Dale 46
Lizada, Christian Gio Biag 19
Lukosch, Heide 96

M
MacCallum, Kathryn 96
Menugonda, Pavan Kumar 19
Michał, Jakubowski 69
Miura, Kento 31
Mizuyama, Hajime 228
Monfort, Amélie 215

N
Nakadegawa, Yuta 31
Nakamura, Mieko 1

O
Ohnuma, Susumu 31

P
Podgórski, Błażej 262

R
Rajavat, Anand 168

S
Sas, Éléonore 182
Sato, Mizuho 228
Shibuya, Takeshi 31
Suzuki, Kengo 31
Szatkowska, Weronika 128

T

Trautwein, Friedrich 155, 249

V
Vesty, Gillian 46

W
Wall, Kieron 96

Wardaszko, Marcin 262
Wątrucki, Piotr 262
Weronika, Szatkowska 69
Wittenzellner, Helmut 239

Z
Zürn, Birgit 239

The manufacturer's authorised representative in the EU is Springer Nature Customer Service Centre GmbH, Europaplatz 3, 69115 Heidelberg, Germany. If you have any concerns regarding our products, please contact ProductSafety@springernature.com

Printed and bound by CPI Group (UK) Ltd, Croydon, CR0 4YY

26/03/2026

02078968-0006